Lingua Latina

111 Interlinear

Latin - English

Conversations

Brian Smith

Introduction

The interlinear method for learning Latin (or any language) is a technique where a text is presented in the original language (Latin in this case) with an English translation directly underneath each word or phrase. The idea is to allow learners to engage with the original Latin text while simultaneously seeing the English meaning, helping them to understand and internalize the structure and vocabulary of the language more effectively. Here's how it works and why it can be a powerful tool for learning Latin:

How the Interlinear Method Works:

1. **Original Latin Text:** The main body of the text is presented in Latin. It is typically classical or historically authentic to give learners exposure to the way the language was used by native speakers.

2. **Direct Translation:** Below each word or phrase is the English translation. This isn't a polished or idiomatic translation but a literal one, designed to stay as close to the Latin as possible. This helps learners see how Latin grammar and word order differ from English while giving them an instant reference.

3. **Grammar Exposure:** As you follow the interlinear translation, you get a direct sense of how Latin grammatical structures like cases, tenses, and word agreements work. You are forced to notice things like noun declensions, verb conjugations, and word endings in context.

4. **Contextual Vocabulary Learning:** The Latin words are accompanied by their English meanings, but in the context of real sentences. This helps learners associate Latin words with specific contexts and situations, leading to better retention compared to learning vocabulary in isolation.

Best Practices for Learning Latin with the Interlinear Method:

1. **Start with Familiarization:** Begin by reading both the Latin and the English translation to get a feel for the text. Pay attention to the structure of the sentence and the role each word plays. This

will help you grasp how the Latin language organizes ideas differently from English.

2. **Focus on Patterns:** As you read, focus on identifying patterns in the language. For example, notice how Latin uses different case endings to convey meaning, how verbs change according to tense or subject, and how word order in Latin is more flexible than in English.

3. **Re-read Without Looking at the Translation:** After you've gone through the text once or twice with the English translation, try reading the Latin on its own. Use the translation only when you don't understand a word or phrase. This encourages you to rely on your growing knowledge of Latin rather than the translation.

4. **Break Down Complex Sentences:** If you encounter a complex sentence, break it down into its components—subject, verb, object, and any modifiers or clauses. Interlinear texts help you see how Latin uses inflection rather than word order to convey relationships between words.

5. **Analyze Grammatical Structures:** Take time to analyze the grammatical structures present in the Latin text. Identify cases, verb forms, and other grammatical elements and see how they correspond to the English translation. This helps to solidify your understanding of Latin grammar.

6. **Build Your Vocabulary:** As you encounter new words, make a note of them and practice using them in different contexts. The more you read, the more frequently you'll encounter words, and soon, you'll start recognizing them without needing to check the translation.

7. **Practice Translation Back to Latin:** For a more advanced step, try translating the English back into Latin. This helps reinforce the vocabulary and grammar rules you've learned, as it forces you to think in Latin.

8. **Move Toward Independence:** Over time, rely less on the English translation and focus more on understanding the Latin

directly. The goal of the interlinear method is to scaffold learning until you're comfortable enough with Latin to read without needing the direct translation.

Why the Interlinear Method is Effective:

- **Immediate Feedback:** You can see immediately if you've understood a word or phrase correctly by glancing at the English translation, which helps reduce frustration and boosts confidence.

- **Grammar in Context:** You learn grammar naturally as it appears in actual usage rather than through isolated drills or memorization. This contextual learning deepens comprehension and retention.

- **Progressive Learning:** The more you read, the less you'll need to rely on the translation, making the interlinear text a stepping stone to reading Latin fluently.

- **Immersive Experience:** The interlinear method allows you to immerse yourself in authentic Latin texts while still having the safety net of an English translation. It's a more engaging and intuitive way to learn compared to traditional methods.

By consistently using the interlinear method and gradually reducing your dependence on the English translations, you can develop a strong ability to read and understand Latin.

De Natalibus – De celebrationibus dierum natalium apud Romanos

Sextus: *Salve, Servilie! Audivi te cras diem natalem tuum celebraturum esse. Estne ita?*

Sextus: Hello, Servilius! I heard you will be celebrating your birthday tomorrow. Is that correct?

Servilius: *Salve, Sexte! Ita est, cras mihi dies natalis est, et familiam meam atque amicos ad cenam invitavi. Volo illum diem non solum convivio laetitiae pleno, sed etiam pietate et gratia erga familiam deosque honorare. Scis enim Romanos natales suos non semper propter opes aut divitias celebravisse, sed etiam ut parentes et deos colerent.*

Servilius: Greetings, Sextus! Indeed, tomorrow is my birthday, and I have invited my family and friends to dinner. I want to honor that day not only with a feast full of joy, but also with piety and gratitude toward my family and the gods. You know that Romans did not always celebrate their birthdays for wealth or riches, but also to honor their parents and the gods.

Sextus: *Bene facis, Servilie! Dies natalis maximo honore dignus est, ut mihi videtur, et memoria cum gratia sociatur. Quid ages in cena? Sacrificiumne erit? Bovem aut porcum immolabis? Tu enim semper rite deos veneraris.*

Sextus: You are doing well, Servilius! A birthday is most worthy of honor, in my view, and is linked with gratitude and remembrance. What will you do at dinner? Will there be a sacrifice? Will you sacrifice an ox or a pig? You always honor the gods with proper rites.

Servilius: *Ita est, Sexte. Sacrificium primum habebimus antequam convivium incipiat. Volo Iovi Optimo Maximo gratias agere, qui meam familiam per annum custodivit. Porcus immolabitur, cum modestia servata, sed tamen ritus magnifice peragetur. Cena ipsa opulenta erit, cum variis cibis: panis albus, olivae, caro apri, et dulcia ex melle facta.*

Servilius: Yes, Sextus. We will first hold a sacrifice before the feast begins. I want to give thanks to Jupiter Optimus Maximus, who has protected my family throughout the year. A pig will be sacrificed, with due modesty, though the rites will still be conducted with grandeur. The feast itself will be abundant, with various dishes: white bread, olives, boar meat, and sweets made from honey.

Sextus: *Opulenta quidem! Fama cenarum et rituum tuorum per urbem iam diu vulgata est. Sed dic mihi, qui convivae aderunt? Solentne amici tui longas orationes habere ut tuam aetatem celebrent?*

Sextus: Truly lavish! The reputation of your dinners and rituals has spread throughout the city for some time. But tell me, who will be the guests? Do your friends often give long speeches to celebrate your age?

Servilius: *Fabulas narras, Sexte! Convivae propinqui et pauci amici fidi aderunt. Inter alios, filius meus, Marcus, aderit, qui brevissimam mihi orationem recitabit, ut suum profectum ostendat. Longae autem orationes me non delectant. Mihi magis placet sermo familiaris et levis, qui graves verborum pondera effugiat.*

Servilius: You're telling tales, Sextus! My close relatives and a few loyal friends will be there. Among others, my son Marcus will attend, and he will deliver a very brief speech to show his progress. But long speeches do not please me. I prefer light and familiar conversation, which avoids the weight of heavy words.

Sextus: *Sapienter loqueris, Servilie. Dies natales non debent graves esse, sed potius ad laetitiam et iocunditatem pertinere. Ego quoque, cum dies meus natalis advenerit, modestum convivium praeferam, ubi amicitia curatur et risus exsurgit. Nec tamen mentiar: quotiens cenam tuam exspecto, praeclara fercula tua mihi dulcissima sunt.*

Sextus: You speak wisely, Servilius. Birthdays should not be serious, but rather inclined toward joy and celebration. When my birthday comes, I too will prefer a modest feast, where friendship is nurtured, and laughter arises. And I won't lie: every time I look forward to your dinner, your excellent dishes are the sweetest for me.

Servilius: *Gratias tibi ago, Sexte! Ego quoque, cum convivas sedentes et cenam laetitia plenam esse videbo, summam voluptatem percipiam. In diebus natalibus non solum pro annis praeteritis gratias agimus, sed etiam spem novorum annorum fovemus. Vale igitur nunc, et cras ad me veni, ut diem illum simul celebremus!*

Servilius: Thank you, Sextus! I too will feel the greatest joy when I see the guests seated and the dinner filled with happiness. On birthdays, we not only give thanks for the past years, but also nurture hope for the new ones. So, farewell for now, and come to me tomorrow so we can celebrate that day together!

Sextus: *Vale, Servilie! Cras pro certo veniam et tibi laetitiam ac felicitatem optabo.*

Sextus: Farewell, Servilius! I will certainly come tomorrow and wish you joy and happiness.

De Servis Inquietis – De servis infelicibus vel seditiosis colloquium

Quintus: *Salve, Marce! Audivi te nuper difficultatem cum servis habuisse. Nonne quidam servi tibi perturbate oboediunt?*

Quintus: Hello, Marcus! I heard you recently had trouble with your slaves. Aren't some of them obeying you poorly?

Marcus: *Salve, Quinte! Ita est, difficulter oboediunt. Hic novus servus, Hermogenes, qui nuper ex Graecia emptus est, multos allicit ad seditionem. Non iam disciplinam recipere vult, et ceteri servi ei favere incipiunt. Sentio rem aliquantum maturandam esse antequam gravius fiat.*

Marcus: Hello, Quintus! Yes, they obey with difficulty. This new slave, Hermogenes, who was recently purchased from Greece, is inciting many toward rebellion. He no longer wants to accept discipline, and the other slaves are beginning to favor him. I feel that something must be done soon before it becomes more serious.

Quintus: *Hoc sane est periculosum, Marce. Servi qui contumaces sunt celeriter perturbant totam familiam. Num tibi videtur poenam graviorem adhibendam esse, ut ceteri discant quid ex iustitia sequatur?*

Quintus: This is certainly dangerous, Marcus. Disobedient slaves quickly disturb the entire household. Do you think a harsher punishment should be applied so the others learn what follows from justice?

Marcus: *Non dubito quin severitatem aliquando necesse sit adhibere, sed conditio rerum, ut ego animadverto, non solum poena corrigitur. Multi servi nunc solliciti sunt, nam audiverunt de manumissionibus et libertate. Timor est ut, si gravius agam, magis contumacia efficiatur.*

Marcus: I don't doubt that severity is sometimes necessary, but the situation, as I see it, is not corrected by punishment alone. Many slaves are now anxious because they've heard about manumissions and freedom. I fear that if I act too harshly, it will lead to greater rebellion.

Quintus: *Intellego. Etiam si servi rebelles sunt, nimia severitas facile causam maioris tumultus moveat. Fortasse sermo cum Hermogene utilem effectum habere possit. Nonne expedit aliquando cum servis colloqui, ut suas querelas aperiant?*

Quintus: I understand. Even if the slaves are rebellious, excessive severity can easily cause greater unrest. Perhaps a conversation with Hermogenes could have a beneficial effect. Isn't it sometimes useful to speak with the slaves so they can express their grievances?

Marcus: *Rem bene mones, Quinte. Censeo me cum eo colloqui debere. Sed quid faciam si contumax manet? Debeo tandem ad poenam reverti? Videtur me inter iustitiam et servitutem fluctuare.*

Marcus: You give good advice, Quintus. I think I should speak with him. But what should I do if he remains defiant? Should I eventually return to punishment? It seems I am torn between justice and servitude.

Quintus: *Fortasse, si sermo parum proficiat, mediocrem viam quaerere possis. Non omnis poena gravis est; nonnumquam levior castigatio, si iusta et rationabilis sit, satis efficit ut servi suum officium intellegant. Denique, auctoritas tua maiorem vim habet si aequitatem probaveris.*

Quintus: Perhaps, if the conversation makes little progress, you could seek a middle way. Not every punishment has to be severe; sometimes a lighter correction, if fair and reasonable, is enough for the slaves to understand their duties. Ultimately, your authority has greater impact if you demonstrate fairness.

Marcus: *Vere locutus es, Quinte. Oportet me principium facere cum sermone modico, et si opus est, gradatim augere severitatem. Ita spero tranquillitatem in familia mea redire posse. Quosdam servos timor tenet, sed si rationem et aequitatem praeferimus, fortasse fidem et laborem eorum restituere poterimus.*

Marcus: You've spoken truly, Quintus. I must start with a moderate conversation, and if necessary, gradually increase severity. I hope that in this way, peace can return to my household. Some slaves are gripped by fear, but if we prioritize reason and fairness, perhaps we can restore their loyalty and diligence.

Quintus: *Nihil melius! Diligentia et moderatione, multae res improbandae vincuntur. Ego quoque, si talibus rebus occurro, primum sermone tempto ac deinde, si necesse sit, paulatim augere castigationem. Fortes domini, qui aeque et sapienter agunt, familiam meliorem faciunt.*

Quintus: Nothing could be better! With diligence and moderation, many issues can be overcome. I too, when faced with such matters, first attempt to resolve things with conversation and then, if necessary, gradually increase punishment. Strong masters, who act fairly and wisely, create a better household.

Marcus: *Gratias tibi, Quinte. Consilia tua mihi multum valent. Mox Hermogenem accersam ut rem discutiamus. Fortasse sermo prudens pacem iterum feret.*

Marcus: Thank you, Quintus. Your advice means a lot to me. I'll soon summon Hermogenes so we can discuss the matter. Perhaps a wise conversation will bring peace again.

Quintus: *Bene facis, Marce. Si quid auxilii necesse erit, ego semper paratus sum. Vale, et utinam omnia secundum voluntatem tuam accidant.*

Quintus: You're doing the right thing, Marcus. If you need any help, I am always ready. Farewell, and may everything go according to your will.

Marcus: *Gratias, Quinte. Vale!*

Marcus: Thank you, Quintus. Farewell!

In Muro Hadriani – Legionarii vigiles ad Murum Hadriani

Drusus: *Salve, Rufe! Longus videtur mihi hic dies, dum in hac parte muri vigilo. Nonne tibi quoque videtur nullae minae hodie ex barbaris Britonibus imminere?*

Drusus: Hello, Rufus! This day seems long to me, while I keep watch on this part of the wall. Don't you also think that there are no threats today from the barbarian Britons?

Rufus: *Salve, Druse! Ita est, et ego eundem sensum habeo. Quamquam hic Hadriani murus nos ab hostibus defendit, saepe hora in horam nihil fit. Sed noli nimis confidere—Britones quidem incerti sunt et saepe repentini impetus eorum magnam cladem intulerunt. Melius est vigilare quam poenam postea accipere.*

Rufus: Hello, Drusus! Yes, I have the same feeling. Although Hadrian's Wall protects us from the enemy, often nothing happens hour by hour. But don't be too confident—the Britons are unpredictable, and their sudden attacks have often brought great disaster. It's better to keep watch than suffer consequences later.

Drusus: *Sane, sermo tuus rectus est. Numquam decet mens legionaria in somno obdormiscere. Sed in hoc remoto loco, tam procul ab urbe et omnibus rei publicae rebus, vita lentior et plena taedii esse videtur. Nonne, Rufe, desideras aliquam rem excitationem ferentem?*

Drusus: Indeed, your words are correct. A legionary's mind must never fall asleep. But in this remote place, so far from the city and all matters of state, life seems slower and filled with boredom. Don't you, Rufus, long for something exciting to happen?

Rufus: *Vere dicis, Druse. In urbe Roma semper est aliquid novi; hic autem solitudinem sentimus, nec saepe multum fit praeter montes et silvas. Sed tamen, nostra est hoc opus sustinere, ut imperium Romanum diu firmum maneat. Si nos neglegimus, quis scit quid barbari his locis efficiant?*

Rufus: You speak truly, Drusus. In the city of Rome, there is always something new; here, however, we feel the solitude, and not much happens except for the mountains and forests. But still, it is our duty to endure this, so that the Roman Empire remains strong. If we neglect it, who knows what the barbarians might do in these lands?

Drusus: *Non omnino erras. Romae mirabile est, sed hic in Britannia videmus quanta necessitas sit periculorum avertendorum. Curatio muri et vigilantia nullum spatium otii permittunt. Praeterea, decessus mensium hibernorum mox aderit, et tum barbari audacissimi fiunt, cum nivibus et ventis murus noster leniorem fecerit.*

Drusus: You are not entirely wrong. Rome is marvelous, but here in Britannia, we see how important it is to avert dangers. The care of the wall and vigilance leave no room for idleness. Besides, the end of the winter months is approaching, and that's when the barbarians become most daring, as snow and winds make our wall more vulnerable.

Rufus: *Sic est, Druse. Hiems hic gravis fit, et cum tempestates frigidae veniunt, barbari propius accedere audent. Itaque cavendum est ut in vigiliis semper alacres simus, etiam si nunc videntur omnia tranquilla. Numquid tamen mens tuarum cogitationum levatur cum nocte sub stellis vigilas?*

Rufus: That's right, Drusus. Winters here are harsh, and when the cold storms come, the barbarians dare to approach closer. So we must always be alert in our watches, even if everything seems calm now. But tell me, don't your thoughts lighten when you watch the night sky under the stars?

Drusus: *Ita, nocte sub caelo claro, inter astra et tacitas silvas, aliquantum solacium est. Spes autem semper est ut aliquando ad Romam revertamur et hic ludus longae stationis terminetur. Tamen, Rufe, non licet hos dies evitare; legionarii sumus, et quod officium imperii est, id nobis praestandum est.*

Drusus: Yes, at night, under a clear sky, among the stars and the silent forests, there is some comfort. But the hope always remains that we might one day return to Rome and that this long stationing here will end. Yet, Rufus, we cannot avoid these days; we are legionaries, and what the empire requires is our duty.

Rufus: *Bene dicisti, Druse. Quamvis, sicut homines, interdum quiescere cupiamus, semper praestanda est fides imperii. Et, cum in Romam* *redeamus, gloriam feremus non tantum quod murum servavimus, sed etiam quod fidem et virtutem nostram probavimus.*

Rufus: Well said, Drusus. Although, like all men, we may sometimes desire rest, we must always maintain loyalty to the empire. And when we return to Rome, we will carry not only the glory of having defended the wall but also of having proven our loyalty and courage.

Drusus: *Valet haec sententia, amice. Sit nobis hoc animus! Nunc tamen, parati simus vigilare, ne quis hostis prope accedat. Fatum legionarium semper incertum est, sed virtute et constantia omnia vincemus.*

Drusus: That sentiment is true, my friend. Let this be our spirit! But now, let us be ready to keep watch, lest any enemy come near. A legionary's fate is always uncertain, but with courage and persistence, we will overcome everything.

Rufus: *Sic erit. Vigilemus igitur et ut decet legionarios pro Roma et imperio stemus.*

Rufus: So it will be. Let us keep watch and stand as true legionaries for Rome and the empire.

De Caesare et Cleopatra – Sermo de Iulio Caesare et Cleopatra

Lucius: *Salve, Marcia! Audivistine quid de Caesare et Cleopatra fertur? Totus populus Romae nunc de hac re fabulatur. Videtur, ut pervulgatum est, Caesarem in Aegypto non tantum bellis vacavisse, sed etiam amorem cum regina Cleopatra egisse.*

Lucius: Hello, Marcia! Have you heard what is being said about Caesar and Cleopatra? All of Rome is talking about this matter now. It seems, as is widely reported, that Caesar in Egypt wasn't just busy with wars but also had an affair with Queen Cleopatra.

Marcia: *Salve, Luci! Certe audivi. Non modicum est quod homines de hac coniunctione loquuntur. Cleopatra, ut dicunt, mulier formosa et summa arte dolorum peritissima est. Sed Caesar, qui sempiterna sapientia praeditus videtur, qui omnia prudenter agere solet, nuncne amoris illecebris captus est? Quid tu censes, Luci?*

Marcia: Hello, Lucius! Yes, I've certainly heard. It's no small thing that people are talking about this relationship. Cleopatra, they say, is a beautiful woman and extremely skilled in the art of deception. But Caesar, who seems to be endowed with eternal wisdom and always acts prudently, has he now been ensnared by the allure of love? What do you think, Lucius?

Lucius: *Haud scio, Marcia. Caesar quidem vir est qui multa antea sapienter administravit, sed, ut dicunt, nihil potentius est quam amor. Videsne quam celeriter eum Cleopatra attraxerit? Dicitur etiam Ptolemaeum principatu spoliavisse et Cleopatram solam reginam effecisse. Nonne haec sunt indicia quam valde illa Caesarem persuaserit?*

Lucius: I don't know, Marcia. Caesar is indeed a man who has wisely handled many matters before, but, as they say, nothing is more powerful than love. Do you see how quickly Cleopatra attracted him? It's even said that he stripped Ptolemy of his throne and made Cleopatra the sole queen. Aren't these signs of how much she has persuaded Caesar?

Marcia: *Quae narras, mirabilia videntur. Cleopatra cunctas mulieres Romanas virtute et gratia superare dicitur. Sed vide: non solum forma muliebris in hac re spectanda est. Prudentia quoque et sollertia sunt,* *quibus regina elegantissime usa est. Certe illa sciebat quo modo virum magnarum opum atque potestatis sibi coniungere posset.*

Marcia: What you're saying sounds incredible. Cleopatra is said to surpass all Roman women in virtue and charm. But look: in this matter, it's not just her beauty that should be considered. Her wisdom and cleverness are also factors that the queen has used most elegantly. Surely, she knew how to bind to herself a man of great wealth and power.

Lucius: *Ita est. Et quod magis miror, Caesar ipsum Alexandriam diu moratus est, tamquam regiae voluptatibus quam negotiis belli deditus. Non solum Cleopatra amorem suum fovet, sed etiam parvulum filium ex Caesare dicitur habere, qui "Caesarion" vocatur. Quid, si ille puer aliquando Romam veniet et de Caesare suo paterno iura requirat?*

Lucius: That's right. And what astonishes me more is that Caesar stayed in Alexandria for such a long time, as if devoted more to the pleasures of the palace than to the business of war. Cleopatra not only nurtures her love for him, but it's said she also has a small son by Caesar, who is called "Caesarion." What if that boy one day comes to Rome and claims rights as Caesar's heir?

Marcia: *Caesarion! Haec quidem nova sunt mihi. Videsne, Luci, quantam perturbationem id afferre possit? Non modo mirum erit si Romani talem filium accipiunt, sed etiam matre ex Aegyptia regina nato...! Populus securus non erit.*

Marcia: Caesarion! This is certainly new to me. Do you see, Lucius, how much turmoil this could cause? Not only would it be surprising if the Romans accept such a son, but one born of an Egyptian queen as his mother...! The people will not feel secure.

Lucius: *Certe! Multi iam de Caesaris potestate suspiciones habent, et si hoc infans reginae Aegyptiae filius suus esse proclamat, quis scit quid populus senatusque facient? Cleopatra, quam ipsae Romanae matronae timere incipiunt, plus imperii fortasse detinet quam plerique sentiunt.*

Lucius: Certainly! Many already have suspicions about Caesar's power, and if this child declares himself the son of the Egyptian queen, who knows what the people and the Senate will do? Cleopatra, whom even

Roman matrons are beginning to fear, might hold more influence than most realize.

Marcia: *Timeo ut fata haec bene confligant, Luci. Cleopatra fortasse reginam magna sapientia se probavit, sed Roma suaque iura defendet. Caesar quidem magnus est, sed numen civitatis Romanae durius esse constabit. Videbimus quid ex his rebus eveniat.*

Marcia: I fear that these fates will not clash well, Lucius. Cleopatra may have proven herself a queen of great wisdom, but Rome will defend its own rights. Caesar is indeed great, but the spirit of the Roman state will prove to be tougher. We'll see what comes from these events.

Lucius: *Sic est. Multa nunc latent, sed brevi in lucem venient. Valeto, Marcia! Scilicet sermo hic non iam in urbe cessabit.*

Lucius: That's true. Many things are hidden now, but they will soon come to light. Farewell, Marcia! Surely, this conversation won't stop in the city anytime soon.

Marcia: *Vale, Luci! Exspectamus quid futura nobis ferant.*

Marcia: Farewell, Lucius! We'll wait to see what the future brings us.

In Taberna Tonsoris – Colloquium apud tonsorem

Crispus: *Salve, Herme! Diu est quod non te vidi in taberna mea. Quid boni tibi accidit? Capilli tui iam longi sunt et satis neglecti, nisi fallor.*

Crispus: Hello, Hermes! It's been a long time since I last saw you in my shop. What good has happened to you? Your hair is already long and quite neglected, if I'm not mistaken.

Hermes: *Salve, Crispe! Ita est, multis negotiis impeditus eram, sed tandem ad te veni ut capillos mihi tondeas. Hic neglegentia sunt aucti! Quid tu agis? Semperne taberna tua frequens est?*

Hermes: Hello, Crispus! Yes, I was busy with many affairs, but I've finally come to you to get my hair cut. It has grown due to my neglect! How are you doing? Is your shop always busy?

Crispus: *Ita, gratias ago, bene me habeo, et semper multi clientes veniunt. Sed, Herme, quid tu velis hodie? Capilline brevissimi tibi placeant, an moderati longitudinis?*

Crispus: Yes, thank you, I'm doing well, and many clients always come. But tell me, Hermes, what would you like today? Do you prefer very short hair or medium length?

Hermes: *Noli omnino brevissimos facere. Velim tamen ut leviores fiant, modo ut decore tondeantur. Frons paulo magis aperta, capilli circum aures puri, ut maior dignitas adsit. Quid dicis, possisne hoc efficere?*

Hermes: Don't make it too short. I'd like it to be lighter, though, trimmed neatly. A bit more of my forehead exposed, the hair around the ears clean, so it adds a bit more dignity. What do you say, can you manage that?

Crispus: *Facillime! Hoc genus tondendi multis placet, et sic formam tuam exornabit. Sed dic mihi, Herme, audivi te nuper cum rerum gestarum scriptore colloquium habuisse. Nonne vere res praeclarae erant?*

Crispus: Very easily! This style of cutting pleases many, and it will suit your look. But tell me, Hermes, I heard that you recently had a conversation with a historian. Were the stories truly remarkable?

Hermes: *Ah, ita est! Loquebar cum Sallustio, homine prudentissimo. Multa narravit de bello Iugurthino, quam expeditionem, ut ipse dixit, cum magno periculo administravit. Vir magnae eloquentiae est, sed, ut ego animadverti, etiam cupidus gloriae. Itaque videtur magnam partem fabularum virtute sua augere.*

Hermes: Ah, yes! I was speaking with Sallust, a very wise man. He told me much about the Jugurthine War, an expedition that, as he said, he managed with great danger. He's a man of great eloquence, but as I've noticed, he's also eager for glory. So, it seems that he tends to enhance a great part of the stories with his own virtue.

Crispus: *Eloquentia quidem est non solum virtus, sed etiam arma. Ego autem puto res omnes in libris his praeclaras narrari, ut etiam posteritas non obliviscatur. Sed pro certo habeo vocem ipsius audire tibi magnum gaudium fuisse.*

Crispus: Eloquence is indeed not only a virtue but also a weapon. However, I believe that all these great events are told in books so that even future generations will not forget them. But I'm sure hearing his voice was a great joy for you.

Hermes: *Certe! Non solum de rei publicae causis locutus est, sed etiam de vita privata principum et quomodo potestas corrumpat. Multa ex verbis eius profeci, et puto eum maximum scriptorem his temporibus esse. Sed satis iam de mea re. Quid novi apud te? Habesne aliquid audire de urbe?*

Hermes: Certainly! He didn't just speak about the affairs of the state, but also about the private lives of the rulers and how power corrupts. I learned a lot from his words, and I think he's the greatest writer of our time. But enough about me. What's new with you? Have you heard anything from the city?

Crispus: *Mihi quidem nihil certi, nisi quod dicitur Cicero mox novam orationem ad Senatum facturus esse. Alii autem murmurant Pompeium Romam celerius rediturum esse cum exercitu. Populus, ut semper, expectatione tenetur. Videbimus quid de rebus accidat.*

Crispus: Nothing certain on my part, except that it's said Cicero will soon give a new speech to the Senate. Others are murmuring that Pompey will return to Rome faster than expected with his army. The people, as always, are full of anticipation. We'll see what happens with these matters.

Hermes: *Sic est. Nuntia haec semper procul incipiunt, sed celeriter urbis aures implent. Ego autem non dubito quin multa mox in Senatu discutiantur. Verum, Crispe, capilli nunc satis decore tondentur. Gratias tibi ago!*

Hermes: That's true. These rumors always start far away, but they quickly fill the ears of the city. I don't doubt that many things will soon be discussed in the Senate. But Crispus, my hair is now trimmed quite nicely. Thank you!

Crispus: *Gaudeo te contentum esse, Herme. Unum tamen noli oblivisci: semper capilli tui ad me spectant, nec per diuturnum tempus negligantur! Vale, et felix esto.*

Crispus: I'm glad you're satisfied, Hermes. But don't forget: your hair is always my responsibility, so don't neglect it for too long! Farewell, and be happy.

Hermes: *Vale, Crispe! Certe iterum brevi reveniam.*

Hermes: Farewell, Crispus! I'll certainly return soon.

De Nuptiis Parandis – De praeparationibus nuptiarum colloquium

Livia: *Salve, Sempronia! Tu scis quod propinquos meos conspicere non possim quomodo praeparationes nuptiarum fluant. Magis magisque sollicitor, cum dies ille tantum appropinquet. Nonne tu es in hac re peritior?*

Livia: Hello, Sempronia! You know I can't keep an eye on how the wedding preparations are going with my relatives. I'm getting more and more anxious as the day approaches. Aren't you more experienced in this matter?

Sempronia: *Salve, Livia! Mirari non possum te sollicitam esse—nuptias parare est res plena laborum. Sed tibi tranquillam mentem suadeo: omnia apte fient, sic ut decet. Dic mihi, quid iam curatum est?*

Sempronia: Hello, Livia! I can't blame you for being anxious—preparing a wedding is full of challenges. But I advise you to keep a calm mind: everything will be done properly, as it should. Tell me, what's been arranged so far?

Livia: *Hodie decretum est ut familiarum nostrarum convivium in horto amplissimo teneatur, et ornamenta iam mandata sunt. Vestem autem nuptialem adhuc non satis firmavi—multa consilia audio, sed incerta sum, quaenam aptissima sit.*

Livia: Today, it was decided that our families' banquet will be held in the largest garden, and the decorations have already been ordered. But I haven't yet finalized my wedding dress—I've heard many suggestions, but I'm uncertain which one is the most suitable.

Sempronia: *Vere locuta es. Vestis nuptialis est res principalis! Habesne aliquid in mente? Magna est varietas stolarum nuptialium, sed, ut scio, candidus color admodum aptus est; simplicis formae, tamen dignitate plenae.*

Sempronia: You've spoken truly. The wedding dress is the main thing! Do you have something in mind? There is a great variety of bridal gowns, but as far as I know, white is a very suitable color; simple in form, but full of dignity.

Livia: *Candidus color mihi quoque placet, sed cupio aliquid paulo ornatius. Fortasse purpura tenuis in limine addi possit, si modo non nimis opulenta videtur. Nonne turpe est, si nimium gloriosa in ipso die videar?*

Livia: I like white as well, but I desire something a bit more ornate. Perhaps a thin purple trim could be added, as long as it doesn't seem too extravagant. Isn't it shameful if I appear too splendid on the day itself?

Sempronia: *Nihil turpe est, Livia, modo decorum servetur. Opulentia decori esse potest, si ratio constat et modus non exceditur. Purpura ad margines sutilis erit divina et non ab elegantia abducet. Memineris enim hunc diem tibi et familiis tuis esse maximi momenti.*

Sempronia: There's nothing shameful, Livia, as long as decorum is maintained. Splendor can be fitting if it's done with thought and doesn't go overboard. Purple embroidery at the edges would be divine and wouldn't detract from the elegance. Remember, this day is of the utmost importance for you and your families.

Livia: *Bene consilium tuum accipio. Sic faciendum est. Nunc de convivio. Puto multas epulas propositas esse, sed cupio quod consuetudines nostras honorat, nec tamen nimium vulgare videtur. Num tu habes aliquod consilium de cibis?*

Livia: I accept your advice. That's how it should be done. Now about the banquet. I believe many dishes are already planned, but I want something that honors our traditions, yet doesn't seem too ordinary. Do you have any suggestions about the food?

Sempronia: *Multum in hac re refert. Certe, fercula proponenda sunt, quae divitias familiarum repraesentant—apri caro, malum Cotona, et dulcia mellita praeclara esse solent. Sed etiam custodienda est varietas. Quid, si exoticas herbas et ficos ex Aegypto adferamus, quo convivae admirentur?*

Sempronia: That's important. Certainly, the dishes should represent the wealth of the families—boar meat, quince, and honeyed sweets are usually excellent. But variety should also be preserved. What if we bring exotic herbs and figs from Egypt to impress the guests?

Livia: *Id quod cogitavi! Non est satis bonum tantum nostras consuetudines sequi; convivium prospectu dignum esse debet. Aegyptii cibi me magis alliciunt. Bene, epulas quoque ita disponam. Sempronia, tua verba spem mihi magnam adferunt!*

Livia: That's exactly what I was thinking! It's not good enough just to follow our traditions; the banquet should be worthy of admiration. Egyptian food entices me more. Good, I'll arrange the dishes like that as well. Sempronia, your words give me great hope!

Sempronia: *Gavisa sum, Livia. Nuptias non solum propter festum diem paras, sed ut familiam novam et spem felicem efficias. Omnia bene evenient, crede mihi. Vale!*

Sempronia: I'm glad to hear that, Livia. You're not just preparing for a festive day, but to establish a new family and foster happy hope. Everything will turn out well, trust me. Farewell!

Livia: *Vale, Sempronia! Grates tibi maximas ago.*

Livia: Farewell, Sempronia! Thank you very much.

In Circo – De quadrigarum cursibus et sponsione colloquium

Aulus: *Salve, Decimiane! Diu te non vidi in Circo. Vide quam multa turba hodie convenerit ad ludos spectandos! Quisnam hodie, censes, victor erit in cursu quadrigarum?*

Aulus: Hello, Decimianus! I haven't seen you in the Circus for a long time. Look at how large the crowd is today to watch the games! Who do you think will be the victor in the chariot race today?

Decimianus: *Salve, Aule! Ego quoque te gaudeo videre. Quattuor factiones in certamen venient, sed mihi spes in Alba est. Semper candidati Albae fidelissimi et celerissimi sunt. Auriga enim eorum, Scorpus, iam multos cursus vicit. Ponisne aliquid pecuniae?*

Decimianus: Hello, Aulus! I'm also glad to see you. Four teams will compete, but I have my hopes on the Whites. The White team's racers are always the most loyal and fastest. Their charioteer, Scorpus, has already won many races. Are you betting any money?

Aulus: *Ita vero! Ego autem magis viridibus fido. Auriga eorum, Flavinus, non solum velocissimus est, sed etiam ingeniosissimus in arte gubernandi. Semper in angustis cunctos praevenit et turbam deceptam relinquit. Vix credo alium ei comparari posse.*

Aulus: Yes, indeed! But I trust more in the Greens. Their charioteer, Flavinus, is not only the fastest but also the most skillful in steering. He always overtakes everyone in the tight turns and leaves the crowd astonished. I can hardly believe anyone can compare to him.

Decimianus: *Flavinus quidem arte sua laudandus est, sed Scorpus celeritate et audacia praestat. Mihi videtur viridis finem non attingere posse, praesertim si in prima spira firme obstet. Non obliviscar quantos profectus Scorpus fecerit postremis ludis, ubi adversarios omnes prostravit.*

Decimianus: Flavinus is certainly to be praised for his skill, but Scorpus surpasses him in speed and daring. I don't think the Green team will reach the finish, especially if Scorpus holds firm in the first turn. I won't forget how Scorpus dominated the last games, where he defeated all his rivals.

Aulus: *Consentio illum magno virtutis gradu esse, sed ne obliviscar, Decimiane, quod virides novam quadrigam habent—equi fortissimi et levissimi sunt. Si auriga satis prudenter eos regit, nihil praeter se pulverem alii visuri sunt. Hodie certe victoriam viridum exspecto.*

Aulus: I agree he is highly skilled, but don't forget, Decimianus, that the Greens have a new chariot—its horses are the strongest and lightest. If the charioteer guides them wisely, the others will see nothing but dust. Today, I certainly expect a Green victory.

Decimianus: *Ha! Fortuna semper variat in his ludis. Nullum certum est praesidium, sed sic ludi iucundi sunt. Ego tamen audacia fretus sum et pecuniam meam in Albam posui. Quam multum tu audes ponere pro viridibus?*

Decimianus: Ha! Fortune always changes in these games. Nothing is certain, but that's what makes the games exciting. However, I rely on boldness and have placed my money on the Whites. How much are you daring to bet on the Greens?

Aulus: *Hodie magna cum fiducia ago, Decimiane. Quinquaginta denarios pro viridibus pono. Nullus est defensor melior quam fortuna, quae mihi propitia est. Non videbis Scorpum hodie victorem esse!*

Aulus: Today, I'm acting with great confidence, Decimianus. I'm betting fifty denarii on the Greens. There's no better protector than fortune, and she's on my side. You won't see Scorpus victorious today!

Decimianus: *Bene, bene! Videbimus, quis nostrum post cursum laetior sit. Fortasse ambo tecta Circi in gaudio resonabimus aut ira frememus. Quicquid acciderit, Aule, certe hilaritas aderit. Spectacula haec delectant et animum fovent.*

Decimianus: Well, well! We'll see which one of us will be happier after the race. Perhaps both of us will cheer loudly under the Circus's roof or rage in anger. Whatever happens, Aulus, there will certainly be joy. These spectacles entertain and lift the spirit.

Aulus: *Ita est! Spes nostras habemus, sed ludus ipsi certamini primum locum dat. Vale igitur, Decimiane! Mox iterum spectemus et quocumque modo prosperet, ludi semper iucundi sunt.*

Aulus: That's right! We have our hopes, but the game itself takes first place in the competition. Farewell, then, Decimianus! Let's watch again soon, and no matter what happens, the games are always enjoyable.

Decimianus: *Vale, Aule! Sit victor quem fortuna iuvet!*

Decimianus: Farewell, Aulus! May the victor be the one whom fortune favors!

De Calamitate Agrorum – De difficultatibus agrariis colloquium

Faustus: *Salve, Lucili! Multa mala hodie de agris nostris audivi. Messis hac aestate visa est nimis tenuis et fructus minus soliti quam annis superioribus. Hoc graviter me sollicitat.*

Faustus: Hello, Lucilius! Today I've heard much bad news about our fields. The harvest this summer seems very meager, and the crops are less abundant than in previous years. This worries me greatly.

Lucilius: *Salve, Fauste! Et mihi eadem difficultas obvenit. Cum arva mea spectavi, vidi quanto cum dolore fruges non creverint. Siccitas et tempestates, ut videtur, maximam partem culpae ferunt. Haud facile erit, si res his modis pergent.*

Lucilius: Hello, Faustus! The same difficulty has befallen me. When I looked over my fields, I saw, with much sorrow, how the crops had not grown. Drought and storms, it seems, bear most of the blame. It will not be easy if things continue this way.

Faustus: *Sic est. Primum siccitas omnia perdidit, deinde, ubi tandem pluvia visa est, nimium vehemens fuit. Fruges inundationem passae sunt. Ita mala tempestas et quasi malum fatum agricolas nostros premit. Videbamus dies multos sine imbre, tum subito caelum nimia aqua oneratum.*

Faustus: That's right. First, the drought ruined everything, and then, when rain finally came, it was too heavy. The crops suffered from flooding. Thus, bad weather and what seems like a curse press down on our farmers. We saw many days without rain, then suddenly the sky was burdened with too much water.

Lucilius: *Non iniuste quereris. Et ego, cum signa tempestatum male vertentium prospexi, satis intellexi fore ut hic annus pessimus agricolis esset. Multi iam inquiunt proventus hordei villam non sufficientes esse ad familiam alendam. Alimenta omnino deficiunt.*

Lucilius: Your complaint is not unjust. When I saw the signs of bad weather coming, I understood well enough that this year would be terrible for farmers. Many are already saying that the barley harvest won't be enough to sustain their households. Food is completely lacking.

Faustus: *Censeo imperatores nostros aliquid pro agricolis facere debere. Quid, si subsidia agris ferantur? Aut si magis aquaeductus utiles efficiantur? Necessarium est non solum de urbibus curare, sed etiam de ruri, unde omnis vita oritur.*

Faustus: I think our leaders should do something for the farmers. What if they provide subsidies for the fields? Or if they improve the aqueducts to make them more useful? It's necessary not only to care for the cities but also for the countryside, where all life originates.

Lucilius: *Utique! Rustici civium fortissimi sunt, et agri nostri columnae Romanae rei publicae. Sine messibus bonis nullus erit cibus in urbibus. Sed tamen mihi videtur etiam de initiis curationis maioris agendum esse, ut tempestas et caelum, quoad fieri potest, provideantur. Quid enim sine ordinata agricultura effici possumus?*

Lucilius: Certainly! The farmers are the strongest of our citizens, and our fields are the pillars of the Roman Republic. Without good harvests, there will be no food in the cities. But it also seems to me that we need to take steps toward better management, so that the weather and sky are accounted for as much as possible. What can we achieve without well-organized agriculture?

Faustus: *Prudentissimum est quod dicis. Non satis est queri de malis; rationem invenire debemus quo modo his calamitatibus obviam ire possimus. Sic multae difficultates praeveniantur. Sed tamen, si periculum hoc anno duram famem adferet, quid faciendum erit ut populus tota hieme subsistat?*

Faustus: What you say is very wise. It's not enough to just complain about the troubles; we must find a way to address these disasters. This way, many difficulties can be prevented. But still, if the danger brings severe famine this year, what will be done to sustain the people throughout the winter?

Lucilius: *Forsitan necesse sit rem publicam intervenire et frumentum ex aliis partibus imperii importare, si res ad extremum periculum veniat. Multae provinciae sunt, ut Aegyptus, quae frumento satis abundant. Ita saltem urbs Roma ali potest, sed agri nostri multum damnum passi sunt et ad reparandum longius tempus erit.*

Lucilius: Perhaps it will be necessary for the state to intervene and import grain from other parts of the empire if things reach a critical point. There are many provinces, like Egypt, that have an abundance of grain. This way, at least the city of Rome can be fed, but our fields have suffered great damage, and it will take a long time to recover.

Faustus: *Ita puto. Spes nostra in provinciis frugiferis est, dum agri nostri reficiuntur. Sed certe oportet imperium nostrum cavere ne talis clades iterum accidat. Vale, Lucili, et si quid audieris de remediis aut subsidiis, certe me fac scire.*

Faustus: I think so too. Our hope lies in the fertile provinces while our fields are being restored. But certainly, our empire must ensure that such a disaster doesn't happen again. Farewell, Lucilius, and if you hear anything about remedies or subsidies, do let me know.

Lucilius: *Vale, Fauste! Cura ut bene naviges per haec tempora difficilia. Simul cooperantes, spero fore ut agrorum felicitas redeat.*

Lucilius: Farewell, Faustus! Take care as you navigate these difficult times. Working together, I hope that the prosperity of our fields will return.

De Bellis Civilibus – De bellis civilibus Romanis colloquium

Valeria: *Salve, Sulpicia! Audivistine quid de novis rerum communium motibus fertur? Iam videtur bellum civile Romae iterum imminere. Non cogitaveram res tam cito in hanc ruinam ituras esse.*

Valeria: Hello, Sulpicia! Have you heard the news about the new political upheavals? It already seems that another civil war is about to break out in Rome. I hadn't thought that things would fall into such ruin so quickly.

Sulpicia: *Salve, Valeria! Audivi, et non sine magno dolore. Tanta discordia in civitate nostra praevalet, ut vix videam quo modo pax diu servari possit. Hi duces, Caesar et Pompeius, invicem certant pro imperii dominatione, et populus, sicut solet, in medio laceratur. Quid tibi videtur, Valeria?*

Sulpicia: Hello, Valeria! I've heard, and not without great sadness. Such discord prevails in our state that I hardly see how peace can be maintained for long. These leaders, Caesar and Pompey, are fighting against each other for domination of the empire, and as usual, the people are torn apart in the middle. What do you think, Valeria?

Valeria: *Haud dissimile sentio. Mihi videtur hos viros praevalentes non tam pro re publica quam pro sua ipsorum gloria et potentia certare. Caesar quidem magna virtute in Gallia rem gessit, sed nimia ambitio eum ad haec bella civilia trahit. Quis scit quid ex hoc certamine eveniat?*

Valeria: I feel the same way. It seems to me that these powerful men are not fighting for the Republic but for their own glory and power. Caesar indeed accomplished great things in Gaul, but excessive ambition drives him into these civil wars. Who knows what will come out of this conflict?

Sulpicia: *Sic est, Valeria. Censeo autem multos Pompeio favere, quippe qui senatum et optimates secum habeat. Caesar, quamquam invictus videtur in bello, saepe auditur se nimis potentem ac regiae potestatis cupidum ostendere. Timor est, ne Roma iam liberum imperium amittat.*

Sulpicia: That's right, Valeria. However, I believe many favor Pompey, as he has the Senate and the aristocrats on his side. Caesar, although seemingly invincible in war, is often heard showing himself too powerful and desirous of royal authority. There's fear that Rome might lose its free government.

Valeria: *Verumne? Senatus Pompeium sequitur, sed Caesarem sequuntur legiones, qui plebem sibi conciliavit. Mihi metuendum est ne una factio vincat et res publica omnino delabatur. Libertas nostra iam inter duos heroes praeda facta est. Sed quid putas, Sulpicia? Qua re potissimum discordiae initium ceperunt?*

Valeria: Is that so? The Senate follows Pompey, but Caesar is followed by the legions, and he has won the favor of the people. I fear that if one faction wins, the Republic will completely collapse. Our freedom has already become the prey of two heroes. But what do you think, Sulpicia? What do you believe was the main cause of this discord?

Sulpicia: *Opinor, ut saepe fit, propter nimiam opum cupiditatem ac honorum certamen. Senatus, ut videtur, ex principibus metuit, ne alter alterum superet, et quisque potentiae suam partem sibi vindicare conatur. Caesaris victoria in Gallia multos sollicitos fecit; procedentes triumphi timorem novi domini auxerunt.*

Sulpicia: I believe, as often happens, it's due to excessive greed for wealth and the competition for honor. The Senate seems to fear that one leader will surpass the other, and each tries to claim their share of power. Caesar's victory in Gaul has made many anxious; his successive triumphs have increased the fear of a new master.

Valeria: *Non minime. Caesar semper audax et celer fuit, nec facile quidquam intermisit quod virtuti suae commodum esset. Quod si Pompeius senatum vicerit, an fore censes ut res ad pristinam formam redigantur?*

Valeria: Absolutely. Caesar has always been bold and swift, and he has never easily set aside anything that would benefit his power. But if Pompey defeats the Senate, do you think things will return to their previous state?

Sulpicia: *Difficile est dicere. Etiam si Pompeius vincat, mutata sunt tempora. Senatus potestatem quam habuit antea iam non retinet. Multi in populo non amplius fidunt in eos, qui olim Romam regebant. Res publica videtur quasi in manibus militum et ducum esse.*

Sulpicia: It's hard to say. Even if Pompey wins, the times have changed. The Senate no longer holds the power it once had. Many among the people no longer trust those who used to govern Rome. The Republic seems to be almost in the hands of soldiers and generals.

Valeria: *Ita verum est. Spes quidem nostra est ut aliquando pax restituatur, sed timeo ne bella haec civilia tam gravia vulnera infligant, ut non facile sanari possint. Orare debemus ut saltem res meliores fiant.*

Valeria: That's true. Our hope is that peace will someday be restored, but I fear that these civil wars will inflict such severe wounds that they won't be easily healed. We must pray that at least things will improve.

Sulpicia: *Nihil magis exopto. Sed tamen, Valeria, in hac turba, fortasse speremus fore ut aliquis vir prudens res moderetur. Spes, quam tenuis sit, numquam deserenda est.*

Sulpicia: I wish for nothing more. But still, Valeria, in this chaos, perhaps we should hope that some wise man will take control of things. Hope, however faint, must never be abandoned.

Valeria: *Verum est, Sulpicia. Dum speramus, fortuna civitatis nostrae, quamvis incerta, tamen conservari potest. Vale, et vigiles nuntiis utinam melioribus.*

Valeria: That's true, Sulpicia. As long as we hope, the fortune of our state, though uncertain, can still be preserved. Farewell, and may you watch for better news.

Sulpicia: *Vale, Valeria! Firma mente permaneamus in his rebus.*

Sulpicia: Farewell, Valeria! Let us remain steadfast in these matters.

De Somniis et Auspiciis – De somniis et auspiciis interpretandis colloquium

Aemilia: *Salve, Rubelle! Hodie valde sollicitata sum propter somnium, quod hac nocte habui. Nullum prius simile vidi, et nunc mirabilius esse videtur. Fortasse tu, qui semper de auspiciis ac somniis multa scis, aliquid mihi de eius significatione explicare potes.*

Aemilia: Hello, Rubellius! Today I am very worried because of a dream I had last night. I've never seen anything like it before, and now it seems even more extraordinary. Perhaps you, who always know a lot about omens and dreams, can explain something about its meaning to me.

Rubellius: *Salve, Aemilia! Bene factum est, quod ad me venisti. Somnia saepe non frustra mentes nostras agitant. Dic mihi, quid tibi apparuerit in somnio, ut fortasse aliquid de eo augurari possim.*

Rubellius: Hello, Aemilia! It's good that you came to me. Dreams often stir our minds for a reason. Tell me what appeared to you in the dream so that I might be able to interpret something from it.

Aemilia: *In somnio video me in magna silva stare, circumdata arboribus altissimis. Subito accedit aquila magna, quae in arbore maxima residet. Primum mihi videtur mitis, sed deinde de caelo devolat et in me impetum facit. Tum ex tenui auro circumdatur, et cum eius ungulas super caput meum conspicerem, subito ex somno excitata sum. Quidnam, Rubelle, censes significare haec omnia?*

Aemilia: In the dream, I see myself standing in a great forest, surrounded by very tall trees. Suddenly, a large eagle appears, which rests on the tallest tree. At first, it seems gentle to me, but then it swoops down from the sky and attacks me. Then it is surrounded by thin gold, and just as I see its claws above my head, I suddenly wake up. What do you think all this means, Rubellius?

Rubellius: *Signa haec minime contemnenda sunt, Aemilia. Silva ipsa saepe significat mentem aut viam incertam, per quam nostrum iter fit. Arbores altissimae potestatem repraesentant, fortasse magnorum virorum vel divinorum propositum. Aquila autem, quippe quae Iovis avis sit, potentiae caelestis et principatus signa ferre solet.*

Rubellius: These signs should not be taken lightly, Aemilia. The forest itself often represents the mind or an uncertain path on which we travel. The tall trees signify power, perhaps of great men or divine purpose. But the eagle, being the bird of Jupiter, usually bears signs of heavenly power and leadership.

Aemilia: *Et quid de impetu ipsius aquilae? Mea quidem sententia, ferox atque terribilis facta est in fine.*

Aemilia: And what about the eagle's attack? In my opinion, it became fierce and terrifying in the end.

Rubellius: *Id quod dicis, propter impetum, admonitio esse videtur. Mutatio status tibi aut in domo tua appropinquat. Non improbabile est res graves de honore aut fortuna tua vertendas esse. Aurum autem, quod aquilam circumdat, potestatem caelestem seu fatum indicare potuit. Formam auri bene interpretari possumus, quod fortuna bona tibi favere videtur.*

Rubellius: What you describe about the attack seems to be a warning. A change in status, either for you or your household, is approaching. It's not unlikely that significant matters related to your honor or fortune may shift. The gold surrounding the eagle could represent divine power or fate. We can interpret the gold favorably, as it seems that good fortune is on your side.

Aemilia: *Atque de significatione finali quid dicis? Haec omnia timorem mihi intulerunt.*

Aemilia: And what do you say about the final meaning? All of this has brought me fear.

Rubellius: *Ne timeas, Aemilia. Praesentia timenda non sunt, sed potius prudentia requirenda est. Somnium tibi ostendit ut vigiles et parata sis ad res novas aut subitas. Aquila, quamquam terribilis, non signum mali periculi est, sed magnitudinis vel potestatis. Consulas deos et sacrificium facias ut fatum tibi propitium sit.*

Rubellius: Do not be afraid, Aemilia. These things are not to be feared, but rather they require caution. The dream shows you that you should be watchful and prepared for new or sudden events. The eagle, though terrifying, is not a sign of evil danger but of greatness or power. Consult the gods and make a sacrifice so that fate may be favorable to you.

Aemilia: *Gratias tibi ago, Rubelle. Certe nunc levior animo sum, quoniam tua sapientia hanc rem interpretari potuisti. Fortasse nunc ibo ad templum Iovis, ut di scrutinis faverent.*

Aemilia: Thank you, Rubellius. Certainly, I feel much lighter now, since your wisdom was able to interpret this matter. Perhaps now I will go to the temple of Jupiter so that the gods may favor my requests.

Rubellius: *Ita fac, Aemilia. Dei immortales semper iis favent, qui eos consulunt. Vale, et spero ut omnia tibi feliciter eveniant.*

Rubellius: Do so, Aemilia. The immortal gods always favor those who consult them. Farewell, and I hope that everything will turn out happily for you.

Aemilia: *Vale, Rubelle! Tuam doctrinam numquam obliviscar.*

Aemilia: Farewell, Rubellius! I will never forget your teachings.

In Via Appia – Colloquium de itinere per viam Appiam

Sextus: *Salve, Plautiane! Longum iter habemus ante nos in hac via praeclara. Via Appia semper mihi videtur fumo et clamore plena, sed etiam magnum Romae opus ac gloriam Romani imperii prae se fert.*

Sextus: Hello, Plautianus! We have a long journey ahead of us on this famous road. The Via Appia always seems to me to be full of smoke and noise, but it also displays the great work of Rome and the glory of the Roman Empire.

Plautianus: *Salve, Sexte! Ita vero, via Appia non est solum iter, sed etiam monumentum ingenii nostri. Quam late extenditur! Videsne quanta multitudo viatorum hic circa nos sit? Mercatores, milites, et peregrini omnes per hanc viam transire solent.*

Plautianus: Hello, Sextus! Indeed, the Via Appia is not just a road but also a monument to our ingenuity. How far it extends! Do you see how many travelers are around us? Merchants, soldiers, and foreigners all travel along this road.

Sextus: *Sane! Non tantum de Roma narratur quanta sit, sed etiam quantum mare terramque domet. Ego multum tempus in urbe exegi, sed cum per hanc viam iter facio, magis magisque sentio quanto spatio imperium nostrum pateat. Quo properas hodie, Plautiane?*

Sextus: Certainly! It's not just how great Rome is that people talk about, but also how much land and sea it controls. I've spent much time in the city, but when I travel along this road, I feel more and more how vast our empire truly is. Where are you headed today, Plautianus?

Plautianus: *Ad Brundisium iter facio, Sexte. Non procul abest, sed res meae commerciales multum negotii poscunt. Multas merces ex orientis partibus exspecto. Tu autem? Quid te hodie in viam adduxit?*

Plautianus: I'm traveling to Brundisium, Sextus. It's not far, but my business matters require a lot of attention. I'm expecting many goods from the eastern regions. And you? What brought you onto the road today?

Sextus: *Ego quoque iter ad Brundisium capio, sed meum est privatorum causa—filium meum ad navem duco, qui studia sua Athenis continuabit.*

Semper me movet, Plautiane, cum video iuvenes in Graeciam studendi gratia proficisci. Quid putas? Num Graecorum doctrina adhuc maiorem vim habet in nostris temporibus?

Sextus: I'm also heading to Brundisium, but for personal reasons—I'm taking my son to the ship, as he will continue his studies in Athens. It always moves me, Plautianus, when I see young men going to Greece to study. What do you think? Does Greek learning still have as much influence in our times?

Plautianus: *Bene rem tangis, Sexte. Etsi Romana industria atque disciplina nos duxerunt ad imperium, multae tamen res quas apud Graecos invenimus, ut philosophia et leges, ad rationem ipsam pertinent. Graeci virtutem mentis praeclare coluerunt; nos autem, cum corpora nostra bellicis rebus exercemus, etiam mentem ex illis discere debemus.*

Plautianus: You touch on an important point, Sextus. Although Roman industry and discipline have led us to empire, many things we've found among the Greeks, such as philosophy and law, relate directly to reason itself. The Greeks cultivated the virtue of the mind admirably; while we train our bodies for war, we must also learn from them how to train the mind.

Sextus: *Ita est. Virtus et disciplina Graecorum multas utilitates nobis protulit. Tamen, Plautiane, ego saepe cogito nonne nimis etiam moveamur Graecorum institutis. Imperium nostrum nonne potius propriis moribus confirmari debeat? Non estne periculum ut nimia adrogantia ex eo oriatur?*

Sextus: That's true. The virtue and discipline of the Greeks have brought us many benefits. But, Plautianus, I often wonder whether we are too influenced by Greek institutions. Shouldn't our empire be strengthened more by our own customs? Isn't there a danger that too much pride could arise from this?

Plautianus: *Vere loqueris, Sexte. Omnia moderatione regenda sunt. Quod ex Graecis accipimus, non semper id imitandum est, sed iudicium nostrum adhibendum. Sic nos Graecorum sapientia utimur, sed Romanis virtutibus dominamur. Cura tamen ut filium tuum bene admoneas ne obliviscatur unde veniat.*

Plautianus: You speak truly, Sextus. Everything must be governed with moderation. What we take from the Greeks isn't always something to be imitated, but something to be judged carefully. Thus, we use Greek wisdom but rule with Roman virtues. Make sure, however, that you remind your son not to forget where he comes from.

Sextus: *Sane, Plautiane. Semper id filio meo praecipio. Multa discet apud Graecos, sed Roma manet rerum domina. Sed videsne quam festinat populus hic in via? Itaque properemus, ne postremi veniamus ad Brundisium.*

Sextus: Certainly, Plautianus. I always teach my son that. He will learn much from the Greeks, but Rome remains the ruler of the world. But do you see how quickly the people are moving along this road? Let's hurry, so we're not the last to arrive at Brundisium.

Plautianus: *Ita faciamus, Sexte! Iter longum est, sed sermo bonus viam breviorem facit. Vale!*

Plautianus: Let's do so, Sextus! The journey is long, but good conversation makes the road shorter. Farewell!

Sextus: *Vale, Plautiane!*

Sextus: Farewell, Plautianus!

In Foro Romano – Colloquium de rebus agendis in Foro Romano

Marcus: *Salve, Gaie! Quo itur hodie?*

Marcus: Hello, Gaius! Where are you heading today?

Gaius: *Salve, Marce! Non longe abeo. Venio ut negotia quaedam in Foro agam. Et tu? Vidistine iam spectaculum gladiatorum?*

Gaius: Hello, Marcus! I'm not going far. I've come to take care of some business in the Forum. And you? Have you already seen the gladiator show?

Marcus: *Minime! Diem in Foro ago, de rebus civilibus cogitans. Sed audivi hodie spectaculum esse insolitum, gladiatores non mediocres certaturos.*

Marcus: Not at all! I'm spending the day in the Forum, thinking about political matters. But I've heard today's show is extraordinary, with more than average gladiators set to compete.

Gaius: *Ita est. Fama fert pugnam gravem fore, praeclari gladiatores ad certamen ducentur. Sed, ut vides, ego plus curo quid hic in Foro geratur quam quod in amphitheatro fit. Multi hodie cum senatoribus colloquuntur.*

Gaius: That's right. Rumor has it that a serious fight is coming, with famous gladiators competing. But, as you can see, I care more about what's happening here in the Forum than what goes on in the amphitheater. Many people are talking with senators today.

Marcus: *Non miror. Tumultus ubique est; res publica, ut videtur, semper labascit. Audivistine aliquid de novis legibus quae agitantur?*

Marcus: I'm not surprised. There's turmoil everywhere; the Republic, it seems, is always faltering. Have you heard anything about the new laws being debated?

Gaius: *Audivi quidem. De fenore agitur et de pecunia multis modis tractanda. Credo multos ornatos viros hodie de sua ipsorum re quietos non esse. Sed, Marce, quid tibi visum est de statu ordinis senatorii?*

Gaius: I have indeed heard. It's about interest rates and managing money in various ways. I believe many distinguished men today are not calm about their own affairs. But, Marcus, what's your opinion on the state of the senatorial order?

Marcus: *Ah, Gaie, magna vis ambitionis inter eos. Raro verum bonum consilium invenimus. Cuncti de honoribus agunt, pro re publica parum curant. Tibi nonne videntur divitias magis quam iura defendere?*

Marcus: Ah, Gaius, ambition is strong among them. We rarely find any real good advice. They're all focused on honors, and care little for the Republic. Don't you think they defend wealth more than justice?

Gaius: *Omnino! Qui divitias tenent, illi iura fingunt. Pauci, ut mihi videtur, ad populum revocant. Sed, quid ego dico? Iam tempus est ad tabularium ire ut nomina curatorum inspiciam. Tu ad senatum perge?*

Gaius: Absolutely! Those who hold wealth shape the laws. Few, it seems to me, think of the people. But what am I saying? It's time for me to go to the records office to check the names of the officials. Are you heading to the Senate?

Marcus: *Fortasse. Sed prius ad bibliothecam contendam, volo enim scriptum quoddam antiquum inspicere. Qui fons scientiae tam plenus quam ipsi libri?*

Marcus: Perhaps. But first, I'm heading to the library, for I want to examine an ancient manuscript. What source of knowledge is as full as books themselves?

Gaius: *Nullus quidem. Sicum locum invenisti. Nunc vale! Forsitan postremo in amphitheatro conveniamus?*

Gaius: None indeed. You've found the perfect place. Now farewell! Perhaps we'll meet later at the amphitheater?

Marcus: *Ita, si denuo in clamoribus fori otium invenerim! Vale, Gaie.*

Marcus: Yes, if I can find some peace in the midst of the Forum's chaos! Farewell, Gaius.

Gaius: *Vale!*

Gaius: Farewell!

In Taberna Vinaria – Colloquium de vino et cibis

Lucius: *Salve, tabernarie! Vinum sumere velim; quid boni habes?*

Lucius: Hello, innkeeper! I'd like to have some wine; what good wine do you have?

Tabernarius: *Salve, Luci! Hodie optimum Falernum tibi offerre possum, vetus ac famosum. Estne hoc quod quaeris?*

Innkeeper: Hello, Lucius! Today I can offer you some excellent Falernian wine, old and famous. Is this what you're looking for?

Lucius: *Falernum quidem nobilissimum est. Sed quid de Cecina vino? Audivi id quoque satis bonum esse, nec tamen tam grave quam Falernum.*

Lucius: Falernian is indeed very noble. But what about Cecina wine? I've heard that it's also quite good, though not as heavy as Falernian.

Tabernarius: *Cecina quoque bonum vinum praebet; si minus nobile, plus tamen levitatis ac suavitatis habet. Id plerumque illi bibunt qui longius sedere volunt, non celeriter inebriari.*

Innkeeper: Cecina also offers good wine; though less noble, it has more lightness and sweetness. It's usually drunk by those who want to sit longer and not get drunk too quickly.

Lucius: *Itaque Cecinam sumam. Fac ut calix mihi celeriter feratur. Quae pretium est?*

Lucius: Then I'll take the Cecina. Make sure the cup is brought quickly. What's the price?

Tabernarius: *Calix unus Cecinae tibi constabit duobus assibus. Falernum, ut scis, multo plus valet.*

Innkeeper: One cup of Cecina will cost you two asses. Falernian, as you know, is worth much more.

Lucius: *Pretium aequum videtur. Nec multum de Falerno dolendum est, quamquam nemini displicet. Sed dic mihi, num recentia cibaria quoque habes? Quidnam porrigere potes, quo vinum melius sapiat?*

Lucius: The price seems fair. And I won't complain much about the Falernian, although no one dislikes it. But tell me, do you have any fresh food as well? What can you offer that would complement the wine?

Tabernarius: *Si vis, olivas recentissimas habemus et panem fragmentatum, cum modico casei veteris. Etiam caro hodie cocta est, sed gravis et fortis gustu. Quid placet?*

Innkeeper: If you wish, we have the freshest olives and broken bread, with a little aged cheese. There's also meat cooked today, but it's heavy and strong in taste. What do you prefer?

Lucius: *Melius mihi videtur olivas sumere cum pane. Sunt satis iucundae ad vinum levius. Fac ut ferantur.*

Lucius: I think it's better for me to take the olives with bread. They're pleasant enough to go with a lighter wine. Have them brought.

Tabernarius: *Sine mora, Luci! Statim omnia afferam. Si post hoc amplius vinum vel cibum quaeris, noli dubitare me vocare.*

Innkeeper: Without delay, Lucius! I'll bring everything right away. If you want more wine or food afterward, don't hesitate to call me.

Lucius: *Gratias, tabernarie. Spero fore ut hodie tranquillus dies sit, ut vinum paulatim gustare liceat.*

Lucius: Thank you, innkeeper. I hope today will be a peaceful day so that I can savor the wine slowly.

Tabernarius: *Ita sit! Iucunditas non semper ex magnis rebus, sed ex modicis et iucundis consistit. Vale dum feram!*

Innkeeper: May it be so! Enjoyment doesn't always come from great things, but from small and pleasant ones. Farewell for now while I bring it!

Lucius: *Bene dixisti! Expectabo.*

Lucius: Well said! I'll be waiting.

In Thermopolio – De cibo et potu emendo apud venditorem viarium

Sextus: *Salve, thermopolium! Esurio atque sitio; quid hodie praebes?*

Sextus: Hello, snack vendor! I'm hungry and thirsty; what do you have today?

Thermopoliarius: *Salve, Sexte! Multa quidem praeparata sunt. Hodie puls, panis calidus, et vinum mulsum ad manum est. Quid tibi libet?*

Thermopoliarius: Hello, Sextus! Many things are ready. Today we have porridge, warm bread, and spiced wine. What would you like?

Sextus: *Puls satis bene sapiens est, sed velim aliquid levius. Fortasse panem cum aliqua condicione? Estne aliquid carnis vel olivarum?*

Sextus: Porridge is fine, but I'd prefer something lighter. Maybe some bread with a topping? Do you have any meat or olives?

Thermopoliarius: *Habeo carnem porcinam bene assatam ac etiam olivas recentissimas. Panem quoque calidum modo e furno attuli. Quid tibi melius videtur?*

Thermopoliarius: I have well-roasted pork and also the freshest olives. I just brought warm bread from the oven. What sounds better to you?

Sextus: *Olivas sumam cum pane, et vinum mulsum mihi affer. Suntne recentia omnia?*

Sextus: I'll take olives with bread, and bring me some spiced wine. Is everything fresh?

Thermopoliarius: *Certe, omnia recentia sunt! Panis hodie coctus, olivae ex agris prope urbem hodie lectae, et vinum mulsum ex melle optimo confectum. Nec nimis dulce nec gravis saporis est.*

Thermopoliarius: Certainly, everything is fresh! The bread was baked today, the olives were picked from fields near the city today, and the spiced wine is made with the finest honey. It's neither too sweet nor too strong in flavor.

Sextus: *Bene; vinum, panis, et olivae satis erunt. Quanti haec omnia sunt?*

Sextus: Good; the wine, bread, and olives will be enough. How much for all this?

Thermopoliarius: *Duobus denariis panis, olivae unum assem valent, et vinum mulsum duobus assibus. Pretium iustum mihi videtur.*

Thermopoliarius: The bread is two denarii, the olives are one as, and the spiced wine is two asses. It seems like a fair price to me.

Sextus: *Satis modicum! Accipio et dico, nihil melius quam cibum bene paratum in thermopolio inveniri.*

Sextus: Quite reasonable! I'll take it, and I say, there's nothing better than well-prepared food found at a snack stall.

Thermopoliarius: *Gratias tibi ago, Sexte! Cibus vulgaris, ut scis, saepe levior est, sed si bene conditur, voluptatem magnam affert. Qui celeriter ambulant, celerem cibum quaerunt.*

Thermopoliarius: Thank you, Sextus! Simple food, as you know, is often lighter, but if it's well-seasoned, it brings great pleasure. Those who walk fast want fast food.

Sextus: *Ita est. Cibus celer, sed tamen iucundus. Nunc, quaeso, vinum prius mihi porrige, ut sitim tollam.*

Sextus: That's right. Fast food, but still enjoyable. Now, please give me the wine first to quench my thirst.

Thermopoliarius: *Ecce vinum mulsum! Sitim facile exstinguit. Si quid aliud posthac quaeris, noli dubitare.*

Thermopoliarius: Here's the spiced wine! It easily quenches thirst. If you need anything else afterward, don't hesitate to ask.

Sextus: *Gratias, faciam. Hodie autem panis et olivae sufficiunt. Vale!*

Sextus: Thanks, I will. But today, bread and olives will be enough. Farewell!

Thermopoliarius: *Vale, Sexte!*

Thermopoliarius: Farewell, Sextus!

In Pistrino – De pane et crustulis emendis colloquium

Publius: *Salve, pistor! Panem emere volo. Quid hodie praebes?*

Publius: Hello, baker! I want to buy some bread. What do you have today?

Pistor: *Salve, Publi! Hodie panes varii parati sunt. Est panis siligineus, candidus ac levis; item panis farreus, crassior et solidior. Quid tibi placet?*

Baker: Hello, Publius! Today we have various breads ready. There's siligineous bread, white and light; and also bread made from spelt, which is thicker and denser. What do you prefer?

Publius: *Panis siligineus mihi magis convenit. Candidus ac levis semper melius sapit, praesertim cum prandium elegans paraturus sim. Quanti constat?*

Publius: The siligineous bread suits me better. White and light always tastes better, especially when I'm preparing an elegant meal. How much does it cost?

Pistor: *Unus panis siligineus duobus assibus venditur. Sed, si plus volueris, pretium commodius faciemus.*

Baker: One siligineous bread is sold for two asses. But if you want more, we can make the price more favorable.

Publius: *Bene, sumam tres panes siligineos. Estne satis recens?*

Publius: Good, I'll take three siligineous loaves. Is it fresh enough?

Pistor: *Certe, hodie mane e furno extractus est, ut adhuc calidus sit. Nihil melius quam panis modo coctus.*

Baker: Certainly, it was taken from the oven this morning, so it's still warm. There's nothing better than freshly baked bread.

Publius: *Id quidem verum est. Nihil iucundius quam odorem panis calidi sentire. Sed dic mihi, quid praeter panem habes? Fortasse aliqua crustula?*

Publius: That's certainly true. There's nothing more pleasant than the smell of warm bread. But tell me, what else do you have besides bread? Perhaps some pastries?

Pistor: *Habeo crustula mellea et placentas parvas cum nucibus conditas. Hae placentae etiam Ciceroni ipsi gratae fuisse dicuntur!*

Baker: I have honey cakes and small cakes filled with nuts. It's said that even Cicero himself enjoyed these cakes!

Publius: *Cicero ipse laudavit? Bene, crustula mellea gustare velim. Quanti sunt?*

Publius: Cicero himself praised them? Well, I'd like to try the honey cakes. How much are they?

Pistor: *Crustulum unum tribus assibus venditur, placenta vero quinque asses constat. Utra tibi melior videtur?*

Baker: One honey cake is sold for three asses, while the small cake costs five asses. Which do you prefer?

Publius: *Crustula mihi satis sunt, praesertim si ita dulcia sunt ut fama fert. Da mihi tria crustula, quaeso.*

Publius: The honey cakes are enough for me, especially if they are as sweet as their reputation suggests. Give me three honey cakes, please.

Pistor: *Ecce! Crustula mellea optime facta. Cum tres panes sumas et tria crustula, erit omne pretium decem assium.*

Baker: Here you go! Perfectly made honey cakes. Since you're taking three loaves and three honey cakes, the total will be ten asses.

Publius: *Accipio. Praeclarum est pistrinum tuum, pistor; semper aliquid iucundi habes!*

Publius: I accept. Your bakery is excellent, baker; you always have something delightful!

Pistor: *Gratias tibi ago, Publi. Si quando iterum panem aut crustula quaesieris, scis ubi me invenire possis.*

Baker: Thank you, Publius. If you ever need bread or pastries again, you know where to find me.

Publius: *Ne dubitavero! Vale et bonum diem habe.*

Publius: I won't hesitate! Farewell and have a good day.

Pistor: *Vale, Publi, et bene ambula!*

Baker: Farewell, Publius, and walk well!

In Bibliotheca – Colloquium de libris et voluminibus

Marcus: *Salve, Gaie! Quid agis? Video te inter scripta veterum versari.*

Marcus: Hello, Gaius! How are you? I see you're engaged with the writings of the ancients.

Gaius: *Salve, Marce! Bene valeo, gratias tibi. Hic in bibliotheca plerumque tempus consumo, libros et volumina antiqua scrutor. Tu autem quid hodie quaeris?*

Gaius: Hello, Marcus! I'm doing well, thank you. I spend most of my time here in the library, studying old books and scrolls. What are you looking for today?

Marcus: *Ego quoque ad scriptum quoddam venio. Volo enim Titi Livii Ab Urbe Condita iterum legere. Historiam Romae praeclarissimam continet, et stilus eius gravis atque elegans est.*

Marcus: I've also come for a certain text. I want to read again Titus Livy's *Ab Urbe Condita*. It contains the most renowned history of Rome, and his style is serious and elegant.

Gaius: *Recte dicis. Livium legere semper voluptatis est. Sed hodie multi libri non minus iucundi inveniuntur. Nuper ego Naturalis Historia Plinii Maioris perlegi. Quid tibi videtur?*

Gaius: You're right. Reading Livy is always a pleasure. But today, many other books are equally enjoyable. Recently, I read Pliny the Elder's *Natural History*. What do you think of it?

Marcus: *Magnopere laudo! Plinius ingentem curiositatem atque scientiam rerum omnium colligit. Nihil est quod in universo orbe non tetigerit. Sed stilus eius interdum paulo difficilior videtur, nimis densus.*

Marcus: I greatly praise it! Pliny gathers an immense curiosity and knowledge of all things. There's nothing in the world he didn't touch upon. But his style sometimes seems a bit difficult, too dense.

Gaius: *Ita est. Copia verborum apud Plinium immensa est! Sed hanc rerum plenitudinem mentis vastitate excusamus. Sunt tamen alii scriptores qui celeriore et leviore stilo leguntur. Mihi placet, exempli gratia, Seneca.*

Gaius: That's true. The abundance of words in Pliny is immense! But we excuse this richness of content because of his vast mind. However, there are other writers who are read in a faster and lighter style. I like, for example, Seneca.

Marcus: *Seneca? Philosophiam eius praeclaram esse scio, sed stilus aliquando brevior quam mihi placeret videtur. Plus amo longas et continuas orationes, ut apud Ciceronem invenimus.*

Marcus: Seneca? I know his philosophy is excellent, but his style sometimes seems shorter than I would like. I prefer long and continuous speeches, like we find in Cicero.

Gaius: *Verum est, Cicero oratoriam rectissime coluit. Nulla ars eius eloquentiam superavit. Sed Seneca, breviter licet, tamen consiliorum plenus est. Mihi placet eius sermo de virtute et fortitudine animi. Hae sunt res quas inter vitae difficultates in animum semper recitare possum.*

Gaius: That's true, Cicero mastered oratory perfectly. No art surpasses his eloquence. But Seneca, though brief, is full of wisdom. I like his discussions on virtue and courage of the soul. These are things I can always recall during life's challenges.

Marcus: *Tibi consentio, Gaie, sed, ut verum fatear, nihil me magis delectat quam historiam legere. Res gestae clarorum virorum, bella, consilia, insidiae — haec omnia animum meum movent. Et quid de Vergilio? Nonne Aeneis saepe tibi ad manus accedit?*

Marcus: I agree with you, Gaius, but to be honest, nothing delights me more than reading history. The deeds of famous men, wars, plans, plots— these all move my mind. And what about Vergil? Don't you often turn to the *Aeneid*?

Gaius: *O Vergilius! Sicut nullum aliud scriptum! Non solum poeta praeclarus est, sed etiam magister morum et vitae praeceptor. Cum Aeneidem lego, videor me ipsum Aeneae comitem esse, per pericula et discrimina.*

Gaius: Oh, Vergil! Like no other text! He's not only a famous poet but also a teacher of morals and a guide to life. When I read the *Aeneid*, I feel as though I am Aeneas' companion, traveling through dangers and trials.

Marcus: *Mirum est! Per scripta poetarum vivere animum nostrum altissime afficit. Ergo nunc Livium quaero, et forsitan posthac ad Vergilium redeam.*

Marcus: It's amazing! Living through the writings of poets affects our soul most deeply. So now I'm looking for Livy, and perhaps later, I'll return to Vergil.

Gaius: *Bene! Ego autem protinus Senecam recitare constitui. Felicem tibi diem in studiis exopto, Marce.*

Gaius: Good! As for me, I've decided to read Seneca immediately. I wish you a productive day in your studies, Marcus.

Marcus: *Gratias tibi, Gaie. Et tu quoque in bona valetudine stude! Vale!*

Marcus: Thank you, Gaius. And you too, study in good health! Farewell!

Gaius: *Vale!*

Gaius: Farewell!

In Schola – Colloquium inter magistrum et discipulos

Magister: *Salvete, discipuli! Hodie de virtute et sapientia disputabimus. Primum dicite mihi, quid sit virtus vestra sententia.*

Teacher: Hello, students! Today, we will discuss virtue and wisdom. First, tell me, what is virtue in your opinion?

Lucius: *Salve, magister. Ego puto virtutem esse fortitudinem animi, cum quis pericula subeat neque metuat, sicut Marcius Scaevola vel Horatius Cocles.*

Lucius: Hello, teacher. I think that virtue is courage of the spirit, when someone faces dangers and does not fear, like Marcius Scaevola or Horatius Cocles.

Magister: *Bene dixisti, Luci. Fortitudo profecto pars magna est virtutis. Sed estne fortitudo sola virtus? Quid ceteri putant?*

Teacher: Well said, Lucius. Courage is indeed a big part of virtue. But is courage the only virtue? What do the others think?

Claudia: *Salve, magister. Ego arbitror virtutem non solum in fortitudine consistere, sed etiam in iustitia et prudentia. Sine iustitia, quid est fortitudo nisi saevitia?*

Claudia: Hello, teacher. I think that virtue does not only consist in courage but also in justice and wisdom. Without justice, what is courage but cruelty?

Magister: *Praeclare, Claudia! Iustitia sine dubio est fundamentum boni civis. Sapientes semper dixerunt iustitiam summam virtutem esse, quae alias regat. Sed quid dicitis de sapientia? Estne pars virtutis?*

Teacher: Excellent, Claudia! Justice is undoubtedly the foundation of a good citizen. The wise have always said that justice is the highest virtue, which governs the others. But what do you say about wisdom? Is it part of virtue?

Gaius: *Ita est, magister. Sapientia mihi videtur prudentia rerum, cum aliquis non solum quod faciendum sit intellegat, sed etiam qua ratione id perficiendum. Si sapientia abest, virtus quoque vacillat.*

Gaius: Yes, teacher. Wisdom seems to me to be the knowledge of things, when someone understands not only what must be done, but also how it should be accomplished. If wisdom is lacking, virtue also wavers.

Magister: *Gai, optime rem explicavisti! Sapientia prudentiam atque consilium continet. Curandum est ut semper rationem et modum in rebus teneamus. Quid ergo putatis de hoc: potestne aliquis esse vir bonus sine sapientia?*

Teacher: Gaius, you explained it excellently! Wisdom includes prudence and good judgment. We must always make sure to keep reason and balance in all things. So what do you think about this: can someone be a good man without wisdom?

Lucius: *Ego credo virum bonum esse posse, si iustus et pius sit, etiam si multam doctrinam non habeat.*

Lucius: I believe someone can be a good man if he is just and dutiful, even if he does not have much knowledge.

Claudia: *At, magister, nonne sapiens est qui intellegit quid sit bonum aut malum? Ergo vix aliquis iustus esse potest nisi etiam sapiens sit.*

Claudia: But, teacher, isn't a wise person someone who understands what is good or bad? So, someone can hardly be just unless they are also wise.

Magister: *Argumenta vestra gravia sunt! Profecto philosophi saepe de hac quaestione disputaverunt, utrum iustitia sine sapientia constare possit. Quod ad me attinet, credo non satis esse virtutem sine ratione conspici. Sapiens est qui secundum naturam vivit, modum tenet, et omnia in rerum ordinem refert. Sed nunc quaeram: quis est exemplum praeclarum sapientis in nostra historia?*

Teacher: Your arguments are weighty! Indeed, philosophers have often debated this question—whether justice can exist without wisdom. As for me, I believe that virtue cannot be fully seen without reason. The wise person is one who lives according to nature, keeps balance, and refers everything to the order of things. But now I ask: who is a famous example of a wise person in our history?

Gaius: *Socrates mihi videtur summum exemplum sapientiae, quia nihil nisi veritatem quaerebat et dicebat se nescire omnia, quod vere sapientis est.*

Gaius: Socrates seems to me to be the highest example of wisdom because he sought nothing but the truth and said that he didn't know everything, which is truly the mark of a wise person.

Magister: *Ita est, Socrates saepe sapientiae summum exemplum habetur. Sed nolimus non recordari nostrorum virorum, ut M. Ciceronis, qui non solum orator praeclarus fuit, sed etiam sapientiae amator. Multa enim de officiis atque virtute scripsit, quae omnibus temporibus legi debent. Bene disputavistis, discipuli! Ergo hoc concludamus: virtus ex sapientia, iustitia, fortitudine, temperantia constare videtur. Nunc in proximam lectionem progrediamur.*

Teacher: That's right, Socrates is often considered the highest example of wisdom. But let us not forget our own men, like Marcus Cicero, who was not only a famous orator but also a lover of wisdom. He wrote much about duties and virtue, which should be read in all times. You have debated well, students! So let us conclude this: virtue seems to consist of wisdom, justice, courage, and temperance. Now let's move on to the next lesson.

Discipuli: *Gratias, magister!*

Students: Thank you, teacher!

Magister: *Valete, discipuli, et memineritis, virtus non in verbis, sed in factis probatur!*

Teacher: Farewell, students, and remember, virtue is proven not in words, but in deeds!

Discipuli: *Vale, magister!*

Students: Farewell, teacher!

De Tempore – Colloquium de tempestate

Gaius: *Salve, Marce! Nubes hodie densissimae caelum operiunt, nec sol quidem cerni potest. Quid tibi de hac tempestate videtur?*

Gaius: Hello, Marcus! The thick clouds are covering the sky today, and not even the sun can be seen. What do you think of this weather?

Marcus: *Salve, Gaie! Ego quidem non miror. Hiems appropinquat, et venti frigidi iam sentiuntur. Tempus mutatur, ut solet, et mox, ut arbitror, pluviae cadent.*

Marcus: Hello, Gaius! I'm not surprised. Winter is approaching, and the cold winds can already be felt. The weather is changing, as usual, and soon, I believe, rain will fall.

Gaius: *Ita vero. Heri quoque pluvia toto die ruit, et agri madidi sunt. Sed quid dicis de hoc frigore? Numquam antea tam mane talem frigiditatem sensi.*

Gaius: Yes, indeed. Yesterday it rained all day, and the fields are soaked. But what do you say about this cold? I've never felt such chill so early before.

Marcus: *Verum est. Initium frigoris hoc anni tempore advenit. Sed hic apud nos ita solet; nihil novi est. Cum venti ab Alpibus veniunt, semper aquilonem et frigus afferunt.*

Marcus: That's true. The start of cold weather comes at this time of year. But this is how it always is here; nothing new. When the winds come from the Alps, they always bring the north wind and cold.

Gaius: *Mihi quidem videtur feriae autumnales hoc anno frigidiores fuisse quam solebant. Spero tamen fore ut vere tempestas meliores ferat.*

Gaius: It seems to me that this year the autumn holidays have been colder than usual. However, I hope that spring will bring better weather.

Marcus: *Sicut Cicero saepe dicebat, omnia tempora moderata sunt. Post hiemem ver venit, et post frigora calores revertuntur. Patientia opus est.*

Marcus: As Cicero often said, all seasons are moderate. After winter comes spring, and after the cold, warmth returns. We just need patience.

Gaius: *Quid tibi visum est de aestate praeterita? Ferocior fuit quam sperabam. Sol ardebat tota die, nec umbra satis refrigerii praebebat.*

Gaius: What did you think of the past summer? It was fiercer than I had hoped. The sun burned all day, and even the shade didn't provide enough relief.

Marcus: *Aestas quidem calidissima fuit, praesertim in Campania. Multi agricolae sine aqua sufficiente palentes messes perdiderunt. Sed nunc tandem frigus consolationem affert.*

Marcus: The summer was indeed very hot, especially in Campania. Many farmers lost their crops, withering without enough water. But now, finally, the cold brings some comfort.

Gaius: *Mirum est ut res mutantur! Tam cito hiemem post aestatem acerbam accipimus. Sed procellas saepe etiam inter tempora tranquillissima oriuntur.*

Gaius: It's amazing how things change! So quickly we receive winter after a harsh summer. But storms often arise even in the calmest of times.

Marcus: *Ita est, Gaie. Tempora et caelum suis legibus aguntur. Nos tamen ad omnia parati esse debemus, et quodcumque caelum ferat fortiter ferre.*

Marcus: That's right, Gaius. The seasons and the weather follow their own laws. We, however, must be prepared for everything, and face whatever the sky brings with courage.

Gaius: *Profecto! Sed nunc, quoniam caelum videtur in pluviam vertere, melius est ut ad domum redeamus. Iam satis ambulavi!*

Gaius: Certainly! But now, since the sky seems to be turning to rain, it's better for us to head back home. I've walked enough!

Marcus: *Consilium bonum! Pluvia cito cadet, nubes eam produnt. Vale, Gaie, et bene te habe.*

Marcus: Good idea! The rain will fall soon, the clouds are revealing it. Farewell, Gaius, and take care.

Gaius: *Vale, Marce, et speremus cito ad meliores caelos reverti!*

Gaius: Farewell, Marcus, and let's hope we return to better skies soon!

In Horto Publico – Colloquium de plantis et natura

Quintus: *Salve, Tite! Laetus te hodie in horto video. Quid tibi de hac amoenitate videtur?*

Quintus: Hello, Titus! I'm glad to see you in the garden today. What do you think of this beauty?

Titus: *Salve, Quinte! Mihi vero haec loca iucundissima sunt. Flores hic varii, arbores umbrosae, rivi leniter murmurantes—haec omnia animum valde delectant. Nihil mihi magis placet quam in huiusmodi locis versari.*

Titus: Hello, Quintus! I truly find these places most delightful. The varied flowers, shady trees, gently murmuring streams—all of this pleases the soul greatly. Nothing gives me more pleasure than spending time in places like these.

Quintus: *Ita est. Horti pleni sunt gratia naturae et tranquillitate. Videsne illas rosas? Tam rubeae sunt ut ignem ardeant. Cura naturae perfecta simillima.*

Quintus: Indeed. Gardens are full of nature's grace and tranquility. Do you see those roses? They're so red they seem to burn like fire. The care of nature is almost perfect.

Titus: *Specta et illas vites quae pergulas circumvolvunt! Numquam tam pulchram coniunctionem arborum et vitium vidi. Natura semper artem vincit.*

Titus: Look at those vines that twine around the pergolas! I've never seen such a beautiful union of trees and vines. Nature always surpasses art.

Quintus: *Bene dicis, Tite. Etsi homines multum laboris impendunt ut hortos excolant, tamen ipsa natura, sponte sua, maximam pulchritudinem praebet. Nihil est quod cum hac varietate comparari possit.*

Quintus: You speak well, Titus. Even though people put in much work to cultivate gardens, nature itself, of its own accord, provides the greatest beauty. Nothing can compare with this variety.

Titus: *Nonne tibi videtur, Quinte, hortus ipsam formam tranquillitatis et otii repraesentare? Hic procul a turba, procul a clamoribus urbis, licet mentem ad se ipsum revocare.*

Titus: Don't you think, Quintus, that the garden represents the very essence of tranquility and leisure? Here, far from the crowd, far from the noise of the city, one can bring their mind back to itself.

Quintus: *Vere! Horti nullo loco melius id faciunt. Nam in mediis frondibus et floribus vivunt et hominibus loquuntur. Herbae quasi tranquilla voce invitare videntur ad consilia secundum naturam capienda.*

Quintus: Truly! Gardens do this better than anywhere else. For among the leaves and flowers, they seem to live and speak to people. The plants seem to invite us with a quiet voice to take advice in accordance with nature.

Titus: *Qualis vox sapientis! Et vides illos cupressos, qui ut proceres inter ramos surgunt? Quotiescumque eos aspicio, mihi videtur tamquam de diuturnitate et stabilitate loquantur.*

Titus: What wisdom in that voice! And do you see those cypress trees, which rise like leaders among the branches? Whenever I look at them, it seems as if they are speaking about endurance and stability.

Quintus: *Cupressus, ut dicis, est arbor stabilitatis atque aeternitatis. Sed etiam illae lauri, quas semper victores in capite gestant, de gloria et honore suo silentio praedicant.*

Quintus: The cypress, as you say, is the tree of stability and eternity. But even those laurels, which victors always wear on their heads, silently proclaim their own glory and honor.

Titus: *Quinte, mi amice, saepe res naturae plus docent quam verba magistrorum. Flores ac folia, fruges ac silvae, si bene observantur, multa de vita hominum ac rebus divinis narrant.*

Titus: Quintus, my friend, often nature's things teach more than the words of teachers. Flowers and leaves, fruits and forests, if observed well, tell us much about human life and divine matters.

Quintus: *Verissimum est. Natura ipsa magistra sapientiae est. Ego saepe huc venio, non solum ob pulchritudinem, sed etiam ut res magnas et parvas meditari possim inter flores et frondes.*

Quintus: That's absolutely true. Nature itself is the teacher of wisdom. I often come here, not only for the beauty but also so I can reflect on great and small matters among the flowers and leaves.

Titus: *Bene facis, Quinte. Forsitan posthac huc simul veniamus et de philosophia, de natura ipsa colloquamur. Tempus hic tantum lente fluit, ut omnia quae dicere velimus dici possint.*

Titus: You do well, Quintus. Perhaps in the future, we can come here together and talk about philosophy, about nature itself. Time flows so slowly here that everything we wish to say can be said.

Quintus: *Libet! Horti quippe se dulcissimos interlocutores praebent. Nunc tamen, vale, Tite, et fruere hoc die amoenissimo.*

Quintus: I'd like that! Gardens, indeed, offer themselves as the sweetest companions. But now, farewell, Titus, and enjoy this most pleasant day.

Titus: *Vale, Quinte, et tibi placidam et felicem diem exopto.*

Titus: Farewell, Quintus, and I wish you a peaceful and happy day.

In Ludo Gladiatorum – Colloquium inter spectatores in certamine gladiatorum

Lucius: *Salve, Gaie! Vide, quantus hominum concursus in amphitheatro! Numquam antea tam magnas turbas vidi. Certamen gladiatorum magnum spectaculum promittit.*

Lucius: Hello, Gaius! Look at how many people have gathered in the amphitheater! I've never seen such large crowds before. The gladiator fight promises to be a grand spectacle.

Gaius: *Salve, Luci! Ita est. Hodie non solum communes gladiatores pugnabunt, sed etiam praeclari et peritissimi. Dicitur etiam retiarius quidam notissimus, cui nomen Hermes est, in arena pugnaturus esse. Virum tam fortem saepe laudant!*

Gaius: Hello, Lucius! That's right. Today, not only ordinary gladiators will fight, but also famous and highly skilled ones. It's said that a well-known *retiarius* named Hermes will fight in the arena. They often praise him as a very strong man!

Lucius: *Hermes? Audivi multos de eo locutos, sed numquam eum spectavi. Ferunt eum dirissimum esse in pugna, sed etiam astutum. Suntne adversarii eius pares?*

Lucius: Hermes? I've heard many people talk about him, but I've never seen him fight. They say he is fierce in battle but also cunning. Are his opponents his equal?

Gaius: *Hodie contra mirmillonem praeclarum, qui Severus vocatur, certabit. Multi Severum pro victore habent, quia magnos et multos honores iam reportavit. Sed Hermes magna dexteritate uti solet, et vix potest praedicari quis victurus sit.*

Gaius: Today, he will fight against a famous *murmillo* named Severus. Many consider Severus the likely victor because he has already won great and numerous honors. But Hermes is known for his great skill, and it's hard to predict who will win.

Lucius: *Hoc certamen magnam expectationem excitat! Ego autem semper mirmillones retiariis praefero. Eis scutum, galea, gladiusque ad* *rem comparatum est; melius oppugnare et defendere possunt. Retiarius mihi magis fugit quam pugnat.*

Lucius: This match is creating great excitement! But I always prefer *murmillos* over *retiarii*. They have shields, helmets, and swords for the task; they can attack and defend better. A *retiarius* seems more like he's running away than fighting to me.

Gaius: *Etiam si retiarii leves et mobiles sunt, non puto eos minus fortes esse. Celeritas et astutia saepe plus valent quam corporis munitio. Videbis, Luci, Hermes forsitan Severum vincet celeritate sua.*

Gaius: Even though *retiarii* are light and mobile, I don't think they are any less strong. Speed and cunning often matter more than bodily armor. You'll see, Lucius, Hermes may very well defeat Severus with his speed.

Lucius: *Fortasse. Sed quid dicis de hac multitudine? Videor iam discedere velle antequam tumultus fiant. Plerique spectatores, cum nimium accenduntur, non sine periculo sunt.*

Lucius: Perhaps. But what do you think of this crowd? I feel like I might want to leave before things get too chaotic. Many spectators, when they get too excited, can be dangerous.

Gaius: *Vera dicis. Ludi gladiatorii saepe ferociam populi excitant. Quidam non modo pugnam spectare volunt, sed etiam crudelitatem. Ego tamen spero me hoc certamen cum voluptate spectaturum esse, sine iis clamoribus qui non delectant.*

Gaius: You're right. Gladiator games often stir up the crowd's ferocity. Some people don't just want to watch the fight but also enjoy the cruelty. However, I hope to watch this match with pleasure, without the kinds of shouts that spoil the enjoyment.

Lucius: *Hora certaminis nondum advenit, sed iam motus in arena videmus. Gladiatores procedunt. Ecce, vide Hermen! Magnam turbam salutat. Numquam talem audaciam vidi.*

Lucius: The time for the match hasn't come yet, but we already see movement in the arena. The gladiators are coming out. Look, there's Hermes! He's greeting the crowd. I've never seen such boldness.

Gaius: *Hermes se bene praeparavit. Constat eum semper prius diligenter exerceri quam in arenam prodeat. Severus non minore audacia est, tamen, ut honorem suum tueatur.*

Gaius: Hermes has prepared himself well. It's well known that he always trains diligently before entering the arena. Severus is no less bold, though, as he's defending his honor.

Lucius: *Spectaculum incipit. Nunc videbimus utrum celeritas an gravitas certaminis dominetur. Vale nunc, Gaie; oculis intentis spectare necesse est!*

Lucius: The show is starting. Now we'll see whether speed or strength dominates the match. Farewell for now, Gaius; I must watch closely!

Gaius: *Vale, Luci! Et felix sit cui victoria decernetur!*

Gaius: Farewell, Lucius! And may victory go to the deserving one!

De Spectaculis Circensibus – Colloquium de cursibus quadrigarum in Circo Maximo

Marcus: *Salve, Publi! Vide quantus clamor e Circo Maximo tollitur! Hodie praeclari agitatores in certamen descendunt. Visne spectare?*

Marcus: Hello, Publius! Look at the roar rising from the Circus Maximus! Today, famous charioteers are entering the competition. Do you want to watch?

Publius: *Salve, Marce! Certe! Nihil mihi magis placet quam ludi circenses. Hodie quadrigae vehementer contendunt, et agitatores nobilissimi pugnabunt. Quibus tibi faves?*

Publius: Hello, Marcus! Of course! Nothing pleases me more than the circus games. Today, the chariots are competing fiercely, and the most renowned charioteers will fight. Who are you rooting for?

Marcus: *Ego semper prasinae factioni faveo. Eorum equi rapidissimi sunt, et agitator princeps, Scorpus, celeritate sua prae cunctos excellit. Tu autem quibus faves?*

Marcus: I always support the green faction. Their horses are the fastest, and their lead charioteer, Scorpus, surpasses everyone with his speed. And you, who do you support?

Publius: *Ego caeruleis favere soleo. Non modo praeclari sunt, sed etiam plerumque victores fuerunt anno proximo. Fortuna enim agitatori eorum Maximo favet. Ille arte et prudentia semper utitur.*

Publius: I usually support the blues. They're not only famous, but they were also the champions last year. Fortune favors their charioteer Maximus. He always uses skill and wisdom.

Marcus: *Maximus quidem peritus est, sed celeritas Scorpi ei praevalere potest. Certe tamen uterque summam peritiam habet. Praeterea equos prasinorum tam robustos numquam vidi. Hodie prasinis victoriam praenuntio.*

Marcus: Maximus is indeed skilled, but Scorpus' speed could overpower him. Surely, though, both have great expertise. Besides, I've never seen horses as strong as those of the greens. Today, I predict victory for the greens.

Publius: *Noli tam celeriter iudicare, Marce. In Circo, fortuna saepe variat. Multi ante cursum finire vincentes videbantur, sed repente eis adversa eveniebant. Equi interdum deficiunt, aut rotarum collisio periculosa vehicula evertit. Ora spectantium clamore replentur ubi sors repente mutatur.*

Publius: Don't judge too quickly, Marcus. In the Circus, fortune often changes. Many seemed to be winning before the race ended, but suddenly things turned against them. Sometimes the horses falter, or a dangerous collision flips the chariots. The stands fill with the roar of spectators when fate suddenly shifts.

Marcus: *Recte dicis. Spes et pericula semper in eo loco sunt. Nihil tamen magis animi excitationem movet quam cursus quadrigarum. Celeritas equorum, clamor populi, et ipsa incertitudo victoriae totam animi intentionem captat.*

Marcus: You're right. Hope and danger are always present there. But nothing stirs excitement more than a chariot race. The speed of the horses, the roar of the crowd, and the uncertainty of victory capture all my attention.

Publius: *Ita est. Sed dic mihi, quid de aliis factionibus sentis? Albi et russati quoque non sunt contemnendi. Paucis abhinc annis russati, quidquid acciderit, saepe vicerunt.*

Publius: That's true. But tell me, what do you think of the other factions? The whites and reds shouldn't be underestimated either. A few years ago, no matter what happened, the reds often won.

Marcus: *Russati antiquitus magnos triumphos fecerunt, sed nunc minus valent. Albi quidem quondam praeclari fuerunt, sed eorum equi nunc minus fortes videntur. Itaque plerique prasinis aut caeruleis favere solent.*

Marcus: The reds won great victories in the past, but they are weaker now. The whites were once famous too, but their horses don't seem as strong anymore. So most people tend to support the greens or blues.

Publius: *Tamen, Marce, in ludis circensibus nemini fidendum est, nisi fors ipsa pro favore decernat. Ecce! Signum datur, quadrigae procedunt. Vide quanta celeritas! Prasini et caerulei iam in primis locis certant.*

Publius: Still, Marcus, in the circus games, you can't rely on anyone unless fortune itself decides. Look! The signal is given, and the chariots are off. Look how fast they are! The greens and blues are already fighting for the lead.

Marcus: *Vere spectaculum! Scorpus et Maximus humeris pugnare videntur. Quis nunc victor erit, nescio. Faciamus ut animum intentum teneamus.*

Marcus: Truly a spectacle! Scorpus and Maximus seem to be battling shoulder to shoulder. Who will be the victor now, I don't know. Let's stay focused and watch closely.

Publius: *Nihil aliud nunc fieri potest nisi spectare. Vale, Marce, dum certamen incipit. Felix sit agitator cui victoria data sit!*

Publius: Nothing else can be done now but to watch. Farewell, Marcus, as the race begins. May fortune favor the charioteer who is granted victory!

Marcus: *Vale, Publi! Spectaculum summum sit, ut solet!*

Marcus: Farewell, Publius! May it be the greatest spectacle, as it usually is!

In Ludo Scholastico – Colloquium inter discipulum et magistrum praeparantem ad lectionem

Magister: *Salve, Sexte! Paratusne es hodie ad lectionem?*

Teacher: Hello, Sextus! Are you prepared for today's lesson?

Sextus: *Salve, magister! Paratus sum, quamquam aliquantulum sollicitus sum de quaestionibus quas mihi hodie propones. Quae res discendae sunt?*

Sextus: Hello, teacher! I am prepared, although I'm a little worried about the questions you might ask me today. What topics will we be learning?

Magister: *Hodie de rebus belli et pacis disseremus. Lectionem ex Libro III Titi Livii Ab Urbe Condita legemus, ubi Fabii de populo Veientium loquuntur. Visne memoriam tuam probare et prompte recitare quae iam legisti?*

Teacher: Today we will discuss matters of war and peace. We will read from Book III of Livy's *Ab Urbe Condita*, where the Fabii talk about the people of Veii. Would you like to test your memory and recite what you've already read?

Sextus: *Certe, magister. Declamationem ex primo capitulo paravi. "Cum Veientes bellum cum Romanis renovarent, senatus populi Romani Fabios ad bellum mittit, viros clarissimos et fortissimos, qui suae domus vires pro re publica dederunt." Ita scriptum est, si recte memini.*

Sextus: Certainly, teacher. I've prepared a recitation from the first chapter. "When the Veientes renewed war with the Romans, the Senate of the Roman people sent the Fabii to war, the most famous and brave men, who gave the strength of their house for the Republic." That is what's written, if I remember correctly.

Magister: *Bene recitas, Sexte. Livius sempiterna exempla virtutis et officii nobis ostendit. Sed quid intellegis de sententia? Cur Fabii soli ad bellum mittuntur?*

Teacher: You recite well, Sextus. Livy presents us with timeless examples of virtue and duty. But what do you understand from the sentence? Why are the Fabii sent to war alone?

Sextus: *Ego puto quod Fabii semper pro re publica prompti erant et consilio sapientiaque sua senatum adiuvabant. Sed, magister, nonne id etiam nobis monere videtur ut causam pro patria nostra semper suscipiamus?*

Sextus: I think it's because the Fabii were always ready to act for the Republic and helped the Senate with their wisdom and counsel. But, teacher, doesn't this also remind us that we should always take up the cause for our homeland?

Magister: *Ita est! Livius non solum historiam narrat, sed etiam virtutes civiles extollit. Nos quoque, si boni cives esse volumus, exempla talium virorum sequi debemus. Sed nunc, quaeso, explica mihi qui fuerint Veientes et quid bellum cum eis difficilius reddidit.*

Teacher: That's right! Livy doesn't just tell history; he also praises civic virtues. We, too, if we want to be good citizens, must follow the examples of such men. But now, please explain to me who the Veientes were and what made the war with them so difficult.

Sextus: *Veientes, ut scis, populus Etruriae fuit, prope Romam situs. Cum tam propinqui essent, saepe de finibus controversiae inter eos et Romanos ortae sunt. Praeterea urbes Etruriae magnae divitiae habebant, itaque bellum cum iis non facile fuit.*

Sextus: The Veientes, as you know, were a people of Etruria, located near Rome. Since they were so close, disputes over borders often arose between them and the Romans. Moreover, the cities of Etruria had great wealth, so the war with them was not easy.

Magister: *Recte dicis. Etrusci semper adversarii firmi et potentes hostes fuerunt. Haec autem lectio nos docet quam promptus Romanus senatus fuerit ad pericula civium sananda et ad bellum gerendum. Videsne exemplum quomodo prudentia et virtus bellum vincant?*

Teacher: You're right. The Etruscans were always strong opponents and powerful enemies. But this lesson shows us how ready the Roman Senate was to address the dangers to its citizens and wage war. Do you see an example of how prudence and virtue can win wars?

Sextus: *Bene video, magister. Sed scisne quid postea Fabiis acciderit? Num bellum contra Veientes victoriam finalem attulit?*

Sextus: I see it well, teacher. But do you know what happened to the Fabii afterward? Did the war against the Veientes bring final victory?

Magister: *Leges, Sexte, cura ut hoc capitulum prosequaris. Fabii quidem in bello magna fortitudine pugnant, sed omnes, praeter unum, in insidiis occiduntur. Unus tamen filius superest, ex quo domus Fabiorum posteros suos habet.*

Teacher: You'll read that, Sextus. Make sure to continue with this chapter. The Fabii fought with great bravery in the war, but all of them, except one, were killed in an ambush. However, one son survived, and from him, the house of the Fabii continued its line.

Sextus: *Tristis finis est, magister, sed simul pulcher propter eorum devotionem. Ponunt vitam pro Roma sine haesitatione.*

Sextus: It's a sad ending, teacher, but also beautiful because of their devotion. They gave their lives for Rome without hesitation.

Magister: *Id verum est. Haec lectio nos admonet de magnitudine animi Romani. Iam satis progredimur. Diligenter te para ad proximam lectionem, ubi plura de virtute Romana tractabimus.*

Teacher: That's true. This lesson reminds us of the greatness of the Roman spirit. We've progressed enough for now. Prepare yourself carefully for the next lesson, where we will discuss more about Roman virtue.

Sextus: *Gratias, magister! Faciam ut me bene proparem. Vale!*

Sextus: Thank you, teacher! I will make sure to prepare well. Goodbye!

Magister: *Vale, Sexte, et in studiis tuis semper progredere!*

Teacher: Goodbye, Sextus, and always make progress in your studies!

In Villa Rustica – Colloquium de vita agraria

Gaius: *Salve, Marce! Quam iucundum est te in hac villa rustica videre! Quid cogitas de vita agraria?*

Gaius: Hello, Marcus! How pleasant it is to see you in this country villa! What do you think of rural life?

Marcus: *Salve, Gaie! Praeclara quidem mihi videtur haec vita. Quam tranquilla sunt omnia! Terra ipsa sua fertilitate delectat, et labor agrorum magnum fructum reddit. Nullus strepitus urbis, nulla sollicitudo negotiorum.*

Marcus: Hello, Gaius! This life seems wonderful to me indeed. How peaceful everything is! The land itself delights with its fertility, and the labor of the fields yields great rewards. No city noise, no business worries.

Gaius: *Vere dicis. Nihil dulcius esse potest quam hoc ruris otium. Hic in agris, sol prima luce oritur, et omnes res secundum naturam fiunt. Quid magis ad animi constantiam convenit quam cura agri sui?*

Gaius: You're right. Nothing can be sweeter than this peace of the countryside. Here in the fields, the sun rises at dawn, and everything happens according to nature. What is better for peace of mind than tending to one's own land?

Marcus: *Quid enim est dulcius, nisi agricola sua manu cibum gignit, dum reliqui urbani de miseriis laborant? Nam quae urbs artificiis et industria parare debet, hic natura ipsa sine labore melius proveniunt.*

Marcus: What could be sweeter than a farmer producing food with his own hands while the rest of the city folk toil with their struggles? For what the city must prepare through craft and industry, here nature herself produces better without effort.

Gaius: *Nihil profecto urbi comparandum est agro. In urbe homines tumultuantur, semper alienis negotiis occupati; in agro autem, qui ruri vivunt, ad suas ipsorum curas et labores revocantur. Ubi maius bonum est quam in sua terra colenda?*

Gaius: Truly, nothing in the city can compare to the countryside. In the city, people are always in turmoil, busy with the affairs of others; but in the fields, those who live in the country focus on their own cares and work. Where is there a greater good than in cultivating one's own land?

Marcus: *Et nonne videtur, Gaie, qui ruri vivimus, etiam sapientiam plus capere ex natura ipsa? Solem, caelum, tempestates cotidie observamus, et quas res alii non animadvertunt, nos intellegimus. Agricultura non solum laborem, sed etiam sapientiam requirit.*

Marcus: And don't you think, Gaius, that those of us who live in the country gain even more wisdom from nature itself? We observe the sun, the sky, and the weather daily, and we understand things that others overlook. Farming requires not only labor but also wisdom.

Gaius: *Recte dicis, Marce. Agricola non modo de terra, sed etiam de caelo, ventis, et annorum vicissitudinibus discit. Sicut veteres agricolae dicebant, agricultura mater omnium artium est. Nihil sine agris fieri potest, neque hominum vita neque civitatis salus.*

Gaius: You're right, Marcus. A farmer learns not only about the land but also about the sky, the winds, and the changing seasons. As the old farmers used to say, farming is the mother of all arts. Nothing can happen without the fields, neither human life nor the safety of the state.

Marcus: *Ita est. Sed quid ceterorum? Hodie operarii in vinea laborant? Vinum hodie exprimitur?*

Marcus: That's right. But what about the others? Are the workers in the vineyard today? Is wine being pressed today?

Gaius: *Ita vero. Hodie operarii in vinea non solum uvas legunt, sed etiam torculo exprimunt. Vinum novum, si natura favet, hac tempestate optime fiet. Si volueris, post prandium ad vineam ire possumus ut labores spectemus.*

Gaius: Yes, indeed. Today, the workers are not only picking grapes in the vineyard but also pressing them in the winepress. If nature is kind, the new wine will turn out wonderfully this season. If you like, we can go to the vineyard after lunch to watch the work.

Marcus: *Laetus veniam! Nihil magis me delectat quam vinum recente torqueri spectare. Sed dic mihi, Gaie, quantum vinum hodie exspectatur? Abundatne hoc anno?*

Marcus: I'd be happy to come! Nothing pleases me more than watching fresh wine being pressed. But tell me, Gaius, how much wine is expected today? Is there an abundance this year?

Gaius: *Hodie vinetum bonum fructum dedit. Annus pluvialis fuit, neque nimium frigidus neque calidus. Ergo spero me satis vini habiturum esse ut urbem et villam sine inopia curem.*

Gaius: The vineyard has produced good fruit today. It's been a rainy year, neither too cold nor too hot. So I hope to have enough wine to supply both the city and the villa without shortage.

Marcus: *Hoc optimum nuntium est! Cura ut sit satis vinum conservandum et bonum ad longas horas hibernas praeparetur. Hic in agris omnia suis temporibus fiunt, et nihil melius pro vita tranquilla est quam suum vinum habere.*

Marcus: That's excellent news! Make sure there's enough wine stored and well-prepared for the long winter hours. Here in the countryside, everything happens in its own time, and nothing is better for a peaceful life than having your own wine.

Gaius: *Ita vero, Marce. Hic in agris homo sibi et suis semper prospicit. Vita simplex, sed plena laboris honesti et fructus suavitatis.*

Gaius: Exactly, Marcus. Here in the fields, a man always provides for himself and his own. It's a simple life, but full of honest labor and sweet rewards.

Marcus: *Speremus diu talem vitam nobis manere. Iam ad prandium conveniamus, et postea ad vineas spectandum ire possumus.*

Marcus: Let's hope this kind of life lasts for us a long time. Let's meet for lunch now, and afterward, we can go to the vineyards to watch.

Gaius: *Placet! Vale interim, Marce, et ad prandium mox te exspecto.*

Gaius: Sounds good! Farewell for now, Marcus, and I'll see you soon for lunch.

Marcus: *Vale, Gaie!*

Marcus: Farewell, Gaius!

De Re Rustica – Colloquium de agricultura et rationibus colendi

Publius: *Salve, Gaie! Te videre semper mihi iucundum est, praesertim cum de re rustica agere possumus. Nihil mihi magis delectabile est quam agri cultura! Dic mihi, quomodo agri tui se habent?*

Publius: Hello, Gaius! It's always a pleasure to see you, especially when we can talk about farming. Nothing pleases me more than agriculture! Tell me, how are your fields doing?

Gaius: *Salve, Publi! Agri mihi bene se habent. Annus hic satis pluviae tulit, itaque fruges bene creverunt. Tamen mihi videtur quaedam de ratione colendi mutanda esse. Nonne tibi videtur utile esse agros aliter excolere?*

Gaius: Hello, Publius! My fields are doing well. This year has brought enough rain, so the crops have grown nicely. However, I think some changes in farming methods might be necessary. Don't you think it's useful to cultivate the fields differently?

Publius: *Certe! In re rustica semper aliquid est quod optime fieri possit. Ego quoque nunc magis attentus sum ad terram excolendam quam antea. Ut exemplum afferam, triticum paulo celerius serere coepi, ut frumenta firmiora fiant antequam imbres saeviant. Nonne id verisimile videtur?*

Publius: Certainly! In farming, there is always something that can be done better. I, too, am paying more attention to how I cultivate the land than before. For example, I started sowing wheat a little earlier, so the grains become stronger before the heavy rains. Doesn't that seem like a good idea?

Gaius: *Bene dicis, Publi. Tempestates enim saepe agricolam praeveniunt, itaque sapientissimum est tempestatibus antevertere. Sed quid dicis de vitibus tuis? Multi nuper suadebant ut vinea vetus recideretur, ut laetiorem fructum gigneret.*

Gaius: You're right, Publius. Weather often gets ahead of the farmer, so it's wise to stay ahead of it. But what do you say about your vineyards? Many have recently suggested that old vines be pruned to produce better fruit.

Publius: *Ita, hoc verum est. Recidere vinetum vetus optimos ramos servat et maiorem vim viribus recentibus praebet. Ego ipse vites post tres annos recidi, et fructus copiosior factus est. Vinum autem, quotiens bene cultum et tempestate adiutum est, dulcius atque plenius fit.*

Publius: Yes, that's true. Pruning old vines preserves the best branches and gives more strength to the newer growth. I pruned my vines after three years, and the harvest became more abundant. Wine, whenever it is well-tended and aided by good weather, becomes sweeter and fuller.

Gaius: *Ne ego quidem id negare possum. Vinum profecto melior custodia fit. Sed quid dicis de ceteris agri partibus? Estne diligentia operariorum tuorum sufficiens in fodiendo et subigendo terram?*

Gaius: I can't deny that either. Wine certainly improves with better care. But what about the other parts of the field? Are your workers diligent enough in digging and working the land?

Publius: *Ego quidem semper magna cura terram fodio et stercoro. Terra exhauriri solet nisi certo modo subigatur. Nam stercus et reliquiae agri ad fundum trahenda sunt, ut veteres auctores docuerunt. Multi tamen haec neglegunt, contenti sine providentia procedere.*

Publius: I always dig and fertilize the land with great care. The soil tends to be depleted unless it's worked in a certain way. For manure and remains of the field must be drawn to the ground, as the old authors taught. However, many neglect this, content to proceed without foresight.

Gaius: *Certe. Agros curare oportet ut fructum perpetuum ferant. Ego quoque omnes agricolas monere soleo ut fossas faciant ad imbrem colligendum, ne terram nimia siccitas aut nimium umor laedat.*

Gaius: Certainly. Fields must be cared for to yield continuous fruit. I also always advise farmers to dig trenches to collect rainwater so that neither excessive dryness nor too much moisture harms the land.

Publius: *Prudentiam tuam laudo, Gaie. Non solum de cultura agri bene cogitas, sed etiam de aquae usu. Nihil enim magis fruges adiuvat quam tempestiva aquae dispensatio. Ego ipse canales fodi in agris meis, ut imbres melius colligantur et fruges praeserventur.*

Publius: I praise your wisdom, Gaius. You think not only about cultivating the land well but also about the use of water. Nothing helps crops more than timely water management. I, myself, have dug channels in my fields so that rainwater can be collected better and preserve the crops.

Gaius: *Sapiens consilium! Propono etiam rationem de variis sementis temporibus et de terram aliis annis aliter excolendo, ut solum ne fatiget. Nam cum fruges varie seruntur, humus semper uberior fit.*

Gaius: Wise decision! I also propose the idea of alternating planting seasons and cultivating the land differently in other years so the soil doesn't become exhausted. When crops are rotated, the soil always becomes more fertile.

Publius: *Hac doctrina uti omni tempore convenit. Vere dicitur: terra ipsa prudentiae discipula fit, si bene colatur. Ex alternatione frugum et cura sementis fit ut proventus melior et constantior sit.*

Publius: This practice should be followed at all times. It's truly said: the land itself becomes a student of wisdom if well cultivated. From crop rotation and careful planting, the harvest becomes better and more reliable.

Gaius: *Ita est, Publi. Et non solum fruges meliores ex agro exspectamus, sed etiam laetitiam et tranquillitatem animi. Nam res rustica ipsa nobis praecepta de vita sapienter agenda praebet.*

Gaius: That's right, Publius. And we expect not only better crops from the land but also joy and peace of mind. For rural life itself gives us lessons on how to live wisely.

Publius: *Haec verba sapientiae plena sunt, Gaie. Omnia quae natura dat, cum industria et conservatione, non solum corporibus sed etiam animis alimenta praebent. Sed iam tempus est mihi ad villam redire et laborem uberem agricolarum recognoscere.*

Publius: These words are full of wisdom, Gaius. Everything nature gives, when combined with hard work and preservation, provides nourishment not only to our bodies but also to our minds. But now it's time for me to return to the villa and check on the fruitful work of the farmers.

Gaius: *Ita vero, Publi. Utinam vilici tui feliciter laborent et tibi satis divitias afferant. Mox autem ad te veniam ut videam quomodo terra tua te remuneret.*

Gaius: Certainly, Publius. May your stewards work successfully and bring you plenty of wealth. I will visit you soon to see how your land rewards you.

Publius: *Gratias tibi ago! Vale, Gaie, et bonam fortunam in agris tuis tibi exopto.*

Publius: Thank you! Farewell, Gaius, and I wish you good fortune in your fields.

Gaius: *Vale, Publi, et bene curato agrum tuum ut tibi delectationem et felicitatem afferat!*

Gaius: Farewell, Publius, and take good care of your land so that it brings you joy and happiness!

In Coquina – Colloquium inter cocum et servum in culina

Servus: *Salve, Caie! Dic mihi, quid hodie in culina praeparas? Dominus pro cena nulla minore consilium cepit, et convivae mox aderunt.*

Servant: Hello, Caius! Tell me, what are you preparing in the kitchen today? The master has planned nothing less than a grand dinner, and the guests will arrive soon.

Cocus: *Salve, Luci! Hodie multa et varia prandia parantur. Iam carnem apri bene assatam atque conditam praeparavi, et murenae in sartagine frixantur. Si volueris, inspicere potes utrum omnia bona sint.*

Cook: Hello, Lucius! Today, many different dishes are being prepared. I have already roasted and seasoned the wild boar well, and the moray eels are frying in the pan. If you'd like, you can check whether everything is in order.

Servus: *Bene sapiunt, ut videtur. Sed dic mihi, caseum adposuistine? Scis enim dominum in cenis suis caseum praecipuum quaerere. Praeterea, quid de holeribus agitur?*

Servant: They smell good, it seems. But tell me, have you set out the cheese? You know the master always insists on special cheese at his dinners. Moreover, what about the vegetables?

Cocus: *Caseus Parmensis iam pridem paratus est. Holera autem ex horto matura lecta sunt: brassica, porrum, et pastinaca cum oleo et aceto mox in mensam ferentur. Num quid aliud praeparari oportet?*

Cook: The Parmesan cheese has long been prepared. As for the vegetables, they were freshly picked from the garden: cabbage, leek, and parsnip will soon be served with oil and vinegar. Is there anything else that needs to be prepared?

Servus: *Miror num ferculum ex malis pomis praeparatum sit. Dominus malorum dulcissimorum semper appetens est. Estne aliquid in delphica?*

Servant: I wonder if a dish with apples has been prepared. The master always has a craving for the sweetest apples. Is there anything in the oven?

Cocus: *Certe! Mala cocta sunt et cum melle mixto condimentis variis sparsa. Item placentae ex farina et melle factae proximo tempore coquentur. Neque deerunt nuces cum passis, quae ad finem cenae optime respondent.*

Cook: Of course! The apples have been cooked and sprinkled with various spices mixed with honey. Also, cakes made from flour and honey will be baked shortly. And we won't be without walnuts and raisins, which are perfect for the end of the meal.

Servus: *Profecto nullam partem promissi in hac cena omisisti, Caie! Convivae quidem has epulas magnopere laudabunt. Quid autem de vino? Vinum novum an vetus praeferetur?*

Servant: Truly, you haven't missed any part of the promise for this meal, Caius! The guests will surely praise these dishes greatly. But what about the wine? Will new or old wine be preferred?

Cocus: *Utrumque paratum est. Vinum Falernum vetus cenam honorabit, sed etiam vinum novum Campanum sitim levabit. Dominus ipse, ut scis, semper Falernum petit, sed multis convivis vinum minus forte magis placet.*

Cook: Both are prepared. Old Falernian wine will grace the meal, but new Campanian wine will quench the thirst. The master himself, as you know, always asks for Falernian, but many guests prefer a lighter wine.

Servus: *Bene providisti! Nunc tibi necesse est properare, quia cena mox servanda est. Convivae intrant, et dominus nihil tardius exspectabit.*

Servant: You've planned well! Now you must hurry because the dinner will be served soon. The guests are arriving, and the master will not wait for anything delayed.

Cocus: *Noli esse sollicitus, Luci. Cena ad tempus parata erit. Ad focum revertar ut omnia ad perfectum perveniant. Quidquid fieri oportet, secure faciam.*

Cook: Don't worry, Lucius. The meal will be ready on time. I'll return to the stove to make sure everything reaches perfection. Whatever needs to be done, I'll handle it confidently.

Servus: *Placet mihi, Caie! Vale, et labores tuos fortuna meliore contexe.*

Servant: That pleases me, Caius! Farewell, and may fortune guide your work to success.

Cocus: *Vale, Luci! Ad laborem redeo, ut cena digna domino et convivis fiat.*

Cook: Farewell, Lucius! I'm returning to work so that the dinner will be worthy of the master and his guests.

De Cena Romana – Colloquium de praeparatione et moribus cenae Romanae

Gaius: *Salve, Marce! Miror te hodie tam sollicitum videri. Quid accidit?*

Gaius: Hello, Marcus! I'm surprised to see you so anxious today. What happened?

Marcus: *Salve, Gaie! Nihil grave accidit, sed multa de cena paranda cogito. Dominus meus hodie magnum convivium dare vult, et ego praeparationes curare debeo. Etiam de regulis et moribus cenae Romanae meminisse oportet.*

Marcus: Hello, Gaius! Nothing serious happened, but I'm thinking a lot about preparing the dinner. My master wants to host a grand banquet today, and I'm responsible for overseeing the preparations. Also, I must remember the rules and customs of a Roman dinner.

Gaius: *Intellego cur sollicitus sis. Cena Romana non solum de bonis cibis, sed etiam de recta disciplina atque moribus agitur. Sed quaenam fercula paratis?*

Gaius: I understand why you're worried. A Roman dinner isn't just about good food but also about proper discipline and etiquette. What dishes are you preparing?

Marcus: *Primum adgustationes ex olivis, ovis, atque herbis variis praeparantur, ut gustus convivarum excitentur. Deinde porcinam et leporem cum variis condimentis in mensam feremus. Postremo garum et mulsum cum frugibus ad ultimum ferculum praeparavimus.*

Marcus: First, we're preparing appetizers of olives, eggs, and various herbs to stimulate the guests' appetites. Then we'll serve pork and hare with various seasonings. Finally, we've prepared garum and honey wine with fruit for the last course.

Gaius: *Garum quidem aptissimum ad carnem molliendam videtur. Si bene memini, Sulla ipse plurimum gari appetebat. At quid de lectis et ordine cenandi? Satisne meministi quo modo convivae recipiendi sint?*

Gaius: Garum is indeed excellent for tenderizing meat. If I remember correctly, Sulla himself was very fond of garum. But what about the couches and the dining order? Have you remembered how the guests should be seated?

Marcus: *Ita! Dominus in loco summo lecti accubiturus est, ut decet. Proximi ad eum sunt viri summi honoris, qui in civitate clarissimi sunt. Paullulum autem dubito de loco qui minoribus convivis tribuendus sit. Nonne ordo et locus multum de honore ipsius cenae significat?*

Marcus: Yes! The master will recline in the place of honor on the main couch, as is proper. Next to him will be men of the highest rank, those most distinguished in the city. However, I'm a little unsure about where to place the less important guests. Doesn't the seating order and position say a lot about the honor of the dinner?

Gaius: *Profecto! Lectus summus semper optimis reservatur, medius proximis amicis, et imus minoribus aut humilitatis gradu dignis. Hoc exemplum tibi erit utile si honorem servare voles. Meministine dominum tuum semper Falerno veteri praeferre?*

Gaius: Absolutely! The main couch is always reserved for the most important guests, the middle for close friends, and the lowest for those of lesser or humble status. This will be useful if you want to maintain the proper honor. Do you remember that your master always prefers old Falernian wine?

Marcus: *Bene memini. Dominus meus semper praeoptat Falernum vetus. Estne quid gravius quo modo pocula temperanda sint?*

Marcus: I remember well. My master always prefers old Falernian wine. Is there anything serious about how the cups should be mixed?

Gaius: *Nihil quidem. Sed vide ut vinum semper cum aqua misceatur, ut prudentia in convivio servetur. Mihi tamen placet etiam vinum musum aut conditum praebere ad delectationem convivarum.*

Gaius: Not really. But make sure the wine is always mixed with water, so moderation is maintained during the dinner. Personally, I also like to serve sparkling or spiced wine for the guests' enjoyment.

Marcus: *Etiam de mulso cogitaveram. Sed quid de sermone convivarum? Saepe animadverti dominum meum dicere convivium non* *debere gravibus disputationibus implicari. Mavult iucundam confabulationem.*

Marcus: I was also thinking about honey wine. But what about the conversation among the guests? I've often noticed my master saying that the dinner should not be involved in heavy debates. He prefers lighthearted conversation.

Gaius: *Sapienter dominus tuus facit. Gravia de re publica vel bellis colloquia non semper apta sunt ad cenam, praesertim ubi voluptas quaeritur. Optima cena iucunda colloquia et laetitiam promittit, magis de vita cotidiana aut amoribus quam de rebus gravibus agitur.*

Gaius: Your master is wise. Serious discussions about politics or wars are not always suitable for dinner, especially when pleasure is the goal. The best dinner promises light conversation and joy, with topics more about daily life or love than serious matters.

Marcus: *Itaque omnia bene cogitavisse videor. Cibi, vinum, et mores convivarum satis praeparata sunt. Mihi solum relinquitur servos admonere ut omnia ad perfectum perveniant.*

Marcus: It seems I've thought of everything well. The food, the wine, and the behavior of the guests are all prepared. Now, all I have left is to remind the servants to ensure everything reaches perfection.

Gaius: *Sine dubio praeclarum erit convivium, Marce. Certus sum convivas de regulis et cibis gratias acturos esse. Fortasse aliquando ipse ad cenam invitaberis, ut dignum est.*

Gaius: Without a doubt, it will be a splendid banquet, Marcus. I'm sure the guests will be grateful for the arrangements and the food. Perhaps one day you'll be invited to the dinner yourself, as you deserve.

Marcus: *Spero id quoque fore, Gaie. Vale nunc, et gratias tibi ago pro consiliis. Sine te haec omnia non tam prospere evenissent.*

Marcus: I hope so too, Gaius. Farewell for now, and thank you for your advice. Without you, none of this would have gone so smoothly.

Gaius: *Vale, Marce! Et bonam cenam domino et convivis exopto.*

Gaius: Farewell, Marcus! And I wish your master and the guests a great dinner.

De Philosophia Stoica – Colloquium de Stoicismo

Marcus: *Salve, Gaie! Nuper multum temporis dedi libris philosophorum, praesertim Stoicorum, qui mihi prudentiam vitae conservandae tradunt. Quid tu sentis de doctrina Stoica?*

Marcus: Hello, Gaius! Recently, I've spent a lot of time reading the books of philosophers, especially the Stoics, who teach me the wisdom of maintaining life's balance. What do you think of Stoic philosophy?

Gaius: *Salve, Marce! Doctrinam Stoicorum semper maximi aestimavi. Nam, sicut sapiens vir in rebus omnibus moderatus et immotus manere potest, ita Stoici nos proponunt vivere secundum naturam et rationem, nec perturbationibus animi cedere. Sed dic mihi, quid in hac doctrina tibi maxime placet?*

Gaius: Hello, Marcus! I've always held Stoic teachings in the highest regard. Just as a wise man can remain balanced and unmoved in all situations, so the Stoics propose that we live according to nature and reason, without yielding to emotional disturbances. But tell me, what do you like most about this philosophy?

Marcus: *Maxime mihi placet quod Stoici fatum et rationem mundi divinam esse docent. Nihil accidit sine causa, et omnia quae in vita nostra fiunt providentia reguntur. Hominem vero nihil magis decet quam sapienter ferre quidquid acciderit, sicut deus ipse omnia aequa mente consulat.*

Marcus: What I like most is that the Stoics teach that fate and reason in the world are divine. Nothing happens without a cause, and everything that happens in our lives is governed by providence. There is nothing more appropriate for a man than to wisely bear whatever happens, just as a god calmly oversees everything.

Gaius: *Quid verius? Quam ob rem fortuna, quam plerique tam vehementer metuunt, nihil per se boni vel mali continet, sed res animo nostro afficere potest modo si ei concedimus. Sapiens autem se fatis devinctum non videt, sed liberum, quia se rationi divinae conformare novit.*

Gaius: What could be truer? This is why fortune, which many fear so intensely, contains nothing inherently good or bad; it only affects us if we allow it to. The wise man does not see himself bound by fate, but free, because he knows how to align himself with divine reason.

Marcus: *Ita est! Praeterea, mihi placet quod Stoici virtutem summum bonum esse statuant, nec ullam rem externam plus valere quam nostras actiones. Si iuste, fortiter, et prudenter agimus, beati sumus, etiamsi res adversae circumstent. Quid putas de hoc?*

Marcus: Exactly! Additionally, I like how the Stoics declare virtue as the highest good, and that nothing external is more valuable than our actions. If we act justly, courageously, and wisely, we are happy, even when faced with adversity. What do you think about this?

Gaius: *Plene adsentior. Stoici enim non aurum, non honores, non opes summum bonum faciunt, sed virtutem ipsam. Non refert quam dives sit aut quam pauper; id quod refert est, utrum virtute utatur. Nam bono viro nihil deest, etiam si nihil possidet.*

Gaius: I fully agree. The Stoics do not make gold, honors, or wealth the highest good, but virtue itself. It doesn't matter whether someone is rich or poor; what matters is whether he uses virtue. For a good man lacks nothing, even if he possesses nothing.

Marcus: *Admodum! At inter homines saepe video eos qui in voluptate vivunt et perturbationibus cedunt Stoicorum doctrinam difficillimam arbitrari. Quomodo tibi videtur hos homines persuaderi posse ut virtutem pro summo bono habeant?*

Marcus: Exactly! But among people, I often see those who live for pleasure and give in to emotions finding Stoic teachings very difficult. How do you think these people can be convinced to value virtue as the highest good?

Gaius: *Non facile, Marce. Nam plerique homines sua voluntate delectantur, nec facile persuadentur ut cupiditates suas reprimant. Sed quicumque doctrinam Stoicorum bene intellegit, non timet res adversas nec quaerit externas voluptates. Sicut Seneca dicit: "nihil malum homini potest accidere nisi quod ipse facit." Ideo persuadere oportet bonum internum omnibus in manibus esse.*

Gaius: It's not easy, Marcus. Most people delight in their desires and aren't easily persuaded to restrain their passions. But whoever truly understands Stoic teachings does not fear adversity nor seek external pleasures. As Seneca says: "Nothing bad can happen to a man unless he brings it upon himself." Thus, we must persuade them that inner goodness is within everyone's reach.

Marcus: *Bene dicis, Gaie. Nihil externum sapiens timet, quia omne bonum in sua potestate continetur. Sed quid sentis de eloquentia Stoicorum? Nam quidam dicunt eos nimis severe et rigide de his rebus loqui.*

Marcus: You speak well, Gaius. The wise man fears nothing external because all goodness lies within his own power. But what do you think about the Stoics' manner of speech? Some say they speak too severely and rigidly about these matters.

Gaius: *Recte mones. Stoici quidem graviter et austere loquuntur, sed id necessarium est ad doctrinam ipsam. Virtus enim, ut aiunt, non mollibus verbis sed firmis et certis praeceptis sustinetur. Non debet esse sermo suavis, sed potius efficax et ad rem aptus. Sicut vita sapientis, ita etiam oratio debet esse stabilis et sincera.*

Gaius: You're right. The Stoics indeed speak gravely and austerely, but that is necessary for the doctrine itself. Virtue, as they say, is not supported by soft words but by firm and certain principles. Speech doesn't need to be pleasant, but rather effective and suited to the matter. Just as the life of a wise man is stable and sincere, so too should his speech be.

Marcus: *Verum est, Gaie. Stoici non quaerunt placere, sed veritatem dicere. Nihilominus, ex doctrina eorum multum sapientiae haurire possumus. Nam cum perturbationibus et incertis rebus vitam agimus, nihil melius est quam rationem et virtutem in fundamento habere.*

Marcus: That's true, Gaius. The Stoics don't seek to please but to tell the truth. Nevertheless, we can draw much wisdom from their teachings. As we live through disturbances and uncertainties, there is nothing better than having reason and virtue as a foundation.

Gaius: *Sapiens consilium, Marce. Et memineris, etiam si difficile videatur, omnia adversa fortiter ferenda esse. Est enim haec summa* *sapientia: agere secundum naturam, et quidquid acciderit, aequo animo suscipere.*

Gaius: Wise advice, Marcus. And remember, even if it seems difficult, all adversity must be borne with strength. This is the ultimate wisdom: to act according to nature and to accept whatever happens with a calm mind.

Marcus: *Ita faciam, Gaie. Gratias tibi ago pro hac collocutione philosophica. Nullus sermo melior animum movet quam is qui virtutem et sapientiam tractat.*

Marcus: I'll do that, Gaius. Thank you for this philosophical conversation. No discussion moves the soul more than one that deals with virtue and wisdom.

Gaius: *Et ego tibi gratias ago, Marce. Vale nunc, et feliciter omnia secundum naturam agas!*

Gaius: And I thank you, Marcus. Farewell for now, and may you succeed in all things according to nature!

Marcus: *Vale, Gaie, et in virtute persevera!*

Marcus: Farewell, Gaius, and persevere in virtue!

De Philosophia Epicurea – Disputatio de Philosophia Epicurea

Titus: *Salve, Luciane! Nuper multum de philosophia Epicuri cogitavi et miror quid tu de illa doctrina sentias. Sicut scis, multi eam reprehendunt, sed mihi videtur Epicurum non satis bene intellectum esse.*

Titus: Hello, Lucian! Recently, I've been thinking a lot about the philosophy of Epicurus, and I wonder what you think about it. As you know, many criticize it, but it seems to me that Epicurus is not well understood.

Lucianus: *Salve, Tite! Etsi ego Stoicis magis favere soleo, doctrinam Epicuri non omnino contemno. Multi quidem eum vituperant, putantes voluptatem summum bonum esse iniquum; sed, si recte perpendimus, voluptas quam Epicurus quaerit non in corporum deliciis consistit, sed potius in tranquillitate animi. Quid ipse censes?*

Lucianus: Hello, Titus! Although I tend to favor the Stoics more, I do not completely dismiss the philosophy of Epicurus. Many criticize him, thinking that pleasure as the highest good is wrong; but, if we consider it properly, the pleasure Epicurus seeks is not in bodily indulgence, but rather in the tranquility of the mind. What do you think?

Titus: *Profecto, id verum est. Epicurus voluptatem summum bonum esse dicit, sed voluptatem quietam, quae ex absentia doloris et perturbationum animi nascitur. Non quaerit ille cibos lautiores aut vinorum copiam, sed modicam vitam, sine curis atque metu. Eadem enim felicitas est et vivere in villa parvula et vivere in palatio, si animus tranquillus est.*

Titus: Indeed, that is true. Epicurus says that pleasure is the highest good, but it's the calm pleasure that comes from the absence of pain and mental disturbances. He doesn't seek fine foods or a surplus of wine, but rather a simple life, free from worries and fear. The same happiness exists whether living in a small house or in a palace, as long as the mind is at peace.

Lucianus: *Sed dic mihi, Tite, nonne Epicurus neglegit officia publica aut amicitiam? Nam dicitur eum secessum ad suam voluptatem quaerendam praeoptavisse, quod mihi videtur rem publicam et civitatem parvi aestimare. Virtus enim nonne est quae rem publicam sustinet?*

Lucianus: But tell me, Titus, doesn't Epicurus neglect public duties or friendship? He is said to prefer retreating to seek his own pleasure, which seems to me to undervalue the state and society. Isn't it virtue that upholds the republic?

Titus: *Hic multi errant, Luciane. Epicurus officium et amicitiam magni facit, sed sua sponte potius quam ex praecepto. Non vult civilem vitam neglegere, sed docet sapientem curas turbidas vitare, quae homines ad anxietatem ducunt. Cum tranquillitas animi summum bonum sit, etiam amicitia maximam voluptatem affert, si est sincera et sine ulla utilitate.*

Titus: Many are mistaken here, Lucian. Epicurus values duty and friendship highly, but by choice rather than obligation. He doesn't want to neglect civic life, but he teaches that the wise man should avoid the turbulent cares that lead people to anxiety. Since mental tranquility is the highest good, even friendship brings great pleasure if it is sincere and without self-interest.

Lucianus: *Intellego. Itaque Epicurus non voluptates corporales corporis praeferre videtur, sed potius animi quietem et pacem. Hoc quidem plus ad sapientiam videtur pertinere quam ad luxum aut libidinem, quem invidi ei criminantur. Fortasse tamen otium et secessus difficilius est omnibus hominibus adsequi.*

Lucianus: I understand. So, Epicurus doesn't seem to prefer bodily pleasures, but rather the peace and quiet of the mind. This seems to pertain more to wisdom than to luxury or lust, for which his critics accuse him. However, perhaps leisure and retreat are harder for everyone to achieve.

Titus: *Ita est. Multi difficile Epicurum intellegunt, quia nemini licet se omnino a negotiis vitae mundanae subtrahere. Sed memento, non re ipsa Epicurus omnes negotiosas res despicit, sed potius monere vult ut has res moderemur nec permittamus vitam nostram perturbari. Sic est etiam cum rebus externis — divitiae, honores, potentia — quae non ipsa bona sunt, nisi animum tranquillum conservamus.*

Titus: Exactly. Many people find it difficult to understand Epicurus because no one can completely withdraw from the affairs of worldly life. But remember, Epicurus doesn't despise all busy matters themselves; he just advises that we moderate these things and not allow them to disturb our lives. It's the same with external things—wealth, honors, power—they are not truly good unless we maintain a tranquil mind.

Lucianus: *Bene pronuntias, Tite. Videor nunc melius Epicurum intellegere. Non omnino refert utrum aliquis pro Epicureo an Stoico censeatur; unum certum est: sapientia ad tranquillitatem ducere debet. Sed quaestio mihi manet: num etiam fatum, quod Stoici tantopere laudant, Epicurus admittit?*

Lucianus: Well said, Titus. I think I understand Epicurus better now. It doesn't entirely matter whether someone identifies as an Epicurean or a Stoic; one thing is certain: wisdom must lead to tranquility. But one question remains for me: Does Epicurus also acknowledge fate, which the Stoics praise so highly?

Titus: *Epicurus fatum reicit, quia docet omnia ex atomis casu moveri, nec ullam necessitatem proventus futurorum esse. Sed hoc non significat imprudenter agere. Ipse suadet ut sapiens providus sit et modum teneat; sic enim ei continget vita sine metu et anxietate.*

Titus: Epicurus rejects fate because he teaches that everything moves by chance through atoms and that there is no necessity for future outcomes. But this doesn't mean acting recklessly. He still advises that the wise person be prudent and maintain moderation; in this way, they can live a life without fear and anxiety.

Lucianus: *Nihil nisi rationem sequendi videtur et mores placidos colendos. Nunc Epicuri doctrina non mihi tam peregrina videtur. Fortasse, cum omnia bene aestimemus, non in principiis tanta diversitas est, quamquam propositum variat.*

Lucianus: It seems like nothing but following reason and cultivating peaceful habits. Now, Epicurus' doctrine doesn't seem so foreign to me. Perhaps, when we assess everything properly, the differences in principles are not that great, although the approaches vary.

Titus: *Sapiens vis. Licet doctrinae diversae sint, finis philosophiae semper est idem: vita beata, qua nihil melius homini dari potest.*

Titus: Wise insight. Even though the teachings may differ, the goal of philosophy is always the same: a happy life, the greatest gift a person can have.

Lucianus: *Gratias tibi ago, Tite. Eloquentia et sapientia me plane docuisti. Fortasse nunc plus Epicurum legam ut intellegam quomodo tranquillitas animi adsequenda sit.*

Lucianus: Thank you, Titus. Your eloquence and wisdom have taught me clearly. Perhaps now I'll read more of Epicurus to understand how to achieve tranquility of mind.

Titus: *Placet mihi quod sermo noster tibi fructum attulit. Vale, Luciane, et tranquillitatem animi semper quaere.*

Titus: I'm glad that our conversation brought you some insight. Farewell, Lucian, and always seek the tranquility of the mind.

Lucianus: *Vale, Tite, et felicitas tibi adsit, quemadmodum Epicurus promittit!*

Lucianus: Farewell, Titus, and may happiness be with you, just as Epicurus promises!

In Thermis – Colloquium in Thermis Romanis

Aulus: *Salve, Sexte! Diu est quod te non vidi. Num saepe ad thermas venire soles?*

Aulus: Hello, Sextus! It's been a long time since I last saw you. Do you usually come to the baths often?

Sextus: *Salve, Aule! Ita vero, ad thermas frequenter venire solebam, sed his diebus variis negotiis distinebar. Nuper multum temporis in agris consumpsi, nunc autem tandem mihi licet in hanc quietem et voluptatem redire. Quid tu agis?*

Sextus: Hello, Aulus! Yes, I used to come to the baths frequently, but lately, I've been occupied with various business matters. Recently, I've spent a lot of time in the countryside, but now I can finally return to this peace and pleasure. How are you?

Aulus: *Bene valeo! Scis enim me thermas non modo corpori lavando, sed etiam animo reficiendo petere. Post diuturna negotia, nihil mihi est iucundius quam hic in vapore sedere et cum amicis libero sermone colloqui.*

Aulus: I'm doing well! You know I come to the baths not only to wash my body but also to refresh my mind. After long work, nothing is more enjoyable to me than sitting here in the steam and chatting freely with friends.

Sextus: *Ita est! Hic non modo corpus, sed etiam animus recreatur. Sed dic mihi, Aule, visistine iam primas partes thermarum — apodyterium et tepidarium — an ad caldarium iam progressus es?*

Sextus: That's true! Here, not only the body but also the mind is restored. But tell me, Aulus, have you already visited the first parts of the baths— the changing room and the warm room—or have you already moved on to the hot room?

Aulus: *Iam tepidarium praeterii atque modo ex caldario egressus sum. Verum dicere, caldarium perplacet mihi, sed modo paulum aestu fatigatus sum. Nunc frigidarium intrare cogito, ut corpus refrigeretur et reficiatur.*

Aulus: I've already passed through the warm room and just came out of the hot room. To be honest, I really enjoy the hot room, but right now, I'm a bit tired from the heat. I'm thinking of entering the cold room now to cool down and refresh my body.

Sextus: *Bene cogitas! Frigidarium post caldarium semper est iucundissimum. Nihil mihi dulcius est quam ille frigoris sensus post vaporem. Quin etiam, post longam balneationem, laconicum interdum viso, ut perspiratio cito finiatur.*

Sextus: Good thinking! The cold room after the hot room is always the most pleasant. Nothing is sweeter to me than the feeling of coolness after the steam. In fact, after a long bath, I sometimes visit the dry sauna so that perspiration ends quickly.

Aulus: *Et ego idem sentio! Laconicum profuit, praesertim cum corpus defatigatum sit. Curare tamen oportet, ne nimium in aestu remaneamus. Sed dic mihi, Sexte, audivistine de novis ornamentis thermarum quae imperator fieri iussit?*

Aulus: I feel the same way! The dry sauna is helpful, especially when the body is exhausted. But we must be careful not to stay too long in the heat. But tell me, Sextus, have you heard about the new decorations in the baths that the emperor ordered to be made?

Sextus: *Audivi! Nova ornamenta, ut ferunt, pulcherrima sunt — columnae marmoreae, lacus spatiosi, piscinae etiam sub die patentes. Imperator quidem magnopere curat ut cives deliciis suis fruantur.*

Sextus: I've heard! The new decorations, as they say, are very beautiful— marble columns, spacious pools, and even open-air swimming areas. The emperor indeed takes great care that the citizens enjoy such luxuries.

Aulus: *Laudabile quidem! Nam cum tantopere laboramus, necesse est locum habere ubi refici possimus. Et quid de palaestra? Nonne post lavationem ibi interdum corpus exerceas?*

Aulus: Indeed, it's commendable! Since we work so hard, it's necessary to have a place where we can refresh ourselves. And what about the exercise yard? Don't you sometimes exercise your body there after bathing?

Sextus: *Ita est. Palaestra mihi locus aptus est ad levem exercitationem, praesertim postquam in aqua calida nervos meos mollivi. Sed non semper, Aule, nimis laboro. Hoc loco saepe magis rerum levium et iucundarum meminisse volo.*

Sextus: Yes, it is. The exercise yard is a suitable place for light exercise, especially after I've relaxed my muscles in the warm water. But I don't always work too hard, Aulus. Here, I often prefer to think about lighter and more pleasant things.

Aulus: *Sapienter dicis. Thermas neque ad laborem neque ad sollicitudinem venimus, sed potius ad relaxationem et colloquia levia. Profecto nihil magis nos reficit quam fida amicitia et sermo amicorum.*

Aulus: You speak wisely. We don't come to the baths for work or worry, but rather for relaxation and light conversation. Indeed, nothing refreshes us more than faithful friendship and the talk of friends.

Sextus: *Bene sentis, Aule. Nunc eamus ad frigidarium, ut corpus reficiamus et deinde, si volueris, sermones de rebus cotidianis continuemus. Multa mihi de novis urbis progressibus narrantur.*

Sextus: You're right, Aulus. Now let's go to the cold room to refresh our bodies, and then, if you like, we can continue our conversation about daily matters. I've heard much about the latest developments in the city.

Aulus: *Libenter venio, Sexte. Post frigidarium confabulatio certe erit iucunda, cum iam refecti animi parati sint ad plura colloquia. Iam vale, et eamus!*

Aulus: I'm happy to join you, Sextus. After the cold room, the conversation will surely be pleasant, as our refreshed minds will be ready for more talk. Now, farewell, and let's go!

Sextus: *Eamus! Vale!*

Sextus: Let's go! Farewell!

De Corpore Exercendo – Colloquium de exercitio corporali et valetudine

Quintus: *Salve, Valeri! Video te hodie in palaestra strenue exercere. Curasne de valetudine magis quam antea?*

Quintus: Hello, Valerius! I see you exercising vigorously in the gym today. Are you paying more attention to your health than before?

Valerius: *Salve, Quinte! Certe, hoc tempore magnam curam adhibeo exercendo corpus. Valetudo enim mihi videtur omnium rerum principium, sine qua nihil recte agere possumus. Tu autem quid agis? Num et ipse aliquos exercitus facis?*

Valerius: Hello, Quintus! Indeed, I am taking great care in exercising my body at the moment. Health seems to me the foundation of everything, without which we can accomplish nothing properly. But what about you? Do you also engage in some exercise?

Quintus: *Ita est, Valeri! Ego quoque palaestram frequento. Exercitatio enim non modo corpus firmat, sed etiam animum alit. Nonne verum est quod veteres dicunt: mens sana in corpore sano?*

Quintus: Yes, Valerius! I also visit the gym regularly. Exercise not only strengthens the body but also nourishes the mind. Isn't it true what the ancients say: a sound mind in a sound body?

Valerius: *Profecto! Nulla res melius ad tranquillitatem mentis valet quam corpus bene exercitatum. Cura corpus, et animus ipse sequetur. Sed dic mihi, Quinte, quo modo te exerces? Utrum cursus, luctatio, an certamen gladiatorium tibi placet?*

Valerius: Absolutely! Nothing benefits mental tranquility more than a well-exercised body. Take care of your body, and the mind will follow. But tell me, Quintus, how do you exercise? Do you prefer running, wrestling, or perhaps gladiatorial contests?

Quintus: *Cursus mihi maxime gratus est. Nihil aequale est celeritati pedum, qua corpus celeriter incitatur et sanguis rapidius fluit. At luctationes quoque non neglego, quia vires firmas requirunt. Sed quid de te? Video te saepius ponderibus uti.*

Quintus: Running is what I enjoy most. There's nothing like the speed of foot, which quickly invigorates the body and makes the blood flow faster. But I don't neglect wrestling either, as it requires strong strength. But what about you? I see you often lifting weights.

Valerius: *Ita, Quinte. Pondus tollere mihi semper placuit, nam ita vires augentur et corpus robustum fit. Sed interdum luctationes quoque me iuvant, quia ars et ingenium ibi aequa manu cum viribus contendunt. Utique tamen cavendum est, ne nimium laboris capiamus. Modus enim in exercitationibus semper servandus est.*

Valerius: Yes, Quintus. I've always enjoyed weightlifting because it increases strength and makes the body robust. But sometimes wrestling helps me too, as skill and intelligence compete equally with strength. Of course, we must be careful not to overwork ourselves. Moderation in exercise must always be maintained.

Quintus: *Recte mones. Nihil nimis! Non diuturnitas aut vehementia curanda est, sed potius constantia et mediocritas studenda. Si corpus nimium fatigatur, magis laeditur quam iuvatur. Etsi medici multum de modo suadent, saepe homines ad hanc doctrinam non satis attendunt.*

Quintus: You're right. Nothing in excess! It's not the duration or intensity that matters, but rather consistency and moderation. If the body is overly fatigued, it's harmed rather than helped. Although doctors advise much about moderation, people often don't pay enough attention to this principle.

Valerius: *Ita est! Homines cupide quaerunt celeres vires, sed obliviscuntur corpus tempus et modum requirere. Neque satis est se exercere; etiam cibus et quies ad valetudinem maxime pertinent. Nam, ut scis, nocte bona atque cena moderata corpus bene recreatur.*

Valerius: Exactly! People eagerly seek quick strength but forget that the body requires time and moderation. It's not enough just to exercise; food and rest are equally important for health. As you know, a good night's sleep and a moderate meal restore the body well.

Quintus: *Nullam sententiam verius dicis. Cibus simplex, temperatus, et bona quies sunt quasi fundamenta bonae valetudinis. Saepe video eos,* *qui vinum multum aut epulas sumunt, labore corporis frustra frui. Nihil adiuvat exercere si corpus excessibus perturbatur.*

Quintus: You speak no truer words. Simple food, moderation, and good rest are like the foundations of good health. I often see those who consume too much wine or indulge in feasts struggling with exercise in vain. It's useless to exercise if the body is disturbed by excess.

Valerius: *Certe! At nulla medicina melior est quam ipsa natura et modus. Sed dic mihi, Quinte, utrum solum propter corpus exercitationes facis an etiam ad certamina?*

Valerius: Certainly! And there's no better remedy than nature and moderation itself. But tell me, Quintus, do you exercise solely for your body, or do you also train for competitions?

Quintus: *Ego vero potius valetudinis causa facio. Certamina mihi grata sunt, sed nullam gloriam quaero. Praefero tranquillitatem corporis mei sani et activitatem potius quam pugnas aut honorem. Tu autem, Valeri, an ad certamen aliquod te paras?*

Quintus: I do it mainly for my health. I enjoy competitions, but I don't seek glory. I prefer the calm of a healthy and active body over fights or honors. But you, Valerius, are you preparing for any competition?

Valerius: *Ego quoque hoc tempore potius corpus firmare quam ad certamina contendere volo. Licet olim cogitaverim me certamen luctationis subiturum esse, nunc malo vires et valetudinem propriam servare. Curare de sana vita est primum.*

Valerius: I too, at this time, prefer to strengthen my body rather than compete. Although I once thought I might enter a wrestling competition, now I'd rather maintain my strength and health. Taking care of a healthy life is my priority.

Quintus: *Recte cogitas, Valeri. Navigandum est cum modo, ut animus simul cum corpore stabilis sit. Valetudo est rerum omnium fundamentum, et si ea servatur, nihil impedit quominus bene vivamus.*

Quintus: You're thinking correctly, Valerius. We must navigate with moderation so that the mind remains stable along with the body. Health is the foundation of everything, and if it's maintained, nothing prevents us from living well.

Valerius: *Plene adsentior, Quinte. Nunc autem, post exercitationem, tempus mihi videtur in thermas descendere et corpus reficere. Venisne quoque?*

Valerius: I fully agree, Quintus. Now, after exercising, it seems like a good time to go down to the baths and refresh the body. Are you coming too?

Quintus: *Profecto! Nihil nunc magis cupio quam quietem post laborem bonum. Eamus et diem bonum expleamus.*

Quintus: Absolutely! There's nothing I want more right now than rest after good exercise. Let's go and finish the day well.

Valerius: *Eamus, Quinte!*

Valerius: Let's go, Quintus!

In Triclinio – Disputatio in convivio

Servilius: *Salve, Fabi! Gaudeo te in convivio nostro adesse. Mihi magna voluptas est amicos prope me accumbere et diem sermonibus lepidis terere. Quomodo te habes?*

Servilius: Hello, Fabius! I'm glad you are here at our dinner. It brings me great pleasure to have friends reclining near me and to spend the day in pleasant conversation. How are you?

Fabius: *Salve, Servili! Ego quidem bene valeo, et gratias tibi ago quod me ad talem cenam vocavisti. Videlicet hodie non solum cibi optimi, sed etiam convivae praestantes sunt. Sed dic mihi, quid primum apponis?*

Fabius: Hello, Servilius! I am doing well, and I thank you for inviting me to such a dinner. Clearly, today we have not only the finest food but also excellent guests. But tell me, what's being served first?

Servilius: *Hodie apponuntur pultes et olivae ad gustum excitandum, deinde caro phasiani variis condimentis praeparata. Praeterea habemus pisces ex Tiberi recens captos et vinum Falernum. Spero fore ut haec omnia convivas delectent.*

Servilius: Today, we're serving porridge and olives to whet the appetite, followed by pheasant meat prepared with various spices. Additionally, we have fish freshly caught from the Tiber and Falernian wine. I hope all these things will please our guests.

Caius: *Eia! Phasiani quidem rari sunt! Sed, Servili, sic decet virum, qui semper lautitiam et urbanitatem cenae sumptuosae exhibet. Et vinum, ut audivi, excellentissimum praebetur.*

Caius: Wow! Pheasants are indeed rare! But, Servilius, this is fitting for a man who always presents elegance and sophistication at a sumptuous dinner. And as I've heard, the wine being served is excellent.

Servilius: *Non tibi mentiar, Cai, vinum hoc Falernum vineis meis coactum est, et maturitate annorum refertum deliciis. Si volueris, poculum celeriter feram, ut ipse gustes.*

Servilius: I won't lie to you, Caius; this Falernian wine was pressed from my own vineyards and is full of the delights of aged maturity. If you'd like, I'll quickly bring a cup for you to taste.

Livia: *O vere praeclarum, Servili! Sed, ut ad me saepe pertinet, quid de cenandi moribus censetis? Mihi videtur antiquitas aliquantulum simplicior fuisse. Nunc cenae multo splendidiores et copiosiores fiunt quam nostri maiores tolerare solebant.*

Livia: Oh, truly splendid, Servilius! But as it often concerns me, what do you think of dining customs? It seems to me that the ancients were somewhat simpler. Now, dinners are much more lavish and abundant than our ancestors used to tolerate.

Fabius: *Recte mones, Livia. Nos praeclara convivia hodie celebramus, sed in mentem mihi saepe venit quanta simplicitate veteres vivebant. Legistine umquam Catonem aut senatores nostros, qui simplicem cibum praeferrebant? Eis panis, herbae, et vinum modicum satis erat.*

Fabius: You're right, Livia. We enjoy grand feasts today, but I often think about how simply the ancients lived. Have you ever read Cato or our senators, who preferred simple food? For them, bread, herbs, and a little wine were enough.

Servilius: *O certe, Fabi. Sed nunc, ut vides, mores multum mutati sunt. Tempora quoque nostra abundantiam ferunt. Quid enim inter amicos dulcius quam cenam commodam et bene conditam proponere? Sic enim, ut Cicero dixit, nihil melius est quam in convivio mens et animus reficiantur.*

Servilius: Oh, certainly, Fabius. But now, as you see, customs have changed greatly. Our times bring abundance. What is sweeter among friends than to present a comfortable and well-prepared meal? For as Cicero said, there's nothing better than refreshing the mind and spirit at a feast.

Caius: *Profecto! Sed non solum cibis bonis, sed etiam sermonibus philosophicis reficiamur. Nonne convivium est locus, ubi de rebus seriis et iucundis disserere licet? Quid dicitis de hac re?*

Caius: Exactly! But let's also refresh ourselves with philosophical discussions, not just good food. Isn't the dinner table the place where we can discuss serious and pleasant matters? What do you think about that?

Livia: *Bene, Cai. Sic est, nihil melius quam in media cena de rebus gravibus et delectantibus colloqui. Ego quidem libenter audio quid alii* *de virtute, de officiis, aut etiam de re publica sentiant. Cena sine sermonibus tamquam corpus sine anima mihi videtur.*

Livia: Well said, Caius. Yes, there's nothing better than discussing important and delightful topics during dinner. Personally, I enjoy hearing what others think about virtue, duties, or even politics. A dinner without conversation seems like a body without a soul to me.

Fabius: *Recte dicis, Livia. In his cenis sermo liberius fluit, et sapientes convivae saepe in sermone profundam doctrinam proferunt. Sed dic mihi, quid censes de officiis amicorum in talibus conviviis?*

Fabius: You're right, Livia. At these dinners, conversation flows freely, and wise guests often share profound knowledge in their words. But tell me, what do you think about the duties of friends at such gatherings?

Livia: *Ego puto amicitiam summam gratiam habere in conviviis. Nihil in cenis melius quam fidem et veras amicitias conservare, quoniam fiducia et animi apertitas ubique sunt bonae vitae fundamentum.*

Livia: I believe that friendship holds the highest value in dinners. There's nothing better at a feast than preserving trust and true friendships because faith and openness of spirit are the foundation of a good life.

Servilius: *Consentio omnino, Livia. In cenis amicitiarum solidatio fit. Quid enim refert cenam sumptuosam habere, nisi mens bona et gratia inter amicos adsint? Sed nunc, convivae, eamus ad dulcia et vinum novum. Nullus sermo iucundior est post cenam.*

Servilius: I completely agree, Livia. Dinners strengthen friendships. What's the point of a lavish meal if good spirits and kindness aren't present among friends? But now, guests, let's move on to desserts and the new wine. No conversation is more pleasant than that which follows dinner.

Caius: *Ita vero! Eamus, et simul loquamur de rerum humanarum varietatibus.*

Caius: Absolutely! Let's go, and at the same time, let's talk about the variety of human affairs.

Fabius: *Placet mihi. Gratias tibi ago, Servili, pro hoc praeclaro convivio. Valeamus, et sermo longior post dulcia meliores afferat voluptates.*

Fabius: I agree. Thank you, Servilius, for this wonderful feast. Let's all stay well, and may a longer conversation after dessert bring even greater pleasures.

Servilius: *Valete, amici, et hunc diem perpetuum faciamus in animo!*

Servilius: Farewell, friends, and let's keep this day forever in our hearts!

De Matrimonio – Disputatio de moribus nuptiarum apud Romanos

Decimus: *Salve, Aemili! Dic mihi, quid de nuptiis et matrimonio Romano sentis? Vidi nuper quoddam coniugium splendidum, et multum mihi profuit cogitare de moribus nostris.*

Decimus: Hello, Aemilius! Tell me, what do you think of Roman weddings and marriage? I recently saw a splendid wedding, and it made me reflect a lot on our customs.

Aemilius: *Salve, Decime! Matrimonium Romanum, ut bene scis, non modo privatos affectus, sed etiam res publicas complectitur. Non est tantum duorum hominum consensus, sed familiae ac dignitatis iunctio. Plerique matrimonium contrahunt non solum propter amorem, sed etiam propter honorem.*

Aemilius: Hello, Decimus! As you know, Roman marriage encompasses not only personal feelings but also public matters. It is not just the agreement of two individuals, but the union of families and dignity. Many enter into marriage not only for love but also for honor.

Decimus: *Ita vero! In matrimonio, res familiaris semper spectatur. Praesertim in nobili genere, uxorem ex digna familia deligere maximi momenti est. Sed dic mihi, Aemili, nonne amori quoque locus est in coniugiis nostris?*

Decimus: Exactly! In marriage, family affairs are always considered. Especially in noble circles, choosing a wife from a respectable family is of utmost importance. But tell me, Aemilius, isn't there also room for love in our marriages?

Aemilius: *Profecto, amori locus est, sed plerumque in consilio et concordia amor reperitur, magis quam in illa ferventia iuvenum, quam Graeci in tragoediis saepe extollunt. Amicitia inter virum et uxorem firmior longius durat quam solus ardor amoris.*

Aemilius: Certainly, there is room for love, but love is mostly found in understanding and harmony, rather than in that youthful passion the Greeks often praise in their tragedies. Friendship between husband and wife lasts longer and is stronger than mere passion.

Decimus: *Recte mones. Amicitia et fides inter coniuges summi momenti sunt. Sed tamen, non possumus pronuntiare amorem omnino abesse in bono matrimonio. Nonne illud est iucundissimum si coniunx non modo honestam familiam, sed etiam animam carissimam habeat?*

Decimus: You're right. Friendship and trust between spouses are of the utmost importance. However, we cannot claim that love is entirely absent from a good marriage. Isn't it most delightful if a spouse not only comes from a respectable family but also has a dear soul?

Aemilius: *Ita quidem, Decime! Optime evenit si vir et uxor non modo coniunctionem familiae sed etiam concordiam animi inveniunt. Quod vere dicis, carissimos se factos esse, id matrimonium summum facit. Sed nonne etiam matrimonium mores nostros custodiendos tradit?*

Aemilius: Yes indeed, Decimus! It's wonderful when a husband and wife find not only a family connection but also harmony of spirit. What you say is true; when they become dear to each other, it makes the marriage perfect. But doesn't marriage also help preserve our customs?

Decimus: *Non potest negari. Matrimonium non solum est res viri et uxoris, sed etiam traditio familiaris. Liberi ex bona stirpe nasci debent, et patres proles suas in moribus et honesta vita instituere tenentur. Hinc maximus honor familiarum prodit.*

Decimus: It cannot be denied. Marriage is not just about the husband and wife but also about family tradition. Children should be born from a good lineage, and fathers are responsible for raising their offspring with good morals and an honest life. From this comes the greatest honor of families.

Aemilius: *Profecto! Liberi enim sunt fundamentum civitatis et posteritatis. Matrimonium non modo ad domesticam tranquillitatem pertinet, sed etiam ad rem publicam ipsam. Nulla maior est responsabilitas quam proles nostras bene instituere.*

Aemilius: Absolutely! Children are the foundation of the state and the future. Marriage pertains not only to domestic peace but also to the state itself. There is no greater responsibility than raising our children well.

Decimus: *Bene dicis, Aemili. Matrimonium, licet res privata videri possit, rem publicam maxime attingit. Sic est etiam cum religionibus et* *caerimoniis quae nuptias comitantur. Matronae flammeo velato capite ambulant, pronubi adhibentur, et laetus hymenaeus cantatur.*

Decimus: You speak well, Aemilius. Even though marriage might seem like a private matter, it greatly affects the state. This is also true with the religious practices and ceremonies that accompany weddings. The brides walk with veils, pronubi are involved, and the joyful wedding hymn is sung.

Aemilius: *Hae caerimoniae profundam significationem habent. Nonne ipsa dextrarum iunctio, quae in nuptiis fit, maximam concordiam et societatem viri et uxoris significat? Et quid dicis de confarreatione? Quae sanctissima habetur apud nos!*

Aemilius: These ceremonies hold deep meaning. Doesn't the very joining of hands, which occurs in weddings, signify the utmost harmony and partnership between husband and wife? And what do you think about confarreatio? It's considered the most sacred among us!

Decimus: *Confarreatio quidem priscum et sacratissimum ritum matrimonii est. Cum panes farrei in sacrificio adhibentur, vir et uxor non solum iunctura humana, sed etiam divina copulantur. Hinc matrimonium initia et deorum beneficiis corroboratur.*

Decimus: Confarreatio is indeed an ancient and most sacred marriage rite. When farro bread is used in the sacrifice, the husband and wife are united not only in a human bond but also in a divine one. Thus, marriage begins and is strengthened by the blessings of the gods.

Aemilius: *Ita est. At, quamquam hi mores antiqui sunt, non credo matrimonium sine vera cura et animo vivere posse. Nihil tam fragile est quam fictum coniugium, quod sine fide et consilio initum est.*

Aemilius: That's right. But even though these customs are ancient, I don't believe a marriage can thrive without real care and spirit. Nothing is as fragile as a marriage that is entered into without trust and wisdom.

Decimus: *Recte sentis, Aemili. Matrimonium fictum nihil proficit, sed matrimonium ex consilio et amicitia firmissime tenetur. Gaudeo nos de hac re locutos esse. Forsitan exemplum matrimonii boni ipse aliquando sequar.*

Decimus: You're absolutely right, Aemilius. A false marriage achieves nothing, but a marriage founded on wisdom and friendship holds firm. I'm glad we've spoken about this. Perhaps I will someday follow the example of a good marriage myself.

Aemilius: *Spero ut ita sit, Decime. Nihil dignius est quam matrimonium bene curatum et virtute subnixum. Vale nunc, et bonam fortunam in omnibus rebus exopto.*

Aemilius: I hope so, Decimus. Nothing is more worthy than a well-cared-for marriage based on virtue. Farewell for now, and I wish you good fortune in all things.

Decimus: *Vale, Aemili, et similem concordiam semper in matrimonio habeas!*

Decimus: Farewell, Aemilius, and may you always have such harmony in your marriage!

In Foro Olitorio – De emptione holerum in foro

Manius: *Salve, Tiberi! Vide quantam multitudinem hodie in foro! Tempus est mihi aliquid herbarum emere. Cur ad forum venisti?*

Manius: Hello, Tiberius! Look at the crowd in the market today! It's time for me to buy some vegetables. Why have you come to the market?

Tiberius: *Salve, Mani! Ego quoque huc veni ut cenae parandae causa olivas et brassicam emam. Nullus locus aptior quam hic est ad optimas fruges inveniendas. Quid autem tu quaeris?*

Tiberius: Hello, Manius! I also came here to buy olives and cabbage for preparing dinner. There's no better place to find the best produce. But what are you looking for?

Manius: *Mihi pastinacae et lactuca praecipue necessariae sunt. Uxor enim hodie convivium parat et vult omnia optima habere. Sed vidi etiam raphanos non male praeberi; fortasse illos quoque emam.*

Manius: I especially need parsnips and lettuce. My wife is preparing a feast today and wants to have the best of everything. But I've also seen some good radishes; perhaps I'll buy those too.

Tiberius: *Bene facis! Raphani enim boni sunt et ad stomachum placandum valent. Sed cavendum est, ne quid nimis sumas, ut semper modum teneas. Ecce, ille tabernarius optimas brassicas habere videtur. Dic mihi, non credisne brassicam admodum salubrem esse?*

Tiberius: You're right! Radishes are good and help soothe the stomach. But be careful not to buy too much, always keep moderation. Look, that vendor seems to have the best cabbages. Tell me, don't you believe cabbage is quite healthy?

Manius: *Profecto! Brassica enim medicina quoque laudatur. Ut Cato ipse scripsit, nihil est salubrius quam brassica cruda ad salutem tuendam. Et praeterea ad cenam bene conditur, si modico aceto additur. Vadamus ad illum venditorem, ut pretium cognoscamus.*

Manius: Absolutely! Cabbage is even praised for its medicinal properties. As Cato himself wrote, nothing is healthier than raw cabbage for maintaining health. And it's well-prepared for dinner when a little vinegar is added. Let's go to that vendor and find out the price.

Tiberius: *Placet! Sed prius dic mihi, quid de his olivis sentis? Videntur satis recentes esse, nec nimis durae. Nonne olivae semper ad cenam necessariae sunt?*

Tiberius: Good idea! But first, tell me, what do you think of these olives? They seem quite fresh and not too hard. Aren't olives always essential for dinner?

Manius: *Certe! Olivae, sicut panis et vinum, sunt sine quibus cena perfecta esse non potest. Ego saepe olivas cum oleo et modico salis condio, quae melius sapiunt. Videmus pretium et emamus, nam domina impatiens erit, si nimis longe moramur.*

Manius: Certainly! Olives, like bread and wine, are things without which a dinner cannot be perfect. I often season olives with oil and a little salt, which makes them taste better. Let's check the price and buy them, as the mistress will be impatient if we take too long.

Tiberius: *Recte mones. Ecce, tabernarius adest. (Tabernario appropinquat) Salve, bone vir! Quanti haec brassica et olivae venduntur?*

Tiberius: You're right. Look, here comes the vendor. (Approaching the vendor) Hello, good man! How much are these cabbages and olives?

Tabernarius: *Salve! Brassica tibi quattuor assibus venditur, olivae tribus. Fruges hodie optimae sunt condicione; hoc mane ipsae lectae sunt ex hortis prope urbem.*

Vendor: Hello! The cabbage is sold for four asses, and the olives for three. The produce is of the best quality today; they were picked this morning from gardens near the city.

Manius: *Quattuor asses brassicae? Pretium iustum esse videtur. Accipio. Olivas quoque sumam, nam uxor mea illas semper in conviviis laudat. Etiam lactucam quaerebam; num lactucam hodie habes?*

Manius: Four asses for cabbage? That seems like a fair price. I'll take it. I'll also take the olives, as my wife always praises them at feasts. I was also looking for lettuce; do you have any today?

Tabernarius: *Lactucam optimam habeo, heri vespere in horto meo coactam. Si placet, decem holera accipies duobus assibus.*

Vendor: I have the best lettuce, picked yesterday evening from my garden. If you like, you can have ten heads for two asses.

Tiberius: *Bene convenit! Lactucam quoque accipiamus, Mani. Curae non sunt minores, sed sic cena erit iucunda. Gratias tibi agimus, tabernarie. Hodie parati sumus ad bonam cenam faciendam.*

Tiberius: That's a good deal! Let's take the lettuce too, Manius. Preparations are not minor, but this way, the dinner will be delightful. Thank you, vendor. We're ready to prepare a good meal today.

Manius: *Ita est, Tiberi. Nunc, cum omnia necessaria habemus, nil amplius morandum est. Vale, bone vir, et bonum diem habe.*

Manius: Indeed, Tiberius. Now that we have everything we need, there's no reason to delay further. Farewell, good man, and have a good day.

Tabernarius: *Valete et vobis dies felix sit!*

Vendor: Farewell, and may you have a fortunate day!

Tiberius: *Vale, Mani! Nunc domum redeamus et omnia cum cura praeparemus.*

Tiberius: Farewell, Manius! Now let's head home and prepare everything with care.

De Rebus Publicis – Disputatio politica de re publica Romana

Gnaeus: *Salve, Marcelle! Audivi te nuper in senatu de rebus publicis graviter locutum esse. Quid sentis de praesenti statu rei publicae? Multi enim credunt rem publicam magnis periculis obire.*

Gnaeus: Hello, Marcellus! I heard you recently speak seriously in the Senate about public affairs. What do you think of the current state of the republic? Many believe the republic is facing great dangers.

Marcellus: *Salve, Gnae! Quid dicam? Status rei publicae me valde sollicitat. Senatus non amplius, ut antea, sapientiam consiliorum et auctoritatem pro suo honore tuetur. Populus etiam turbidior fit, et tribuni plebis, qui potestatem moderari debent, saepe se ad popularem gratiam promovent. Quid tibi videtur?*

Marcellus: Hello, Gnaeus! What can I say? The state of the republic worries me greatly. The Senate no longer, as before, defends the wisdom of its decisions and its authority for its own honor. The people are becoming more restless, and the tribunes of the plebs, who ought to moderate their power, often promote themselves for popular favor. What do you think?

Gnaeus: *Plene adsentior, Marcelle. Haec turba populi, cum de iuribus suis nimium contendat, rem publicam periclitari cogit. Quamquam tribuni potestate fruuntur ad populum tuendum, video tamen perniciem, cum plerique leges non iam respectant. Hic senatus interdum nimium remissus videtur.*

Gnaeus: I completely agree, Marcellus. This unruly crowd, when they argue too much about their rights, puts the republic in danger. Although the tribunes enjoy power to protect the people, I see destruction, as most no longer respect the laws. The Senate sometimes seems too lenient.

Marcellus: *Senatus, dico vere, mollis factus est. Ubi sunt viri, qui sicut Fabricius aut Cincinnatus ad dignitatem rei publicae conservandam magna prudentia et integritate se praestiterunt? Nunc videmus non consilia bona, sed ambitionem regere. O tempora, o mores!*

Marcellus: The Senate, I tell you truly, has become soft. Where are the men, like Fabricius or Cincinnatus, who showed themselves with great wisdom and integrity to preserve the dignity of the republic? Now we see not good decisions, but ambition ruling. Oh, the times, oh, the morals!

Gnaeus: *Ita est, et haec cupiditas honorum tantam discordiam inter cives creavit. Vide exempla recentia: certamina inter nobiles et plebem semper increscunt. Populus, qui alienatus ab ordine senatorio videtur, non amplius senatui fidit. Periculum est, ne res publica ad interitum decurrat, si nulla concordia inter cives restituatur.*

Gnaeus: Exactly, and this desire for honors has created such discord among citizens. Look at recent examples: the conflicts between the nobles and the common people are always increasing. The people, who seem alienated from the senatorial order, no longer trust the Senate. There is a danger that the republic will fall into ruin if no harmony is restored among the citizens.

Marcellus: *Quae nunc dicis, Gnae, verissima sunt. Sed quid, tua sententia, fieri debet? Ubi remedium inveniamus? Mihi quidem videtur, nisi leges rigores redintegrantur et magistratus cum maiore gravitate agant, spes nostra admodum tenuis sit.*

Marcellus: What you say now, Gnaeus, is very true. But in your opinion, what should be done? Where will we find a remedy? It seems to me that unless the strictness of the laws is restored and the magistrates act with greater seriousness, our hope is very slim.

Gnaeus: *Remedium, Marcelle, forsitan in reformatione morum ipsorum iaceat. Debemus revocare virtutes antiquas, ut honores et officia non pro propria utilitate, sed pro re publica suscipiamus. Si magistratus exemplum virtutis proponant, cives etiam secuti essent. Sed hoc nunc rarum fit.*

Gnaeus: The remedy, Marcellus, perhaps lies in the reform of our morals. We must revive the ancient virtues, so that honors and duties are undertaken not for personal gain, but for the republic. If the magistrates offer an example of virtue, the citizens would follow. But this is rare nowadays.

Marcellus: *Sicut loqueris, Gnae, ita agendum est. Virtus est salus rei publicae. Non infractae leges, sed animi honesti et fortes res publicas* *sustinent. Quod si per ornamenta et simulacra honoris ambulamus, frustra sperare possumus ut populus nos sequatur.*

Marcellus: As you say, Gnaeus, this is the way to act. Virtue is the salvation of the republic. It is not broken laws, but honest and strong minds that sustain republics. If we walk through the symbols and facades of honor, we can hope in vain that the people will follow us.

Gnaeus: *Sed, Marcelle, nonne etiam tibi videtur externa pericula ad augendam hanc domesticam discordiam contribuere? Bella cum populis barbaris ac bellum civile semper latent. Etsi nunc pax videtur, mox nova certamina prosperitatem Romae perditura sunt, nisi consilia maiora capiuntur.*

Gnaeus: But, Marcellus, doesn't it also seem to you that external dangers contribute to this growing internal discord? Wars with barbarian peoples and civil wars are always lurking. Even though there seems to be peace now, soon new conflicts will destroy Rome's prosperity unless greater plans are made.

Marcellus: *Profecto! Etsi extraneam vim domandam putamus, verum periculum intus est. Dum in bellis foris vincimus, discordia intus cor nostrum consumit. Ubi concordia deest, consilium et fortitudo nullam vim habent. Sicut dicitur, bellum intestinum semper est peius quam externum.*

Marcellus: Certainly! Even if we think we are conquering external forces, the real danger is within. While we win battles abroad, discord within is consuming our heart. Where there is no harmony, neither wisdom nor courage has any power. As they say, internal war is always worse than external.

Gnaeus: *Bene dixisti! Si inter nos ipsos concordiam et aequitatem non tenemus, fortitudo nostra frangitur. Spero tamen nos modum invenire posse, si tantum senatus iterum auctoritatem suam servet et populus ad virtutem incitetur.*

Gnaeus: Well said! If we do not maintain harmony and fairness among ourselves, our strength will be broken. But I hope we can find a way if only the Senate preserves its authority again and the people are inspired toward virtue.

Marcellus: *Spero et ego, Gnae, sed tempus narrabit. Nos quidem omnia facienda suscipere debemus pro patria. Fortuna saepe virtutes miratur, et Roma humanis opibus non tam indiget quam bonis exemplis.*

Marcellus: I hope so too, Gnaeus, but time will tell. Indeed, we must take up all necessary actions for our country. Fortune often admires virtue, and Rome needs good examples more than human resources.

Gnaeus: *Ita est. Vale nunc, Marcelle, et memento semper pro rei publicae causa pugnare!*

Gnaeus: That's right. Farewell for now, Marcellus, and always remember to fight for the cause of the republic!

Marcellus: *Vale, Gnae, et fidelem tibi virtutem pro re publica semper custodias!*

Marcellus: Farewell, Gnaeus, and always keep your faithful virtue for the republic!

In Curia – Disputatio in Senatu

Appius: *Patercule, hodie gravissimam rem in Curia tractamus. Quaestio de foedere cum populis externis est. Ego quidem censeo bellum vitandum esse et pacem curandam, ut vires nostras internas firmemus. Quid tu sentis?*

Appius: Paterculus, today we are discussing a most serious matter in the Senate. The question is about making treaties with foreign peoples. I believe we must avoid war and ensure peace in order to strengthen our internal forces. What do you think?

Paterculus: *Appi, semper sapiens es, sed in hac re dissentio. Pax quidem bona est, sed non semper durare potest. Hostes, sicut Germani et Daci, virtutem nostram timere debent. Si nimium cedamus, prospicito, hi barbari mox audaciores fient et muros ipsos Romae percutient.*

Paterculus: Appius, you are always wise, but I disagree on this matter. Peace is good, yes, but it cannot always last. Our enemies, like the Germans and Dacians, must fear our strength. If we give in too much, mark my words, these barbarians will soon become bolder and strike at Rome's very walls.

Appius: *Intellego tuam sollicitudinem, Patercule, sed nonne satius est sedatione potius quam armis omnia comparare? Bella Romanos defessos et exsangues fecerunt. Res publica nostra a discordiis internis adflicta est, et multum sanguinis iam perditum est. Cur non potius diplomatia utimur?*

Appius: I understand your concern, Paterculus, but isn't it better to achieve everything through negotiation rather than arms? Wars have left Romans exhausted and bloodless. Our republic is afflicted by internal discord, and much blood has already been lost. Why not use diplomacy instead?

Marcellus: *Vos ambo gravia pronuntiatis, Appi et Patercule. Ego autem media via incedo. Nec bellum semper quaerendum est, nec pax sine virtute stabit. Fortuna nostra semper in virtute militari fundata est, sed non minus arte pacis conservandae. Si pax consequi potest sine ignavia, eam amplectamur; sin bellum necessarium fit, non recedamus.*

Marcellus: Both of you speak weighty truths, Appius and Paterculus. However, I take the middle path. War is not always to be sought, nor will peace stand without strength. Our fortune has always been founded on military valor, but no less on the art of maintaining peace. If peace can be achieved without cowardice, let's embrace it; but if war is necessary, let us not retreat.

Paterculus: *Marcelle, verba tua non contemno, sed hos barbaros diplomatia regi non credo. Vires externae solas vires internas confirmant. Hostes diplomatia moveri non possunt, nisi antea ferro subacti sunt. Quis enim sine timore in re publica nostra fidem collocabit?*

Paterculus: Marcellus, I do not dismiss your words, but I don't believe these barbarians can be ruled by diplomacy. Only external strength strengthens internal strength. Diplomacy cannot move our enemies unless they have first been subdued by the sword. Who will place their trust in our republic without fear?

Appius: *At dic mihi, Patercule, quot bella conferemus, dum finem quaerimus? Quot iuvenes in armis peribunt, dum potestas belli nos vivere non sinet? Quaeramus viam pacis per rationem, non per ferrum. Ut dicebant antiqui: summum ius summa iniuria. Si bellum semper quaerimus, tandem nos ipsi exhauriemus.*

Appius: But tell me, Paterculus, how many wars will we wage while seeking an end? How many young men will die in arms, while the power of war will not let us live? Let's seek the way of peace through reason, not through the sword. As the ancients said: the highest law brings the highest injustice. If we always seek war, in the end we will exhaust ourselves.

Marcellus: *Firmiter crede, Appi, neque bellum neque pax absque periculo sunt. Sed meminisse oportet populum Romanum cum gloria bellum semper gessisse, sed etiam consilio egregio pacem comparasse. Qui vires nostras contemnat, ultimum fatum sibi petit. Qui autem pacem cupit, non ignorare debet virtutem nostram. Uterque modus, belli ac pacis, prudentiam exigit.*

Marcellus: Trust me, Appius, neither war nor peace is without danger. But we must remember that the Roman people have always waged war with glory, yet have also secured peace with wise counsel. Those who despise our strength invite their own doom. But those who desire peace should not ignore our might. Both approaches, war and peace, require wisdom.

Paterculus: *Dignus es, Marcelle, et verba tua sedationem afferunt. Sed bellum necesse est, ut Romam muniamus, non modo urbem ipsam, sed totam rem publicam. Extremis temporibus fortitudine et promissis pacis servamus civitatem.*

Paterculus: You are worthy, Marcellus, and your words bring calm. But war is necessary to defend Rome, not just the city itself, but the entire republic. In extreme times, we protect the state through strength and the promises of peace.

Appius: *Patercule, nihil ego contra virtutem militarem dico. Sed cave ne nimis confidamus in vi nuda. Quid si Roma ipsa ab intus corrumpitur, dum foris bellum geritur? Alio modo constituamus concordiam inter cives nostros, tum extranea pericula minoris momenti erunt. Civitas recte gubernata neque bello neque pace frangetur.*

Appius: Paterculus, I say nothing against military strength. But beware of trusting too much in brute force. What if Rome itself is corrupted from within while we wage war abroad? Let's establish harmony among our citizens in another way, then external dangers will be of less importance. A rightly governed state will not be broken by either war or peace.

Marcellus: *Rem certe difficillimam tractamus, Appi et Patercule. Sed, proficiamus! Propositum belli sine prudentia non quaeramus, neque sine fortitudine pacem quaeramus. Pax atque virtus semper sociatae sint.*

Marcellus: Indeed, we are dealing with a very difficult matter, Appius and Paterculus. But let us proceed! Let us not seek war without wisdom, nor peace without courage. Peace and strength must always be linked.

Appius: *Ita sit. Senatus ipse nunc decernat quid optimum rei publicae videatur.*

Appius: So be it. The Senate itself must now decide what is best for the republic.

Paterculus: *Verum est. Si consilium commune captum fuerit, utrumque modum in honore habebimus. Valete, Appi et Marcelle. Spero fore ut res publica virtute et pace servetur.*

Paterculus: That is true. If a common decision is reached, we will honor both paths. Farewell, Appius and Marcellus. I hope that the republic will be preserved through strength and peace.

Marcellus: *Valete, patres conscripti, et prudentia et fortitudine utamur!*

Marcellus: Farewell, senators, and let us use both wisdom and courage!

Appius: *Valete!*

Appius: Farewell!

De Officiis – Disputatio de officiis et responsabilitatibus

Julius: *Salve, Corneli! Video te sollicitum esse hodie. Quid accidit? An de officiis tuis gravioribus cogitas?*

Julius: Greetings, Cornelius! I see that you seem troubled today. Has something happened? Are you thinking about your heavier responsibilities?

Cornelius: *Salve, Juli! Recte animadvertis. Multa mihi in mente versantur de officiis, quae vir bonus pro familia et re publica sustinere debet. Oneris pondus interdum nimium videtur, sed scis quam necessaria officia sint.*

Cornelius: Greetings, Julius! You've noticed correctly. Many thoughts about the duties a good man must bear for his family and the state are weighing on my mind. Sometimes the burden seems too great, but you know how essential these responsibilities are.

Julius: *Profecto, Corneli. Sine officiis, neque familia neque civitas stare potest. Nam sic dixit Cicero ipse: officium est quod decet personam eius, qui vir bonus haberi vult. Officium igitur firmamentum est dignitatis nostrae et stabilis virtutis. Sed quid tua sententia primum officium viri boni est?*

Julius: Indeed, Cornelius. Without duties, neither family nor the state can stand. For, as Cicero himself said: duty is what befits the character of one who wishes to be considered a good man. Therefore, duty is the foundation of our dignity and stable virtue. But in your opinion, what is the foremost duty of a good man?

Cornelius: *Censeo primum officium esse familiae prospicere et eam sustentare. Nam familia, si bene administratur, fundamentum est totius vitae. Paterfamilias curare debet ut liberi sui bonis exemplis et disciplina utantur. Hic honores externi minoris sunt, si domus ipsa ruat. Quid tu censes?*

Cornelius: I believe that the first duty is to provide for and support the family. For if the family is well-managed, it is the foundation of all life. The head of the household must ensure that his children are guided by good examples and discipline. External honors mean little if the household itself falls apart. What do you think?

Julius: *Mihi quidem placet tua sententia. Nihil est maius quam domus bene gubernata, quippe quae procreatio futurae generationis sit. Sed etiam censeo virum non solum familiam suam, sed rem publicam spectare debere. Officia civitatis omni tempore praeponderare videntur; nam sine re publica sana, familiarum salus quoque minuitur.*

Julius: I agree with your view. There is nothing more important than a well-managed household, as it is the foundation of future generations. However, I also believe that a man should not only consider his family but also the state. The responsibilities of the state seem to take precedence at all times; for without a healthy republic, the welfare of families also diminishes.

Cornelius: *Recte mones, Juli. Sed tibi nonne videtur quod saepe difficultates oriuntur inter privata officia et officia publica? Saepe fit ut aliquis inter proprias res et communes dividatur, nesciatque quid potissimum agendum sit.*

Cornelius: You're right, Julius. But don't you also find that difficulties often arise between private and public duties? It often happens that someone is torn between personal matters and public concerns and doesn't know which should take priority.

Julius: *Ita est! Hic discrimen invenimus inter ea, quae civitas requirit, et ea, quae familia. Sed sapiens vir, ut Cicero suadet, modum invenit. Nec privatis curis omnino vacandum est, nec res publica omnino neglegenda. Mediocritas et temperantia in officiis maxime laudantur.*

Julius: Exactly! This is where we find the distinction between what the state requires and what the family demands. But a wise man, as Cicero advises, finds balance. We must neither entirely neglect private concerns nor completely disregard public matters. Moderation and temperance in fulfilling duties are greatly praised.

Cornelius: *Mediocritas profecto laudanda est. Sed quod te nunc rogare velim, est: quid agendum est, si officii nostri propositum cum nostra vita privata videtur confligere? Curabisne tuos aut magistratus potius defendere?*

Cornelius: Moderation is indeed commendable. But what I want to ask you now is this: what should we do if our duty conflicts with our private life? Would you prioritize your family or defend your official responsibilities?

Julius: *Hic, Corneli, ratio agendi ad rem singularem spectat. Si familia summo periculo agit, patet primum familiam curari. Sed si res publica gravior oratur, id est quod primum agendum est. Principium omnium officiorum est iustitia, ut omnibus id quod suum est reddatur. Sine iustitia, ne officium quidem manere potest.*

Julius: Here, Cornelius, the course of action depends on the specific situation. If the family is in great danger, it's clear that the family must be cared for first. But if a greater matter concerning the state arises, that is what must come first. The foundation of all duties is justice, to give everyone what is theirs. Without justice, duty itself cannot stand.

Cornelius: *Verba tua sapiunt summam sapientiam, Juli. Officia, ut dicis, iustitiae subiecta sunt. Nam in omnibus rebus, et privatis et publicis, summa auctoritas iustitiae est. Fortasse hic inveniatur propositum: omnia officia ex principio iustitiae moderari debent.*

Cornelius: Your words reflect great wisdom, Julius. Duties, as you say, are subject to justice. For in all things, both private and public, justice holds the highest authority. Perhaps here lies the answer: all duties must be governed by the principle of justice.

Julius: *Ita est, Corneli. Nihil est dignitati viri boni accommodatius quam ratio iusta et moderata. Si hoc principium sequimur, neque familia, neque res publica umquam neglegetur. Haec est summa officii: nihil iniustum facere, omnia pro dignitate.*

Julius: Exactly, Cornelius. Nothing is more fitting to the dignity of a good man than a just and measured approach. If we follow this principle, neither the family nor the state will ever be neglected. This is the essence of duty: do nothing unjust, and always act with dignity.

Cornelius: *Bene conclusisti, Juli. Ego hoc diem meliorem sentio, quia de officiis nostris sic consideravimus. Virtus et officium virum semper tenent.*

Cornelius: You've concluded well, Julius. I feel that this day has improved, thanks to our reflection on our duties. Virtue and duty always hold a man steady.

Julius: *Ita vero, Corneli. Vale nunc, et memento semper officium summum decus esse viri sapientis.*

Julius: Indeed, Cornelius. Farewell for now, and always remember that duty is the highest honor of a wise man.

Cornelius: *Vale, Juli, et omnia tua officia cum honore perficias!*

Cornelius: Farewell, Julius, and may you fulfill all your duties with honor!

In Nave – Disputatio in nave Romana

Caius: *Salve, nauta! Vide quanta tranquillitas maris hodie sit. Cura est, ut hoc iter tam placidum perpetuum sit, an saepe mutatur natura maris?*

Caius: Greetings, sailor! Look at how calm the sea is today. Do you think this journey will remain as peaceful, or does the nature of the sea often change?

Nauta: *Salve, Cai! Maris tranquillitatem numquam fidam esse scimus. Hodie fortasse vides aequora placida, sed cras venti saevire possunt. Tamquam fortuna ipsa, mare saepissime mutatur. Sed bene est sperare. Hodie venti favent.*

Sailor: Greetings, Caius! We know that the calmness of the sea is never reliable. Today you may see peaceful waters, but tomorrow the winds could rage. Like fortune itself, the sea changes very often. But it's good to be hopeful. Today, the winds are in our favor.

Caius: *Bene monitum. Ego quidem, cum primum in navem ascendi, timebam de tempestatibus, sed nunc, videns mare tam placidum, aliquantulum refectus sum. Dic mihi, quotiens his fluctibus navigasti? Certe huius maris mores bene novisti.*

Caius: Well said. When I first boarded the ship, I was afraid of storms, but now, seeing the sea so calm, I feel somewhat reassured. Tell me, how many times have you sailed these waters? You must know the ways of this sea very well.

Nauta: *Multas quidem navigationes feci, Cai. Hoc mare nostrum mihi non ignotum est. Multos annos per vicissitudines tempestatum iter feci, et prope omnes portus orarum nostrarum vidi. Semper tamen est aliquid quod miror in mari; nihil umquam omnino idem manet.*

Sailor: I've made many voyages, Caius. This sea is no stranger to me. I've sailed for many years through changing storms, and I've seen nearly all the ports of our coasts. But still, there's always something about the sea that amazes me; nothing ever stays the same.

Caius: *Incredibile! Videtur ut mare, quamquam saepe visum, semper alicuius novi sit auctore. At dic mihi, nauta, quid sit maxime periculosum* *in huius maris navigatione? Suntne scopuli, tempestates, an aliae naves quae cavendae sunt?*

Caius: Incredible! It seems that the sea, though often seen, always has something new to offer. But tell me, sailor, what is the most dangerous thing in navigating these waters? Are there rocks, storms, or other ships to watch out for?

Nauta: *Maxima pericula, Cai, ab tempestatibus oriuntur, praesertim si repentini surgunt. Sed etiam scopuli, quos oculus non cernit, saepissime naufragia faciunt. Aliquando quoque piratae, praesertim prope insulas sparsas, magnos dolos agunt. Navigare necesse est cum magna prudentia.*

Sailor: The greatest dangers, Caius, come from storms, especially when they arise suddenly. But also, unseen rocks frequently cause shipwrecks. At times, pirates, especially near scattered islands, carry out great deceptions. One must always navigate with great caution.

Caius: *Nihil facilius videtur dicere, "navigare necesse est," sed prudentiam, ut ais, maxime requirit. Sed dic, quid facias, si tempestas magna repente oriatur? Numquam antea mari periclitatus sum, et scire volo quid fieri debeat.*

Caius: It seems easy to say, "it is necessary to sail," but as you say, it requires great wisdom. But tell me, what do you do if a great storm suddenly arises? I've never faced danger at sea before, and I want to know what should be done.

Nauta: *Si tempestas subito oriatur, prima res est ventis obsistere et vela stringere, ut navis nimio impetu non frangatur. Remi adhibentur, si necesse est, ut navis rectum cursum teneat. Prudentia et constantia sunt duae virtutes navigantium. Ne metuas, Cai, si praecipitationem evitare poterimus.*

Sailor: If a storm arises suddenly, the first thing is to resist the winds and tighten the sails, so the ship isn't broken by too much force. Oars are used, if necessary, to keep the ship on course. Prudence and perseverance are the two virtues of sailors. Don't fear, Caius, as long as we can avoid rushing into danger.

Caius: *Prudentiam tuam laudo, nauta. Ego quidem hoc iter cum animo tranquillo feram, sciens te rerum maritimarum peritissimum esse. Utrum credas nos cito portum adventuros?*

Caius: I praise your wisdom, sailor. I will continue this journey with a calm mind, knowing that you are highly skilled in maritime matters. Do you think we will reach the port soon?

Nauta: *Si venti hodie suaves manebunt, portum intra paucos dies attigemus. Sic, ut spero, iter nostrum securum erit, sed, ut semper in mari, nihil certum pronuntiare possum. Fortuna maris est instabilis.*

Sailor: If the winds remain gentle today, we'll reach the port within a few days. So, I hope, our journey will be safe, but as always at sea, nothing can be predicted with certainty. The fortune of the sea is unpredictable.

Caius: *Bene intellego. Fortunam navium firmamus consilio fortitudineque. Vale nunc, nauta, et in prudentia tua semper permaneas.*

Caius: I understand well. We strengthen the fortune of ships with wisdom and courage. Farewell for now, sailor, and may you always remain steadfast in your wisdom.

Nauta: *Vale, Cai! Et spero ut iter nostrum prospere conficere possimus.*

Sailor: Farewell, Caius! And I hope that we can complete our journey successfully.

De Bello Gallico – Disputatio de expeditionibus Iulii Caesaris in Gallia

Servius: *Salve, Quintine! Audivi te librum Iulii Caesaris De Bello Gallico legisse. Quid sentis de rebus ab eo gestis? Nonne haec expeditio magnas glorias et virtutes Romanae extollit?*

Servius: Greetings, Quintinus! I heard you've read Julius Caesar's *De Bello Gallico*. What do you think of the deeds he accomplished? Doesn't this expedition exalt the great glory and virtues of Rome?

Quintinus: *Salve, Servi! Certe, librum legi, et profecto tantam audaciam atque consilium Caesaris admiror. Bellum Gallicum non solum Romae imperium late extulit, sed etiam promptam et celerem militarem disciplinam populus noster ostendit. Sed, dic mihi, quid tibi videtur? Quomodo proventus belli aestimas?*

Quintinus: Greetings, Servius! Indeed, I've read the book, and I greatly admire Caesar's boldness and strategy. The Gallic War not only expanded Rome's empire far and wide, but also displayed the quick and disciplined military skill of our people. But tell me, what's your opinion? How do you assess the outcomes of the war?

Servius: *Ego quidem gloriam Caesaris magnam esse censeo. Nihil minus quam Romanam potentiam in Gallia fundavit, et multos populos feroces sub iugum misit. Praesertim victoria contra Vercingetorigem ad Alesiam me miratum affecit. Quid enim audacius aut clarius fieri potuit?*

Servius: I think Caesar's glory is immense. He established Roman power in Gaul and subdued many fierce tribes. The victory over Vercingetorix at Alesia particularly amazed me. What could have been more daring or brilliant than that?

Quintinus: *Profecto, Alesia summum belli momentum fuit. Circumventae Caesaris legiones a Gallis, ipse tamen duplicem obsidionem sicut mirabilem rem gerens, tam extra quam intus copias continuit. Ingenium et consilium eius nullum par habet. Sed aliqui, Servi, dicunt Caesarem nimis crudelem fuisse. Quid dicis de hoc?*

Quintinus: Certainly, Alesia was the climax of the war. Caesar's legions were surrounded by the Gauls, yet he managed a double siege, controlling forces both inside and outside. His genius and strategy have no equal. But some, Servius, say that Caesar was too cruel. What do you think about this?

Servius: *Certe, audivi aliquos eum crudelitatis accusare, sed bellum ipsum feritatem requirit. Si consulas iura belli, mirari non debes. Galli erant populus periculosus, et si Caesar minus severe ageret, Roma fortasse civitates Gallorum numquam subiectas haberet. Imperium sine virtute et dura iustitia servari non potest.*

Servius: Surely, I've heard some accuse him of cruelty, but war itself demands harshness. If you consider the laws of war, you shouldn't be surprised. The Gauls were a dangerous people, and had Caesar acted less severely, Rome might never have subdued them. Empire cannot be maintained without strength and strict justice.

Quintinus: *Vera pronuntias. In bello, crudelitas interdum necessaria fit ad metum iniiciendum, et sic pax longius diurnabitur. Nihilominus, mihi quoque videtur Caesarem non tam pro re publica quam pro suis commodis bellum gessisse. Ambitio eius ad summum imperium petendum perspicua erat. Quid tu censes?*

Quintinus: You speak truth. In war, cruelty is sometimes necessary to instill fear, and thus peace will last longer. However, it also seems to me that Caesar waged war not so much for the republic as for his own benefit. His ambition to seek supreme power was obvious. What do you think?

Servius: *Non possum negare, Quintine. Ambitionem Caesari negare non possumus; multa eius facta non solum pro re publica, sed etiam pro sua gloria egisse videtur. Sed quaestionem tamen proferam: num gloria personalis et salus rei publicae semper dissociandae sunt? Mihi videtur, interdum summi viri suae virtutis praemium quaerere possint.*

Servius: I can't deny it, Quintinus. We can't ignore Caesar's ambition; many of his actions seem to have been done not only for the republic but also for his own glory. But I ask you this: are personal glory and the welfare of the republic always at odds? It seems to me that at times great men can seek the reward of their virtues.

Quintinus: *Fortasse. Caesar enim victoria sua Romam amplificavit et magnam vim copiarum et opum comparavit. Sed hoc quoque verum est, bellum Gallicum rei publicae mirabilem potestatem dedit, quae tandem* *ad civilia bella duxit. Num gloria Romae aequatur damnum, quod discordia interna paene civitatem perdidit?*

Quintinus: Perhaps. Caesar did expand Rome with his victory and gained a great deal of forces and wealth. But it's also true that the Gallic War gave the republic immense power, which eventually led to civil wars. Can Rome's glory really outweigh the damage caused by internal discord that nearly destroyed the state?

Servius: *Hoc quidem gravius est. Caesar bello Gallico propulit et auxit potentiam, sed eodem tempore civitatem fragiliorem fecit. Cum Roma tantis divitiis et potentiae nondum parata esset ad cives concordia continendos, ad civile bellum inevitabiliter evoluta est. Sed sic est fortuna, quae semper cum virtute ac periculo coniungitur.*

Servius: That's indeed a serious point. Caesar propelled and increased power through the Gallic War, but at the same time, he made the state more fragile. When Rome wasn't yet ready to handle such wealth and power with unity among its citizens, civil war became inevitable. But that's how fortune is—it's always tied to virtue and danger.

Quintinus: *Ita est, fortuna cum virtute saepe iungitur, sed interdum magno pretio id vidimus. Nihilominus, Caesar magnus dux fuit, et, quamquam ambitionis sui accusatur, humanum est res miras cum gloria quaerere. Illum neglegere in nostra historia non possumus.*

Quintinus: Yes, fortune and virtue often go hand in hand, but we've seen that sometimes at a great price. Nonetheless, Caesar was a great leader, and although he is accused of ambition, it's human to seek greatness with glory. We cannot ignore him in our history.

Servius: *Recte mones, Quintine. Caesar semper pro exemplo manebit prudentiae et audaciae militaris. De factis eius iudicium aliquando variat, sed sine dubio bellum Gallicum restat magnum et memorabile tempus. Valet Roma, dum vires tales in suis finibus generat.*

Servius: You're right, Quintinus. Caesar will always remain an example of military wisdom and boldness. Opinions on his actions may vary, but without a doubt, the Gallic War remains a great and memorable period. Rome endures as long as it produces such strength within its borders.

Quintinus: *Vale, Servi! Et quotiens de Caesaris factis cogitamus, memento: historia semper utramque faciem ostendit.*

Quintinus: Farewell, Servius! And whenever we think of Caesar's deeds, remember: history always shows both sides.

Servius: *Ita est! Vale, amice, et ad proximas rationes magnorum virorum revertamur.*

Servius: Indeed! Farewell, my friend, and let's return to the matters of great men next time.

In Horto Domestico – Disputatio de cura horti domestici

Lucius: *Salve, Gaie! Vidi te hodie in horto tuo operantem. Quid praeparas? Videntur tibi omnia floribus et herbis fructiferis abundare.*

Lucius: Greetings, Gaius! I saw you working in your garden today. What are you preparing? It seems that your garden is full of flowers and fruitful herbs.

Gaius: *Salve, Luci! Gaudeo te hortum meum spectare. Hodie rosas novas sero et aliquot herbas condimentarias colo, ut thymum et mentham. Non solum ad pulchritudinem, sed etiam ad cenas familiares hic hortus mihi usui est.*

Gaius: Greetings, Lucius! I'm glad you're looking at my garden. Today, I'm planting new roses and cultivating some culinary herbs, such as thyme and mint. This garden is useful to me not only for beauty but also for preparing family meals.

Lucius: *Rosas quidem splendidas habes. Nihil magis delectat quam odor rosarum florentium sub sole matutino. Sed quid de herbis? Videntur tibi satis bene crescere?*

Lucius: Your roses are indeed splendid. Nothing is more delightful than the scent of blooming roses under the morning sun. But how are the herbs? Do they seem to be growing well?

Gaius: *Ita vero! Thymus et menta bene consistunt, quoniam solem amant et umiditatem mediocrem postulant. Cotidie aquam modicam affero, ut ne nimis sit humidum, sed satis ut virides maneant. Fortasse etiam aliquot lactucas seram, si locus superest.*

Gaius: Indeed! The thyme and mint are doing well since they love sunlight and need moderate moisture. I water them lightly every day, making sure the soil isn't too wet but stays green enough. I might even plant some lettuce if there's enough space.

Lucius: *Lactuca profecto aptissima est ad hortum domesticum. Nihil facilius est quam propriam lactucam ex horto ad mensam adferre. Sic semper habes fruges recentes. Sed dic mihi, Gaie, quid facis ut herbas tuas ab insectis tuearis? Saepe vidi herbas ab illis vastari.*

Lucius: Lettuce is certainly perfect for a home garden. Nothing is easier than bringing fresh lettuce straight from the garden to the table. So, tell me, Gaius, what do you do to protect your herbs from insects? I've often seen herbs destroyed by them.

Gaius: *Hoc verum est. Multa insecta sunt quae hortos nostros vexant. Ego tamen, sicut veteres faciebant, alium aut absinthium inter herbas sero, quod multas pestes arcet. Praeterea, modicum oleum ex olea arboribus affero, ut foliis infundatur. Hoc res parvas nocentes inhibet.*

Gaius: That's true. Many insects do trouble our gardens. But as the ancients did, I plant garlic or wormwood among the herbs, which helps keep many pests away. I also apply a bit of olive oil to the leaves, which prevents small harmful creatures.

Lucius: *Ingeniosum consilium! Veteres recte monent: res simplices saepe maxima adiumenta afferunt. Sed quid de fructibus arborum? Vidi ficus et malos granatos in horto tuo crescere. Bene crescuntne?*

Lucius: Ingenious idea! The ancients were right: simple things often bring the greatest help. But what about your fruit trees? I've seen fig trees and pomegranate trees growing in your garden. Are they thriving?

Gaius: *Bene scis, Luci! Ficus et mala granata celeriter crescunt, praesertim postquam pluviae anni satis superque iuverunt. Ficus iam maturae sunt, et mala granata autumno colligam. Nihil iucundius est quam arbores fructiferas curare, quae non modo pulchritudinem oculorum, sed etiam fructum mensae praebent.*

Gaius: You know well, Lucius! The fig and pomegranate trees are growing quickly, especially since this year's rains have helped greatly. The figs are already ripe, and I'll harvest the pomegranates in autumn. There's nothing more pleasing than caring for fruit trees, which not only provide visual beauty but also fruit for the table.

Lucius: *Certe, hortus tuus optime videtur! Ego quoque cogito aliquid simile in villa mea facere, sed locus mihi admodum parvus est. Non satis est spatium ad magnas arbores, sed fortasse herbas aut parvas vites serere possim.*

Lucius: Certainly, your garden looks excellent! I'm thinking of doing something similar at my villa, but my space is quite small. There's not enough room for large trees, but perhaps I could plant herbs or small vines.

Gaius: *Etiam in parvo loco multa fieri possunt. Herbae aromaticae et parvae plantae non multum spatium exigunt. Si locum ad flores habes, etiam parvas vites serere potes ad pergulam vel parvum hortulum. Natura ipsa semper locum novis rebus invenit.*

Gaius: Even in a small space, much can be done. Aromatic herbs and small plants don't require much room. If you have space for flowers, you could even plant small vines along a pergola or in a small garden bed. Nature always finds room for new things.

Lucius: *Benigne monuisti, Gaie. Cogito nunc parvum hortulum condere in parte villae quae solem accipit. Tua consilia mihi magnum auxilium dabunt.*

Lucius: You've given me great advice, Gaius. I'm now thinking of setting up a small garden in the part of my villa that gets sunlight. Your suggestions will be of great help to me.

Gaius: *Nihil melius est quam humi manus nostras in serendo adhibere. Sic et animus et corpus reficitur. Si umquam consilium opus erit aut auxilium in horto, libenter veniam.*

Gaius: There's nothing better than getting our hands into the soil when planting. It refreshes both the mind and the body. If you ever need advice or help in the garden, I'll gladly come.

Lucius: *Gratias tibi ago, Gaie. Sine dubio hortus tuus pro exemplo mihi erit. Vale nunc, et fruere tuis operibus horti!*

Lucius: Thank you, Gaius. Without a doubt, your garden will serve as an example for me. Farewell for now, and enjoy your work in the garden!

Gaius: *Vale, Luci, et utinam hortus tuus, quem mox condes, semper floreat et fruges optimas afferat!*

Gaius: Farewell, Lucius, and may your garden, which you will soon plant, always flourish and bring forth the best fruits!

De Religione Romana – Disputatio de deis Romanis et ritibus religiosis

Marcus: *Salve, Publi! Nuper multa de religione Romana cogitavi, praesertim de ritibus quos patres nostri servabant. Videsne quanta vis deorum in vitam nostram quotidianam influat?*

Marcus: Greetings, Publius! Lately, I have been thinking a lot about Roman religion, especially the rituals our ancestors followed. Do you see how much influence the gods have on our daily lives?

Publius: *Salve, Marce! Profecto, dei omnes res nostras regunt. Sicut scis, nullam rem protinus agere debemus nisi divino nuntio accepto. Auspicia et auguria semper consulenda sunt, ut sciamus utrum favere dei vel adversari velint.*

Publius: Greetings, Marcus! Indeed, the gods govern all our affairs. As you know, we must not undertake anything without first receiving a divine message. Omens and auguries must always be consulted to know whether the gods are favorable or opposed.

Marcus: *Ita est. Augurum pronuntiatio magna est. Quoties curia nostra aut imperatores bella gerere constituunt, auspicia ex avibus aut aliis signis caeli sumpta sunt. Sed dic mihi, Publi, quis deorum tibi principem locum tenet?*

Marcus: That's right. The declarations of the augurs are significant. Whenever our senate or generals plan to wage war, omens are taken from birds or other celestial signs. But tell me, Publius, which god holds the highest place for you?

Publius: *Mihi quidem Iuppiter Optimus Maximus principatum tenet. Est enim rex deorum et hominum, cuius thronus in Capitolio summo loco stat. Iuppiter caelum regit, tempestates moderatur, et ius hominum custodit. Nonne omnes ad eum preces effundimus cum urbi aut familiis nostris periculum imminet?*

Publius: For me, Jupiter Optimus Maximus holds the highest place. He is the king of gods and men, whose throne stands on the highest place on the Capitoline Hill. Jupiter governs the sky, controls the weather, and protects human law. Don't we all offer prayers to him when danger threatens our city or families?

Marcus: *Certe, Iuppiter ipse omnium consilia et arma regit. Sed ego quoque Martem magno honore habeo. Is enim bellum et virtutem militarem custodit, et sine Martis favore imperium Romae numquam constitisset. Ad bellum proficiscens, consuetudo est Martem sacrificiis placare, ut victoriam de hostibus feramus.*

Marcus: Certainly, Jupiter rules all decisions and weapons. But I also hold Mars in high regard. He governs war and military virtue, and without Mars' favor, the Roman Empire would never have been established. Before setting out for war, it is customary to appease Mars with sacrifices to ensure victory over our enemies.

Publius: *Recte dicis, Marce! Militaris potentia sine Martis beneficiis impar fuisset. Mihi tamen Venus quoque maxima dignitate est. Ipsa enim amorem et pulchritudinem inter homines divino fulgore dono fecit. Non solum proelia et res bellicae nobis recte gerendae sunt, sed etiam amores et amicitiae, quae societates coniungunt. Venus in templis suis semper cum gratia colitur.*

Publius: You're right, Marcus! Military power would be incomplete without Mars' blessings. However, I also hold Venus in high esteem. She has bestowed love and beauty among humans with her divine radiance. It's not only battles and war that must be managed, but also love and friendships, which bind societies together. Venus is always honored with great devotion in her temples.

Marcus: *Venus, ut scis, etiam mater Aeneae, fundatoris generis Romani, est. Itaque Venus non solum amoris dea est, sed etiam custos posteritatis nostrae. Bene quidem Roma templis suis et sacra deorum celebrat, sicut Ianus et Vesta, qui ipsam domum et familiam protegunt.*

Marcus: As you know, Venus is also the mother of Aeneas, the founder of the Roman people. So, Venus is not only the goddess of love but also the guardian of our lineage. Rome honors its temples and the sacred rites of the gods well, such as Janus and Vesta, who protect the home and family itself.

Publius: *Ah, Ianus! Ipse est deorum portarum custos. Nonne sacrificium ad initium cuiusque mensis Iano faciendum est? Porta Iani semper aperta in bello, clausa in pace, et reges nostri consuetudinem hanc magna cum cura coluerunt.*

Publius: Ah, Janus! He is the keeper of the gods' gates. Isn't a sacrifice to Janus required at the beginning of each month? The doors of Janus are always open in war and closed in peace, and our kings have followed this tradition with great care.

Marcus: *Ianus quidem portas rerum novarum aperit, Vesta autem ignem perpetuum tenet, qui domum Romanam custodit. Quam sacrum et magnum munus Vestalium Virginum, quae sacrum ignem numquam exstingui sinunt! Mirum est quo modo dei omnes vitam nostram totam complexi sint.*

Marcus: Indeed, Janus opens the doors to new beginnings, while Vesta holds the eternal flame that protects the Roman home. What a sacred and great duty the Vestal Virgins have, who never let the sacred fire go out! It's amazing how the gods encompass our entire life.

Publius: *Ita est. Nihil in Romana vita sine religione fit. Quod exemplum quoque dat, ut pietatem colamus et divinis semper gratiam referamus. Templa, sacra, sacrificia—omnia ad benevolentiam deorum et salutem populi pertinent.*

Publius: Exactly. Nothing in Roman life happens without religion. It sets an example for us to practice piety and always show gratitude to the divine. Temples, rites, sacrifices—all are for the goodwill of the gods and the safety of the people.

Marcus: *Recte dicis, Publi. Pietas nostra non modo propter metum, sed etiam propter amorem deorum servatur. Si civitas nostra pietatem neglegeret, di non tam benigne nos respicerent. Nunc autem Roma, deorum favore, in omnibus rebus prosperat.*

Marcus: You speak rightly, Publius. Our piety is maintained not just out of fear but also out of love for the gods. If our city neglected piety, the gods wouldn't look upon us so kindly. But now, thanks to the gods' favor, Rome prospers in all things.

Publius: *Sapiens es, Marce. Sine dubio, quamdiu religionem nostram curamus et deos honoramus, Roma manebit invicta. Vale nunc, et preces tuas deis semper effundas!*

Publius: You are wise, Marcus. Without a doubt, as long as we maintain our religion and honor the gods, Rome will remain undefeated. Farewell for now, and may you always offer your prayers to the gods!

Marcus: *Vale, Publi! Et tibi favorem deorum semper exopto.*

Marcus: Farewell, Publius! And I always wish the gods' favor upon you.

De Sacrificiis – Disputatio de processu et necessitate sacrificiorum

Sextus: *Salve, Opiter! Audivi te hodie ad aram Martis sacrificium obtulisse. Quid te movit ad hunc ritum peragendum?*

Sextus: Hello, Opiter! I heard that you offered a sacrifice at Mars' altar today. What moved you to perform this ritual?

Opiter: *Salve, Sexte! Ita est, Marti bovem immolavi pro salute exercitus nostri. Mihi visum est, si victoriam quaerimus, nihil melius esse quam ipsi deo belli sacrificium offerre. Martis favor sine dubio magnam vim in cursum belli habet.*

Opiter: Hello, Sextus! Yes, I sacrificed a bull to Mars for the safety of our army. It seemed to me that if we seek victory, nothing is better than offering a sacrifice to the god of war himself. Without a doubt, Mars' favor greatly influences the course of war.

Sextus: *Bene factum! Curare ut di faveant maximum officium est. Sed dic mihi, quomodo ritus ipse peractus est? Multi saepe loquuntur de minutis, sed pauci vere sciunt quanta sit gravitas in singulis partibus sacrificii.*

Sextus: Well done! Ensuring the gods' favor is of utmost importance. But tell me, how was the ritual itself performed? Many often talk about the details, but few truly understand the gravity in every part of the sacrifice.

Opiter: *Primum victima ipsa cura eligenda est. Bovem fessum aut imperfectum offerre nefas est; victima integra et in meliore statu semper praeparanda est. Tum sacerdos praeit, dicta ritus formula, et mox victima ad aram adducitur. Vidi quoque augurem aspectum caeli observare ut auspicia non adversa essent.*

Opiter: First, the victim must be carefully chosen. It is forbidden to offer a tired or imperfect bull; the sacrifice must always be in its best condition and fully intact. Then, the priest leads with the ritual formula, and soon the victim is brought to the altar. I also saw the augur observing the sky to ensure that the omens were favorable.

Sextus: *Bene, profecto nihil sine auguribus fieri debet. Auspicia enim sic petuntur, ut sciamus an di ritum accipiant. Quid autem postea secutum est? Num omnia secundum consuetudinem facta sunt?*

Sextus: Good, indeed nothing should be done without the augurs. Omens are sought this way to know if the gods accept the ritual. What happened next? Was everything done according to custom?

Opiter: *Ita. Postquam augur faustum signum dedit, victima per sacerdotem ad aram admota est. Cum precibus et verbis sollemnibus dictis, victima immolata est, et cor bovi adflavit. Statim flammae sublatae sunt et igni holocaustum datum est. Tum cera litabilis et spelta sacrificialis in ignem iacta sunt, ut di benevolentia nostras supplicationes acciperent.*

Opiter: Yes. After the augur gave a favorable sign, the victim was brought to the altar by the priest. With prayers and solemn words spoken, the victim was sacrificed, and the bull's heart was offered. Immediately, the flames were raised, and the holocaust was given to the fire. Then, wax and sacrificial spelt were cast into the fire so the gods would accept our supplications with goodwill.

Sextus: *Iuvenes quidem saepe ritum illum vident, sed raro intus intellegunt. Omnis pars sacra est, et neglegi nihil potest. Mihi quoque memoria tenet quod pater meus, cum ad Apollinis templum iret, maxima cum reverentia omnia verba sacerdotis audivit, ne quod peccatum sacrum fieret.*

Sextus: Young men often see that ritual, but rarely do they understand its depth. Every part is sacred, and nothing can be neglected. I also remember that when my father went to the temple of Apollo, he listened to the priest's words with the utmost reverence, lest any sacred mistake be made.

Opiter: *Ita est, Sexte. Multi ritum faciunt, sed sapientes sciunt veram pietatem intus esse, non solum in externis moribus. Pater tuus verum dixerat: sine consilio et attenta mente sacrificium quasi inanimum est. Quid de sacrificiis ad Lares? Saepissime ii ritus familiares parvi aestimantur, sed magnam vim habent.*

Opiter: That's right, Sextus. Many perform the ritual, but the wise know that true piety lies within, not just in the outward practices. Your father was right: without careful thought and attention, a sacrifice is nearly lifeless. What about sacrifices to the Lares? Those family rites are often undervalued, but they hold great significance.

Sextus: *Recte dicis! Sacra familiaris ad Lares domesticos saepius neglecta sunt, sed illa sunt quae fundamentum familiae tenent. Vinum, fruges, ac modicum incensi saepe Laribus offero, et semper credo familiam meam sub eorum custodia manere. Quod est fas, sacrificium et pietas familiae primum locum habent.*

Sextus: You're right! Family rites to the household Lares are often neglected, but they are what hold the family together. I often offer wine, fruits, and a little incense to the Lares, and I always believe my family remains under their protection. As it should be, sacrifice and family piety hold the highest place.

Opiter: *Bene! Cum Lares domum tueantur et Martis favor bellum adiuvet, vere possumus sperare ut et familia et res publica prospere gerantur. Nihil enim homini magis necessarium est quam bonorum deorum gratiam habere.*

Opiter: Good! With the Lares guarding the home and Mars aiding in war, we can truly hope that both family and state will prosper. Nothing is more necessary for humans than to have the favor of the benevolent gods.

Sextus: *Ita vero! Ne dubitemus deis semper debita reverentia sacrificia ferre. Sic enim civitas nostra aeternum stare poterit. Vale, Opiter, et utinam di tibi faveant!*

Sextus: Indeed! Let us never hesitate to offer sacrifices with due reverence to the gods. In this way, our state can stand forever. Farewell, Opiter, and may the gods always favor you!

Opiter: *Vale, Sexte, et di te tuosque semper tueantur!*

Opiter: Farewell, Sextus, and may the gods always protect you and your family!

In Foro Piscario – De emendo pisce in foro

Afer: *Salve, Lupule! Quid tibi hodie placet in foro piscario? Vidi te inter tabernas circumspicere. Num pisces aliquos optimos quaeris?*

Afer: Hello, Lupulus! What do you fancy today in the fish market? I saw you browsing among the stalls. Are you looking for some choice fish?

Lupulus: *Salve, Afer! Bene animadvertisti. Hodie piscem novum et recens ad cenam quaero, sed non facile est decernere quem sumam. Multa genera piscium offeruntur, sed pretium interdum non respondet qualitati. Quid censes? Utrum tibi haec merx bona videtur?*

Lupulus: Hello, Afer! You noticed correctly. Today I'm looking for fresh fish for dinner, but it's not easy to decide which one to choose. Many types of fish are offered, but sometimes the price doesn't match the quality. What do you think? Does this catch look good to you?

Afer: *Etsi plerique hic pisces bene parati sunt, vide quam recentes sint. Mihi videtur mulus iste ruber, qui in sinu nostro capi solet, satis bene crevisse. Carne sua delicatissimus est, et in cenis Romanis non contemnitur. Sed primum odorem cura; nam nihil est fallacius quam piscis vetus sub nova specie.*

Afer: Although most of the fish here are well prepared, look at how fresh they are. That red mullet, which is usually caught in our bay, seems to have grown well. Its meat is very delicate, and it's not overlooked in Roman feasts. But first, check the smell; nothing is more deceptive than an old fish disguised as fresh.

Lupulus: *Recte dicis. Odor semper primum indicium bonitatis est. (Piscem circumspicit) Hic videtur satis bonus. Quid de hispide illo censes? Audivi illum piscem admodum laudari propter mollitiem carnis.*

Lupulus: You're right. The smell is always the first sign of quality. (Examines the fish) This one looks quite good. What do you think of that sea bream over there? I've heard it's highly praised for the tenderness of its flesh.

Afer: *Hispis profecto bonam famam habet, et mollitiem carnis iucundam. Multi illum ad domos villas vehunt cum convivas laute accipiunt. Sed pretium eius, ut vides, altius est quam muli. Si festivus est usus, fortasse* *hispis magis aptus erit; si autem simplicem cenam domi praeparas, mulus sufficiat.*

Afer: The sea bream indeed has a good reputation, with its tender flesh being quite pleasant. Many bring it to their villas when entertaining guests with elaborate meals. But as you can see, its price is higher than the mullet. If it's for a special occasion, perhaps the sea bream is more fitting; but if you're preparing a simple dinner at home, the mullet should suffice.

Lupulus: *Mihi nunc propositum est cenam non tam lautam, sed iucundam amicis proponere. Forsitan mulus magis idoneus sit. Sed quid de piscium parvulis? Num illos in hac taberna pretium aequum tenent?*

Lupulus: My plan is to prepare a pleasant, though not too fancy, dinner for friends. Perhaps the mullet would be more suitable. But what about the small fish? Do they have a fair price here?

Afer: *Minuti pisces, ut sardinae, parvo pretio veniunt et saepe bene frixi aut ad acetum conditi comeduntur. Eos libenter emo, cum aliquid rapide parandum est. Hic tamen paulum rari sunt hodie. Non tam abunde capti sunt.*

Afer: Small fish, like sardines, usually come at a low price and are often fried or pickled in vinegar. I buy them when I need to prepare something quickly. However, they are a bit scarce today. They haven't been caught in large numbers.

Lupulus: *Bene monuisti. Forsitan hodie mulum sumam, nam pretium videtur iustum, et piscis ipse satis bene spectat. (Tabernarium vocat) Quanti hic mulus est?*

Lupulus: Good advice. Perhaps I'll take the mullet today, as the price seems fair, and the fish looks quite good. (Calls the vendor) How much is this mullet?

Tabernarius: *Salve, domine! Hic mulus tribus assibus venditur. Praesto est, hodie mane captus in sinu. Qualitatem suam celeriter videbis.*

Vendor: Hello, sir! This mullet is being sold for three asses. It was caught this morning in the bay. You'll quickly see its quality.

Lupulus: *Tribus assibus? Satis iustum videtur. Accipio hunc mulum. Ad cenam mihi necessarius est. (Tabernario pecuniam tradit)*

Lupulus: Three asses? That seems fair enough. I'll take this mullet. It's just what I need for dinner. (Hands the money to the vendor)

Tabernarius: *Gratias tibi ago, domine! Utinam piscis tibi et convivis tuis maxime placeat.*

Vendor: Thank you, sir! I hope the fish greatly pleases you and your guests.

Afer: *Bene egisti, Lupule. Nihil magis in cena quam piscis bene conditus delectat. Vale nunc, et fruare cena!*

Afer: You made a good choice, Lupulus. Nothing pleases at dinner more than a well-seasoned fish. Farewell for now, and enjoy your meal!

Lupulus: *Vale, Afer, et gratias tibi pro bono consilio. Sine dubio cena bene succedet!*

Lupulus: Farewell, Afer, and thanks for the good advice. Without a doubt, the dinner will turn out well!

De Rhetorica – Disputatio de arte rhetorica et oratoria

Severus: *Salve, Lucili! Quid censes de rhetorica hodie? Videor aliquot iudices in foro audivisse, sed non satis callide orati sunt. Quid tibi videtur? Nonne ars rhetorica iam minus valet?*

Severus: Hello, Lucilius! What do you think of rhetoric today? I've heard several judges in the forum, but their speeches weren't delivered skillfully enough. What do you think? Isn't the art of rhetoric less valued now?

Lucilius: *Salve, Severe! Profecto, saepe mihi videtur ars rhetorica non eodem honore coli quam olim. Oratores veteres, ut Cicero, summam eloquentiam habebant, sed nunc multi contenti sunt rebus mediocribus. Ut scis, rhetorica non tantum verba quaerit, sed rationem prudentiamque.*

Lucilius: Hello, Severus! Indeed, it often seems to me that the art of rhetoric is no longer held in the same esteem as it once was. The old orators, like Cicero, possessed the highest eloquence, but now many are content with mediocrity. As you know, rhetoric seeks not just words, but reason and wisdom.

Severus: *Recte dicis. Cicero ipse docet non solum ornatum esse quaerendum verborum, sed propositum persuadendi et veritatem explicandi. Vidi autem multos, qui magis ad pompam verba effundunt quam ad rem tractandam. Quidnam causam huius declinationis esse putas?*

Severus: You're right. Cicero himself teaches that not only should the embellishment of words be sought, but also the aim of persuasion and the explanation of truth. I've seen many who speak more for show than to address the issue. What do you think is the cause of this decline?

Lucilius: *Haud difficile dictu est, Severe. Multi, qui honorem et potentiam ex orationibus petunt, magis famam quaerunt quam veram artem. Ambitio, non virtus, saepe propositum est. Vides enim, cum in senatu aut in iudicio quidam orationem habeant, praeclaram et sonoram vocem proferunt ad publicam scenam, sed consilium et ratio in obscuro manent.*

Lucilius: It's not hard to say, Severus. Many who seek honor and power through speeches are more interested in fame than in the true art. Ambition, not virtue, is often the goal. You see, when some give speeches in the senate or in court, they project grand and resonant voices for the public stage, but their reasoning and purpose remain obscure.

Severus: *Ita est. Rhetorica enim, si bene colitur, animi virtutes manifestat, non tantum linguarum acumen. Qui oratores recte pro loquuntur, non solum ad populum persuadendum sed etiam ad bonum civitatis constituendum. Audivistine nuper quosdam oratores in causis publicis versari?*

Severus: Exactly. When rhetoric is cultivated properly, it reveals the virtues of the mind, not just linguistic sharpness. Good orators speak not only to persuade the people but also to promote the good of the state. Have you recently heard any orators involved in public cases?

Lucilius: *Audivi, sed, ut ferunt, pauci sunt qui in Ciceronis vestigia insistunt. Multi enim mediocres sunt et verba vana proferunt, ubi magna causa postulabatur. Quid autem tu, Severe, censes esse optima praecepta rhetoricae, quae oratorem bene instituant?*

Lucilius: I've heard some, but it's said that few follow in Cicero's footsteps. Many are mediocre and speak empty words where a great cause called for more. What do you think are the best principles of rhetoric to train a good orator?

Severus: *Mihi videtur primum esse ut orator veritatem quaerat, deinde ut verba apta atque ad rem accommodata eligat. Necessarium est et copia verborum et gravitas in sententiis. Eloquentia sine sapientia flos sine fructu est. Producere enim in oratione plus valet honestas quam pulchritudo sola. Praeterea, et rhythmus et mensurae colendae sunt, ut oratio auribus iucunda sit.*

Severus: I believe the first thing is for the orator to seek truth, then choose words that are appropriate and relevant. Both a wealth of words and weight in the arguments are necessary. Eloquence without wisdom is like a flower without fruit. In delivering a speech, integrity is worth more than mere beauty. Moreover, rhythm and cadence must also be cultivated so that the speech is pleasing to the ears.

Lucilius: *Sapientia plena verba tua sunt. Ut dixit Cicero, summa laus oratoris est docere, delectare, movere. Docere vere opus est rationemque afferre; delectare, ut animi liberaliter audiant; movere, ut ad finem persuasionis veniamus. Omnia haec tria arti rhetoricae necessaria sunt.*

Lucilius: Your words are full of wisdom. As Cicero said, the highest praise for an orator is to teach, delight, and move. Truly, it's necessary to teach and bring reason; to delight, so that the audience listens willingly; and to move, so that we achieve the goal of persuasion. All three of these are essential to the art of rhetoric.

Severus: *Profecto. Sed quaeram a te, Lucili: Utrum malis orationes brevibus viribus, an longa ornataque sententia redintegratas? Ego quidem brevibus veris magis favere soleo, sed interdum longitudinem necessariam intellego.*

Severus: Indeed. But let me ask you, Lucilius: do you prefer speeches with brief force, or those rich with long and ornate sentences? I myself favor brief but true words, although I understand that sometimes length is necessary.

Lucilius: *Mihi quidem brevitas praeferenda videtur, nisi res ipsa longior exposcatur. Nihil est molestius quam oratio prolixa sine necessitate, quae animos fatigat. Sed, ubi causa magna est, et longitudo requirenda est, dummodo ratio verbis iuncta sit. Cicero ipse longas orationes habebat, sed numquam sine causa.*

Lucilius: I prefer brevity unless the situation calls for something longer. Nothing is more tiresome than an unnecessarily lengthy speech, which wearies the audience. But when the matter is great, length is also necessary, provided that reason is joined to the words. Cicero himself gave long speeches, but never without cause.

Severus: *Sapienter respondisti. In omnibus autem, aequitas et ratio prima debet esse. Nihil tam praeclarum est quam orator qui neque nimis breviter neque nimis longe loquitur, sed semper rem optime et apte exponit.*

Severus: You answered wisely. In all things, fairness and reason must come first. Nothing is as admirable as an orator who speaks neither too briefly nor too long, but always presents the matter in the best and most fitting way.

Lucilius: *Ita est, Severe. Si ad hanc doctrinam revocari possumus, forsitan ars rhetorica iterum florebit. Utinam iuvenes magis discant, quam spectare decent.*

Lucilius: That's right, Severus. If we can return to this principle, perhaps the art of rhetoric will flourish again. I hope the young learn more than just how to perform.

Severus: *Sicut semper, Lucili, magna sperare debemus. Vale nunc, et rhetoricae studio non intermittamus!*

Severus: As always, Lucilius, we must hope for great things. Farewell for now, and let's not neglect our study of rhetoric!

Lucilius: *Vale, Severe, et semper vivamus ut oratio et actio in consilio sint.*

Lucilius: Farewell, Severus, and let us always live so that our words and actions align with wisdom.

In Amphitheatro – Disputatio ante certamen gladiatorium

Nerva: *Salve, Otho! Hodie diem exspectatum tandem adfuimus. Gladiatores in arenam mox descendent, et ego iam magnam excitationem sentio. Numquid et tibi similis est animus?*

Nerva: Hello, Otho! We have finally arrived at the long-awaited day. The gladiators will soon descend into the arena, and I already feel great excitement. Do you feel the same way?

Otho: *Salve, Nerva! Ita vero, gladiatorium certamen semper me maxime movet. Nihil est quod animos nostros ita exsuscitet quam videre fortes viros, mortis metu contemptu, in certamen descendere. Utrum credis hodie meliorem victorem fore?*

Otho: Hello, Nerva! Indeed, the gladiatorial games always stir me deeply. There's nothing that excites our spirits as much as watching brave men, with contempt for the fear of death, step into battle. Who do you think will emerge victorious today?

Nerva: *Hodie Spiculus principem locum tenere videtur. Gladiator ille magnam famam habet et saepe adversarios in arena superavit. Celeritas eius et armorum dexteritas omnibus nota sunt. Tu autem cui faves?*

Nerva: Today, Spiculus seems to hold the top position. That gladiator has a great reputation and has often defeated opponents in the arena. His speed and skill with weapons are well known to all. But who do you support?

Otho: *Spiculum prope invictum esse fama est, sed ego more solito Daxionem sustineo, qui non minus viribus praeclarus est. Etiamsi minus famae habet, fortis et prudens est in pugna. Videsne quantum robur habeat et quomodo gladium ferat? Certa mihi victoria videtur.*

Otho: Spiculus is famed as nearly unbeatable, but as usual, I support Daxio, who is no less renowned for his strength. Though he has less fame, he is strong and skilled in battle. Do you see how much power he has and how he wields his sword? Victory seems certain to me.

Nerva: *Daxio profecto vir fortis est, sed adversus Spiculum pugna gravis erit. Sed dic mihi, Otho, quid censes de hoc genere spectaculi? Nonne* *interdum nimis cruentum videtur? Multi philosophi de crudelitate huiusmodi certaminum loquuntur.*

Nerva: Daxio is indeed a strong man, but the fight against Spiculus will be tough. But tell me, Otho, what do you think of this kind of spectacle? Doesn't it sometimes seem too bloody? Many philosophers speak of the cruelty of such contests.

Otho: *Profecto, cruentum est, sed gladiatorium certamen pars non minima est morum Romanorum. Etsi crudelitas inest, tamen fortitudinem et virtutem spectamus, quae decus hominis sunt. Gladiatores ipsi sciunt periculum, et non sine honore in arena decertant. Cur igitur nos, qui spectamus, minus audere debemus quam illi, qui in ipsa mortis umbra stant?*

Otho: Certainly, it is bloody, but gladiatorial combat is an essential part of Roman tradition. Even though cruelty is present, we are witnessing bravery and virtue, which are the glory of humanity. The gladiators themselves know the danger, and they fight with honor in the arena. So why should we, as spectators, be less courageous than they, who stand in the very shadow of death?

Nerva: *Bene quidem dicis. Spectaculum hoc eo valere videtur ut animos ad fortitudinem erigat, et ut Romani proponantur exempla virtutis. Quid enim, nisi vires et audacia virorum nostrorum, rem publicam sustinet? Et tamen, philosophi non nihil habent de humanitate. Haec certamina in eo sunt ut animum moveant, sed non semper laetitiam afferunt.*

Nerva: You speak well. This spectacle seems to serve the purpose of uplifting our spirits to courage and offering examples of Roman virtue. For what else but the strength and bravery of our men sustains the Republic? And yet, philosophers have something to say about humanity. These contests move the soul, but they do not always bring joy.

Otho: *Ita est, Nerva. Philosophiam ipsam non contemno, sed saepe nos ab asperitate vitae separat. Res publica viros fortes requirit, non tantum in consilio sed etiam in armis. Gladiatores, etsi servi vel damnati sunt, saepe exemplum virtutis proferunt. Nos autem spectatores discimus quomodo pericula sustinenda sint.*

Otho: That's true, Nerva. I do not disregard philosophy, but it often separates us from the harshness of life. The Republic needs strong men, not only in counsel but also in arms. Gladiators, even though they are slaves or condemned men, often offer examples of virtue. We, as spectators, learn how to endure dangers.

Nerva: *Vere loqueris. In arena nihil falsum, nihil simulatum est; ibi vere periculum et vere audacia apparet. Mihi quidem placet horum virorum constantiam spectare, et si quis dignus victoria fuerit, laetus eius triumphum celebrabo.*

Nerva: You speak truly. In the arena, nothing is false, nothing is feigned; there, danger and bravery truly appear. I, for one, enjoy watching the perseverance of these men, and if someone deserves victory, I will happily celebrate their triumph.

Otho: *Hodie igitur videbimus utrum Spiculus an Daxio fortior sit. Quisquis victoriam feret, nos spectaculo iucundissimo fruemur. Ecce, signum datur! Gladiatores in arenam intrant!*

Otho: Today, then, we will see whether Spiculus or Daxio is the stronger. Whichever one wins, we will enjoy a most delightful spectacle. Look, the signal is given! The gladiators are entering the arena!

Nerva: *Eamus nunc spectare! Vale, Otho, et bonum spectaculum exopto!*

Nerva: Let's go now to watch! Farewell, Otho, and I wish you a good spectacle!

Otho: *Vale, Nerva! Haec pugna memorabilis erit!*

Otho: Farewell, Nerva! This fight will be unforgettable!

De Architectura – Disputatio de aedificiis Romanis et architectura

Quintilius: *Salve, Serviane! Nuper in urbem redii postquam novum templum ad Capitolium spectavi. Non possum satis laudare artem architectorum nostrorum. Nonne tibi videtur Roma nunc magis quam umquam antea magnificentia fulgere?*

Quintilius: Hello, Servianus! I recently returned to the city after viewing the new temple on the Capitol. I can't praise the skill of our architects enough. Don't you think Rome now shines with more magnificence than ever before?

Servianus: *Salve, Quintili! Plene adsentio. Architectura nostra praeclara et egregia est, et templum illud quod in Capitolio extruxerunt dignum est omni honore. Sed, ut scis, non solum in templis, sed etiam in thermis, basilicis, et theatris res nostras maxime exornamus. Architecti nostri, ut Vitruvius dixit, semper tria spectant: firmitas, utilitas, et venustas.*

Servianus: Hello, Quintilius! I completely agree. Our architecture is extraordinary, and that temple they built on the Capitol is worthy of all honor. But as you know, it's not just temples—we embellish our city with baths, basilicas, and theaters as well. Our architects, as Vitruvius said, always focus on three things: durability, usefulness, and beauty.

Quintilius: *Verissima sunt verba Vitruvii! Firmitas quidem prima est, nam quid proficimus si aedificium statim ruat? Sed utilitas et venustas eadem ex parte curandae sunt. Nihil de decore negligendum est, et tamen opus ei officio servire debet, quod propositum est. Vidi enim basilicam novam, quae non solum pulchra, sed etiam commodissima esset ad iudicia et mercatus agendos.*

Quintilius: Vitruvius' words are absolutely true! Durability is essential—what good is a building if it collapses right away? But usefulness and beauty must also be equally attended to. Nothing should be neglected in terms of decoration, yet the building must still serve its intended purpose. I saw a new basilica that was not only beautiful but also extremely practical for conducting trials and markets.

Servianus: *Mihi quoque placet quod, quamquam aedificia pulchritudine praeclara sunt, semper etiam ad rem publicam et communem usum* *spectant. Basilicas non modo iudicibus aut magistratibus dicamus, sed omni populo Romano. Eas plebi et senatoribus communiter apertas esse nonne magna sapientia factum est?*

Servianus: I also appreciate that, while these buildings are renowned for their beauty, they are always designed with public use in mind. We dedicate basilicas not only to judges and officials but to the entire Roman people. Isn't it a wise decision to have them open to both the plebeians and the senators?

Quintilius: *Nihil sapientius. Roma ipsa non solum imperii sed etiam concordiae et societatis domicilium est. Basilicas et fori et theatra omnia haec confirmant, dum cives non solum laborant, sed etiam in ludis et negotiis iucundam vitam agunt. Quid censes de thermis nostris? Nuper audiebam thermas novas prope Aventinum factas esse splendidissimas.*

Quintilius: Nothing could be wiser. Rome itself is the center not only of empire but also of harmony and society. The basilicas, forums, and theaters all reinforce this, as citizens work and enjoy pleasant lives in games and business. What do you think of our baths? I recently heard that new baths near the Aventine are absolutely magnificent.

Servianus: *Oh, thermas! Quis recte Romam laudare possit nisi thermarum eius meminerit? Non solum pro corporum munditia sed etiam pro animi refectione valent. Thermas Aventini splendidas esse audio, plenas marmoreis lacubus et columnarum insignium. Piscinae late patent, et vapores qui inde subeunt mirabiles dicuntur. Visne eas ipse aliquando visitare?*

Servianus: Oh, the baths! Who can rightly praise Rome without mentioning its baths? They serve not only for physical cleanliness but also for mental refreshment. I've heard the baths on the Aventine are splendid, filled with marble pools and impressive columns. The pools are vast, and the steam that rises from them is said to be marvelous. Would you like to visit them sometime?

Quintilius: *Certe! Nihil iucundius est quam post labores diuturnos in thermis requiescere et cum amicis colloqui. Sed, Serviane, pro certo habeo non solum thermas aut basilicas esse spectaculo. Nuper etiam viaductus et pontes nostrorum architectorum multum laudati sunt. Quid* *tibi videtur de Pontibus Agrippae, qui aquam tam diu et tam longe in urbem ducunt?*

Quintilius: Certainly! There's nothing more enjoyable than resting in the baths after long work and chatting with friends. But, Servianus, I'm sure it's not just the baths or basilicas that are worth admiring. Recently, our architects' aqueducts and bridges have been highly praised. What do you think of Agrippa's bridges, which carry water so far and so steadily into the city?

Servianus: *Ei pontes et aquaeductus, Quintili, maximi miraculi sunt. Nam ne Roma omni sua aqua uno flumine penderet, architecti nostri modum invenerunt aquam ex montibus et longinquis locis in urbem vehendi. Pontes Agrippae et Aqua Claudia magnam laudem merentur, quippe qui non solum utilitatem praebeant, sed etiam ipsi spectaculum sint cum arcus eorum in caelo surgunt.*

Servianus: Those bridges and aqueducts, Quintilius, are truly marvelous. Instead of relying on just one river for all its water, our architects have found a way to transport water from the mountains and distant places into the city. Agrippa's bridges and the Aqua Claudia deserve great praise, as they not only provide a practical benefit but are also a spectacle in themselves, with their arches rising into the sky.

Quintilius: *Non potuisti melius dicere! Architectura Romana nemini secunda est. In omnibus usibus nostris, a labore ad divinos honores, aedificia praeclara spectamus quae et firmitatem et pulchritudinem iungunt. Profecto nobis multum gloriae sunt architecti, qui hanc civitatem pulchriorem et potentiorem fecerunt.*

Quintilius: You couldn't have said it better! Roman architecture is second to none. In all aspects of our lives, from work to divine honors, we see magnificent buildings that combine both durability and beauty. Truly, we owe much of our glory to the architects who have made this city more beautiful and powerful.

Servianus: *Ita est, amice. Roma in marmore stabit dum haec ingenia prosperant. Vale nunc, Quintili, et utinam in proximo thermas illas novas simul spectemus!*

Servianus: Indeed, my friend. Rome will stand in marble as long as these talents thrive. Farewell for now, Quintilius, and I hope we can soon visit those new baths together!

Quintilius: *Vale, Serviane! Ego primum tibi promitto ut thermas illas visitemus, simulque gaudeamus quanta sit gloria architecturae nostrae.*

Quintilius: Farewell, Servianus! I promise you, we will visit those baths first, and together we'll enjoy the full glory of our architecture!

De Medicis et Medicina – Disputatio de medicis et arte medica in urbe Roma

Afer: *Salve, Salvidene! Vidi te nuper in taberna medici fuisse. Quid accidit? Num aegrotas, an consilium medici quaesivisti pro familia?*

Afer: Hello, Salvidenus! I saw you recently at the doctor's shop. What happened? Are you ill, or were you seeking advice for your family?

Salvidenus: *Salve, Afer! Consilium pro me ipso quaesivi. Gravis tussis me iam aliquot dies vexat, et medicus mihi herbas et syrupum commendavit. Etsi raro medicis confido, dixerunt veteres: nihil sine medico, et fortasse iuste.*

Salvidenus: Hello, Afer! I was seeking advice for myself. I've had a bad cough for several days, and the doctor recommended some herbs and syrup. Although I rarely trust doctors, the ancients said: "Nothing without a doctor," and perhaps they were right.

Afer: *Ita, recte dicis, Salvidene. Medici quidem nullam parvam partem in vita nostra sustinent. Sicut apud Graecos Hippocrates, ita et apud nos medici summam scientiam habere dicuntur. Sed dic mihi, quid medicus tibi praescripsit? Num pro remediis Graecis, quae nunc valde celebrantur, usus est?*

Afer: Yes, you're right, Salvidenus. Doctors indeed play no small part in our lives. Just as the Greeks have Hippocrates, we too say our doctors possess great knowledge. But tell me, what did the doctor prescribe? Did he use the Greek remedies that are now so popular?

Salvidenus: *Ita vero! Multa remedia ex Graecia advecta mihi commendavit. Syrupus ex melle et hysopo mixtus est, cum modica parte papaveris, ut somnum faciat et pectora leniat. Sed audivi quoque eum de Galeni praeceptis loqui, qui dicit medicinam non solum ex remediis, sed etiam ex ratione totius vitae curandam esse.*

Salvidenus: Indeed! He recommended many remedies brought from Greece. The syrup was mixed with honey and hyssop, with a small amount of poppy to induce sleep and soothe the chest. But I also heard him speak of Galen's principles, who says medicine is not only about remedies but also about managing one's entire way of life.

Afer: *Galenus profecto sapiens fuit. Ei medici praeclari sunt qui non tantum de herbis aut potionibus cogitant, sed etiam de corporis cura et animi ordine. Nonne dixit ipse Galenus modum vivendi ad valetudinem maxime pertinere? Non herbae solae, sed temperantia in cibis et quies sine sollicitudinibus bonam valetudinem custodiunt.*

Afer: Galen was indeed wise. The best doctors don't just think about herbs or potions; they also consider the care of the body and the order of the mind. Didn't Galen himself say that lifestyle is essential for good health? It's not just about herbs—moderation in food and rest without worries are what truly maintain good health.

Salvidenus: *Bene meministi! Medicus mihi praeclarum praeceptum dedit: corpora laboribus exercendo servanda sunt. Ei remedia saepe necessaria fiunt, cum homines vitiis laboris aut otii corpus suum corrumpunt. Sed quid tibi videtur de nostra medicina Romana? Num censes nostros medicos meliores esse quam Graecos?*

Salvidenus: You remembered well! The doctor gave me an excellent piece of advice: our bodies must be maintained through exercise. Remedies often become necessary when people ruin their bodies through too much work or idleness. But what do you think of our Roman medicine? Do you believe our doctors are better than the Greeks?

Afer: *Difficultatem proponis. Quidam quidem praeferunt nostros medicos, qui magis ad simplices modos curandi revertuntur. Apud nos multa ex natura adhibentur, et simplicia remedia saepe magis proficiunt quam illa exotica. At tamen Graeci plurimam scientiam habent, et Galenus propter sapientiam suam multum laudandus est. Mihi quidem videtur medicina Romana et Graeca miscenda esse.*

Afer: You raise a difficult question. Some people prefer our Roman doctors, who tend to return to simpler healing methods. We often use natural remedies, and simple treatments can often be more effective than exotic ones. However, the Greeks have much knowledge, and Galen, for his wisdom, is greatly respected. I think Roman and Greek medicine should be combined.

Salvidenus: *Sapiens consilium! Nam multi Romani etiam nunc remedia ex agris aut hortis suis praeparant. Ego ipse saepe lauro et salvia utor ad levandam tussim. Sed recte dicis, medicinam Graecam non esse* *omnino contemnendam. Denique curare animos et corpora pari modo est omni populo.*

Salvidenus: Wise advice! Many Romans still prepare remedies from their fields or gardens. I myself often use laurel and sage to ease my cough. But you're right, Greek medicine should not be entirely dismissed. In the end, caring for the mind and body is important for everyone.

Afer: *Ita est. Sed numquid meministi Fabiam, quam dicunt familiam antiquissimam habere? Nuper audivi eam a medico Gallico curatam esse, qui non remedia Graeca sed Gallica adhibebat. Quae res non minima admiratione erat.*

Afer: Exactly. But do you remember Fabia, who is said to come from a very ancient family? I recently heard she was treated by a Gallic doctor, who used not Greek but Gallic remedies. This was quite surprising.

Salvidenus: *Vere? Gallicus medicus? Haec nova est! Gallici quidem multa rerum occultarum scire putantur, sed plerique eos superstitionibus plus quam arte medicinae studere existimant. Quae remedia praecepit?*

Salvidenus: Really? A Gallic doctor? That's news! The Gauls are thought to know many hidden things, but most believe they focus more on superstition than on the art of medicine. What remedies did he prescribe?

Afer: *Aiunt illum herbas ex silvis Gallicis adhibuisse, et mixtum quoddam ex corticibus arborum, cum aqua fluvii montani, ad bibendum dedisse. Valere eam postea firme dicunt, sed ego dubito utrum felicitas sit in arte an fortuna.*

Afer: They say he used herbs from Gallic forests and a mixture of tree bark with water from a mountain stream for her to drink. They claim she recovered well, but I wonder whether it was due to his skill or just good fortune.

Salvidenus: *Fortuna et medicina saepe iunguntur, sed certe, si bene valuit, praeter curam medici, etiam fortuna favit. Quidquid sit, bene est, ut res successit. Mihi autem nunc gratias ago, quod tuo sermone animum relevavi. Medicinam curabo, et modum vivendi conservabo.*

Salvidenus: Fortune and medicine often go hand in hand, but certainly, if she recovered, fortune must have favored her along with the doctor's care. Whatever the case, it's good that things turned out well. Now I thank you for this conversation—it has eased my mind. I'll take my medicine and keep a healthy lifestyle.

Afer: *Vale, Salvidene! Cura te diligenter, et utinam remedia tibi optime proficiant!*

Afer: Farewell, Salvidenus! Take good care of yourself, and I hope the remedies work well for you!

Salvidenus: *Vale et tu, Afer! Et te in valetudine optima habeas!*

Salvidenus: Farewell, Afer! And may you remain in the best health!

In Aedibus Senatoriis – Disputatio in domo senatoris

Sulpicius: *Salve, Oppiane! Gaudeo te domum meam vidisse. Sed dic mihi, quid tibi nunc in mentem versatur? Nuper te in Curia graviter disseruisse audivi. Nonne de novis legibus et re publica curas?*

Sulpicius: Hello, Oppianus! I'm glad to see you in my home. But tell me, what's on your mind? I recently heard you speak passionately in the Senate. Are you concerned about the new laws and the state of the republic?

Oppianus: *Salve, Sulpici! Ita est, et gratias tibi ago pro benigna hospitalitate. Rei publicae status me valde sollicitat. Leges quidem novae, quae in senatu recens propositae sunt, multorum civium animos turbant. Multi censent eas non ad populi bonum tendere, sed magis ad singularum familiarum potentias firmandas. Quid tu censes?*

Oppianus: Hello, Sulpicius! Yes, and I thank you for your kind hospitality. I'm very concerned about the state of the republic. The new laws recently proposed in the Senate are troubling many citizens. Many believe they're not aimed at the good of the people but rather at strengthening the power of certain families. What do you think?

Sulpicius: *Oppiane, sententias tuas sapiens iudico. Non novi sunt qui sua consilia pro populo fingant, dum suam ipsorum potentiam augent. Leges autem non solum iustae, sed etiam salubres esse debent. Ego pro eo contendo, ut populi voluntas non negligatur et ut magistratus ipsi virtutem prae solo lucro habeant.*

Sulpicius: Oppianus, I find your views wise. It's nothing new for some to claim they're acting for the people while really advancing their own power. But laws must not only be just but also beneficial. I believe that the will of the people should not be ignored, and magistrates should prioritize virtue over personal gain.

Oppianus: *Iusta loqueris, Sulpici. Sed tamen videmus nunc homines, qui in re publica versantur, propriorum commodorum magis quam civitatis dignitatis curam habere. Curia nostra saepius ad rixas et divitias spectat quam ad rem publicam bene gerendam. Et, ut puto, periculum est ne discordia interna Romam labefactet.*

Oppianus: You speak rightly, Sulpicius. But we see now that those involved in public affairs care more about their personal interests than the dignity of the state. Our Senate often seems more focused on quarrels and wealth than on governing the republic properly. And I fear that internal discord may weaken Rome.

Sulpicius: *Profecto, Oppiane, cavendum est ne interni dissensus maiora mala procreent. Senatores non memoriam maiorum nostrorum colunt, qui virtute et concordia rem publicam sustinuerunt. Quorundam cupiditas effecit ut honores, qui bonis viris conveniunt, nunc per fraudem et ambitionem quaerantur.*

Sulpicius: Indeed, Oppianus, we must beware that internal divisions don't create greater dangers. Senators no longer honor the memory of our ancestors, who sustained the republic through virtue and unity. The greed of some has led to the pursuit of honors, once reserved for good men, now gained through deceit and ambition.

Oppianus: *Eadem tibi sentio. Non iam praeclari mores in senatu videntur, sed pecunia atque ambitio magis regunt. Sed quid faciendum est, Sulpici? Quomodo res publica ad meliores mores reducenda sit? Videtur mihi nunc difficultates multas obstare.*

Oppianus: I feel the same as you. Virtue is no longer seen in the Senate—money and ambition rule instead. But what can be done, Sulpicius? How can the republic be restored to better morals? It seems to me that many obstacles stand in our way.

Sulpicius: *Non facile est, Oppiane, rem publicam ad vetustam virtutem revocare. Sed primum necesse est ut magistratus iusti et sapientes praeferantur, qui exemplum probatarum vitarum proponant. Item, populus ipse monendus est, ne falsis promissis aut vanis spebus fallatur. Honos reddendus est eis, qui digni sunt, non eis qui per dolos et largitiones ad summum perveniunt.*

Sulpicius: It's not easy, Oppianus, to bring the republic back to its old virtues. But first, we must ensure that only just and wise magistrates are elected, who can set an example of honorable lives. Also, the people must be warned not to be deceived by false promises or vain hopes. Honor should be given to those who deserve it, not to those who rise through trickery and bribery.

Oppianus: *Nihil verius! Cives nostri, si veram iustitiam et virtutem ex magistratibus exspectarent, haud dubie meliores duces haberent. Sed etiam mihi videtur populus aliquando de qua re publica sit bene recta oblitum esse. Ita fit, ut honores maiores plus privatis quam publicis commodis tribuantur.*

Oppianus: Nothing could be truer! If our citizens expected real justice and virtue from their magistrates, they would undoubtedly have better leaders. But it also seems to me that the people sometimes forget what makes a well-governed republic. As a result, greater honors are often given for private rather than public benefit.

Sulpicius: *Ita est. Nam pervenit ad me rumor quidam de magistratu qui per largitiones et donorum spe ad summam potestatem ascendere conatur. Si hic mos crescit, Roma ipsa paulatim labefactabitur. Ego autem in senatu de eis rebus pronuntiare statuo.*

Sulpicius: Indeed. I've heard a rumor of a magistrate who's trying to rise to great power through bribes and promises of gifts. If this practice grows, Rome itself will gradually be undermined. I plan to speak about these matters in the Senate.

Oppianus: *Oratio tua, Sulpici, necessaria erit, ut spes in senatu adhuc iustae virtutis sit. Nam si nemo loquatur et iustitiam postulet, nihil mutabitur. Ego quoque delectabor, si tu in senatu haec vitia publice reprehenderis.*

Oppianus: Your speech, Sulpicius, will be necessary if there's still hope for true virtue in the Senate. For if no one speaks and demands justice, nothing will change. I too will be pleased if you publicly denounce these vices in the Senate.

Sulpicius: *Bene faciam, et spero ut alii senatores non ignavi sint. Rem publicam ipsam tutabimur si nos virtutem et fidem prae omnibus curemus. Vale nunc, Oppiane, et si quid aliud occurrat, me certiorem fac.*

Sulpicius: I will do my best, and I hope that other senators will not be cowardly. We will protect the republic if we place virtue and loyalty above all else. Farewell for now, Oppianus, and if anything else comes up, let me know.

Oppianus: *Vale, Sulpici! Exspectabo te mox in Curia loquentem et spero ut verba tua auctoritatem habeant!*

Oppianus: Farewell, Sulpicius! I will look forward to hearing you speak soon in the Senate and hope that your words will carry weight!

In Templo – De Sacrificiis et Ritibus Religiosis

Valerius: *Salve, Atratine! Vidi te hodie in templo Iovis sacrificium sollemne facientem. Num aliquid maioris momenti celebrabas? Multitudo enim adfuit, et magni divinorum officiorum ritus visi sunt.*

Valerius: Hello, Atratinus! I saw you today performing a solemn sacrifice in the temple of Jupiter. Were you celebrating something of greater importance? For a crowd was present, and the rituals of the divine duties appeared grand.

Atratinus: *Salve, Valeri! Ita est, sacrificium hodie pro familia mea feci. Non ita pridem filius meus in morbum gravem incidit, et nunc, postquam di faverunt et sanus factus est, Iovi sacrificium gratulationis obtuli. Nec minoris momenti fuit; ritus omnes maxima cum diligentia praeparavi.*

Atratinus: Hello, Valerius! Yes, I performed a sacrifice today for my family. Not long ago, my son fell seriously ill, and now, after the gods showed favor and he recovered, I offered a thanksgiving sacrifice to Jupiter. It was not of little importance; all the rituals were prepared with the greatest care.

Valerius: *Laudabile factum, Atratine. Nihil gratius est quam dis sacrificium debitum persolvere, praesertim cum sana familia gaudeamus. Sed dic mihi, quo ritu id sacrificium perfecisti? Ut audivi, Iovi Optimo Maximo bos candidissimus immolatur. Num ornatus et victimae cura similiter summa fuit?*

Valerius: A praiseworthy deed, Atratinus. Nothing is more pleasing than paying the owed sacrifice to the gods, especially when we rejoice in the good health of our family. But tell me, by what ritual did you perform the sacrifice? As I've heard, a pure white ox is sacrificed to Jupiter Optimus Maximus. Was the attention to the adornments and the victim equally great?

Atratinus: *Profecto! Victima bos candidissimus fuit, sine macula. Primum victimam ad aram admovi cum verbis sollemnibus, et postea sacerdos manus suas ad caelum sustulit, divinas preces firmiter proferens. Tum hostia, ut mos est, immolata est, et viscera in flammas posita sunt. Ara ipsa flamma accensa est, cum primi fumus ad caelum a Iove acceptus est.*

Atratinus: Indeed! The victim was a pure white ox, without blemish. First, I led the victim to the altar with solemn words, and then the priest raised his hands to the sky, firmly reciting the divine prayers. Then the sacrifice, as is the custom, was offered, and the entrails were placed into the flames. The altar itself was lit, and the first smoke was accepted by Jupiter as it rose to the heavens.

Valerius: *Magnifice! Ipsa fumus de sacrificio ascendens, ut aiunt, dis signum est acceptum ritum esse. Si flamma bene ardeat et sine vento nimio, id est bonum omen. Sed dic mihi, quid de auguriis? Nonne auspicia quoque capta sunt ante sacrificium?*

Valerius: Magnificent! The very smoke rising from the sacrifice, as they say, is a sign that the gods have accepted the ritual. If the flame burns well and without too much wind, it is a good omen. But tell me, what about the auguries? Weren't the auspices also taken before the sacrifice?

Atratinus: *Ita vero, auspicia pro ritu sumpta sunt. Augur nobiscum adfuit, qui volatum avium spectavit. Cum avis laeva ex parte prospere volavit, id bonum omen fuisse crediderunt. Nihil magis mihi gaudium attulit quam videre omnia prospere ire et dis favorem ostendere.*

Atratinus: Indeed, the auspices were taken for the ritual. An augur was present with us, who observed the flight of birds. When a bird flew prosperously from the left side, it was considered a good omen. Nothing brought me more joy than seeing everything go well and show the gods' favor.

Valerius: *Nulla res pulchrior est quam spectare deorum benevolentiam per auspicia et ritus. Nuper ipse Marti sacrificium obtuli pro integritate exercitus. Victima illa bellicis armis ad aram instructa est, et post sacrificium, augurio fausto accepto, exercitus laetus in proelium processit. Nihil sine deis gerendum!*

Valerius: Nothing is more beautiful than witnessing the benevolence of the gods through auspices and rituals. Recently, I myself offered a sacrifice to Mars for the integrity of the army. That victim was prepared at the altar with warlike arms, and after the sacrifice, with the auspices favorable, the army happily marched into battle. Nothing must be undertaken without the gods!

Atratinus: *Sapiens es, Valeri! Sine fide et pietate non possumus sperare ut opera nostra prosperent. Mihi quidem semper videtur religio et ritus non tantum pro salute singularum familiarum esse, sed etiam pro tota civitate. Si populus non colat deos, Roma ipsa vacillabit.*

Atratinus: You are wise, Valerius! Without faith and piety, we cannot hope that our efforts will prosper. To me, it always seems that religion and rituals are not only for the well-being of individual families but also for the entire state. If the people do not honor the gods, Rome itself will falter.

Valerius: *Vere pronuntias, Atratine. Nam, ut veteres scripserunt, pietas Romam condidit et eadem custodit. Nos quidem privatim familias nostras servamus, sed maiores et divinorum officiorum observatio rem publicam tuentur. Vale igitur, amice, et di tecum sint!*

Valerius: You speak truly, Atratinus. For, as the ancients wrote, piety founded Rome, and it is the same that guards it. We indeed privately protect our families, but the ancestors and the observance of divine duties safeguard the republic. Farewell then, my friend, and may the gods be with you!

Atratinus: *Vale, Valeri! Dis fidem serva et fortuna Romae semper fida manebit.*

Atratinus: Farewell, Valerius! Keep faith with the gods, and the fortune of Rome will always remain loyal.

In Thermopolio Pompeiano – De Cibo in Thermopolio Ordinando

Numerius:

Salve, Macrine! Hodie non procul ab Amphitheatro ambulabam, cum fames me superavit. Vidi hoc thermopolium admodum frequentari, et nunc aliquid edere velim. Quid mihi censeas optimum esse in loco tam celebri?

Numerius: Hello, Macrinus! Today, I was walking not far from the Amphitheater when hunger overcame me. I saw this thermopolium being quite busy, and now I'd like to eat something. What do you think is the best thing to have in such a famous place?

Macrinus:

Salve, Numeri! Etsi hoc thermopolium parvum est, edulia hic laudantur. Ego saepe huc veni ut puls lenticulam aut garum sumam. Cibus hic simplex sed saporibus plenus est. Cur non hordeum cum olivis aut panem et vinum capis?

Macrinus: Hello, Numerius! Even though this thermopolium is small, the food here is praised. I often come here to have lentil porridge or garum. The food is simple but full of flavor. Why not have barley with olives or bread and wine?

Numerius:

Bene, sic faciam. Hoc tempore primum aliquid parvi et levis quaero. Censeo hordeum cum olivis mihi aptissimum esse, et postea fortasse aliquid robustius. Sed dic mihi, Macrine, quid vini prope sit? Solumne Falernum dant, an plura genera?

Numerius: Good, I'll do that. Right now, I'm looking for something small and light. I think barley with olives is the best choice for me, and maybe later something more substantial. But tell me, Macrinus, what wine is nearby? Do they only serve Falernian, or are there more options?

Macrinus:

Sic est, Falernum in primis laudatur, sed habent quoque vinum ex Campania. Utrumque bonum est, sed ego praesertim Campanum consuevi bibere cum edo. Leve, et tamen saporem amarum habet. Hoc vino, si volueris una cum pane condito, nihil amabilius erit.

Macrinus: That's right, Falernian is especially praised, but they also have wine from Campania. Both are good, but I especially like to drink Campanian wine when I eat. It's light, yet it has a bitter taste. With this wine, if you'd like it with seasoned bread, nothing would be more delightful.

Numerius:
Bene suades! Tunc vinum Campanum accipiam. (Ad tabernarium vertitur) Heus, bone vir! Dic mihi, quanti hordeum cum olivis et vinum Campanum vendis?

Numerius: You give good advice! Then I'll take the Campanian wine. (Turning to the shopkeeper) Hey, good man! Tell me, how much do you charge for the barley with olives and Campanian wine?

Tabernarius:
Salve, domine! Hordeum cum olivis tibi assem unum constabit, et vinum Campanum duobus assibus venditur. Bene matutinum frigus accipies, nam et vinum et cibum pro victu semper recentes habemus.

Shopkeeper: Hello, sir! The barley with olives will cost you one as, and the Campanian wine is sold for two asses. You'll enjoy the cool of the morning well, as we always have fresh food and wine.

Numerius:
Optimum! Accipio utrumque. Nihil gratius est quam cibum modicum et vinum salubre hodie sumere. (Tabernario pecuniam tradit)

Numerius: Excellent! I'll take both. Nothing is more pleasing than having a modest meal and healthy wine today. (He hands the money to the shopkeeper)

Tabernarius:
Gratias ago, domine. Ecce tibi hordeum et vinum. Utinam bene sapiant!

Shopkeeper: Thank you, sir. Here is your barley and wine. May they taste great!

Macrinus:
Mihi semper bene hic cenatur, Numeri. Cibus paratus et sapidus est, neque vinum nimis gravat. Nonne tibi videtur Pompeii thermopolia praeter cetera in aliis urbibus excellere?

Macrinus: I always eat well here, Numerius. The food is well-prepared and tasty, and the wine isn't too heavy. Don't you think the thermopolia of Pompeii surpass those in other cities?

Numerius:

Profecto! Thermopolia Pompeiana et varia ciborum abundantia et hospitio pleno notissima sunt. Etsi simplex cibus est, modus et sapor mirabiles sunt. Hic sermone et cena frui magna voluptate est.

Numerius: Absolutely! The thermopolia of Pompeii are well-known for their variety of food and full hospitality. Even though the food is simple, the presentation and taste are remarkable. Enjoying a conversation and a meal here is a great pleasure.

Macrinus:

Vere dicis. Valetudo post levem et iucundum prandium semper melior est. Vale nunc, Numeri, et, cum aliud sit tempus, iterum huc redeamus!

Macrinus: You speak truly. Health is always better after a light and pleasant lunch. Farewell now, Numerius, and when there's time again, let's return here!

Numerius:

Vale, Macrine! Huc sic venire semper delectabit.

Numerius: Farewell, Macrinus! It will always be a delight to come here.

De Mutua Amicitia – Disputatio de Amicitia et Fide

Scaevola:

Salve, Pomponi! Videor multum hodie de amicitia cogitavisse, praesertim cum plures cives nostri in suas privatas res magis quam in amicorum fidem incumbere videantur. Nonne recte sentio quod amicitia, sicut olim inter nostros maiores fuit, nunc paulatim evanescit?

Scaevola: Hello, Pomponius! I seem to have been thinking a lot about friendship today, especially as many of our fellow citizens appear to focus more on their personal affairs than on the loyalty of their friends. Don't you think I'm right in feeling that friendship, as it once was among our ancestors, is now gradually disappearing?

Pomponius:

Salve, Scaevola! Recte quidem sentis. Haec nostra tempora, cum amicitia simulata plus quam vera regnat, mihi quoque saepe sollicitudinem afferunt. Qui multum in rerum externarum commodis versantur, pauca fidem aut veram amicitiam colunt. Non satis est nunc amicos verbis aut blanditiis fovere; operibus probandi sunt.

Pomponius: Hello, Scaevola! You are indeed right. These days, when simulated friendship reigns more than true friendship, I too often feel concern. Those who dwell much on external advantages seldom cultivate loyalty or true friendship. Now, it's not enough to nurture friends with words or flattery; they must be proven through deeds.

Scaevola:

O, quam verum! Illa vetus amicitia, quam Cicero ipse laudabat in suo libro De Amicitia, iam inter paucos tantum invenitur. Erat olim consensio animorum in omnibus rebus humanis et divinis, et fides inter amicos non solum constantiam sed etiam virtutem imperabat. Tu autem quid sentis? Quid censes causam esse huic ruinae amicitiae?

Scaevola: Oh, how true! That old friendship, which Cicero himself praised in his book *De Amicitia*, is now found among only a few. Once there was a harmony of minds in all human and divine matters, and loyalty between friends commanded not only constancy but also virtue. But what do you think? What do you believe is the cause of this decline in friendship?

Pomponius:

Mihi videtur, Scaevola, quod cupiditas et avaritia vincunt virtutem in animis multorum. Nunc plerique pro suo quaestu amicitias fingunt, et ubi utilitas desinit, illi quoque amici recedunt. Veteres amicitias, ut Fabii aut Scipiones, propter honestatem et fidem coluerunt, non propter lucrum aut honorem. Haec iam perdita videntur.

Pomponius: It seems to me, Scaevola, that greed and avarice overpower virtue in the minds of many. Now, most people forge friendships for their own gain, and when the benefit ends, so do those friendships. The old friendships, like those of the Fabii or Scipios, were cultivated for honesty and loyalty, not for profit or honor. These seem lost now.

Scaevola:

Ita, veteres sicut Laelius et Scipio exempla praestiterunt verae amicitiae, quae nec fortunis nec adversis casibus mutari poterat. Nullus metus, nulla ambitio eos dividebat. Sed quid facere possumus? Estne spes ut haec virtus iterum colatur?

Scaevola: Yes, the ancients like Laelius and Scipio provided examples of true friendship, which could not be changed by fortune or adverse circumstances. No fear, no ambition could divide them. But what can we do? Is there hope that this virtue will be cultivated again?

Pomponius:

Spes quidem semper est, sed difficile videtur, nisi homines ipsi virtutem prae se ferant et commodis suis respuant. Si ex studio honestatis et iustitiae amicitias colamus, fortasse non omnia perdidimus. Curandum est ut honor amicorum sit sine simulatione aut fraudibus. Amicitia, si vera est, ad multas res bonas ducit.

Pomponius: There is always hope, of course, but it seems difficult unless people themselves carry forth virtue and reject their own interests. If we cultivate friendships from a sense of honesty and justice, perhaps not all is lost. We must ensure that the honor of our friends is maintained without pretense or deceit. True friendship, if it exists, leads to many good things.

Scaevola:

Profecto. Etenim amicitia sine iustitia et fide quasi corpus sine anima est. Sed dic mihi, Pomponi, habesne ipse amicum cuius fidem prope exemplo tibi videas?

Scaevola: Indeed. For friendship without justice and loyalty is like a body without a soul. But tell me, Pomponius, do you yourself have a friend whose loyalty you see as an example to you?

Pomponius:

Habeo, Scaevola! Amicus mihi est Vettius, vir probitatis summae, qui numquam suum commodum prae meo posuit. Cum difficilia passus essem, ille primus me adiuvit, nec quaesivit quid sibi esset ex hoc lucri. Hoc in amicitia semper quaerendum est, ut sine spe mercedis amicus adiuvetur.

Pomponius: I do, Scaevola! My friend is Vettius, a man of the highest integrity, who has never placed his own interest above mine. When I was going through difficulties, he was the first to help me, and he didn't ask what profit he could gain from it. This is always what should be sought in friendship: to help a friend without expecting a reward.

Scaevola:

Bene te felicem iudico, Pomponi. Ego quoque paucos habeo, sed firmissimos amicos. Cerno autem hoc: non est multitudo amicorum quaerenda, sed paucorum fides tenenda. Pro amicitia enim constantia opus est, quae tempore probatur, non verbis.

Scaevola: I consider you lucky, Pomponius. I too have a few, but very loyal friends. However, I see this: it's not the multitude of friends we should seek, but the loyalty of a few that must be held. For in friendship, constancy is needed, which is tested by time, not by words.

Pomponius:

Ita est. Ut ait Cicero, amicitia nisi inter bonos esse non potest. Nam qui ipse non probus sit, neque fidem amicorum tueri poterit neque fidem suam praebere. Virtus est fundamentum omnium bonarum rerum, etiam amicitiae.

Pomponius: That's right. As Cicero said, friendship cannot exist except among the good. For he who is not good himself cannot protect the loyalty of his friends nor offer his own. Virtue is the foundation of all good things, even friendship.

Scaevola:

Sapientia plena sunt verba tua, Pomponi. Si amicitia diu et firmiter manere debet, virtus et honestas sunt necessariae. Videmus quidem exempla eorum qui fidem amicorum violaverunt pro suis commodis, sed hi in fama perpetua male notantur.

Scaevola: Your words are full of wisdom, Pomponius. If friendship is to last long and firmly, virtue and honesty are necessary. We do see examples of those who have betrayed the loyalty of their friends for their own gain, but they are forever marked in infamy.

Pomponius:

Recte dicis. Amicitiam veram colere non solum honorem affert, sed etiam animi tranquillitatem et fiduciam. Vale igitur, Scaevola, et fides tua semper sit intemerata!

Pomponius: You speak rightly. Cultivating true friendship not only brings honor but also peace of mind and trust. Farewell then, Scaevola, and may your loyalty always remain untainted!

Scaevola:

Vale, Pomponi, et amicitiae nostrae semper praeclaram fidem habeamus!

Scaevola: Farewell, Pomponius, and may the loyalty of our friendship always remain outstanding!

In Foro Boario – Emptio pecorum in foro

Sextus: *Salve, Decime! Video te hodie in Foro Boario esse. Num boves aliquos comparare vis? Ego quoque animo ad pecus emendum sum, praesertim postquam novi agri mihi tributi sunt.*

Sextus: Hello, Decimus! I see you are at the Forum Boarium today. Are you thinking of buying some oxen? I too am planning to buy cattle, especially since new land has been allotted to me.

Decimus: *Salve, Sexte! Ita est, hodie boves emere cogito, nam res agrariae meae ampliores factae sunt, et plus iuvamenti in agris necessarium habeo. Sed non semper facile est bonum pecus invenire. Nonne tibi videtur melius pro certo caput spectare quam totum venditorem fidei credere?*

Decimus: Hello, Sextus! Yes, today I am thinking of buying oxen, for my agricultural affairs have expanded, and I need more help in the fields. But it is not always easy to find good livestock. Don't you think it's better to inspect the animal yourself than to trust entirely in the seller's word?

Sextus: *Vere loqueris, Decime! Oculis ipsis confidere oportet. Ego semper prius pedes et cornua animalis considero, deinde pellem specto, ut videam an sana sit. Multi, ut scis, pecus non sine fraude vendunt. Et, sicut dicitur: ubi pecunia, ibi fides rara.*

Sextus: You speak truly, Decimus! You must trust your own eyes. I always first examine the feet and horns of the animal, then I inspect its skin to see if it's healthy. Many, as you know, sell livestock not without deceit. And, as they say: where money is, trust is rare.

Decimus: *Sapiens consilium! Dic mihi tamen, Sexte, quem modum emptionis sequi soles? Ego primum numerum annorum quaero, quoniam iuvenci recentes ad laborem multo diutius et firmiores sunt.*

Decimus: Wise advice! But tell me, Sextus, what buying method do you usually follow? I first look at the age, since young oxen are much stronger and last longer for work.

Sextus: *Primum quidem aetatem curare necesse est, ut dicis. Iuvenci duorum triumve annorum optimi ad laborem sunt. Tum etiam corpus integrum specto: nec nimis magnum nec nimis parvum esse debet. Mihi* *placet medium robur et bene firmata membra. Ecce autem, videsne illum venditorem prope stabulum? Boves sui satis bene spectant.*

Sextus: Indeed, it's necessary to consider age first, as you say. Young oxen of two or three years are best for work. Then I also inspect the body: it shouldn't be too big or too small. I prefer medium strength and well-built limbs. But look, do you see that seller near the stable? His oxen look quite good.

Decimus: *Cerno! Non male videntur, praesertim ille qui in sinistra stat. Corpus iusto maius videtur, sed robustus et confidens. Fortasse ad illum vadamus et pretium quaeramus.*

Decimus: I see! They don't look bad, especially the one standing on the left. His body seems larger than average, but he looks strong and confident. Perhaps we should go to him and ask the price.

Sextus: *Placet. (Approchantes venditorem) Salve, bone vir! Quanti est hic bos? Mihi is, qui in sinistra stat, placet.*

Sextus: Agreed. (Approaching the seller) Hello, good man! How much is this ox? I like the one standing on the left.

Venditor: *Salvete, domini! Hic bos, quem spectatis, quattuor denariis venditur. Firmus est, et eadem nocte bene cubavit. Promitto vobis illum paratum esse ad quemlibet laborem, et plurimae fiduciae praestabit.*

Seller: Hello, sirs! This ox you're looking at is sold for four denarii. He is strong, and last night he rested well. I promise you that he is ready for any kind of work and will prove to be very reliable.

Decimus: *Quattuor denarii? Profecto videtur pretium non modicum. Numquam audivi pretium tam altum pro bove! Sed dic mihi, quae sit causa huius pretii? Estne pecus ex stirpe praeclara?*

Decimus: Four denarii? That certainly seems like no small price. I've never heard of such a high price for an ox! But tell me, what is the reason for this price? Is the cattle from a noble lineage?

Venditor: *Dico vere, domine, pecus hoc natum esse ex grege optimo. Genus suum praeclarum est, et nulla in parte vitium reperietis. Hoc animal non solum ad laborem, sed etiam ad procreandos iuvencos idoneum est.*

Seller: I tell you truly, sir, this cattle was born from the best herd. Its lineage is excellent, and you will find no flaw in it. This animal is not only good for work but also for breeding young oxen.

Sextus: *Fortasse verum est, sed tamen, Decime, censeo ut paulo minore pretio offeratur. Si tantam pecuniam nunc dedam, futurum est ut plus de agrorum cultu desum. Numquid licet tibi paulum pretii demittere?*

Sextus: Perhaps that's true, but still, Decimus, I think it should be offered at a slightly lower price. If I give this much money now, it will take away more from the cultivation of the fields. Could you lower the price a little?

Venditor: *Bene, quia videtur vos graviorem numerum pecudum velle, tres denarios ponam. Non possum minorem summam accipere; sed certo scio bovem hunc vobis satis placiturum.*

Seller: Well, since it seems you want a larger number of cattle, I will set it at three denarii. I can't accept less, but I'm certain this ox will satisfy you.

Decimus: *Bene, tres denarii mihi videntur aequi. Accipio. Sexte, quid tibi videtur? Ego hunc bovem accipiam et domum ducam, ut in agris nostris laboret.*

Decimus: Good, three denarii seem fair to me. I accept. Sextus, what do you think? I will take this ox and lead him home to work in our fields.

Sextus: *Consentio. Videtur honestum animal, et pretium iam ad aequitatem adductum est. Vende igitur, Decime, et gratias age viro.*

Sextus: I agree. It seems like a good animal, and the price has now been made fair. Go ahead and buy it, Decimus, and thank the man.

Decimus: *Gratias tibi, bone vir! Pecuniam accipe et vale! Hunc bovem mecum duco.*

Decimus: Thank you, good man! Take the money and farewell! I will lead this ox with me.

Venditor: *Gratias vobis! Utinam bos bene laboret in agris vestris. Valete!*

Seller: Thank you! May the ox work well in your fields. Farewell!

De Virtutibus Romanis – De virtute et honore Romanorum sermo

Mummius: *Salve, Torquate! Saepe mihi in mentem venit de virtutibus Romanis cogitare, praesertim cum tempora nostra videantur eas paulatim oblivisci. Quid tibi videtur? Nonne fortitudo, fides, et honestas iam minus coluntur quam olim?*

Mummius: Hello, Torquatus! I often find myself thinking about Roman virtues, especially since it seems that our times are gradually forgetting them. What do you think? Is it not true that courage, loyalty, and honor are now less respected than they once were?

Torquatus: *Salve, Mumme! Non procul a vero dicis. Eae virtutes, quae Romam ad tantam gloriam perduxerunt, video paucis nunc in honore esse. Fortitudo quondam rerum omnium fundamentum erat, sed nunc homines plus in luxu et voluptatibus quam in labore et virtute spem collocant.*

Torquatus: Hello, Mummius! You're not far from the truth. The virtues that once led Rome to such great glory, I see now, are honored by few. Courage was once the foundation of all things, but now people place their hope more in luxury and pleasure than in hard work and virtue.

Mummius: *Ita est. Vide exempla pristina: qui maiores nostri non fortitudine et patientia non solum bellorum pericula vicerunt, sed etiam domesticas difficultates? Quid de Lucio Quinctio Cincinnato? In agros suos revertens postquam dictaturam gessit, rem publicam salvis manibus reliquit. Quis hodiernus vir ad tantam modestiam descenderet?*

Mummius: That's right. Look at the examples of the past: didn't our ancestors overcome not only the dangers of war with their courage and endurance, but also domestic challenges? What about Lucius Quinctius Cincinnatus? After holding the dictatorship, he returned to his fields and left the republic in safe hands. Which man today would descend to such modesty?

Torquatus: *Nemo, ut puto, Mumme. Cincinnatus propter honorem suum magis quam propter gloriam actus est. Eius exemplum omnes Romani imitari debent. Sed quid de fide? Romani semper in fide magni fuimus, et tamen nunc plerique, ut videtur, pro suo lucro pacta violant. Nonne hanc virtutem iam prope discimus oblivisci?*

Torquatus: No one, I think, Mummius. Cincinnatus was driven by honor rather than by glory. All Romans should imitate his example. But what about loyalty? Romans were always great in their loyalty, yet now most people, it seems, break their promises for personal gain. Are we not on the verge of forgetting this virtue?

Mummius: *Fides olim vere sacra erat! Nemini plus quam sibi ipsi fidere vir bonus debebat. Sed nunc homines proditiones dolosque quaerunt, ut suum commodum faciant. Multi ex amicis falsis nihil aliud quaerunt nisi rem sibi utilem, quasque amicitias pro lucro fingunt. Priscus moris huius diu lusus videtur.*

Mummius: Loyalty was once truly sacred! A good man was to trust no one more than himself. But now people seek betrayal and deceit to benefit themselves. Many false friends seek nothing but what's useful to them, and they forge friendships for profit. The old way of this seems long gone.

Torquatus: *Quid etiam de pietate, Mumme? Pietas, quam ut summum decus semper coluimus, nunc vix apparet. Paterfamiliae, di, patria—his omnibus fidem et cultum semper praestare debemus. Sed plerique nunc rei publicae neglegentiorem operam dant, et familias suas male curant. Nonne hoc gravissimum defectum prospicis?*

Torquatus: What about piety, Mummius? Piety, which we always revered as the highest honor, now scarcely appears. To the father of the family, the gods, the homeland—we must always show loyalty and devotion to them all. But now most people give little care to the republic and neglect their families. Don't you see this as a grave failing?

Mummius: *Videtur mihi vero magnum periculum esse, si pietas amittatur. Nam patria ipsa pietate firmata est: si nemo patriae fidem servat, quomodo Roma manebit? Video tamen non omnes perdidisse hoc officium. Sunt viri qui virtutem colant et iustitiam prae omnibus habeant. Sed spero ut plura exempla talia sequamur, antequam haec virtus pereat.*

Mummius: It seems to me there is a great danger if piety is lost. For the homeland itself is built on piety: if no one maintains loyalty to the homeland, how will Rome endure? Yet I see that not everyone has lost this duty. There are men who cultivate virtue and hold justice above all else. But I hope we follow more such examples before this virtue perishes.

Torquatus: *Ita est, spes adhuc restat. Custodire virtutem debemus non solum verbis sed etiam factis. Fortitudo, fides, pietas: haec tria fundamenta sunt quibus res publica nixa manet. Si has virtutes Romani servare possumus, nihil metuendum est.*

Torquatus: Yes, hope still remains. We must safeguard virtue not only with words but also with deeds. Courage, loyalty, piety: these three are the foundations on which the republic stands. If Romans can preserve these virtues, there is nothing to fear.

Mummius: *Oratio tua sapiens est, Torquate. Nos ipsi virtutem agere primum curemus, et exemplum maiorum nostrorum in rei publicae curam referamus. Vale nunc, amice, et semper ad Romanam gloriam animos intendamus!*

Mummius: Your speech is wise, Torquatus. Let us first see that we act virtuously ourselves and carry the example of our ancestors into our care for the republic. Farewell now, my friend, and let us always focus our minds on Roman glory!

Torquatus: *Vale, Mumme! Virtute nostra et fide, Roma in aeternum firma manebit!*

Torquatus: Farewell, Mummius! With our virtue and loyalty, Rome will remain strong forever!

In Aula Imperatoris – A conversation in the emperor's court

Faustulus: *Salve, Flavi! Hodie in aula imperatoris multus tumultus fuit. Vidi multos senatores et legatos circumstare, atque ipse imperator sermonibus gravibus intentus videbatur. Quid accidit? Numquid novus sermo de bello aut aliis rebus promulgatus est?*

Faustulus: Hello, Flavius! Today there was a lot of commotion in the emperor's court. I saw many senators and envoys standing around, and the emperor himself seemed engrossed in serious conversations. What happened? Has there been any new announcement about war or other matters?

Flavius: *Salve, Faustule! Ita est, multa gravia hodie in aula disceptata sunt. Imperator nuper de Germanis inquietis audivit; itaque hodie principes militiae convocavit ut consilium caperent. Bellum foris semper Romam sollicitat, sed imperatori nunc etiam internorum dissensionum cura est.*

Flavius: Hello, Faustulus! Yes, many serious matters were discussed in the court today. The emperor recently heard about unrest among the Germans, so today he summoned the military leaders to make plans. War abroad always concerns Rome, but the emperor is now also worried about internal dissensions.

Faustulus: *O, difficile est principem esse, cum et bella foris gerenda sint et inter cives discordiae reprimendae. Sed dic mihi, Flavi, quid de his internis dissensionibus audisti? Num senatores adhuc propria quaerunt potius quam rem publicam communem?*

Faustulus: Oh, it is difficult to be a ruler when wars must be fought abroad and discord among the citizens must be suppressed. But tell me, Flavius, what have you heard about these internal dissensions? Are senators still seeking their own interests rather than the common good?

Flavius: *Profecto, magna dissensio est inter aliquos senatores. Quidam imperatori fidem promittunt, dum alii potentiam suam augere cupiunt. Imperator se magnopere laborare ait ut civitatem in concordiam redigat. Hoc profecto est principis gravissimum officium—pacem domi et finem bellorum foris curare.*

Flavius: Indeed, there is great dissension among some senators. Some promise loyalty to the emperor, while others seek to increase their own power. The emperor says he is working hard to restore harmony to the city. This, surely, is the most important duty of a ruler—to ensure peace at home and bring an end to wars abroad.

Faustulus: *Vere dicis, amice. Nulla res gravior est imperatori quam unitas civitatis. Sine concordia, etiam maxima bellorum victoria, res publica labefactatur. Sed quid censes? Possumusne internas discordias componere si foris bellum geritur?*

Faustulus: You speak truly, my friend. There is nothing more important to the emperor than the unity of the state. Without harmony, even the greatest victory in war will shake the republic. But what do you think? Can we resolve internal discord if a war is being fought abroad?

Flavius: *Id quidem difficile videtur. Dum hostes foris oppugnamus, inter cives tumultus oriri solent. Res enim Romanae primum ex consensu et fide conservantur, ut senatus populusque simul agant. Sed imperator prudentiam magnam ostendit in his causis tractandis, et spero fore ut pacem domi stabiliat, priusquam bellum longius protrahatur.*

Flavius: That indeed seems difficult. While we fight enemies abroad, unrest tends to arise among the citizens. The Roman state is preserved primarily through consensus and loyalty, with the senate and people acting together. But the emperor has shown great wisdom in handling these issues, and I hope he will establish peace at home before the war drags on too long.

Faustulus: *Sapiens visus est semper imperator noster, et magna cum iustitia rem publicam moderatur. Sed memini de principibus Graecis et aliis populis, qui dum bella foris quaerebant, domi omnia perdiderunt. Roma, nisi unitas servetur, eandem sortem passura est.*

Faustulus: Our emperor has always appeared wise, and he governs the state with great justice. But I remember the Greek leaders and other nations, who while seeking wars abroad, lost everything at home. Unless unity is maintained, Rome will suffer the same fate.

Flavius: *Recte mones, Faustule. Vetera exempla semper memoranda sunt. Graeci quidem sua discordia se in exitium dederunt, dum foris* *victorias quaerebant. Quod Romae non proderit, nisi interna concordia nitimur. Melius est vires nostras domi firmare quam longinqua bella intulerimus.*

Flavius: You are right, Faustulus. Old examples should always be remembered. The Greeks indeed destroyed themselves with their own discord while seeking victories abroad. This will not benefit Rome unless we strive for internal harmony. It is better to strengthen our forces at home than to wage distant wars.

Faustulus: *Spero igitur, ut consilia imperatoris ad bonum finem ducant. Mihi quidem placet quomodo ipse moderationem et fidem pollicetur, et si senatus secum steterit, omnia bene procedent. Sed animadverto te plura scire de exercitus statu. Quid de legionibus nuper audivisti?*

Faustulus: I hope, then, that the emperor's plans lead to a good outcome. I do like how he promises moderation and loyalty, and if the senate stands with him, everything will go well. But I notice you know more about the state of the army. What have you heard about the legions recently?

Flavius: *Exercitus bene se habet, sed longis itineribus et proeliis fatigatus est. Legiones in Germania positae magna virtute pugnant, sed multi milites iam bellosas condiciones ac diuturnam ab urbe absentiam queruntur. Imperator autem iussit ut militibus fortissimis honores tribuantur, ut eorum fides et animus retineantur.*

Flavius: The army is doing well, but it is fatigued from long marches and battles. The legions stationed in Germany are fighting with great courage, but many soldiers are now complaining about the harsh conditions and the long absence from the city. The emperor, however, has ordered honors to be given to the bravest soldiers so that their loyalty and spirit may be maintained.

Faustulus: *Id laudabile est. Non solum bellum gloria et fortitudine geritur, sed etiam cura et honore eorum qui pro patria pugnaverunt. Imperatorem laudo, qui tam sollicitus sit de militibus suis. Sed videamus quid futurum sit. Vale, Flavi, et speremus ut res meliores fiant!*

Faustulus: That is commendable. War is waged not only with glory and courage, but also with care and honor for those who have fought for their country. I praise the emperor, who is so concerned for his soldiers. But let's see what happens. Farewell, Flavius, and let's hope things improve!

Flavius: *Vale, Faustule! Spes nostra in sapientia imperatoris et in concordia civium manet.*

Flavius: Farewell, Faustulus! Our hope rests in the wisdom of the emperor and the unity of the citizens.

De Diis et Fatis – Disputatio philosophica de fato et diis

Aulus: *Salve, Nigidi! Saepe mihi in animo est de fatis cogitare et quo modo dei omnes res gubernent. Multi credunt omnes hominum actus pro certo fato praeordinatos esse. Tu quid censes? Num omnes res ad deos redeunt, an aliquid in nostra potestate sit?*

Aulus: Hello, Nigidius! I often find myself thinking about fate and how the gods govern all things. Many believe that all human actions are predetermined by fate. What do you think? Do all things return to the gods, or is there something within our own power?

Nigidius: *Salve, Aule! Haec quaestio magna est et saepe tractata ab antiquis sapientibus. Ego quidem arbitror fata partem magnam vitae nostrae regere, sed non ita ut omnes actus nostri praefiniti sint. Est enim aliquid quod nos ipsi possumus agere, et virtute nostra quaedam fata mutare. Dei quidem gubernant, sed non sine nostra voluntate.*

Nigidius: Hello, Aulus! This is a great question and has often been discussed by the ancient philosophers. I believe that fate governs a large part of our lives, but not in such a way that all our actions are predetermined. There is something we ourselves can do, and through our virtue, we can change certain fates. The gods govern, but not without our will.

Aulus: *Humanum consilium inter deorum propositos? Mirabilis haec vis! At tamen dic mihi, Nigidi, qui homines saepe cladibus opprimuntur sicut Ilium aut Remus ipse, numquid poterant se suis fatis eripere? An non, ut poetae dicunt, "fata ineluctabilia" fuerunt?*

Aulus: Human choice among the gods' plans? This is a marvelous power! But tell me, Nigidius, those men who are often overcome by disasters, like Ilium or Remus himself, could they have escaped their fates? Or were they, as the poets say, "inescapable fates"?

Nigidius: *Profecto, Aule, sunt fata quae ne quidem summi viri effugere possunt. Non omnia sunt in potestate nostra. Ut enim Iuppiter in fatis Homericis sua stabat in arbore, res mortales terras hominum mirum in modum regi iubet. Sed nos, quamvis fatis subiciamur, non omnino sine facultate agendi sumus. Virtus in malis et fortitudo in adversis magnopere commendatur.*

Nigidius: Indeed, Aulus, there are fates that not even the greatest of men can escape. Not everything is within our control. As Jupiter, standing in the Homeric fates, commands the mortal affairs of men to be governed in a wondrous way. But although we are subject to fate, we are not entirely without the power to act. Virtue in misfortune and courage in adversity are greatly valued.

Aulus: *Ita, intellego. Fata quidem suum cursum tenent, sed homines etiam in fortuna adversa suam viam per virtutem invenire possunt. Sed quid dices de oraculis? Si fata iam praeordinata sunt, quid est utilitatis in oraculis quaerendis?*

Aulus: Yes, I understand. Fate indeed follows its course, but people can also find their way through virtue even in adverse fortune. But what will you say about oracles? If fates are already predetermined, what use is there in seeking oracles?

Nigidius: *Bene rogas. Oracula sunt instrumenta, per quae dei cum hominibus loquuntur, sed non semper responsa aperta praebent. Saepe fatum tibi demonstrat, sed modum ad eos eventus ferendos ipse eligere debes. Sicut apud Delum aut Pythiam, quotiens homines fatum suum quaerunt, saepe ambiguitas in responsis apparet. Tamen, oracula nos ad prudentiam et cautelam vocant.*

Nigidius: That is a good question. Oracles are tools through which the gods speak to humans, but they do not always provide clear answers. They often show you fate, but you must choose how to handle those events. Just as at Delos or Delphi, when people seek their fate, ambiguity often appears in the responses. However, oracles call us to wisdom and caution.

Aulus: *Vere dicis, responsa oraculorum plerique vix intellegunt nisi cum malum iam factum est. Sed vellem non solum de fatis, sed etiam de deorum ipsorum voluntate quaerere. Nonne omnipotens est Iuppiter, qui potest omnium fatorum ordinem mutare?*

Aulus: You speak truly; most people hardly understand the answers of oracles until the harm is already done. But I would like to ask not only about fate but also about the will of the gods themselves. Isn't Jupiter omnipotent, able to change the entire order of fate?

Nigidius: *Potest quidem, Aule, sed dei saepe leges ipsas, quibus mundus et res caelestes reguntur, servare volunt. Iuppiter fatum tenet, sed non tamquam tyrannus, qui omnia pro sua voluntate flectit. Ipse rerum ordo, quem dei constituerunt, fortitudine et iustitia manet. Ita fit ut, quamquam dei magnorum modorum auctores sunt, homines etiam pars illius ordinis sint.*

Nigidius: He can indeed, Aulus, but the gods often wish to uphold the very laws by which the world and celestial matters are governed. Jupiter holds fate, but not as a tyrant who bends everything to his will. The very order of things, which the gods have established, remains in strength and justice. Thus, while the gods are authors of great forces, humans are also a part of that order.

Aulus: *Quid dicis, Nigidi, de eo quod fata et virtutes hominum vinci non possunt? Vere fata et dei animos mutare nequeunt nec commovere: quid igitur rei homines curant?*

Aulus: What do you say, Nigidius, about the idea that fate and human virtues cannot be overcome? Truly, fate and the gods cannot change or be swayed: so why should men care about their actions?

Nigidius: *Humana consilia pro virtute et fide sempiternis sunt.*

Nigidius: Human decisions for virtue and loyalty are eternal.

In Foro Argentario – De gemmis et argentariis mercandis

Lentulus: *Salve, Sergi! Video te in foro argentario versari. Quaerisne aliquid gemmarum aut argentum, an fortasse ornamentum uxori tuae?*

Lentulus: Hello, Sergius! I see you are walking in the jewelry market. Are you looking for some gems or silver, or perhaps an ornament for your wife?

Sergius: *Salve, Lentule! Ita est, uxoris dies natalis appropinquat, et mihi in animo est donum elegans emere. Cogitavi de armilla aut fortasse fibula argentea, sed nondum certum habui quid praeferre velim. Tu quid censes? Hic argentarii bene sunt laudati.*

Sergius: Hello, Lentulus! Yes, my wife's birthday is approaching, and I plan to buy her an elegant gift. I've been thinking about a bracelet or maybe a silver brooch, but I haven't decided what I prefer yet. What do you think? The jewelers here are highly praised.

Lentulus: *Profecto, hic in foro argentario multa pulchra invenies. Argentum huius loci semper laudatur ob artem et nitorem. Mihi quidem videtur fibula elegantissima esse, praesertim si gemmis ornata sit. Videsne illum tabernarium prope? Ars eius per totam urbem praeclara est.*

Lentulus: Certainly, you'll find many beautiful things here in the jewelry market. The silver from this place is always praised for its craftsmanship and shine. To me, a brooch seems most elegant, especially if adorned with gems. Do you see that shopkeeper nearby? His craftsmanship is renowned throughout the city.

Sergius: *Videamus igitur! (Ambulant ad tabernarium) Salve, bone vir! Quaero fibulam argenteam uxori meae donandam. Habesne aliquid quod sit dignum et elegans?*

Sergius: Let's take a look then! (They walk to the shopkeeper) Hello, good man! I'm looking for a silver brooch to gift to my wife. Do you have something that is worthy and elegant?

Tabernarius: *Salve, domine! Certe! Multas fibulas habemus, et in argento caelatas et gemmis ornatas. Hic cernas fibulam cum gemma* *carbunculi et alias cum sapphiris vel smaragdis. Omnia opere perfecta artis. Quid tibi placet?*

Shopkeeper: Hello, sir! Certainly! We have many brooches, both engraved in silver and adorned with gems. Here you can see a brooch with a garnet and others with sapphires or emeralds. All are works of perfect craftsmanship. What do you like?

Sergius: *Pulcherrimae sunt! Haec fibula cum carbunculo mihi quidem placet; nitor et figura eius excellit. Sed dic mihi, quanti haec venditur?*

Sergius: They are very beautiful! This brooch with the garnet pleases me; its shine and design are excellent. But tell me, how much is this sold for?

Tabernarius: *Fibula haec, qua te delectari video, quinque denariis venditur. Est opus praestantissimum, et nihil in ea reminisci potes quod non arte perfectum sit.*

Shopkeeper: This brooch, which I see you admire, is sold for five denarii. It is an excellent piece of work, and there is nothing about it that you could not call perfectly crafted.

Lentulus: *Certe, Sergi, haec fibula digna videtur pretio. Nihil in foro elegantius inveniri potest. Sed fortasse potes pretium paulo minorem facere, bone tabernarie? Amici sumus qui semper ad tuam tabernam venimus.*

Lentulus: Certainly, Sergius, this brooch seems worth the price. Nothing more elegant can be found in the market. But perhaps you could lower the price a bit, good shopkeeper? We are friends who always come to your shop.

Tabernarius: *Bene, quia vos amici estis et saepius apud me emistis, ponam pretium in tres denarios et semissem. Nihil minus offerre possum, sed certo scito hanc fibulam uxori tuae maxime placituram esse.*

Shopkeeper: Well, since you are friends and have bought from me many times, I will set the price at three and a half denarii. I can't offer less, but I'm certain this brooch will greatly please your wife.

Sergius: *Haud dubium est! Pretium iam aequum videtur. Accipio hanc fibulam. (Pecuniam tradit) Gratias tibi ago, bone vir. Nulla res melius laetitiam uxori meae afferre poterit.*

Sergius: There is no doubt! The price now seems fair. I'll take this brooch. (He hands over the money) Thank you, good man. Nothing could bring my wife more joy.

Tabernarius: *Gratias tibi, domine. Utinam donum tuum magnam uxori delectationem ferat. Vale et iterum veni cum aliquid pulchrum quaeris!*

Shopkeeper: Thank you, sir. May your gift bring great delight to your wife. Farewell, and come again when you seek something beautiful!

Sergius: *Vale! Lentule, quid tibi videtur? Mihi quidem placet et fiducia est uxorem meam magnopere hanc fibulam laudaturam.*

Sergius: Farewell! Lentulus, what do you think? I really like it and am confident that my wife will greatly praise this brooch.

Lentulus: *Profecto! Nihil melius elegisti, Sergi. Ornamentum istud summa arte factum est et uxori tuae profecto placebit. Vale igitur, et natalem uxoris tuae iucunde celebres!*

Lentulus: Absolutely! You couldn't have chosen better, Sergius. That ornament is crafted with the utmost skill, and your wife will surely love it. So, farewell, and may you celebrate your wife's birthday joyfully!

Sergius: *Gratias tibi, Lentule. Vale et tu!*

Sergius: Thank you, Lentulus. Farewell to you too!

De Rebus Militaribus – De rebus militaribus et vita militis colloquium

Manlius: *Salve, Rufine! Audivi te nuper de castris et rebus militaribus discere. Dic mihi, quinam sunt mores exercitus nostri, et quomodo milites nostri proelia bene gerant?*

Manlius: Hello, Rufinus! I heard you have recently been learning about the military camps and military affairs. Tell me, what are the customs of our army, and how do our soldiers fight well in battles?

Rufinus: *Salve, Manli! Ita est, multas res in castris discere cogor, quoniam non satis est virtutem in bello habere; consilium quoque et disciplina summo loco habentur. Ex omnibus praeceptis, firmiter aciem servare et imperiis parere primum habetur. Nam in unitate exercitus potissimum res consistit.*

Rufinus: Hello, Manlius! Yes, I am compelled to learn many things in the camps, because it is not enough to have courage in war; strategy and discipline are also held in the highest regard. Of all the rules, keeping the battle line firm and obeying orders are considered the most important. For in the unity of the army lies the greatest strength.

Manlius: *Nihil verius dicis. Disciplina semper prima virtus militum fuit. Ne sine ordine aut praecipiti impetu certandum est. Etsi animi magnitudo necessaria est, sine prudentia in agmine vix victoria sperari potest. Num etiam de locorum natura et itineribus in castris didicisti?*

Manlius: You speak nothing but the truth. Discipline has always been the foremost virtue of soldiers. You must not fight without order or with reckless haste. Although courage is necessary, without wisdom in the ranks, victory can hardly be hoped for. Have you also learned about the nature of the terrain and the routes in the camps?

Rufinus: *Ita vero. Locus maximi momenti est in proelio. Dux semper spectat ut milites locum praeoccupent, ut superiores sint. Profecto, si hostes in loco altiore stant, victoria difficilis erit. Itaque montes, colles, et pontes pro viribus occupare praeceptum est. Navigia quoque et fossae saepe ad defensionem adhibentur.*

Rufinus: Yes, indeed. Location is of the greatest importance in battle. A commander always makes sure the soldiers occupy the terrain first so that they have the advantage. Certainly, if the enemy stands on higher ground, victory will be difficult. Therefore, taking control of mountains, hills, and bridges with strength is a key rule. Ships and ditches are also often used for defense.

Manlius: *Recte! Eadem res et in historia nostra memorata est. Cum Hannibal in Italia bellum gerebat, id quod eum per montes et saltus iter facientem iuvit, scientia locorum fuit. Sed dic mihi, Rufine, quid de vita cotidiana in castris? Estne difficilis?*

Manlius: Correct! The same thing is mentioned in our history. When Hannibal waged war in Italy, it was his knowledge of the terrain that helped him while traveling through the mountains and passes. But tell me, Rufinus, what about daily life in the camps? Is it difficult?

Rufinus: *Certe, vita in castris neque facilis neque delicata est. Milites assidue exercentur, et disciplina severe observatur. Cotidie ad arcum, hastam, et gladium milites exercentur. Cibus autem est simplex: panis, frumentum, et aqua. Nam in exercitu nihil peius est quam luxuria, et corpora ad laborem parata esse debent.*

Rufinus: Certainly, life in the camps is neither easy nor delicate. The soldiers are constantly trained, and discipline is strictly observed. Every day, soldiers train with the bow, spear, and sword. The food, however, is simple: bread, grain, and water. For in the army, nothing is worse than luxury, and the bodies must be prepared for labor.

Manlius: *Non mihi quidem alia responsa exspectanda erant! Quippe Romani milites ab antiquo non voluptate sed labore et frugalitate ceteris gentibus praeferuntur. In eo ipso laus militiae posita est, ut in difficultate corporis et fortitudine animi spes sit. Num etiam de hostium moribus et armis doceris?*

Manlius: I expected no different answers! Indeed, Roman soldiers from ancient times have been preferred to other peoples not for pleasure but for labor and frugality. The praise of the military lies precisely in this, that in bodily hardship and mental fortitude lies hope. Have you also been taught about the customs and weapons of the enemy?

Rufinus: *Sic! De Gallis, Germanis, et Persis multa disco, quia hostium procedendi modum et arma scire necesse est. Galli celeres sunt in* *impetu, sed disciplinam ferre non possunt. Germani longas hastas praeferunt, sed saepe sine ordine pugnant. Persae autem sagittas longe iaciunt et procul pugnant, quare cum eis celeriter et munito exercitu agendum est.*

Rufinus: Yes! I am learning a lot about the Gauls, Germans, and Persians, because it is necessary to know the enemy's ways of advancing and their weapons. The Gauls are swift in attack but cannot withstand discipline. The Germans prefer long spears, but they often fight without order. The Persians, however, shoot arrows from afar and fight at a distance, so they must be dealt with quickly and with a fortified army.

Manlius: *Quam docte dicis! Scientia hostium non minoris pretii est quam virtus nostri exercitus. Si milites non solum viribus, sed etiam astu et prudentia vincimus, victoria certe paratur. Vale igitur, Rufine, et in studiis tuis perge!*

Manlius: How wisely you speak! Knowledge of the enemy is no less valuable than the virtue of our army. If we defeat our enemies not only with strength but also with cunning and wisdom, victory is surely secured. Farewell then, Rufinus, and continue in your studies!

Rufinus: *Gratias tibi ago, Manli! Vale et tu, et fortunam in bello tibi prospicere exopto!*

Rufinus: Thank you, Manlius! Farewell to you as well, and I wish you success in war!

In Campo Martio – De exercitatione athletica in Campo Martio sermo

Lucius: *Salve, Statilia! Vidi te hodie in Campo Martio exerceri. Multi quidem in hunc locum veniunt ad corporis vires confirmandas. Dic mihi, quid hodie praeclarum egisti? Num militaribus ludis exercuisti, an aliud genus exercitationis malle soles?*

Lucius: Hello, Statilia! I saw you exercising today in the Field of Mars. Many people indeed come to this place to strengthen their bodies. Tell me, what did you accomplish today? Did you engage in military exercises, or do you prefer another type of training?

Statilia: *Salve, Luci! Ita vero, hodie arcum et sagittam propius spectavi. Sagittando me exerceo, nam et magnam consensum manuum et oculorum requirit et corporis agilitatem servat. Sed tibi, Luci, quid praeferendum est in Campo Martio? Equitatu te vidi saepe gloriari.*

Statilia: Hello, Lucius! Yes, today I focused more on archery. I practice shooting with a bow and arrow, as it requires great coordination between hands and eyes and helps maintain agility. But what about you, Lucius? What do you prefer in the Field of Mars? I've often seen you take pride in horseback riding.

Lucius: *Equitatus mihi admodum placet. Nihil est quod me magis exsuscitet quam cursus equorum in aperto campo. Non solum vires requirit, sed etiam celeritatem mentis et constantiam. Sed confiteor, sagitta quoque virtus non minor est. Arcus tamen firmum et bene tensum nervum habere debet, si bene velis iacere.*

Lucius: I greatly enjoy horseback riding. Nothing excites me more than galloping horses in the open field. It requires not only strength but also mental quickness and steadiness. But I admit, archery is also no lesser skill. The bow, however, must have a strong and well-tensed string if you want to shoot well.

Statilia: *Profecto, arcus quidem bene tendendus est. Sed praeter sagittam et equitatum, plures aliae disciplinae in Campo Martio exercitantur. Video multos, qui pilae ludo delectantur aut hastilio certant. Quid tibi de illis videtur?*

Statilia: Indeed, the bow must be well-tensed. But besides archery and horseback riding, many other disciplines are practiced in the Field of Mars. I see many who enjoy playing ball games or competing in javelin throwing. What do you think about those?

Lucius: *Pila et hastilia probatissima sunt ad iuvenum corpora firmanda. Pila, cum agilitatem et celeritatem foveat, etiam amicitiam inter ludentes auget. Hastilia autem certaminis ac militiae causa magnopere usui sunt. Sed ego, Statilia, semper admiratione video viros qui discum aut iaculum longe iaciunt.*

Lucius: Ball games and javelin throwing are excellent for strengthening young bodies. Ball games foster agility and speed while also promoting friendship among the players. Javelin throwing, on the other hand, is very useful for competition and military training. But I always admire the men who throw the discus or the spear over great distances.

Statilia: *Ita est, Luci, iaculum ad proelium maxime aptum est. Cerno saepe viros qui diu iaculum in campo iaciunt, ut dexteritatem suam in proelio augeant. Ipsa tamen longum spatium in cursu praefero, qui vires militares simul cum perseverantia comprobare potest.*

Statilia: That's right, Lucius, the javelin is especially suited for battle. I often see men throwing the javelin in the field for a long time to improve their skill in combat. As for me, I prefer long-distance running, which tests both military strength and endurance.

Lucius: *Cursus longus, ut bene dicis, est optimus ad virtutes et ad animi tenaciam exercendas. Fortitudo in cursu semper probatur, praesertim si homo longum spatium sine lassitudine superet. Sed dic mihi, Statilia, num saepe in Campo Martio venire consuevisti?*

Lucius: Long-distance running, as you say, is excellent for exercising virtues and mental toughness. Strength is always tested in running, especially if a person can cover a long distance without tiring. But tell me, Statilia, do you often come to the Field of Mars?

Statilia: *Saepissime! Nihil melius est quam corpus agile et validum servare. Utique, post diuturnam sedentariam vitam in urbe, huc advenio, ut verum laborem sentiam. Et tu, Luci? Quotiensne ad hunc locum reverti soles?*

Statilia: Very often! There is nothing better than maintaining a body that is agile and strong. Of course, after a long sedentary life in the city, I come here to feel real physical effort. And you, Lucius? How often do you come to this place?

Lucius: *Ego quidem cotidie, si licet, huc venio. Exerceor enim non solum corporis causa, sed etiam ut militaria officia semper prompta et parata teneam. Nam, ut scis, Romano viro semper ad bellum paratum esse oportet.*

Lucius: As for me, I come here daily, if possible. I exercise not only for my body's sake but also to always keep my military duties ready and prepared. For, as you know, a Roman man must always be prepared for war.

Statilia: *Sapiens es, Luci. Non solum ad virtutem sed etiam ad provinciam Romanam defendendam corpus et animus semper praeparandus est. Spero ut semper in viribus et valetudine maneamus.*

Statilia: You are wise, Lucius. Both body and mind must always be prepared not only for virtue but also for defending the Roman province. I hope we always remain strong and healthy.

Lucius: *Bene optas, Statilia. Vale nunc, et in viribus et in honore semper manebis!*

Lucius: You wish well, Statilia. Farewell now, and may you always remain strong and honorable!

Statilia: *Vale, Luci! Et utinam semper ad virtutem progressum habeamus!*

Statilia: Farewell, Lucius! And may we always make progress toward virtue!

De Historia Urbis Romae – Sermo de urbis Romae historia

Servilia: *Salve, Calpurni! Saepe de urbis Romae initiis cogito, praesertim quomodo tam parva urbs ad tantam imperii magnitudinem creverit. Dic mihi, quid tibi videtur, quae sunt primariae causae progressus huius civitatis?*

Servilia: Hello, Calpurnius! I often think about the beginnings of the city of Rome, especially how such a small city grew to the vast size of an empire. Tell me, what do you think, what are the primary causes of this city's progress?

Calpurnius: *Salve, Servilia! Non sine causa te haec movent. Initia Romae, ut nostri historici referunt, minima quidem fuerunt, sed virtus et industria maiorum nostrorum civitatem tamquam flamma per totam Italiam et denique orbem terrarum auxerunt. Ut aedificium ex solidis fundamentis oritur, sic Roma virtute, iustitia, et bellorum disciplina crevit.*

Calpurnius: Hello, Servilia! Your thoughts are well-founded. Rome's beginnings, as our historians recount, were indeed small, but the virtue and diligence of our ancestors spread the city like a flame throughout all of Italy and, ultimately, the entire world. Just as a building rises from solid foundations, so Rome grew through virtue, justice, and the discipline of war.

Servilia: *Bene meministi, Calpurni! Legendum est de Romulo et Remo, qui ipsam urbem condiderunt, sed etiam de Sabinis et regibus primis, qui consilia civitatis firmaverunt. Mirum est quomodo, inter tanta bella et discordias, Roma semper progressa sit.*

Servilia: You remember well, Calpurnius! We must recall Romulus and Remus, who founded the city itself, but also the Sabines and the first kings, who solidified the plans of the state. It's remarkable how, amid so many wars and conflicts, Rome always advanced.

Calpurnius: *Ita est. Romulus primus non solum urbem condidit, sed etiam senatum instituit, qui consilium et auctoritatem Romae perpetuo servaret. Post eum, reges Romani, ut Numa et Servius Tullius, non minus prudentia quam fortitudine urbem confirmarunt. Mihi quidem videtur res* *publica Romana primum ex mixtura regiae potestatis et populi virtutis profectam esse.*

Calpurnius: That's right. Romulus not only founded the city, but also established the Senate, which would perpetually maintain the counsel and authority of Rome. After him, the Roman kings, like Numa and Servius Tullius, strengthened the city not less with wisdom than with courage. It seems to me that the Roman Republic first arose from a blend of royal power and the virtue of the people.

Servilia: *Numa Pompilius profecit quidem religionem inter cives Romanos collocare, quod magna pars stabilitatis fuit. Sed post reges, mihi videtur Roma veram gloriam sub re publica adeptam esse. Quid censes de temporibus post Tarquinium Superbum?*

Servilia: Numa Pompilius indeed succeeded in establishing religion among the Roman citizens, which was a great part of stability. But after the kings, it seems to me that Rome achieved its true glory under the Republic. What do you think about the times after Tarquin the Proud?

Calpurnius: *Fines regiae cum Tarquinio Superbo clausi sunt, et, profecto, res publica nata est ex cupiditate libertatis, quae cives incitavit ut sibi ipsis imperarent. Brutus et Collatinus primi consules non solum tyrannidem finiverunt, sed etiam posteris exemplum praeclarum praebuerunt. Bella cum Etruscis, Gallis, et Samnitibus, quae postea secuta sunt, magno industriae et fortitudinis testimonio fuerunt.*

Calpurnius: The royal power ended with Tarquin the Proud, and indeed, the Republic was born out of the desire for freedom, which inspired the citizens to rule themselves. Brutus and Collatinus, the first consuls, not only ended tyranny but also provided a great example for future generations. The wars with the Etruscans, Gauls, and Samnites, which followed, were a great testimony to Roman diligence and courage.

Servilia: *Quam fortunati fuerunt Romani illi consules! Virtute eorum et armis civitas tutata est. Post multos annos, cum Hannibale bellum Punicum gessimus, res tamen difficillima fuit. Sed dic mihi, Calpurni, quid de Scipione Africano putas? Nonne ille Romam servavit in ultima necessitate?*

Servilia: How fortunate were those Roman consuls! Through their virtue and arms, the city was protected. Many years later, when we fought the Punic War against Hannibal, the situation was extremely difficult. But tell me, Calpurnius, what do you think of Scipio Africanus? Didn't he save Rome in its greatest crisis?

Calpurnius: *Scipio Africanus, sine dubio, fuit unus ex summis ducibus Romae. Hannibal ipse, quamvis in bello mirabilis esset, tandem Romana industria et Scipionis ingenio superatus est. Pugna apud Zamam finem attulit Hannibalis victoriis et imperium maris Mediterranei Romae asseruit. Illa quidem tempora Punicis bellis finem posuerunt et dominationem Romae in totum orbem definirent.*

Calpurnius: Scipio Africanus, without a doubt, was one of Rome's greatest generals. Hannibal himself, though he was remarkable in war, was ultimately defeated by Roman diligence and Scipio's genius. The Battle of Zama brought an end to Hannibal's victories and secured Rome's control of the Mediterranean. Those times indeed marked the end of the Punic Wars and defined Rome's domination of the entire world.

Servilia: *Quam grandia haec facta! Et tamen post tam multa bella, res publica non in bellis tantum, sed etiam in legibus et moribus profecit. Quid censes de M. Tullio Cicerone? Nonne eius orationes et prudentia multum ad rem publicam adiuverunt?*

Servilia: How grand these deeds are! And yet, after so many wars, the Republic made progress not only in wars but also in laws and customs. What do you think of Marcus Tullius Cicero? Didn't his speeches and wisdom greatly benefit the Republic?

Calpurnius: *Cicero summum exemplum oratoris et consulis prudentis fuit. Eius orationes contra Catilinam rem publicam ab interitu servaverunt. Et quamquam res publica tunc iam laborare coeperat sub potentia singularum familiarum, Cicero tamen eloquentia sua virtutem et iustitiam semper defendit.*

Calpurnius: Cicero was the highest example of a wise orator and consul. His speeches against Catiline saved the Republic from destruction. And although the Republic was already beginning to struggle under the power of individual families, Cicero always defended virtue and justice with his eloquence.

Servilia: *Bene dixisti. Res publica non solum gladiis, sed etiam verbis et iustitiae studio servata est. Quodcumque futurum sit, semper Romae maiores nostri primam virtutem et sapientiam coluerunt. Vale, Calpurni, et gratias tibi ago pro tanta doctrina.*

Servilia: You've spoken well. The Republic was preserved not only by swords but also by words and a devotion to justice. Whatever the future holds, our ancestors in Rome always upheld virtue and wisdom above all. Farewell, Calpurnius, and thank you for such knowledge.

Calpurnius: *Vale, Servilia! Gaudeo tecum de istis rebus locutus esse, et semper paratus sum ad discendum de nostra gloriosa urbe!*

Calpurnius: Farewell, Servilia! I'm glad to have spoken with you about these matters, and I'm always ready to learn more about our glorious city!

In Athenis – Sermo de visitatione Athenarum

Quintus: *Salve, Iulia! Audivi te nuper Athenas profectam esse. Quid tibi visum est in urbe tam praeclara, ubi sapientiae et philosophiae doctrinae proferuntur?*

Quintus: Hello, Julia! I heard you recently traveled to Athens. What did you think of such a famous city, where teachings of wisdom and philosophy are shared?

Iulia: *Salve, Quinte! Athenae mihi omnium urbium praestantissimae visae sunt. Cum ad illam urbem venissem, magnitudo sui et vetustas mox me occupavit. Templa, porticus, ac ipsi ludi philosophorum omnes animos rerum divinarum plenos fecerunt. Videre ipsa loca ubi Socrates, Plato, et Aristoteles docuerunt... nonne id est quod omnium animum commoveat?*

Iulia: Hello, Quintus! Athens seemed to me the most magnificent of all cities. When I arrived in that city, its grandeur and antiquity soon overwhelmed me. The temples, porticos, and even the teachings of the philosophers filled every mind with thoughts of divine matters. To see the very places where Socrates, Plato, and Aristotle taught... doesn't that stir everyone's heart?

Quintus: *Nullum dubium est, Iulia! Athenae semper fons doctrinae et virtutis fuisse dicuntur. Dic mihi, quid primum te delectavit? Nonne Acropolis ipsa, quae omnium oculos statim rapit?*

Quintus: There's no doubt, Julia! Athens is always said to have been the fountain of learning and virtue. Tell me, what impressed you most at first? Wasn't it the Acropolis itself, which immediately captures everyone's eyes?

Iulia: *Primum quidem Acropolis mihi visa est, sublimis et nitidissima sub solis luce. Templum Parthenon, quod Minervae dicatum est, immota dignitate stabat, omni arte supra modum exornatum. Inter columnas marmoreas ambulans, me quasi ad ipsam aetatem auream Athenarum revocatam esse sentiebam.*

Iulia: The Acropolis was the first thing that struck me, lofty and shining under the sunlight. The Parthenon, dedicated to Minerva, stood with unshakable dignity, adorned with art beyond measure. Walking among its marble columns, I felt as though I had been transported back to Athens' golden age.

Quintus: *Parthenon sine dubio exemplum summum est artis Graecae. Sed quid de philosophis? Num ad Lyceum aut Academiam venisti, ubi sapientes hi ipsi congregabantur?*

Quintus: The Parthenon is without doubt the highest example of Greek art. But what about the philosophers? Did you visit the Lyceum or the Academy, where these wise men themselves used to gather?

Iulia: *Profecto! Ad Lyceum veni, ubi Aristoteles olim discipulos suos docebat. Nunc locus quidem silet, sed vis priscae sapientiae quasi in aere pendet. In Academia Platonis etiam subsistens, mihi videbatur somnium quoddam esse, ut in eis locis essem ubi philosophi tantum genus humanum docuerunt.*

Iulia: Certainly! I went to the Lyceum, where Aristotle used to teach his students. Now the place is silent, but the force of ancient wisdom seems to hang in the air. Standing in Plato's Academy as well, it seemed like a dream to me, to be in the very places where such philosophers taught humanity.

Quintus: *Quam felix es, quod illas praeclaras porticus et gymnasia vidisti! Videtur mihi Athenis non solum sensus, sed etiam animi nutriri. Sed quid de populo Atheniensium? Suntne non minus spectabiles quam urbs ipsa?*

Quintus: How lucky you are to have seen those famous porticoes and gymnasia! It seems to me that in Athens not only the senses but also the soul are nourished. But what about the people of Athens? Are they as impressive as the city itself?

Iulia: *Athenienses mirabili consuetudine et comitate pleni sunt. Graeci sapientia et studiis suis noti sunt, sed etiam hospitibus honores tribuunt. Multos homines ad portum Piraeum conveni, mercatores et nautae ex variis terris, qui commercium agunt et Athenas locum peregrinationis faciunt. Omnia in illa urbe tam varia, tam viva sunt.*

Iulia: The Athenians are full of remarkable hospitality and kindness. The Greeks are known for their wisdom and learning, but they also show great respect to their guests. I met many people at the port of Piraeus—

merchants and sailors from various lands—who trade and make Athens a place of pilgrimage. Everything in that city is so diverse, so lively.

Quintus: *Vere Athenae magnum centrum esse videntur et nationum et doctrinae. Estne aliquid aliud, quod Athenis tibi praecipue in memoria manet?*

Quintus: Truly, Athens seems to be a great center of both nations and learning. Is there anything else that remains especially memorable for you in Athens?

Iulia: *Bene memoriam tenebo theatrum Dionysi, ubi tragoediae et comoediae pro ludis publicis fiebant. Ibi stans, putavi me Euripidem aut Sophoclem ipsos spectaturam esse. Et vidi prope aram Athenienses ipsos honori deorum sacrificia facientes. Tanta erat reverentia cum artibus et diis coniuncta, ut Athenae vere domus sapientiae et pietatis visae sint.*

Iulia: I will surely remember the Theater of Dionysus, where tragedies and comedies were performed as public games. Standing there, I felt as if I were about to watch Euripides or Sophocles themselves. I also saw Athenians offering sacrifices to honor the gods near the altar. There was such reverence connected to the arts and the gods that Athens truly seemed like the home of wisdom and piety.

Quintus: *Athenae videntur urbs, ubi omnia — philosophia, ars, et religio — in eundem locum coeunt. Mirum est, quantam auctoritatem et pulchritudinem Graeci per tantum tempus servare potuerunt. Ego ipse iam Athenas videre exopto.*

Quintus: Athens seems to be a city where everything—philosophy, art, and religion—comes together in one place. It's amazing how much authority and beauty the Greeks have been able to preserve for so long. I myself now long to see Athens.

Iulia: *Mirum in modum, Athenae tibi plenas animi laetitia offerent, si umquam eas visitabis. Vale nunc, Quinte, et forsitan aliquando Athenis conveniamus!*

Iulia: Amazingly, Athens will offer you full joy of the spirit if you ever visit. Farewell for now, Quintus, and perhaps we will meet someday in Athens!

Quintus: *Vale, Iulia! Utinam Athenas spectem et earum sapientia fruar!*

Quintus: Farewell, Julia! May I see Athens and enjoy its wisdom!

De Rebus Graecis – De cultura et philosophia Graecorum sermo

Timaeus: *Salve, Terentia! Audivi te nuper de litteris Graecis studiosissimam esse. Quid tibi videtur de doctrinis Graecorum? Nonne ea philosophia et ars maxime excellunt inter omnium gentium culturas?*

Timaeus: Hello, Terentia! I heard that you have recently been very studious about Greek literature. What do you think of the teachings of the Greeks? Isn't their philosophy and art the most excellent among the cultures of all nations?

Terentia: *Salve, Timae! Ita est, mihi quidem videntur Graeci sapientia et artibus omnibus gentibus praeclari fuisse. Philosophi eorum, ut Socrates, Plato, et Aristoteles, rationem scrutantur non modo de humana vita, sed etiam de rebus divinis et mundi natura. Nihil est, ut mihi videtur, quod eorum ingenium non attigit.*

Terentia: Hello, Timaeus! Yes, it seems to me that the Greeks were distinguished above all nations in wisdom and the arts. Their philosophers, such as Socrates, Plato, and Aristotle, investigated reason not only regarding human life but also about divine matters and the nature of the world. There is nothing, it seems to me, that their intellect did not touch upon.

Timaeus: *Recte pronuntias, Terentia. Platoni quidem maximam laudem tribuo, quippe qui ideas ipsas — rerum aeternam formam — meditaretur. Sed et Aristoteles praeclarus est, qui res in singulas partes dispertiit et de cunctis artibus ac scientiis diligenter disputavit. Quid de hoc philosopho sentis?*

Timaeus: You speak rightly, Terentia. I give the greatest praise to Plato, who contemplated the very ideas—the eternal forms of things. But Aristotle is also outstanding, as he divided things into their individual parts and carefully discussed all the arts and sciences. What do you think of this philosopher?

Terentia: *Mihi quidem Aristoteles summam mentem habuisse videtur. Dissertationes eius de rerum causis et principiis tam sunt subtiles et profundae, ut nihil in philosophia excedere possit. Profuit autem non solum in theoria, sed etiam in praxi, quippe qui de rerum naturalium ordinibus atque ethica hominum scripserit. Ego tamen etiam Socraten* *magnopere admiror, qui nihil non interrogavit et suis discipulis semper quaerere imperavit.*

Terentia: It seems to me that Aristotle possessed the highest intellect. His discourses on the causes and principles of things are so subtle and profound that nothing in philosophy can surpass them. Moreover, he was beneficial not only in theory but also in practice, as he wrote about the order of natural things and human ethics. However, I also greatly admire Socrates, who questioned everything and always commanded his disciples to keep asking.

Timaeus: *Quod verum est! Socrates enim, licet nihil se scire dictitaret, omnium mentes scrutatus est et sua methodo interrogandi ad veritatem pervenire conabatur. At dic mihi, Terentia, quid de cultura Graeca ipsa? Nonne etiam in artibus, poesi, atque rerum pulchritudine excellunt?*

Timaeus: That's true! Socrates, though he claimed to know nothing, examined everyone's minds and tried to reach the truth through his method of questioning. But tell me, Terentia, what about Greek culture itself? Don't they also excel in the arts, poetry, and the beauty of things?

Terentia: *Sine dubio, Graeci artem et pulchritudinem summo opere coluerunt. Vide, quaeso, tragoedias Aeschyli, Sophoclis, Euripidis, quae non solum mores humanos scrutantur, sed etiam de deorum et fati potestatibus loquuntur. Et in artibus visualibus quoque summi fuerunt. Templa, sicut Parthenon, et sculpturae ut Fidiae—haec omnia non modo pulchritudinem ostendunt, sed etiam honorem deorum et humanam sapientiam.*

Terentia: Without a doubt, the Greeks held art and beauty in the highest regard. Look, for example, at the tragedies of Aeschylus, Sophocles, and Euripides, which not only examine human behavior but also speak about the powers of the gods and fate. And they were also supreme in the visual arts. Temples like the Parthenon and sculptures like those of Phidias—all of these not only display beauty but also honor the gods and human wisdom.

Timaeus: *Profecto. Artium Graecarum forma et symmetria insignes sunt. Non solum dei in marmorea effigie laudantur, sed etiam ipsa natura et humana figura summa cum ratione exprimuntur. Quid tibi videtur de*

Graecorum theatro? Poetae et spectacula eorum non minus gravitatem quam iucunditatem ferunt.

Timaeus: Indeed. The form and symmetry of Greek arts are remarkable. Not only are the gods praised in marble statues, but also nature and the human form are expressed with the highest sense of reason. What do you think of the Greek theater? Their poets and performances carry as much seriousness as they do entertainment.

Terentia: *Graecum theatrum mihi omnino mirandum est. Non enim levia ludusque sunt spectacula eorum, sed gravia ratione mores et fatalitatem discutiunt. Tragoedias, ut iam dixisti, profundas esse intellegimus; sed etiam comoediae Aristophanis, licet iocosae, tamen de rei publicae et societatis vitiis loquuntur. Nihil est in Graecorum theatro quod animos nostros non excitaret.*

Terentia: The Greek theater is truly something to marvel at. Their performances are not light or frivolous, but they deeply explore human behavior and fate through reason. As you said, the tragedies are profound; but even the comedies of Aristophanes, though humorous, speak about the flaws of the state and society. There is nothing in Greek theater that doesn't stir our spirits.

Timaeus: *Bene verum dicis, Terentia. Graeci omni arte profecerunt, sed etiam in philosophia praecipuam sibi laudem vindicaverunt. Quid censes de Stoicis aut Epicureis? Num aliae philosophiae sunt eorum aemulae?*

Timaeus: You speak truly, Terentia. The Greeks excelled in every art, but they also claimed the highest praise for themselves in philosophy. What do you think of the Stoics or the Epicureans? Are there any other philosophies that rival theirs?

Terentia: *Et Stoici et Epicurei magna cum sapientia suas doctrinas exponunt. Stoici virtutem summum bonum esse iudicant et fato cedendum esse praeceptum habent, dum Epicurei voluptatem, sed non intemperantiam, summum finem hominis statuunt. Amborum sententiae profundae sunt, sed ego Stoicis magis faveo, quippe qui firmissimam mentem et constantiam in adversis proponant.*

Terentia: Both the Stoics and the Epicureans explain their doctrines with great wisdom. The Stoics judge virtue to be the highest good and teach that one must submit to fate, while the Epicureans regard pleasure, though not excess, as the ultimate goal of life. Both schools have profound teachings, but I favor the Stoics more because they propose the firmest mind and constancy in adversity.

Timaeus: *Equidem censeo Stoicos Romanis virtutibus aptissimos esse. Fortitudo eorum et sapiens contemptus doloris nostris moribus congruunt. Sed semper pulchrum est de diversis doctrinis discere et videre quomodo Graeci et Romani una philosophia et arte vitam excoluerint.*

Timaeus: I indeed believe that the Stoics are most suited to Roman virtues. Their strength and wise disregard for pain align with our values. But it is always wonderful to learn about different doctrines and see how the Greeks and Romans have enriched life together through philosophy and art.

Terentia: *Bene dixisti, Timae. Doctrinae Graecae non solum Romam sed totum orbem terrarum inlustraverunt. Sapientia eorum aeterna fama digna est. Vale nunc, et semper de philosophis Graecis mecum loqui gaudebo!*

Terentia: You've spoken well, Timaeus. Greek teachings have illuminated not only Rome but the entire world. Their wisdom is worthy of eternal fame. Farewell for now, and I will always be glad to talk about Greek philosophers with you!

Timaeus: *Vale, Terentia! Etiam ego tibi gratias ago pro huius sermonis iucunditate.*

Timaeus: Farewell, Terentia! I also thank you for the pleasure of this conversation.

De Musica et Poesi – Sermo de musica et poesi

Marcellus: *Salve, Flaccilla! Audivi te nuper de poesi et musica multa cogitare. Utrum magis tibi placet: carmina poetarum an melodiae tibicinum?*

Marcellus: Hello, Flaccilla! I heard you have recently been thinking a lot about poetry and music. Which do you prefer more: the verses of poets or the melodies of flute players?

Flaccilla: *Salve, Marcelle! Ego quidem utrumque magna delectatione amplector. Nihil enim pulchrius est quam verba poetarum musica adiuvare. Si tamen me roges, utrum praeferam, poesis mihi cordi est, quippe quae non solum auditu iucunda sit, sed etiam mentem nostram ad alta et graviora consilia inclinet.*

Flaccilla: Hello, Marcellus! I truly embrace both with great delight. For nothing is more beautiful than to enhance the words of poets with music. But if you were to ask me which I prefer, poetry holds a special place in my heart, as it not only pleases the ear but also inclines our minds toward lofty and weighty thoughts.

Marcellus: *Bene dicis, Flaccilla. Poesis omnino animum ad sapientiam et veras rationes evehit. Cernere possumus quomodo Vergilius in Aeneide non solum bella canat, sed etiam de fato, pietate, et humana fortitudine disserat. Sed quid de musica? Nonne vis ac numerus musicae animos nostros graviter movet?*

Marcellus: You speak well, Flaccilla. Poetry indeed elevates the soul toward wisdom and true reason. We can see how in the *Aeneid*, Virgil not only sings of wars but also discusses fate, piety, and human strength. But what about music? Doesn't the power and rhythm of music deeply move our souls?

Flaccilla: *Non nego, Marcelle. Musica, si modeste et cum arte fit, miras res efficit. Vide quid faciunt citharoedi aut tibicines in conviviis! Ipsi qui adsunt, quamvis sermonibus delectentur, tamen musica plus alliciuntur. Et cum lyra aut cithara carmina poetarum cantantur, quasi deus ipse sonat.*

Flaccilla: I don't deny it, Marcellus. Music, when done with moderation and skill, accomplishes wondrous things. Look at what the lyre players or flute players do at banquets! Those present, though they may enjoy conversation, are even more drawn in by music. And when the verses of poets are sung with a lyre or harp, it's as though a god himself is playing.

Marcellus: *Nihil vere pulchrius est quam carmen apte cum musica iunctum. Sed, ut scias, ego musicam magis ad vitam cotidianam atque ad militarem disciplinam pertinentem admiror. Nonne tibiae in castris et tubarum clangores milites excitant atque ad proelia incitant?*

Marcellus: Nothing is truly more beautiful than a song properly joined with music. But, you should know, I admire music more for its role in daily life and military discipline. Don't the flutes in the camps and the blaring of trumpets stir up soldiers and drive them to battle?

Flaccilla: *Recte meministi, Marcelle. Militariae tibiae et cornua non solum ad ludum sunt, sed milites ipsos ad fidem et fortitudinem vocant. Mirum est quomodo sonus bene moderatus animos hominum tam valde permoveat. Itaque videmus musicam in omnibus vitae partibus suum locum habere.*

Flaccilla: You remember correctly, Marcellus. Military flutes and horns are not just for ceremony, but they call the soldiers themselves to loyalty and courage. It's amazing how a well-controlled sound can move the minds of men so powerfully. Thus, we see that music has its place in all parts of life.

Marcellus: *Cerno te sapientia plenam esse in his rebus, Flaccilla. Sed dic mihi, quis poeta tibi magis placet? Mihi quidem Ovidius maxime delectavit ob suam elegantiam et facilitatem in verbis exprimendis. Sicut fluvius verborum fluit, ita et carmina sua animos nostros implent.*

Marcellus: I see that you are full of wisdom in these matters, Flaccilla. But tell me, which poet do you like the most? For me, Ovid has delighted me the most for his elegance and ease in expressing words. Just as a river of words flows, so too do his poems fill our hearts.

Flaccilla: *Ovidius quidem mirabilis est, praesertim cum de amore et natura humana loquitur. Sed ego praefero Catullum, qui brevibus verbis acutissimas rationes et emotiones exprimere potest. Nihil tam simplex videtur, sed multa in brevitate latent. Et cum carmina Catulli musica canuntur, quasi musica et poesis unum efficiunt corpus.*

Flaccilla: Ovid is indeed marvelous, especially when he speaks of love and human nature. But I prefer Catullus, who can express the sharpest thoughts and emotions with just a few words. Nothing seems so simple, but much is hidden in brevity. And when Catullus' poems are sung with music, it's as if music and poetry form one body.

Marcellus: *Catullus profecto sensus sublimes habet. Cum legas illa verba de Lesbia, cernis amoris et doloris profunditatem. Sed etiam Horatius mihi videtur dignus, qui philosophiae et sapientiae doctrinam cum ludo atque gratia iungat. Carmina sua saepe, sicut musica levis, animos serenant.*

Marcellus: Catullus certainly has sublime sentiments. When you read those words about Lesbia, you perceive the depth of love and sorrow. But I also think Horace is worthy, as he joins the teachings of philosophy and wisdom with playfulness and grace. His poems often, like gentle music, calm the soul.

Flaccilla: *Horatius certe solide ac sapienter loquitur, praesertim cum de moderatione vitae et fato loquitur. Nihil superfluum, nihil nimium; omnia suo modo temperata. Carmina eius non solum animum sed etiam mentem pascunt. Vides ut poesis et musica simul ad omnem vitam pertineant.*

Flaccilla: Horace certainly speaks solidly and wisely, especially when he talks about moderation in life and fate. Nothing is excessive, nothing is lacking; everything is balanced in its own way. His poems nourish not only the soul but also the mind. You see how poetry and music together pertain to all aspects of life.

Marcellus: *Ita est, Flaccilla. Musica et poesis omni tempore nostram animam alunt atque ad vivendum sapienter et iucunde nos hortantur. Vale nunc, et gaudeo tecum de his pulcherrimis rebus collocutam esse!*

Marcellus: That's right, Flaccilla. Music and poetry nourish our souls at all times and encourage us to live wisely and joyfully. Farewell for now, and I'm glad to have spoken with you about these most beautiful things!

Flaccilla: *Vale, Marcelle! Semper iucundum est de artibus et poetis loqui. Utinam musica et poesis vitam tuam semper iucundam faciant!*

Flaccilla: Farewell, Marcellus! It's always a pleasure to talk about the arts and poets. May music and poetry always make your life joyful!

In Foro Romano Post Mortem Caesaris – De rebus post Caesaris necem

Aemilius: *Salve, Tullia! Romam hodie subito turbatam esse cernis. Post mortem Gaii Caesaris, omnia in urbe versantur. Nullus senatus, nulla plebs quieta est. Quid tu de his rebus censes?*

Aemilius: Hello, Tullia! You see how Rome is suddenly thrown into chaos today. After the death of Gaius Caesar, everything in the city is in turmoil. The Senate is in disarray, and the common people are not at peace. What do you think of these events?

Tullia: *Salve, Aemili! Causa profecto gravissima est. Mors Caesaris non solum virum, sed spem imperii subvertit. Multi ei favebant, multi eum oderant. Nunc Roma ipsa scinditur. Audivistine quae dicta sunt de Bruto et Cassio? Aiunt eos pro libertate id fecisse, sed plures metum et periculum videre coeperunt.*

Tullia: Hello, Aemilius! The cause is indeed a serious one. Caesar's death has not only taken a man but also shaken the hope of the empire. Many favored him, and many hated him. Now Rome itself is divided. Have you heard what's been said about Brutus and Cassius? They claim to have acted for liberty, but more and more people are starting to see fear and danger ahead.

Aemilius: *Audivi, et nescio an vere libertatem restituere voluerint aut propriis cupiditatibus impulsi id fecerint. Caesaris imperium multis iniustum visum est, sed ipse quoque, ut dicitur, consilia Romae magnifica proposuerat. Nonne populus eum amabat? Nonne multa bona in urbem et foras attulit?*

Aemilius: I've heard, and I don't know whether they truly wanted to restore liberty or were driven by their own desires. Caesar's rule seemed unjust to many, but he also, as it is said, had grand plans for Rome. Didn't the people love him? Didn't he bring many benefits to the city and beyond?

Tullia: *Ita est. Plebs, praesertim, eum magnopere amabat. Donos et cibos saepe largitus est, et victorias magnas reportavit. Non ignoro autem senatores et nobiles eum timuisse. Eius potestas nimium* *constantem rei publicae ordinem vertebat, ut existimabant. Sed nunc, quid expectandum est? Bellum civile?*

Tullia: Yes, indeed. The common people, especially, loved him greatly. He often gave out gifts and food, and he won great victories. But I understand that the senators and nobles feared him. His power seemed to overturn the stable order of the republic, or so they believed. But now, what can we expect? Civil war?

Aemilius: *Bellum civile quidem timendum videtur. Cum Octavianus, qui Caesari suffectus est, et Marcus Antonius contra Brutum et Cassium consurgant, certe erit sanguinem domi fundi. Nullum diem sine tumultu videre potuimus post Caesaris mortem. Roma iam tandem in discordiam prolapsa est.*

Aemilius: A civil war certainly seems to be feared. With Octavian, who has succeeded Caesar, and Mark Antony rising against Brutus and Cassius, there will surely be bloodshed at home. We haven't seen a day without turmoil since Caesar's death. Rome has now finally fallen into discord.

Tullia: *Si hoc bellum exardescet, nescio quomodo Roma salvari possit. Duo omnino exercitus in urbe non valent. Quid putas de Octaviano? Multi eum cognatu Caesaris sequi incipiunt, sed ipse adhuc iuvenis est.*

Tullia: If this war ignites, I don't know how Rome can be saved. Two armies in the city cannot stand together. What do you think of Octavian? Many are beginning to follow him as Caesar's heir, but he is still young.

Aemilius: *Octavianus, quamvis iuvenis sit, ingenium acutum habere videtur. Imperatoris dignitatem proponere cernitur, et Marcus Antonius eum ut detractabilem aut facile deludendum minime putat. Sed, Tullia, quid de Bruto censes? Fuit enim amicus Caesaris, tamen manum contra eum sustulit.*

Aemilius: Octavian, though young, seems to have sharp intelligence. He is seen as aiming for the dignity of an emperor, and Mark Antony certainly does not consider him weak or easily deceived. But, Tullia, what do you think of Brutus? He was Caesar's friend, yet he raised his hand against him.

Tullia: *Quid dicam, Aemili? Brutus non tantum propter Caesarem agebat, sed pro Romae libertate, ut sibi persuasit. Ego tamen nescio utrum senatores ipsi fidem habuerint aut, ut saepe fit, cupiditate propriae auctoritatis ducti sint. Brutus et Cassius, quamquam verbis pulchris locuti sunt, post tantum facinus aequa culpa tenentur.*

Tullia: What can I say, Aemilius? Brutus did not act solely because of Caesar but for the liberty of Rome, or so he convinced himself. However, I don't know if the senators themselves were sincere or, as often happens, were driven by their own thirst for power. Brutus and Cassius, though they spoke beautiful words, are equally guilty after such a deed.

Aemilius: *Sapiens es, Tullia. Verba de libertate saepe dicuntur, sed post hanc mortem non tam libertatem quam potentiam quaesiverunt. Nunc nos in media rerum versamur, et ignoramus quid ex hoc tumultu nascetur. Forsitan nova res publica surgat, aut rursus tyrannis.*

Aemilius: You are wise, Tullia. Words about liberty are often spoken, but after this death, it seems they sought power more than freedom. Now we find ourselves in the midst of things, and we do not know what will arise from this turmoil. Perhaps a new republic will emerge, or tyranny will return.

Tullia: *Utinam Roma meliores dies videat! Sed timeo ne discordia civitatem nostram ad ultimum exitium ducat. Vale, Aemili, et speremus ut dis placitum sit Romam servare.*

Tullia: I hope that Rome will see better days! But I fear that discord will lead our city to its ultimate ruin. Farewell, Aemilius, and let us hope that it pleases the gods to save Rome.

Aemilius: *Vale, Tullia! Si fata sinant, res Romana iterum in pace stabit.*

Aemilius: Farewell, Tullia! If the fates allow, the Roman state will stand again in peace.

De Rebus Aegyptiis – Sermo de Aegypto et eius cultura

Severus: *Salve, Drusiana! Nuper ex Aegypto redii, et necesse est tibi de illa praeclara terra narrare. Mihi profecto videtur Aegyptus inter omnium gentium mirabilissimas esse. Quid tu de Aegyptiis et eorum cultura audivisti?*

Severus: Hello, Drusiana! I recently returned from Egypt, and I must tell you about that remarkable land. To me, Egypt seems one of the most wondrous nations of all. What have you heard about the Egyptians and their culture?

Drusiana: *Salve, Severe! Ego quoque multa de Aegyptiorum sapientia et rituum antiquitate audivi. Videmus templis et monumentis eorum nihil esse simile in toto orbe. Dic mihi, quid primum te Aegyptiis delectavit?*

Drusiana: Hello, Severus! I too have heard much about the wisdom of the Egyptians and the ancient nature of their rituals. We see that nothing in the world compares to their temples and monuments. Tell me, what first delighted you about the Egyptians?

Severus: *Mihi primum oculos rapuit magnitudo et altitudo pyramidum. Vidi pyramidem Cheopis, quae ad caelum prope surgere videtur! Structura ipsa tanta aetate, tot saeculis, immota stetit. Non modo magnitudinem sed etiam artem eorum cogitavi. Quis non stupefactus esset?*

Severus: What first caught my eye was the magnitude and height of the pyramids. I saw the Pyramid of Cheops, which seems to rise up to the sky! The structure itself has stood immovable for such a great age, through so many centuries. I thought not only of their size but also of their artistry. Who wouldn't be astounded?

Drusiana: *Vere dicis, Severe. Pyramides semper admirationem excitant. Sed audivi etiam de deis Aegyptiis, qui ritibus et sacris praeclarissimi sunt. Num templum Isidis vidisti? Aiunt eam apud Aegyptios maxime coli.*

Drusiana: You speak truly, Severus. The pyramids always inspire awe. But I have also heard about the Egyptian gods, who are renowned for their rites and ceremonies. Did you see the Temple of Isis? They say she is worshiped most highly among the Egyptians.

Severus: *Sane, templum Isidis Alexandriae visum est mihi. Omnia illic maxima cum sollemnitate administrantur. Sacerdotes albis vestibus induti, fumo suffimentorum divitissimo deam honorant. Quid dicam de mysteriis? Ipsi Aegyptii mihi dixerunt tantam venerationem habere ut Isidem reginam caeli putent.*

Severus: Indeed, I saw the Temple of Isis in Alexandria. Everything there is carried out with the greatest solemnity. The priests, dressed in white robes, honor the goddess with the richest incense smoke. What can I say about the mysteries? The Egyptians themselves told me they hold such great reverence for Isis that they consider her the queen of heaven.

Drusiana: *Iuste faciunt, cum tanta res sit consociata cum dea sua. Sed, Severe, quid de flumine Nilo? Audivi eum omnium rerum principem esse in Aegyptiorum vita. Num prospexisti flumen ipsum?*

Drusiana: Rightly so, given how much is connected with their goddess. But, Severus, what about the Nile River? I've heard that it is the source of everything in Egyptian life. Did you see the river itself?

Severus: *O, Drusiana, Nilus ipsa vita Aegypti est! Omnes agricolae, mercatores, et cives ad Nilum suas spes adiungunt. Ubi Nilus fluctus et aquas praebet, omnia vigent; ubi non, fames et egestas sequuntur. Videbam navigia plena frumenti et homines flumini ipsi quasi deo sacrificia offerentes. Ritus aquarum certe sacer est apud Aegyptios.*

Severus: Oh, Drusiana, the Nile is the very life of Egypt! All farmers, merchants, and citizens tie their hopes to the Nile. When the Nile provides its waters and floods, everything flourishes; when it does not, famine and poverty follow. I saw boats full of grain and people offering sacrifices to the river as if it were a god. The rituals of the waters are certainly sacred among the Egyptians.

Drusiana: *Quam diversa haec vita ab nostra Romana videtur! Atque tamen puto Aegyptum sapientia eorum et doctrinis praeclaram esse. Aiunt Aegyptios astrorum scientiam maximam habere. Num aliquid de astrologia aut mathematicis audivisti?*

Drusiana: How different this life seems from our Roman one! And yet, I believe that Egypt is renowned for its wisdom and teachings. They say the Egyptians have great knowledge of the stars. Did you hear anything about astrology or mathematics?

Severus: *Ita vero! Aegyptii sunt peritissimi in scrutandis caeli motibus. Vidi observatoria, ubi sacerdotes stellas per multa saecula notaverunt. Inde annos et menses certissime diviserunt. Tempora sacra, propitiationes, et omnes ritus ad caeli cursus accommodant. Putant enim caelo regi non solum vitam, sed et fatum singulorum hominum.*

Severus: Indeed! The Egyptians are highly skilled in observing the movements of the sky. I saw observatories where priests have recorded the stars for many centuries. From this, they have divided the years and months with great precision. They align sacred times, offerings, and all their rituals with the course of the heavens. For they believe that not only life but also the fate of each individual is governed by the stars.

Drusiana: *Quantus honor est eis qui caelum tale contemplantur! Mihi quidem videtur Aegyptus locum sapientiae et rerum occultarum esse. Putasne etiam reges eorum, ut Ptolemaeus aut Cleopatra, hanc doctrinam secutos esse?*

Drusiana: What an honor it must be for those who contemplate the heavens like that! It seems to me that Egypt is a place of wisdom and mysteries. Do you think that even their rulers, like Ptolemy or Cleopatra, followed this teaching?

Severus: *Certe! Cleopatra ipsa dicitur non solum pulchritudine, sed etiam ingenio summo praeclara fuisse. Multi philosophi Alexandriam venerunt ut cum ea colloquerentur. Nec mirum est, cum Aegyptus ipsa sit quasi centrum omnium doctrinarum Orientis et Occidentis. Philosophia, rerum naturalium scrutatio, deorum cultus—omnia in Aegypto unum efficiunt.*

Severus: Certainly! Cleopatra herself is said to have been famous not only for her beauty but also for her great intellect. Many philosophers came to Alexandria to speak with her. And it's no wonder, as Egypt itself is like the center of all the teachings of the East and West. Philosophy, the study of natural things, the worship of gods—all come together in Egypt.

Drusiana: *Vere res mirabiles narras, Severe. Mihi nunc magis magisque Aegyptum videre et discere desiderium est. Tanta varietas in illa terra et sapientia, ut Roma ipsa eos non contemnere possit.*

Drusiana: Truly, you tell amazing things, Severus. Now I have an even greater desire to see and learn about Egypt. There is such variety and wisdom in that land that even Rome cannot look down on them.

Severus: *Sane, Drusiana. Etsi Roma imperium tenet, multa ab Aegyptiis discere possumus. Vale igitur, et si umquam in Aegyptum iter facias, certe me certiorem fac!*

Severus: Certainly, Drusiana. Even though Rome holds the empire, we can still learn much from the Egyptians. Farewell then, and if you ever make a journey to Egypt, be sure to let me know!

Drusiana: *Vale, Severe! Spero me aliquando eandem terram mirabilem visuram esse!*

Drusiana: Farewell, Severus! I hope that someday I will see that wondrous land myself!

In Amphitheatro Flavio – De spectaculis in Colosseo

Marcia: *Salve, Celer! Vix credere possum hodie me in Amphitheatro Flavio sedere, ubi tot milia hominum spectacula magnifica cernunt. Quid exspectas? Certamina gladiatorum tibi magis placent, an venationes?*

Marcia: Hello, Celer! I can hardly believe that today I am sitting in the Flavian Amphitheater, where thousands of people witness magnificent spectacles. What are you looking forward to? Do you prefer gladiator fights or the wild beast hunts?

Celer: *Salve, Marcia! Utrumque genus spectaculi mihi placet, sed gladiatores magnopere admiror, quippe qui cum animo et arte pugnare sciunt. Venationes autem magnificae sunt cum feris bestiis, quas Roma ex Africa aut Asia importat. Sed vide, Marcia! Iam signum datum est, et gladiatores armati in arenam prodeunt!*

Celer: Hello, Marcia! I enjoy both types of spectacle, but I greatly admire the gladiators, as they know how to fight with courage and skill. The hunts are also magnificent, especially with the wild beasts that Rome imports from Africa or Asia. But look, Marcia! The signal has been given, and the armed gladiators are entering the arena!

Marcia: *Ecce, quam fortes et decori sunt! Multi quidem ex eis videntur viri liberi fuisse, sed nunc gladium pro vita sua ferunt. Quid censes de hac re? Num dignum est, homines tam praeclaros inter se pugnare ad mortem?*

Marcia: Look, how strong and dignified they are! Many of them seem to have once been free men, but now they bear the sword for their lives. What do you think of this? Is it right for such noble men to fight each other to the death?

Celer: *Res haud facilis est iudicando. Fortasse quidam indigni sunt eo certamine, sed milites aut gladiatores arte pugnae praeclari sunt. Mirabile est quomodo fortitudo et virtus eorum in pugna emineat. Et ne obliviscamur populum, qui semper delectatur victoriis ac mortibus eorum in arena.*

Celer: It's not easy to judge. Perhaps some are unworthy of this combat, but soldiers and gladiators are renowned for their fighting skill. It's amazing how their courage and virtue shine in battle. And let's not forget the people, who always delight in their victories and deaths in the arena.

Marcia: *Ita est. Nullus tamen me magis movet quam ille retiarius, qui cum fusili et rete armatus stat. Videsne quo modo ad impetum securus et sine pavore praeparatur? Constat eum saepe vicisse.*

Marcia: That's true. But no one impresses me more than that *retiarius*, who stands armed with a trident and a net. Do you see how calmly and fearlessly he prepares for an attack? It's said that he's won many times.

Celer: *Non solum arte sed etiam consilio pugnat. Gladiatorum generibus variis Roma non solum vires sed ingenium quoque exigit. Atque specta, quomodo adversarius eius, murmillo, mature scuto et gladio movetur! Certamen hoc haud dubie memorabile erit.*

Celer: He fights not only with skill but also with strategy. In the various types of gladiators, Rome demands not just strength but also intelligence. And look, how his opponent, the *murmillo*, moves swiftly with his shield and sword! This will no doubt be a memorable contest.

Marcia: *Iam audivi multos principes et senatores his ludis delectari, nec non ipse imperator saepe adsidet. Quid tu censes, Celer? Qua re tanta multitudo in his ludis gaudeat?*

Marcia: I've heard that many nobles and senators enjoy these games, and even the emperor often attends. What do you think, Celer? Why do so many people take pleasure in these spectacles?

Celer: *Populus Romanus semper bellosas res admiratur. Bella, victoriae, mortes—haec omnia partem magni imperii significant. Quotiens gladiatores aut bestiae pugnant, Roma ipsa, ut ita dicam, in arena triumphat. Hic locus non tantum delectationis, sed etiam pro certa victoria et honore est.*

Celer: The Roman people have always admired warlike things. Battles, victories, deaths—all of these symbolize the greatness of the empire. Whenever gladiators or beasts fight, Rome itself, so to speak, triumphs in the arena. This place is not only for entertainment but also for certain victory and honor.

Marcia: *Vere dicis, et tamen interdum cogito, quid sentiant illi qui pugnare coguntur. Nonne alii spem habent liberandi se, si satis vires in certamine ostenderint?*

Marcia: You speak truly, and yet I sometimes wonder what those forced to fight must feel. Don't some hope for their freedom if they show enough strength in combat?

Celer: *Ita est. Multi gladiatores spem habent, si bene pugnaverint et gratiam populi aut imperatoris adepti fuerint, se ad libertatem perventuros esse. Non pauci ex servis liberati sunt, qui multa in arena proelia superaverunt. Est quidam gloria in eo pugnare, sed periculum semper imminet.*

Celer: That's right. Many gladiators hope that if they fight well and gain the favor of the people or the emperor, they will achieve freedom. Quite a few former slaves have been freed after winning many battles in the arena. There is a certain glory in fighting, but danger always looms.

Marcia: *Vide! Proelium iam incipit. Quam ferox est murmillo cum scuto et gladio! Sed retiarius celeriter movetur, et rete ad hostem iacit. Nunc suspensi sumus! Utrum vincet?*

Marcia: Look! The fight is starting. How fierce the *murmillo* is with his shield and sword! But the *retiarius* moves quickly and throws his net at his opponent. Now we're on edge! Who will win?

Celer: *Res incertae sunt! Gladiatorum certamen saepe exspectationem praevenit. Sed hoc sciamus: utrumque eorum fortissime agere et populum laudes dare non cessare. Quidquid fiat, spectaculum hoc diu memorabimus.*

Celer: The outcome is uncertain! Gladiator contests often defy expectations. But one thing we know: both are fighting with great courage, and the crowd never ceases to cheer. Whatever happens, we will remember this spectacle for a long time.

Marcia: *Ita vero, Celer. Hoc amphitheatrum non solum est locus ubi virium et virtutis testimonia dantur, sed etiam ubi fortuna et fatum in oculis nostris manifestantur. Vale igitur, et spero ut semper talia certamina cum vi et sapientia spectes!*

Marcia: Indeed, Celer. This amphitheater is not only a place where strength and courage are displayed but also where fate and fortune manifest themselves before our eyes. Farewell then, and I hope you always watch such contests with both strength and wisdom!

Celer: *Vale, Marcia! Utinam semper fortuna in arena Romanorum animos erigat et gloriam augeat!*

Celer: Farewell, Marcia! May fortune always lift the spirits of the Romans in the arena and increase their glory!

De Thermae Constructione – Sermo de aedificatione thermarum Romanarum

Agrippa: *Salve, Larcia! Audivi te promississe novas thermas in urbe aedificaturas esse. Valde admiratione teneor, nam thermarum aedificatio ars magna est, et multum decoris et usus in se continet. Quid iam progressi estis?*

Agrippa: Hello, Larcia! I heard that you have promised to build new baths in the city. I am filled with admiration, for building baths is a great art, and it contains much beauty and utility. How far have you progressed?

Larcia: *Salve, Agrippa! Ita est, thermas magnificas in mente habeo, quae non solum ad lavandum sed etiam ad conveniendum et discendum aptae erunt. Architecti iam loca elegerunt, et fundamenta iaciuntur. Proximae thermis erunt palaestrae et bibliothecae, ut non solum corporibus, sed etiam animis serviamus.*

Larcia: Hello, Agrippa! Yes, I have in mind magnificent baths, which will not only be suitable for bathing but also for meeting and learning. The architects have already chosen the locations, and the foundations are being laid. Next to the baths, there will be gymnasiums and libraries, so that we may serve not only the bodies but also the minds.

Agrippa: *Admirabile propositum! Nihil pulchrius Romanis civibus quam thermarum conventus, ubi lavatur, exercetur, atque interdum philosophiae aut orationi vacatur. Sed dic mihi, qua ratione aquae tam multa et varia loca implebuntur? Scis quantae copiae aquarum ad thermas maximas requirantur.*

Agrippa: Admirable plan! There is nothing more beautiful for Roman citizens than gathering at the baths, where they bathe, exercise, and sometimes engage in philosophy or public speaking. But tell me, how will so many different areas be supplied with water? You know how vast the water supply must be for the largest baths.

Larcia: *Bene quaeris, Agrippa. Curabimus ut aquaeductus aucti et emendati efficiantur, qui ex montibus circumiectis aquam perducant. Thermae ipsae habebunt alveos marmoreos et hypocaustum novissimis modis adhibitum, ut calores ad omnes partes aeque ferantur. Nihil nisi summae artis mechanicae adhibebitur.*

Larcia: Good question, Agrippa. We will ensure that the aqueducts are expanded and improved to bring water from the surrounding mountains. The baths themselves will have marble basins and a hypocaust system implemented with the latest techniques, so that heat will be distributed equally to all areas. Nothing but the finest mechanical craftsmanship will be used.

Agrippa: *Hypocaustum recte meministi, Larcia. Nihil tantum ad voluptatem ac commoditatem quam caliditas bene per omnes locos diffusa. Et certe marmora et munimenta lapidea erunt in summo decore, ut convivae thermarum magnitudinem loci ipsi sentiant. Quid tamen de ornatu? Aiunt thermas non solum ad corpus fovendum sed etiam ad oculos animosque alliciendos esse.*

Agrippa: You rightly remembered the hypocaust, Larcia. Nothing adds as much to pleasure and comfort as heat well distributed throughout all areas. And certainly, the marble and stone structures will be of the highest beauty, so that visitors to the baths will feel the grandeur of the place. But what about decoration? They say that the baths are not only for caring for the body but also for delighting the eyes and the mind.

Larcia: *Profecto, Agrippa! Marmora et mosaica variis coloribus ex toto imperio afferentur. In caldario et tepidario videbuntur depictae scenae ex fabulis heroum, ut Achilles aut Hercules, ut homines non solum ad corporis curam sed etiam ad exempla virtutis animarentur. Statuae praeclarae deorum quoque instituentur, ut Minervae et Neptuni, qui aquis favet.*

Larcia: Certainly, Agrippa! Marble and mosaics in various colors will be brought from all over the empire. In the hot and warm baths, scenes from the legends of heroes like Achilles or Hercules will be displayed, so that people will be inspired not only to care for their bodies but also by examples of virtue. There will also be splendid statues of the gods, like Minerva and Neptune, who favors the waters.

Agrippa: *Admirabile consilium, Larcia. Mihi quidem videtur thermas tuas non solum ad corporum renovationem, sed etiam ad maiestatem urbis augendam magnopere profuturas esse. Quis enim non delectabitur tam pulcherrimo loco, ubi artes et otium in unum confluunt?*

Agrippa: A marvelous plan, Larcia. It seems to me that your baths will not only serve to refresh the body but also to greatly enhance the majesty of the city. Who would not be delighted by such a beautiful place, where art and leisure flow together?

Larcia: *Ita spero, Agrippa. Nam curas mihi magnas facio ut thermas non solum divitibus sed etiam plebi propitias efficiam. Omnibus gradibus hominum locus fiet ad communem rem et consentaneam vitam habendam. Regulae temperatae erunt, et pretium accedendi modicum, ut thermae idem populi atque nobilitatis sedes sint.*

Larcia: I hope so, Agrippa. I am making great efforts to ensure that the baths will be favorable not only to the wealthy but also to the common people. There will be a place for people of all social classes to gather and live in harmony. The rules will be moderate, and the entrance fee will be modest, so that the baths will serve as a place for both the people and the nobility.

Agrippa: *Tua prudentia et humanitas maximam laudem merentur, Larcia. Nihil enim aptius urbis statu quam locus ubi omnis civitas ad eundem usum conveniat. Valde exspecto ut has thermas cernam perfectas et ad studia omnia paratas.*

Agrippa: Your wisdom and humanity deserve the highest praise, Larcia. Nothing is more fitting for the state of the city than a place where the entire community can come together for the same purpose. I eagerly await seeing these baths completed and ready for all activities.

Larcia: *Gratias tibi ago, Agrippa! Profecto de thermarum nostrarum opere optimam curam habebimus. Spero ut brevi te in thermis ipsis videre possim, ut testis sis tantae pulchritudinis. Vale!*

Larcia: Thank you, Agrippa! We will certainly take the greatest care with the work on our baths. I hope to see you soon in the baths themselves, so you may witness such beauty firsthand. Farewell!

Agrippa: *Vale, Larcia! Exspecto diem, cum haec praeclara opera oculis nostris pateant!*

Agrippa: Farewell, Larcia! I look forward to the day when these splendid works will be revealed to our eyes!

De Navigatione et Mercatoribus – Sermo de mercatura Romana maritima

Publius: *Salve, Faustine! Audivi te nuper de navigationibus tuis rediisse. Quid tibi visum est in illis longinquis terris, ubi mercatores Romani tantas opes ex mari conferunt?*

Publius: Hello, Faustinus! I heard that you recently returned from your voyages. What did you think of those distant lands, where Roman merchants gather such wealth from the sea?

Faustinus: *Salve, Publi! Navigatio quidem non semper placida fuit, sed praeda et commoda mercatorum quae ex toto oceano vehuntur, omnia pericula superant. Ex Aegypto Alexandriā frumentum advexi; ibi hominum multitudo et opulentia mirabilis est. Sed veras divitias Asiae et Orientis ibi cognovi.*

Faustinus: Hello, Publius! The voyage was not always calm, but the spoils and profits that merchants bring from across the sea surpass all dangers. I brought grain from Alexandria in Egypt; the multitude of people and the wealth there are remarkable. But it was there that I truly came to know the riches of Asia and the East.

Publius: *Profecto! Alexandria semper mercatorum regina fuisse dicitur. Omnia ibi invenire possis: gemmas, aromata, textilia. Sed dic mihi, Faustine, quomodo mercatores Romani navigatione in tam longinquas regiones progrediuntur? Nonne saevitia maris aut piratae periculum afferunt?*

Publius: Indeed! Alexandria is always called the queen of merchants. You can find everything there: gems, spices, textiles. But tell me, Faustinus, how do Roman merchants venture into such distant regions by sea? Doesn't the fury of the sea or pirates pose a danger?

Faustinus: *Navigatio semper incerta est, praesertim cum longe a litore remigamus. Tempestates multas vidimus, sed naves Romanae bene armatae sunt et gubernatores periti. De piratis quidem audivisti: periculum est. Sed postquam Caesar quondam illos in Ciliciā fudit, minus iam metui solent. Mercatores enim nunc sub imperii protectore navigant, et classes semper circum mare vigilare solent.*

Faustinus: The voyage is always uncertain, especially when we row far from the shore. We saw many storms, but Roman ships are well-armed, and the captains are experienced. You've surely heard of pirates: they are a danger. But since Caesar once defeated them in Cilicia, they are now less feared. Merchants now sail under the protection of the empire, and fleets constantly patrol the sea.

Publius: *Laetitia est audire mare nostrum iam plus tutum esse. Sed quid de variis gentibus, quas in itineribus tuis vidisti? Curabantne eas rem mercatoriam sicut Romani? Quid spectandum tibi praecipue visum est?*

Publius: It's a relief to hear that our sea is now safer. But what about the different peoples you saw on your journeys? Do they handle commerce as the Romans do? What stood out to you the most?

Faustinus: *Multa cernuntur. In Phoeniciā, mercatorii periti homines sunt, praeclari in navigando et negotiis tractandis. In Indiā, gemmae et aromata maxima exornant mercatores, sed mores eorum multo simpliciores quam nostri. Et in Arabiā, ubi multi camelis utuntur, incensum et myrrham semper vehunt. Magnam divitiarum copiam ex his partibus Roma percipit.*

Faustinus: Many things are observed. In Phoenicia, the people are skilled merchants, renowned for their navigation and business dealings. In India, gems and spices adorn the merchants, but their customs are much simpler than ours. And in Arabia, where many use camels, they always transport incense and myrrh. Rome receives a great abundance of wealth from these regions.

Publius: *Mirum est quantae divitiae ad Romam ex illis longinquis locis afferantur. Non miror quod urbs nostra tantis rebus abundet, cum tot terrarum fruges et opes per mare vehantur. Sed nescio, Faustine, num nostra merces illis gentibus tam grata sit. Quae res ex Roma ad eas portatur?*

Publius: It's amazing how much wealth is brought to Rome from those distant places. I'm not surprised that our city is so full of riches when the produce and wealth of so many lands are carried by sea. But I wonder, Faustinus, are our goods as appreciated by those peoples? What do we send from Rome to them?

Faustinus: *Multae res, Publi. Ex urbe nostra et tota Italiā ad Orientem vehi solent vina, oleum, vestes purpureae, atque ferrum et aeneae statuae. Etiam nostri fictiles vasi et laneae stolae inter illos magno in honore sunt. Vides quomodo omnes gentes mercatura efficiantur.*

Faustinus: Many goods, Publius. From our city and all of Italy, we usually send wine, olive oil, purple garments, as well as iron and bronze statues to the East. Even our clay vessels and woolen robes are highly valued among them. You see how all peoples are shaped by commerce.

Publius: *Quam sapienter hoc Romani instituerunt! Nam per merces et communes usus non solum divitiae, sed etiam coniunctio cum externis populis augetur. Num igitur iterum navigare cogitas? An forte satis tibi est cum tanta periculorum varietate?*

Publius: How wisely the Romans have set this up! For through trade and shared commodities, not only wealth but also connections with foreign peoples are strengthened. Are you planning to sail again then? Or have you perhaps had enough of such a variety of dangers?

Faustinus: *Iterum proficiscar, sic res publica et negoti ratio postulant. Quamquam mare pericula semper habet, lucrum et honor mercatoris magnum pretium esse videtur. Sed, si dis placet, secunda navigatio erit. Ad multas gentes iterum eundum est, Publi, ut opes Romae semper augeantur.*

Faustinus: I will sail again, as both the state and the nature of trade demand it. Although the sea always holds dangers, the profit and honor of the merchant seem a great reward. But, if the gods will it, the next voyage will be smooth. We must return to many lands again, Publius, so that Rome's wealth will always increase.

Publius: *Bene tibi faveant dei, Faustine, et utinam mare tranquilla tibi sit et merces tuas tutas vehas! Vale, amice, et bonam navigationem tibi opto.*

Publius: May the gods favor you, Faustinus, and may the sea be calm for you and your goods safely carried! Farewell, my friend, and I wish you a good voyage.

Faustinus: *Vale, Publi! Gratias tibi ago, et fortunam optimam tibi quoque desidero!*

Faustinus: Farewell, Publius! Thank you, and I wish you the best of fortune as well!

In Foro Romano Ad Vesperum – Sermo Levis in Foro Romano Vesperi

Cornelia: *Salve, Materne! Video te iterum in Foro vesperi ambulantem. Hic locus semper plenus vitae videtur, etiam sole occidente. Num frequenter ad vesperum huc venire soles?*

Cornelia: Hello, Maternus! I see you walking in the Forum again this evening. This place always seems full of life, even as the sun sets. Do you often come here in the evening?

Maternus: *Salve, Cornelia! Saepe huc ad vesperum venio, ut diem placide finiam. Forum Romanum, etiam cum multitudo discessit, maiestatis plenum manet. Curas diurnas deponere atque colloquiis levibus animum reficere mihi saepe iucundum est. Tu autem quid agis?*

Maternus: Hello, Cornelia! I often come here in the evening to peacefully end the day. The Roman Forum, even when the crowds have left, remains full of majesty. It is often pleasant for me to put aside the day's worries and refresh my mind with light conversations. But what about you? How are you?

Cornelia: *Non multum, Materne. Post labores diesque negotiosos, placet mihi paulisper huc ambulare, Fori spatia et monumenta antiqua contemplari. Hodie in basilica Pauli fui, ubi causae pro iure agebantur. Iudices quidem attenti erant, sed sermo nonnumquam ad res leviores inclinabat.*

Cornelia: Not much, Maternus. After busy days and work, I like to take a short walk here, to contemplate the open spaces of the Forum and the ancient monuments. Today I was in the Basilica of Paulus, where legal cases were being argued. The judges were indeed attentive, but at times the conversation leaned towards lighter matters.

Maternus: *Sic est. In basilicis semper iuris consulti et oratores disputant, sed interdum cernere potes iocos et convivia propius quam graves sermones. Quid de causis iudicandis audivisti? Estne aliquid praeclarum quod tibi occurrit?*

Maternus: That's true. In the basilicas, legal experts and orators are always debating, but sometimes you can see more jokes and gatherings than serious discussions. Did you hear anything notable about the cases being judged? Was there anything that caught your attention?

Cornelia: *Nihil admiratione dignum, sed una quaestio de agri litibus me sollicitavit. Dives quidam agrum pauperiori per dolum abstulerat, et nunc ille res suas recuperare conabatur. Iudex, quamvis argumenta utriusque partis aeque audivit, mihi visus est favere diu expulso.*

Cornelia: Nothing particularly remarkable, but one case about land disputes concerned me. A rich man had deceitfully taken land from a poorer man, and now the latter was trying to recover his property. The judge, though he listened fairly to both sides, seemed to favor the man who had been long dispossessed.

Maternus: *Bene audivisti, Cornelia. Multis locis talia iudicia versantur. Non omnia semper aeque geruntur in rei publicae causis. Aliquando favor aut pecunia fidem superat, quamvis iudex oculos iustos praebeat. Sed hoc fatum saepe in urbe nostra invenitur.*

Maternus: You heard well, Cornelia. Such cases happen in many places. Not everything is always handled fairly in the affairs of the republic. Sometimes favoritism or money outweighs justice, even when the judge seems impartial. But this fate is often found in our city.

Cornelia: *Ita vero, Materne. Nihil novi sub sole, ut aiunt. Sed cur plus de curis loquimur? Vespere fruamur et spiremus hanc Fori auram serename. Videsne illa monumenta, quae sub luce declinante pulchriora videntur? Columnae templi Saturni in caelum surgentes mihi semper magna cum reverentia videntur.*

Cornelia: That's true, Maternus. There's nothing new under the sun, as they say. But why do we talk more about worries? Let's enjoy the evening and breathe in the calm air of the Forum. Do you see those monuments, which seem even more beautiful in the fading light? The columns of the Temple of Saturn rising into the sky always seem to me to carry great reverence.

Maternus: *Vere debes videre. Hic locus non tantum negotio, sed etiam pietati et rerum antiquarum memoriae deditus est. Ubi sub vesperum omnia tranquilla sunt, videtur quasi ipsa Roma, cum omnibus suis* *victoriis ac tempestatibus, respiret. Columnae illius templi quasi testes aeternitatis stant.*

Maternus: You're right to see it that way. This place is dedicated not only to business but also to piety and the memory of ancient times. When everything is calm at dusk, it seems as if Rome itself, with all its victories and tempests, is breathing. The columns of that temple stand as if they are witnesses to eternity.

Cornelia: *Quam pulchre dicis, Materne. Re vera, Forum nostrum quasi animam Romae continet—hic victoriae et clades, triumphi et tragoediae ad oculos rediturae videntur. Quotiens in hac via ambulo, memoria antiquorum temporum me circumfusam tenet.*

Cornelia: How beautifully you speak, Maternus. Truly, our Forum contains the very soul of Rome—here victories and defeats, triumphs and tragedies seem to return before our eyes. Every time I walk down this road, the memory of ancient times surrounds me.

Maternus: *Sic omnes sentimus, Cornelia. Quidquid agimus, Forum Romanum semper prae oculis habemus, et in omnium vitas nostras conspectu manet. Sed iam sol paulatim declinat, et umbrae adveniunt. Me certe domum revocant negotia diei crastini.*

Maternus: We all feel that way, Cornelia. Whatever we do, the Roman Forum is always before our eyes, and it remains in view in all our lives. But now the sun is slowly setting, and the shadows are approaching. The business of tomorrow is certainly calling me home.

Cornelia: *Etiam ego paulatim domum redire incipiam. Gratum fuit tecum sermones habere et vesperem in tranquillitate peragere. Vale, Materne, et sit tibi vesper serenus!*

Cornelia: I'll also slowly start heading home. It was a pleasure to have this conversation with you and spend the evening in peace. Farewell, Maternus, and may you have a serene evening!

Maternus: *Vale, Cornelia! Utinam cras iterum te in foro videam, ut sermone iterum delectemur.*

Maternus: Farewell, Cornelia! I hope to see you in the Forum again tomorrow, so we may enjoy another conversation.

De Vita Senatoria – Sermo de officiis senatoris

Laelius: *Salve, Nigidia! Audivi patrem tuum nuper in senatu summa cum gravitate locutum esse. Est profecto summus honos in curia sedere et rem publicam moderari. Dic mihi, quid ipse tibi de vita senatoria narraverit? Nonne est onus ingens?*

Laelius: Hello, Nigidia! I heard that your father recently spoke with great authority in the senate. It is certainly a great honor to sit in the curia and govern the republic. Tell me, what has he told you about the life of a senator? Isn't it a heavy burden?

Nigidia: *Salve, Laeli! Ita est, pater meus saepe de oneribus vitae senatoriae loquitur. Non tantum honorem esse dicit, sed etiam multum laborem atque sollicitudinem. Omnia res publica ad senatum spectat, et saepe gravissimis de rebus consilia deorum hominumque invocanda sunt. Non semper iucunda est haec cura.*

Nigidia: Hello, Laelius! Yes, my father often speaks of the burdens of senatorial life. He says it is not only an honor, but also much work and concern. Everything in the republic depends on the senate, and often advice must be sought from both gods and men on the gravest matters. This responsibility is not always pleasant.

Laelius: *Intellego. Nam saepe videmus senatores inter bellorum minas et discordias civiles versari. Quae est, ut patrem tuum audisti, maxima difficultas in ipsa senatus actione? Num militaria decreta graviora videntur, an interna ordinanda maioris momenti sunt?*

Laelius: I understand. We often see senators dealing with the threats of war and civil discord. From what you've heard from your father, what is the greatest difficulty in senate proceedings? Do military decrees seem more serious, or are domestic affairs of greater importance?

Nigidia: *Pater meus semper dicit quaestiones belli et pacis acerrimas esse, sed res domesticas saepe magis contentiosas. Bellum foris geritur, sed domi senatores de legibus, tributis, et frumento populi deliberant. Vides quanta multitudo hominum Romae sit, et quibus rationibus sustentanda sit. Militaris tamen cura necessaria est, nam sine pace domi et finibus munitis nihil potest florere.*

Nigidia: My father always says that questions of war and peace are the most critical, but domestic matters are often more contentious. War is waged abroad, but at home the senators deliberate about laws, taxes, and the people's grain supply. You can see how large the population of Rome is, and how it must be sustained. Still, military matters are essential, for without peace at home and secure borders, nothing can thrive.

Laelius: *Quam verum dicis! Populus neque ullis rebus publicis contentus erit nisi frumentum et pacem domi habeat. Sed dic mihi, Nigidia, cur senatus tam saepe dissensionibus premitur? Nonne est in senatu idem propositum omnibus, ut patria bene gubernetur?*

Laelius: How true that is! The people will not be content with any public matters unless they have grain and peace at home. But tell me, Nigidia, why is the senate so often pressed by dissension? Isn't there the same purpose for all in the senate, to govern the country well?

Nigidia: *Utinam ita esset, Laeli. Sed dicere solet pater meus senatores saepe inter ambitionem et privatam curam dissentire. Multi magis pro suis familiis aut clientibus quam pro ipsa re publica curant. Et tamen sunt qui semper de consilio et iustitia publica disputent. Sed inter potentes et ambitiosos homines semper difficilis erit concordia.*

Nigidia: If only it were so, Laelius. But my father often says that senators frequently disagree between ambition and private concerns. Many care more for their own families or clients than for the republic itself. And yet there are those who always debate public justice and counsel. But among powerful and ambitious men, harmony will always be difficult.

Laelius: *Non satis ergo est honorem habere, sed summam virtutem et sapientiam exigere, ut quis rebus publicis recte prosit. Putasne igitur patrem tuum his temporibus in senatu maiora pericula Romae videre?*

Laelius: So it is not enough to have honor, but supreme virtue and wisdom are required for someone to properly serve the state. Do you think, then, that your father sees greater dangers for Rome in the senate at this time?

Nigidia: *Ita prorsus, Laeli. Patrem meum saepe audivi dicere Romam nunc sub umbra belli civilis latere. Tanti duces et exercitus sunt, ut vix* *omnia sub una cura contineri possint. Ipse timeo ne senatus mox potius spectator quam rector imperii fiat.*

Nigidia: Yes, exactly, Laelius. I have often heard my father say that Rome now lies under the shadow of civil war. There are such great leaders and armies that it is difficult for everything to be held under one control. I fear myself that the senate may soon become more a spectator than a ruler of the empire.

Laelius: *Quid tum facere potest senatus, Nigidia? Num potest inter discordias ducum auctoritatem suam retinere? An forte militari potentiae semper cessandum est?*

Laelius: What can the senate do then, Nigidia? Can it retain its authority amid the leaders' discord? Or must it perhaps always yield to military power?

Nigidia: *Pater meus censet nihil magis necessarium esse quam ut senatus prudentiam et auctoritatem conservet. Nam, quamvis milites et duces magnam vim habeant, leges et mores Romani in senatu conduntur. Si senatus suam virtutem ostendere debet, non vi sed consilio et iustitia opus est.*

Nigidia: My father believes that nothing is more necessary than for the senate to preserve its wisdom and authority. For although soldiers and leaders hold great power, Roman laws and customs are established in the senate. If the senate must show its virtue, it needs not force but counsel and justice.

Laelius: *Spero ut senatus semper prudentia et sapientia imperium gubernet. Virtus et consilium, ut cerno, in manibus senatorum sunt, si patriam servare volunt. Gratias tibi, Nigidia, quod de re publica mecum sermocinata es.*

Laelius: I hope that the senate will always govern the empire with wisdom and prudence. Virtue and counsel, as I see, are in the hands of the senators if they wish to save the country. Thank you, Nigidia, for discussing the republic with me.

Nigidia: *Gratias tibi, Laeli! Utinam res Romanae meliores fiant, et senatores, qui patriam amant, semper recte consulant. Vale, amice, et bonam fortunam in omnibus tibi opto!*

Nigidia: Thank you, Laelius! May Roman affairs improve, and may the senators, who love their country, always govern rightly. Farewell, my friend, and I wish you good fortune in all things!

Laelius: *Vale, Nigidia!*

Laelius: Farewell, Nigidia!

In Portu Ostiae – Sermo in portu Ostiae

Sulpicius: *Salve, Marcellina! In portu Ostiae tu quoque hodie versaris? Video naves ex variis partibus maris huc advenisse. Multa bona ex Graecia, Aegypto, atque etiam Hispania hodie ventura esse audivi. Quid tibi propositum est?*

Sulpicius: Hello, Marcellina! Are you also here in the port of Ostia today? I see ships arriving here from various parts of the sea. I've heard that many goods from Greece, Egypt, and even Spain are coming today. What brings you here?

Marcellina: *Salve, Sulpici! Ita vero, huc veni ut viderem utrum merces ex Aegypto iam appulsae essent. Pater meus magno in negotio frumenti est, et speravit hanc classem Alexandriae exspectatam tandem pervenisse. Sed tu, quid hic agis? Negotiarisne aut aliis rebus intentus es?*

Marcellina: Hello, Sulpicius! Yes, I came here to see if the goods from Egypt have arrived. My father is deeply involved in the grain trade, and he hoped that this long-awaited fleet from Alexandria has finally arrived. But what about you? Are you here for business or something else?

Sulpicius: *Profecto, Marcellina, negotiis intentus sum. Frumentum, ut bene scis, est res maximi momenti, sed ego etiam oleum ex Hispania importandum curo. Vide, illae naves iam apparent in portu! Quae bona ex longinquis terris vehunt, nonne id semper mirabile est?*

Sulpicius: Indeed, Marcellina, I'm focused on business. Grain, as you well know, is of the utmost importance, but I also manage the import of oil from Spain. Look, those ships are already appearing in the port! Isn't it always amazing to see goods being transported from distant lands?

Marcellina: *Profecto mirabile spectaculum est! Naves plenae rerum, quae totam urbem Romam alant et divitias augeant. Curare quidem huiusmodi merces magnum opus est. Sed dic mihi, Sulpici, num difficilius fit negotium tuum his tempestatibus? Audivimus multas naves in tempestatibus aut piratarum manibus perire.*

Marcellina: It truly is a marvelous sight! Ships full of goods that will feed the entire city of Rome and increase its wealth. Managing such cargo is certainly a great task. But tell me, Sulpicius, has your business become more difficult with the current weather? We've heard of many ships lost to storms or pirates.

Sulpicius: *Tempestates, Marcellina, semper periculum afferunt, sed nostrae naves bene armatae sunt et peritos gubernatores habent. De piratis autem, post victorias contra eos reportatas, minus timoris est. Tamen, nullus mercator sine cura navigat. Spes enim nostrarum opum in secunda fortuna semper pendet.*

Sulpicius: Storms, Marcellina, always bring danger, but our ships are well-armed, and we have experienced captains. As for pirates, after the victories over them, there is less fear. Still, no merchant sails without worry. The hope for our wealth always hangs on favorable fortune.

Marcellina: *Verum dicis. Ego autem semper miror quanta vis operae in portu sit. Vide hos laboratores naves solventes et merces trahentes. Otium quidem non apparet, sed tantum labor et negotium.*

Marcellina: You speak the truth. I always marvel at the sheer amount of work that happens in the port. Look at those workers unloading the ships and pulling the cargo. There's no sign of leisure here, only labor and business.

Sulpicius: *Sic est, Marcellina. Portus est quasi cor Romae, ubi omnia vehuntur, omnia distribuuntur. Sine hoc loco, urbs ipsa deficeret. Non modo merces, sed ipsa vita populi nostri per portum fluere videtur.*

Sulpicius: That's right, Marcellina. The port is like the heart of Rome, where everything is transported and distributed. Without this place, the city itself would fail. Not only goods, but the very life of our people seems to flow through the port.

Marcellina: *Sapienter loqueris, Sulpici. Nihil verius esse potest quam portum Ostiae vitam Romae continere. Tamen, licet admiratione teneamur, negotia nostra non diutius morari possumus. Spero naves Alexandrinas in tempore adventuras esse!*

Marcellina: You speak wisely, Sulpicius. Nothing could be more true than the fact that the port of Ostia sustains the life of Rome. However, though we may be in awe, we cannot delay our business any longer. I hope the Alexandrian ships will arrive on time!

Sulpicius: *Certe, Marcellina! Bona spes est; et si fata nobis favent, omnia prospere gerentur. Vale nunc, et fortunam tuam in omnibus curis exopto!*

Sulpicius: Certainly, Marcellina! There is good hope; and if the fates are with us, everything will go well. Farewell for now, and I wish you good fortune in all your concerns!

Marcellina: *Gratias tibi, Sulpici! Vale et tu, et utinam negotia tua prospera sint et naves tuto perveniant!*

Marcellina: Thank you, Sulpicius! Farewell to you as well, and may your business prosper and your ships arrive safely!

In Circo Maximo – Sermo de ludis circensibus

Aurelia: *Salve, Flavi! Ecce, populus confluit ad Circum Maximum! Romani certe nihil magis amant quam ludos circenses. Nonne animus tuus delectatur spectaculis huius diei?*

Aurelia: Hello, Flavius! Look, the crowd is gathering at the Circus Maximus! The Romans surely love nothing more than the circus games. Doesn't your spirit delight in today's spectacle?

Flavius: *Salve, Aurelia! Ita vero, animus valde movetur cum equos et aurigas in curribus ad certamen procedentes video. Cum vincentibus navis, clamores totius circi quasi resonare videor. Sed dic mihi, utri aurigae magis faves—albis, russatis, viridibus an caeruleis?*

Flavius: Hello, Aurelia! Yes indeed, my heart is greatly stirred when I see the horses and charioteers heading into the race. When the winners take the palm, I can almost feel the entire Circus echoing with cheers. But tell me, which charioteers do you support the most—the Whites, Reds, Greens, or Blues?

Aurelia: *Ego semper russatis faveo! Audistine quanta laus eorum esse dicatur? Non tantum propter virtutem in cursu, sed etiam propter ingeniosa consilia. Et ipse auriga eorum, Scorpus, ut aiunt, iam viginti palmas reportavit.*

Aurelia: I always support the Reds! Have you heard how much praise they receive? Not only for their skill in the race, but also for their clever strategies. And their charioteer, Scorpus, they say, has already won twenty palms.

Flavius: *Ah, Scorpus praeclarus quidem est, sed mihi virides potius placent. Auriga eorum, Eutyches, cum peritissime currum regat, etiam summam fortunam habet. Saepe videas eum in periculis angustiis superare et in ultimo momento victoriam obtinere. Miror quo modo ipse quattuor equos admotos tam firmiter moderetur.*

Flavius: Ah, Scorpus is indeed famous, but I prefer the Greens. Their charioteer, Eutyches, not only expertly drives the chariot but also seems to have incredible luck. You often see him overcome tight spots and snatch victory at the last moment. I marvel at how he so skillfully controls the four horses.

Aurelia: *Ita est, sunt qui Eutychi laudem maximam tribuant. Sed nonne cernis quomodo russati iam paene semper eos superent? Atque illi equi eorum tam celeres sunt ut vix oculis sequi possis! Nihil mihi gratius est quam cum currus concitati volent quasi venti flantes.*

Aurelia: That's true, many give Eutyches the highest praise. But don't you see how the Reds almost always beat them now? And their horses are so fast you can barely follow them with your eyes! Nothing delights me more than when the chariots rush forward like the blowing wind.

Flavius: *Verum dicis, nihil magis spectaculi in urbe videtur quam currus ad metam properantes. Sed meministine ultimum certamen, ubi albi quasi ab ipsa morte ad palmam evaserunt? Tunc omnes exspectabant ut caerulei vincerent, sed in ultimis metis omnia mutata sunt.*

Flavius: You speak the truth, there is nothing more spectacular in the city than the chariots racing toward the turning post. But do you remember the last race, when the Whites escaped victory almost from the jaws of defeat? Everyone was expecting the Blues to win, but everything changed at the final turn.

Aurelia: *Quam bene memini! Tanta erat clamorum vis ut nihil nisi tumultus et gaudia audiretur. Sed quamquam palmae saepe variant, ego semper fidelis russatis maneo. Videsne tamen quantus populus hodie circum Circum sedet? Nemo absens esse vult cum tanta fortuna deciditur.*

Aurelia: How well I remember! The shouts were so loud that you could hear nothing but uproar and joy. But even though the palm changes hands often, I remain ever faithful to the Reds. Do you see how many people are seated around the Circus today? No one wants to be absent when such fortune is at stake.

Flavius: *Sic est! Toti Romani, a divitibus ad pauperes, huc confluunt ut aurigas et equos spectent. Et ne obliviscamur quomodo etiam imperatores ipsi saepe his certaminibus favent. Sed dic mihi, Aurelia, quid censes de periculis huiusmodi certaminum? Nam saepe audimus aurigas ipsos cadere aut currus frangi.*

Flavius: That's right! All Romans, from the wealthy to the poor, gather here to watch the charioteers and horses. And let's not forget how even emperors themselves often favor these races. But tell me, Aurelia, what do you think of the dangers in such contests? We often hear of charioteers falling or the chariots breaking apart.

Aurelia: *Fortuna quidem semper in huiusmodi certaminibus versatur. Sunt pericula, ita est, sed sine periculo hoc spectaculum tantae voluptatis non esset. Aurigae ipsi non timere videntur, quippe qui ad palmam et honorem omnia pericula superare constituunt. Nos autem in tuto sedemus et clamamus!*

Aurelia: Fortune indeed always plays a part in such contests. There are dangers, yes, but without danger, this spectacle wouldn't bring so much delight. The charioteers themselves don't seem afraid, for they are determined to overcome all dangers for the palm and honor. Meanwhile, we sit safely and cheer!

Flavius: *Bene dicis, pericula sunt, sed ipsorum virtus est, quod nos tantopere delectat. Et fortasse ipsorum animi usus est magis quam timor. Vale nunc, Aurelia, certamen iam incipit! Spero ut virides palmam reportent!*

Flavius: You speak well, there are dangers, but it is their courage that so delights us. And perhaps their skill is driven more by daring than by fear. Farewell now, Aurelia, the race is starting! I hope the Greens win the palm!

Aurelia: *Vale, Flavi! Sed cura ut paulum tibi pro russatis invideas, nam vincere certo russati equi non dubito!*

Aurelia: Farewell, Flavius! But be sure to reserve a bit of envy for the Reds, because I have no doubt their horses will win!

De Artibus et Sculptura – Sermo de arte Romana et sculptura

Livia: *Salve, Decime! Audivi te nuper spectaculum artis Romanae in hortis Palatinis vidisse. Multae statuae et picturae ibi exhibitae sunt, ut ferunt. Quid tibi maxime placuit in tanto artis opere?*

Livia: Hello, Decimus! I heard that you recently saw a display of Roman art in the Palatine Gardens. Many statues and paintings were exhibited there, so they say. What impressed you the most in such a great display of art?

Decimus: *Salve, Livia! Ita est, profecto mirabilia vidi. In hortis Palatinis non solum artes Graecorum imitabatur, sed etiam ingenium Romanum ostendebatur. Statuae marmoreae deorum et heroum magnorum cernendae erant, et quidam artifices animam vivam in marmore exprimebant.*

Decimus: Hello, Livia! Yes, indeed, I saw marvelous things. In the Palatine Gardens, not only were the arts of the Greeks imitated, but Roman ingenuity was also showcased. Marble statues of gods and great heroes were on display, and some artists managed to express a living soul in the marble.

Livia: *Quam praeclarum! Maximam venerationem habeo pro sculptoribus nostris, qui marmoris duritiam ita mollire possunt, ut vivos homines spectare videamur. Sed dic mihi, quis tibi praeclarior videtur: Graeci sculpturae magistri, ut Phidias, an nostri Romani, qui non minus eximia opera praestant?*

Livia: How magnificent! I have the utmost admiration for our sculptors, who can soften the hardness of marble so that it seems we are looking at living people. But tell me, who do you think is more remarkable: the Greek masters of sculpture, like Phidias, or our Romans, who also create extraordinary works?

Decimus: *Phidias et alii Graeci summam elegantiam in artibus attigerunt, sed Romani aliquid peculiare addunt—gravitatem et dignitatem, quae Romae propriae sunt. Vidi statuam Augusti ex marmore, qua non solum imperatoris decor, sed etiam maiestas rerum publicarum exprimitur. Romani non solum pulchritudinem, sed etiam virtutem exprimere videntur.*

Decimus: Phidias and the other Greeks reached the height of elegance in the arts, but the Romans add something unique—gravity and dignity, which are proper to Rome. I saw a marble statue of Augustus, where not only the emperor's beauty but also the majesty of the state was expressed. The Romans seem to express not only beauty but also virtue.

Livia: *Verum dicis, Decime. Sculpturae nostrae semper aliquid ex fundamentis virtutis et maiestatis continent. Non satis est, ut mihi videtur, pulchritudinem imitari; oportet animi magnitudinem, res gestas, aut deorum potestatem demonstrare. Quid autem censes de picturis? Audivi etiam multa picta opera ibi fuisse.*

Livia: You speak the truth, Decimus. Our sculptures always contain something of the foundations of virtue and majesty. It's not enough, in my opinion, to merely imitate beauty; there must be a demonstration of greatness of spirit, deeds, or the power of the gods. But what do you think about the paintings? I heard there were many painted works there as well.

Decimus: *Certe! Erant ibi mirabiles picturae, in quibus Romanae victoriae et triumphi celebrabantur. Poteras, exempli gratia, Parthicam victoriam spectare, aut templum Iovis Capitolini in caelesti luce refulgens. Colores quasi vivebant, et totam rem pulchriorem efficiebant.*

Decimus: Certainly! There were marvelous paintings there, in which Roman victories and triumphs were celebrated. You could see, for example, the Parthian victory, or the Temple of Jupiter on the Capitol glowing in celestial light. The colors seemed almost alive, and they made the entire scene more beautiful.

Livia: *Tu quidem bene meministi, Decime. Pictura ad animos movendos non minus valet quam sculptura. Cum videas nostras victorias per picturas revivisci, quasi testis temporis praeteriti esse videaris. Sed dic mihi, praeferisne sculpturam aut picturam? Utrum magis tibi cordi est?*

Livia: You remember it well, Decimus. Painting has as much power to move the soul as sculpture. When you see our victories brought to life through paintings, it's as if you're witnessing the past yourself. But tell me, do you prefer sculpture or painting? Which is more dear to you?

Decimus: *Difficile mihi proponis, Livia! Utrumque genus mirabile est. Sed forsan sculptura mihi magis cordi est. Cur? Quia in marmore* *aeternitas confirmatur; nihil mutatur, nihil obliviscitur. Statuam contemplari, qua homo aut deus perpetuo colitur, maximum mihi videtur.*

Decimus: You pose a difficult question, Livia! Both forms are marvelous. But perhaps sculpture is more dear to me. Why? Because in marble, eternity is confirmed; nothing changes, nothing is forgotten. To contemplate a statue, where a man or a god is honored forever, seems to me the greatest thing.

Livia: *Intellego, Decime. Ego autem picturam magis admiror propter colorum et luminis varietatem, quae conspectu delectant et mentem alliciunt. Tamen, et sculptura et pictura magnae artis partes sunt, quae non solum oculis, sed etiam animis voluptatem praebent.*

Livia: I understand, Decimus. I, however, admire painting more because of the variety of colors and light, which delight the eye and captivate the mind. Still, both sculpture and painting are great parts of art, which provide pleasure not only to the eyes but also to the soul.

Decimus: *Sane, Livia. Utrumque artis genus summa dignitate celebratur. Quicumque Romae statuam aut picturam creat, magnum honorem habere debet. Vale nunc, et, si Di volent, iterum in hortos adibimus!*

Decimus: Certainly, Livia. Both forms of art are celebrated with the highest dignity. Whoever creates a statue or painting in Rome deserves great honor. Farewell for now, and, if the gods are willing, we will visit the gardens again!

Livia: *Vale, Decime! Utinam iterum illa praeclara opera simul spectemus!*

Livia: Farewell, Decimus! I hope we will once again admire those splendid works together!

De Fide et Superstitione – Sermo de religione et superstitione

Servius: *Salve, Fabia! Nuper in templo Iovis Capitolini te vidi sacra facientem. Mihi quidem videtur res divina necessaria esse, sed saepe cogito, utrum fides vere colenda sit, an plerique superstitionibus nimis occupentur. Quid tu de hac re censes?*

Servius: Hello, Fabia! Recently, I saw you performing sacrifices in the Temple of Jupiter on the Capitoline. It seems to me that divine worship is necessary, but I often wonder whether true faith should be honored or if many are too occupied with superstitions. What do you think about this?

Fabia: *Salve, Servi! Fidem in deos et pietatem magna reverentia colere necesse est, quoniam di immortales omnia regunt. Sed confiteor multos esse, qui nimis in vana auguria et falsas superstitiones incidant. Nam inter res sacras et superstitionem discrimen habendum est.*

Fabia: Hello, Servius! It is necessary to honor faith in the gods and piety with great reverence, since the immortal gods govern all things. But I admit that many fall too much into empty omens and false superstitions. There must be a distinction between sacred matters and superstition.

Servius: *Recte dicis. Saepe enim video homines ex qualibet re levi auspicium petere, ut cum avis aliter volat aut cum fulmen descendit. Nonne putas illud animi timidioris esse quam rectae fidei? Curo enim ut pietas solida sit, non ad casus incertos referenda.*

Servius: You speak rightly. Often I see people seeking omens from the slightest things, like when a bird flies differently or when lightning strikes. Don't you think that reflects a timid mind rather than true faith? I'm concerned that piety should be solid, not tied to uncertain events.

Fabia: *Verum quidem! Fides ex virtute et recta ratione nasci debet, non ex metu aut superstitionis insidiis. Dicunt enim aliqui, si munuscula vel sacrificia non offerant, malum sibi evenire. At haec non est pietas, sed servitus falsi timoris.*

Fabia: Indeed, that's true! Faith should arise from virtue and right reason, not from fear or the traps of superstition. Some people say that if they don't offer small gifts or sacrifices, harm will come to them. But this isn't piety; it's the servitude of false fear.

Servius: *Equidem saepe proprium exemplum memini: quondam haruspices audiebam, qui ominibus semper minabantur, si sacrificium non prompte fieret. Tamen, cum postremo nihil accidit, intellexi falso me timuisse. Nonne melius est fortiter vivere et deos vera virtute venerari quam auguriis falsis vacare?*

Servius: I often remember my own experience: I once listened to soothsayers who constantly threatened with omens if a sacrifice wasn't made promptly. But in the end, nothing happened, and I realized I had feared in vain. Isn't it better to live bravely and honor the gods with true virtue rather than obsess over false omens?

Fabia: *Certe! Di immortales non tam verbis aut ritibus moventur quam actionibus et animo sincero. Si pietatem bonosque mores servamus, dei favebunt. Nam ipsi non hominum anxias superstitiones, sed iustitiam et honestatem laudant.*

Fabia: Certainly! The immortal gods are not moved so much by words or rituals as by actions and a sincere heart. If we maintain piety and good morals, the gods will favor us. They praise justice and honesty, not the anxious superstitions of men.

Servius: *Hanc sententiam plurimum amo, Fabia. Non sine causa vivimus, sed sub spe et voluntate deorum. Ei autem non aves aut fulgura observant, sed honesta facta et iustas cogitationes.*

Servius: I greatly love this idea, Fabia. We don't live without purpose, but under the hope and will of the gods. They don't watch for birds or lightning, but for honorable deeds and just thoughts.

Fabia: *Ita est, Servi! Non debemus metu terreri, si quid adversi acciderit, sed semper consilio prudente deos venerari. Spes nostra in ipsis providentia caelesti est, non in credulis metibus. Quid autem de populi consuetudine censes, qui nimis auguriis et signis deorum addictus est?*

Fabia: Exactly, Servius! We shouldn't be frightened if something adverse happens, but always honor the gods with wise counsel. Our hope rests in their divine providence, not in foolish fears. What do you think about the habits of the people, who are too devoted to omens and divine signs?

Servius: *Populus saepe imprudens in superstitionem incidit. Multi bona mente agunt, sed cupiditas saepe firmitatem iusti consilii obruit.*

Curandae sunt res publicae et fama, sed non auguriis incertis innitendae. Si in honorem deorum et in bonam fidem perstamus, omnia bene evenient.

Servius: The people often fall into superstition out of ignorance. Many act with good intentions, but desire often overcomes the firmness of just decisions. We must take care of public affairs and our reputation, but not rely on uncertain omens. If we persist in honoring the gods and with good faith, all will turn out well.

Fabia: *Spero ut tota Roma sapientia et prudentia fidem sinceram colat et superstitiones repudiet. Vale nunc, Servi, et dis immortalibus gratias agamus, qui rectam viam hominibus ostendunt.*

Fabia: I hope that all of Rome will honor true faith with wisdom and prudence and reject superstitions. Farewell for now, Servius, and let us give thanks to the immortal gods, who show the right path to men.

Servius: *Vale, Fabia! Vera fide deos veneremur et animi tranquillitate ad vitae virtutem properemus.*

Servius: Farewell, Fabia! Let us honor the gods with true faith and hasten toward virtue in life with peace of mind.

In Schola Grammatici – Sermo inter grammaticum et discipulos

Grammaticus: *Salvete, discipuli! Hodie in schola nostra de arte grammatica disseremus. Primum, quid est grammatica? Cur tam magnae curae sit vobis, explanare volo. Claudia, quid dicis? Quid tibi videtur grammatica esse?*

Grammaticus: Greetings, students! Today in our school, we will discuss the art of grammar. First, what is grammar? I want to explain why it's so important for you. Claudia, what do you say? What do you think grammar is?

Claudia: *Salve, magister! Grammatica, ut opinor, est ars bene loquendi et scribendi. Per eam discimus quomodo verba coniungantur et sententiae ordinentur.*

Claudia: Hello, teacher! Grammar, in my opinion, is the art of speaking and writing well. Through it, we learn how words are connected and how sentences are arranged.

Grammaticus: *Bene dixisti, Claudia! Grammatica est proficiendi fundamentum, nam sine recta locutione ne ratio quidem explicari potest. Sed, Luci, dic mihi, quae res primaria est in grammatica docenda?*

Grammaticus: Well said, Claudia! Grammar is the foundation of progress, for without proper speech, even reason cannot be explained. But Lucius, tell me, what is the primary thing to be taught in grammar?

Lucius: *Magister, primum censeo nomina, verba, et ceterae partes orationis discendae esse, ut intellegamus quomodo verba inter se apte coniungantur.*

Lucius: Teacher, I think first we must learn nouns, verbs, and the other parts of speech, so we can understand how words are properly connected.

Grammaticus: *Verissimum est! Partes orationis sunt omnis locutionis fundamentum. Sunt octo: nomen, pronomen, verbum, participium, adverbium, coniunctio, praepositio, et interiectio. Quis ex vobis, discipuli, potest mihi nomen et verbum bene explicare? Marce, te interrogo.*

Grammaticus: Very true! The parts of speech are the foundation of all expression. There are eight: noun, pronoun, verb, participle, adverb, conjunction, preposition, and interjection. Which one of you, students, can explain a noun and a verb well? Marcus, I ask you.

Marcus: *Nomen, magister, est vocabulum quod rem aut hominem significat, ut "homo" aut "urbs." Verbum est, quod actionem aut statum significat, ut "currit" aut "sedet."*

Marcus: A noun, teacher, is a word that signifies a thing or a person, like "man" or "city." A verb is something that signifies an action or a state, like "runs" or "sits."

Grammaticus: *Optime, Marce! Nomina personas aut res designant, verba actus aut statum. Sed quaestio difficilior sequitur: quid est discrimen inter nomina declinare et verba coniugare?*

Grammaticus: Excellent, Marcus! Nouns designate people or things, verbs designate actions or states. But here comes a more difficult question: What is the difference between declining nouns and conjugating verbs?

Claudia: *Nomina, magister, secundum casus declinantur, ut "hominis, homini, hominem," sed verba secundum personas et tempora coniugantur, ut "curro, curris, currit."*

Claudia: Nouns, teacher, are declined according to case, like "of the man, to the man, the man," but verbs are conjugated according to person and tense, like "I run, you run, he runs."

Grammaticus: *Recte habes, Claudia! Videmus nomina per casus et verba per tempora mutari. Et quidem, haec diversitas linguae nostrae pulchritudinem reddit. Sed quaero nunc, Luci, quid sit participium, et quomodo a verbo differat?*

Grammaticus: You are right, Claudia! We see that nouns change by case and verbs by tense. Indeed, this diversity gives beauty to our language. Now, I ask you, Lucius, what is a participle, and how is it different from a verb?

Lucius: *Participium est quoddam medium inter nomen et verbum, magister. Actionem significat ut verbum, sed declinatur ut nomen, ut "amans" aut "scriptus."*

Lucius: A participle is something halfway between a noun and a verb, teacher. It signifies an action like a verb but is declined like a noun, like "loving" or "written."

Grammaticus: *Bene dicis, Luci! Participium admodum necessarium est in nostra locutione. Sed nunc vobis exercitatio dabitur. Componite sententiam qua nomen, verbum, et participium uno loco coniungantur. Claudia, a te incipiam!*

Grammaticus: Well said, Lucius! The participle is indeed necessary in our speech. But now you will have an exercise. Compose a sentence in which a noun, a verb, and a participle are combined. Claudia, I'll start with you!

Claudia: *Dico, magister. "Vir amans librum legit." Hic "vir" est nomen, "legit" verbum, "amans" participium.*

Claudia: I'll say, teacher. "The man reading the book." Here "man" is the noun, "reads" the verb, "reading" the participle.

Grammaticus: *Optime factum, Claudia! Tam verba quam partes orationis apte coniungis. Curate, discipuli, ut semper in locutione vestra claritatem et elegantiam servetis. Valete, et cras parati ad novum diem veniatis.*

Grammaticus: Well done, Claudia! You combine the words and the parts of speech well. Take care, students, that you always maintain clarity and elegance in your speech. Farewell, and come prepared for a new day tomorrow.

Discipuli: *Vale, magister!*

Students: Farewell, teacher!

De Lingua Latina et Graeca – Sermo de linguis Latina et Graeca

Aemilia: *Salve, Callistrate! Audivi te nuper Graece discere coepisse. Scisne quid censeam? Nihil praeclarius est quam utramque linguam, Latinam et Graecam, scire. Dic mihi, quid tibi de lingua Graeca videtur?*

Aemilia: Hello, Callistratus! I heard that you've recently started learning Greek. Do you know what I think? There's nothing more admirable than knowing both Latin and Greek. Tell me, what do you think of the Greek language?

Callistratus: *Salve, Aemilia! Ita est, Graecam linguam studere incepi, et fateor, initium difficillimum fuit. Multa enim non sunt similia linguae nostrae Latinae. Sed eadem lingua subtilitate et pulchritudine abundat. Philosophi eorum, ut Socrates et Plato, eam sua ratione excoluerunt.*

Callistratus: Hello, Aemilia! Yes, I've started studying Greek, and I admit the beginning was very difficult. Many things aren't similar to our Latin language. But the Greek language is full of subtlety and beauty. Their philosophers, like Socrates and Plato, refined it with their reasoning.

Aemilia: *Prorsus! Lingua Graeca, cum omnium artium fons sit, non solum rationem philosophicam continet, sed etiam elegantiam poeticam. Nonne in tragoediis Sophoclis aut Euripidis vivaces expressiones invenimus? Sed dic mihi, difficile tibi fuit litteras Graecas discere?*

Aemilia: Exactly! Greek, being the source of all arts, contains not only philosophical reasoning but also poetic elegance. Don't we find vivid expressions in the tragedies of Sophocles or Euripides? But tell me, was it difficult for you to learn the Greek letters?

Callistratus: *Initio paulum offendebar, nam Graecae litterae a Latinis multum differunt. Sed postquam earum modum intellexi, facilius factum est. Sonitus tamen alii sunt, et accentus magis variat quam in Latina lingua. Quid tu, Aemilia? Nonne Graecae linguae studuisti? Scilicet in Latina bene profecisti.*

Callistratus: At first, I was a bit confused, for Greek letters are very different from Latin ones. But once I understood their system, it became easier. However, the sounds are different, and the accent varies more than in Latin. What about you, Aemilia? Didn't you study Greek? Clearly, you've excelled in Latin.

Aemilia: *Ego quidem paulum Graecae linguae studui, sed Latinam semper praefero. Non quod Graeca minor sit, sed quia lingua nostra claritatem ac gravitatem maiorem habet, ut opinor. Latina verba breviora et apertiora videntur; non totum in sono vel melodia, sed in ipsa substantia reconduntur.*

Aemilia: I did study Greek a little, but I always prefer Latin. Not because Greek is lesser, but because our language, in my opinion, has greater clarity and dignity. Latin words seem shorter and more direct; it's not all in the sound or melody, but in the substance itself.

Callistratus: *Bene dicis, Aemilia. Lingua Latina sua gravitate ac soliditate propior est rebus, si ita loquar. Graeca plus formam ac lumen quaerit, cum Latina magis rem definit et ordinem clare stabilit. Sed nonne tibi Graeca flexiones verborum plures et magis variae videntur? Multas terminationes per discrimen sexus et generis habet, quas Latina lingua minus variat.*

Callistratus: You speak well, Aemilia. The Latin language, with its gravity and solidity, is closer to things themselves, if I may say so. Greek seeks more form and brilliance, while Latin defines things more clearly and establishes order. But don't you find that Greek verb conjugations are more numerous and varied? It has many endings depending on gender and number, which Latin varies less.

Aemilia: *Ita, in Graeca multae sunt terminationes, et fortasse ideo difficilius Graeca intellegitur a Romanis. Latina autem, ut scis, simpliciores formas et structuram firmiorem servat. Quod mihi gratissimum est, nam perspicuitas Latina nostra verba aptiora ad orationes politas reddit. Nonne tibi videtur ut Latina sit lingua magis idonea ad imperium et iura statuenda?*

Aemilia: Yes, there are many endings in Greek, and perhaps that's why it's harder for Romans to understand Greek. But Latin, as you know, keeps simpler forms and a more solid structure. I like this very much because the clarity of Latin makes our words better suited for polished speeches. Don't you think that Latin is more suited for establishing law and governance?

Callistratus: *Est quidem. Latina aptissima est ad leges et orationes publicas, quia brevitatem et vim quaerit. Quotiens lego Ciceronem, animadverto quam arte verba sua componat ad persuadendum. Sed Graeca, ut dicam, magis ad philosophiam et subtilitatem loquendi in poesi adhibetur, praesertim ubi abstracta cogitatio perscrutanda est.*

Callistratus: Indeed. Latin is best suited for laws and public speeches because it seeks brevity and force. Whenever I read Cicero, I notice how skillfully he arranges his words to persuade. But Greek, as I would say, is more used in philosophy and the subtlety of speech in poetry, especially when abstract thought is being examined.

Aemilia: *Id verissimum est. Cicero noster multa ex Graecis hausit, sed Latina eloquentia ad summam pervenit. Graeci, licet philosophiam invenerint, Romani tamen in rebus administrandis profecerunt. Sed dic mihi, Callistrate, cur Graecam linguam discere maluisti? Quae pars tuae mentis ad eam transiit?*

Aemilia: That's very true. Our Cicero drew much from the Greeks, but Latin eloquence reached its peak. The Greeks may have discovered philosophy, but the Romans excelled in governance. But tell me, Callistratus, why did you choose to learn Greek? What part of your mind led you to it?

Callistratus: *Ego autem, Aemilia, semper ad philosophiam et historias Graecorum tractandas me incitari sentiebam. Narrationes Herodoti et Thucydidis me delectant, ut videre possim quomodo Graeci de sua re publica et bellis disseruerint. Nec minus poetas, ut Homerum, legere volui, qui divinas res sua lingua tam profunde expressit.*

Callistratus: As for me, Aemilia, I always felt drawn to study the philosophy and histories of the Greeks. The narratives of Herodotus and Thucydides delight me because I can see how the Greeks discussed their republic and wars. And I also wanted to read poets like Homer, who expressed divine matters so profoundly in their language.

Aemilia: *Intellego! Homerus quidem est summus poeta, qui non solum Graecis, sed omnibus litteris formam dedit. Forsitan aliquando et ego ad studia Graeca redibo, ut meliores res intellegam. Vale nunc, Callistrate, et bene stude!*

Aemilia: I understand! Homer is indeed the greatest poet, who not only shaped Greek literature but all literature. Perhaps one day I'll return to Greek studies to better understand important matters. Farewell for now, Callistratus, and study well!

Callistratus: *Vale, Aemilia! Utinam utramque linguam perficere possimus, ut non solum fidem nostrarum rerum, sed etiam sapientiam omnium gentium complectamur!*

Callistratus: Farewell, Aemilia! I hope that we can master both languages so that we can embrace not only the knowledge of our own affairs but also the wisdom of all peoples!

De Inventione Aquae – Colloquium de aquaeductibus et aqua urbis Romanae

Tullius: *Salve, Drusilla! Audivi nuper de novo aquaeductu, qui per montes aquam in urbem Romam ducit. Nonne mirabile est quomodo Romani tanta arte aquas inveniant et distribuere sciant? Dic mihi, quid tibi de aquaeductibus videtur?*

Tullius: Hello, Drusilla! I recently heard about the new aqueduct that brings water into the city of Rome through the mountains. Isn't it amazing how the Romans, with such skill, can find and distribute water? Tell me, what do you think of aqueducts?

Drusilla: *Salve, Tulli! Profecto, nihil mirabilius inter opera Romana esse censeo. Aequo animo videmus Romam sine fine aquas fluere, cum paene per totum orbem fruges nostrae urbi apportentur. Aquaeductus ipsi, ut scias, non solum ad usum populi, sed etiam ad balneas et hortos maximo splendore conservandos sunt.*

Drusilla: Hello, Tullius! Indeed, I think there is nothing more marvelous among Roman works. We calmly observe water flowing endlessly into Rome, as resources are brought to our city from nearly the whole world. The aqueducts, as you know, are not only for the people's use but also for maintaining the baths and gardens with great splendor.

Tullius: *Ita est! Non solum necesse est aquas ad domesticos usus afferre, sed etiam balneae et thermae publicae aqua abundare debent, ut cives salubribus modis utantur. Nuper in Thermis Agrippae fui, ubi aquaeductus Claudianus aquam per arcus magnifice vehit. Num hi aquaeductus etiam in montibus exstructi sunt?*

Tullius: That's right! It's not only necessary to supply water for domestic uses, but the public baths and thermae also need to be filled with water so that citizens can use them healthily. Recently, I was at the Baths of Agrippa, where the Claudian aqueduct magnificently carries water through its arches. Are these aqueducts built even in the mountains?

Drusilla: *Ita, Tulli, ex ipsis montibus Sabinis aquam deferunt. Nam sine montium altitudine, fluxus aquarum in urbem minus facilis esset. Cernere potes arcus illos ingentes, qui per planities extenduntur, portantes aquam* *de locis altissimis in plana Romae. Multae structurae fiunt, ut gravitas ipsa aquam trahat.*

Drusilla: Yes, Tullius, they carry water directly from the Sabine mountains. Without the height of the mountains, it would be much harder for the water to flow into the city. You can see those huge arches stretching across the plains, carrying water from the highest places to the flat areas of Rome. Many structures are built to allow gravity itself to pull the water down.

Tullius: *Miror quanta ingenia ad hoc opus necessaria fuerint! Architecti et fabri mirabili modo tam longas et duras structuras sine ullo moderno instrumento perfecerunt. Aquae in Roma numquam deficiunt, etiam si pluviae raro cadant. Sed dic mihi, Drusilla, quid tibi videntur fontes publici, qui per totam urbem sunt?*

Tullius: I marvel at how much ingenuity must have been needed for this work! Architects and builders, in a miraculous way, completed such long and durable structures without any modern tools. Water in Rome never runs out, even if it rarely rains. But tell me, Drusilla, what do you think of the public fountains scattered across the city?

Drusilla: *Fontes mihi valde placent! Non solum pro utilitate, sed etiam pro ipsa pulchritudine. Multi fontes, ut ille Apollinis aut Castoris et Pollucis, ornamentis praeclari sunt. Aqua haud modo vitam, sed etiam decus urbis nostrae affert. Huc populus non solum ad aquam hauriendam, sed etiam ad spectandum convenit.*

Drusilla: I love the fountains! Not only for their utility but also for their beauty. Many fountains, like the ones of Apollo or Castor and Pollux, are adorned with splendid decorations. Water not only brings life but also adds beauty to our city. People come here not only to fetch water but also to admire the view.

Tullius: *Prorsus! Hoc etiam mihi videntur maiores nostri prudentissime providisse—ut aquaeductus non tantum servirent ad res domesticas, sed etiam ut urbs ipsa decoraretur. Quotiens per urbem ambulo et fontes videns, sentio quasi Roma ipsa sua aqua vigescat.*

Tullius: Exactly! It seems to me that our ancestors wisely foresaw that the aqueducts would not only serve for domestic matters but also to beautify the city itself. Whenever I walk through the city and see the fountains, I feel as if Rome itself thrives on its water.

Drusilla: *Verum est. Sine aqua, urbs nostra vix tanta pulchritudine et vi floreat. Nonne tu quoque, Tulli, putas hanc aquam esse quoddam fundamentum ipsius Romae? Non sine causa Romani aquam inter primas necessitates semper numeraverunt.*

Drusilla: That's true. Without water, our city would hardly flourish with such beauty and vitality. Don't you also think, Tullius, that this water is one of the foundations of Rome itself? It's not without reason that Romans have always counted water among their most essential needs.

Tullius: *Sic est, Drusilla. Nulla pars vitae sine aqua administrari potest. Curaverunt Romani, ut ipsa aquae summa munificentia ostenderetur, et hinc etiam maiestatem suam urbs ostendit. Aquaeductus sunt quasi venae urbis nostrae.*

Tullius: That's right, Drusilla. No part of life can be managed without water. The Romans made sure to display the greatest generosity in supplying water, and in this way, the city also displays its majesty. The aqueducts are like the veins of our city.

Drusilla: *Certe, et quod me maxime iuvat, aquaeductus nostri tam diu manebunt quam ipsa urbs Roma. Haec opera, quae nunc spectamus, ad aeternitatem pertinent. Vale nunc, Tulli, et si placet, iterum per thermas et aquaeductus ambulemus!*

Drusilla: Certainly, and what pleases me the most is that our aqueducts will last as long as the city of Rome itself. These works, which we now see, are built for eternity. Farewell for now, Tullius, and if you'd like, let's walk again through the baths and aqueducts!

Tullius: *Vale, Drusilla! Cum per thermas iterum ambulaveris, nuntia mihi! Semper gaudeo talia opera conspicere.*

Tullius: Farewell, Drusilla! When you walk through the baths again, let me know! I always enjoy seeing such great works.

De Praemiis et Poenis – Colloquium de praemiis et poenis in iuribus Romanis

Manlius: *Salve, Caelia! Hodie in curia fui et iudicium de latrocinio audivi. Iudex hominem furti damnavit, poenamque gravem imposuit. Miratus sum quanta sit severitas in his rebus apud Romanos. Quid tibi videtur de praemiis et poenis in legibus nostris?*

Manlius: Hello, Caelia! Today I was in the courthouse and listened to a trial about robbery. The judge convicted the man for theft and imposed a severe penalty. I was surprised by the level of strictness in these matters among the Romans. What do you think about rewards and punishments in our laws?

Caelia: *Salve, Manli! Recte quidem dicis, quippe Romani summam gravitatem in iure publico observant. Poenae enim non solum ad sceleratos reprimendos institutae sunt, sed etiam ut ceteri timore afficiantur. Iustitia sine poena florere non potest. Sed dic mihi, quam poenam iudex illi imposuit?*

Caelia: Hello, Manlius! You are right, for the Romans observe great seriousness in public law. Punishments are not only established to restrain criminals but also to instill fear in others. Justice cannot flourish without punishment. But tell me, what punishment did the judge impose on him?

Manlius: *Homo, qui furtum magnum commiserat, damnatus est ut in carcerem detrudatur et omnia bona sua amittat. Videtur mihi iustissimum esse; si quis res aliorum violat, dignam poenam ferre debet. Sed haec severitas tibi iusta videtur?*

Manlius: The man, who committed grand theft, was sentenced to imprisonment and the loss of all his property. It seems to me to be very just; if someone violates others' belongings, they should face a fitting punishment. But does this severity seem fair to you?

Caelia: *Profecto. Severitas necessaria est ubi societas tuta esse debet. Nam sine recta poena scelera augebuntur et libertas honestorum civium periculo obiicietur. Poena exemplum ponit, ut alii a maleficiis deterrentur. Sed non semper poenae gravissimae deligendae sunt.*

Nonnumquam levior poena magis efficax est, si ex ipsa culpa proficiscitur.

Caelia: Certainly. Severity is necessary where society needs to be safe. For without proper punishment, crimes will increase, and the freedom of honest citizens will be jeopardized. Punishment sets an example to deter others from wrongdoing. But the harshest penalties are not always the best choice. Sometimes a lighter punishment is more effective, depending on the nature of the crime.

Manlius: *Ita cerno. Leges nostras aequabilitate et moderatione praeclaras esse scimus. Cuncta pro magnitudine delicti temperanda sunt. Sed quaero, quid de praemiis? Nonne etiam res publica magnarum virtutum hominibus praemia tribuere debet?*

Manlius: I understand. We know our laws are renowned for their balance and moderation. Everything must be measured according to the gravity of the crime. But I wonder, what about rewards? Shouldn't the state also grant rewards to people of great virtue?

Caelia: *Certe, Manli! Praemia sunt alia facies iustitiae. Si pro scelere poena datur, pro virtute meritum honorari debet. Spes et metus semper in animis hominum versantur. Quomodo enim optimi in re publica laudem petent, si praemia virtutis non offerantur?*

Caelia: Certainly, Manlius! Rewards are another side of justice. If punishment is given for crime, then merit must be honored for virtue. Hope and fear are always present in the minds of people. How else will the best citizens seek honor in the state if rewards for virtue are not offered?

Manlius: *Iuste loqueris. Virtutem sine praeconio relinquere nihil aliud est quam labores eorum contemnere, qui rem publicam bene gerunt. Vide quantas praemia militibus tribuantur: res gestae magnorum ducum laudantur, coronae, statuae, triumphi... omnia haec ad honorem ducunt.*

Manlius: You speak rightly. To leave virtue without recognition is nothing less than to disdain the efforts of those who serve the state well. Look at the rewards given to soldiers: the deeds of great commanders are praised, crowns, statues, triumphs... all of these lead to honor.

Caelia: *Praecipue in bello, ut vides, civitas non solum praemiis sed etiam honoribus illustres homines celebrat. At non tantum in militari re, sed etiam in civili vita, auctores rerum honestarum laudandi sunt. Non potest res publica sine virtute florere. Ergo praemia et poenae tamquam duo pila iustitiae sunt.*

Caelia: Especially in war, as you can see, the state celebrates distinguished individuals with not only rewards but also honors. But not only in military matters, even in civilian life, those who contribute to worthy causes should be praised. The state cannot flourish without virtue. Therefore, rewards and punishments are like two pillars of justice.

Manlius: *Quid igitur censes, Caelia? Num poena acrior quam praemium in legibus nostris ponderatur?*

Manlius: What do you think then, Caelia? Is punishment weighed more heavily than rewards in our laws?

Caelia: *Non, nisi ubi necessitas id poscit. Plus quidem praemiorum dignitas commendanda est, sed poenae severitas ultimum remedium esse debet. Nam timor mali plus homines cogit quam spes boni.*

Caelia: No, except where necessity demands it. The dignity of rewards should indeed be more commendable, but the severity of punishment should be the last resort. For the fear of evil compels people more than the hope of good.

Manlius: *Profecto, sapiens sententia. Leges Romanae videntur bene moderatae inter metum et spem, inter praemium et poenam. Quisquis virtute praeclaret, honoribus decorandus est; quisquis scelere violat, poena reprimendus.*

Manlius: Indeed, a wise opinion. Roman laws seem well-balanced between fear and hope, between reward and punishment. Whoever excels in virtue should be honored with rewards; whoever violates with crime should be restrained with punishment.

Caelia: *Ita est. Et spero ut nostra civitas semper iustitiam aequam custodiat, ut neque praemia neque poenae ultra modum vagentur. Vale nunc, Manli, et gratias tibi ago quod de hac re philosophati sumus.*

Caelia: That's right. And I hope our city always upholds fair justice so that neither rewards nor punishments go beyond measure. Farewell for now, Manlius, and thank you for discussing this matter with me.

Manlius: *Vale, Caelia! Gratum mihi fuit de legibus et iure publico sermonem habuisse.*

Manlius: Farewell, Caelia! It was a pleasure to have had this conversation about laws and public justice.

In Horto Antiquo – Sermo de arte hortulana in antiquitate

Sulpicius: *Salve, Polla! Hodie in horto tuo te occupatam vidi, flores et herbas disponere. Semper miror quomodo tam pulchre hortum cultum teneas. Dic mihi, quae praecepta sequi soleas in hac arte tam delicata?*

Sulpicius: Hello, Polla! Today I saw you busy in your garden, arranging flowers and herbs. I always marvel at how beautifully you keep the garden cultivated. Tell me, what principles do you usually follow in this delicate art?

Polla: *Salve, Sulpici! Nihil magis me delectat quam horti cura. Multum enim studium et prudentia ad hoc opus necessaria sunt. Primum quidem, ubertas soli multum valet. Si terram bene aras et stercoribus instruis, flores atque herbae facilius crescunt.*

Polla: Hello, Sulpicius! Nothing pleases me more than caring for the garden. Much study and wisdom are necessary for this work. First of all, the richness of the soil is very important. If you till the earth well and enrich it with fertilizers, the flowers and herbs grow more easily.

Sulpicius: *Vere loqueris. Ego quoque scio fructus terram bene foventem semper magno opere respondere. Sed dic mihi, Polla, quid de aqua faciendum sit? Nonne etiam usum modumque rigandi curare debemus?*

Sulpicius: You speak truly. I also know that crops always respond greatly to well-nourished soil. But tell me, Polla, what should be done about watering? Shouldn't we also take care of the use and method of irrigation?

Polla: *Ita profecto! Aqua est vita horti. Sed ne nimium riges neve parum; temperantia semper adhibenda est. Praeterea, flores et herbae ex umbra aut sole secundum cultum mutati fieri debent. Omnia ex loco, quo sata sunt, pendent.*

Polla: Indeed! Water is the life of the garden. But do not water too much nor too little; moderation must always be applied. Furthermore, flowers and herbs must be adapted to shade or sun according to their cultivation. Everything depends on the location where they are planted.

Sulpicius: *Sagaciter videntur tibi omnia perpendisse. Estne etiam tempus sationis aliud floribus, aliud frugibus? Nonnumquam certo tempore semen adhibendum esse dicitur.*

Sulpicius: You seem to have considered everything wisely. Is the planting season different for flowers than for fruits? Sometimes it's said that seeds should be sown at a certain time.

Polla: *Tempus sationis omnino a natura rerum definitur. Verum est, flores melius in vere seri, cum sol tepere incipit et terra mollis est. Fruges autem—praesertim vineae et poma—autumno magis crescunt, cum pluviae multae et dulcis aura vires augent.*

Polla: The planting time is completely determined by the nature of things. It's true, flowers are better sown in spring, when the sun begins to warm and the earth is soft. Fruits, however—especially vines and apples—grow better in autumn, when many rains and the sweet breeze increase their strength.

Sulpicius: *Vidi quoque tuas vineas bene cultas esse. Quid censes de coloribus et specie horti? Tune solum pulchritudinem quaeris, an etiam utilitatem?*

Sulpicius: I have also seen that your vines are well cultivated. What do you think about the colors and appearance of the garden? Do you seek only beauty, or also utility?

Polla: *Ego semper pulchritudinem et utilitatem coniungere conor. Flores, sicut rosae et lilia, propter decorem coluntur, sed herbae utilitatem afferunt. Laurus, thymum, et mentham si bene seras, et oculis et sensibus prosunt.*

Polla: I always try to combine beauty and utility. Flowers, like roses and lilies, are grown for their beauty, but herbs bring usefulness. If you plant bay, thyme, and mint well, they benefit both the eyes and the senses.

Sulpicius: *Quam eleganter et prudenter hortum tuum administras! Verba tua mihi persuadent, Polla, ut etiam ipse hortum meliorem struendum curem. Estne aliquid aliud quod ad hunc cultum conferre possis?*

Sulpicius: How elegantly and wisely you manage your garden! Your words convince me, Polla, that I too should take care to build a better garden. Is there anything else you can contribute to this cultivation?

Polla: *Ratio praecipui modi semper est diligentia. Sic in horto, quem modo teneris manibus crescentem vides, patientia et sollicitudo multum valent. Non satis est sementem facere, nisi postea spectes et omnes partes cures. Aliud aliunde trahitur, et plantas saepe mutandas esse discimus.*

Polla: The main rule is always diligence. Thus in the garden, which you see growing under careful hands, patience and care are very important. It's not enough to sow the seeds unless you later watch and tend to all parts. One thing is drawn from another, and we often learn that plants must be moved.

Sulpicius: *Intellego. Itaque horti curam tamquam quamdam disciplinam accipere oportet, ubi labor et ars in unum coeunt. Gratias tibi ago, Polla, pro sapientia et monitis.*

Sulpicius: I understand. So, we must approach the care of a garden as a kind of discipline, where labor and skill come together. Thank you, Polla, for your wisdom and advice.

Polla: *Gratias tibi, Sulpici! Gaudeo, si quid ex meo sermone didicisti. Vale, et si hortum tuum crescere videbis, benevolentiam deorum laudabis!*

Polla: Thank you, Sulpicius! I'm glad if you learned something from my words. Farewell, and if you see your garden grow, you will praise the favor of the gods!

Sulpicius: *Vale, Polla! Recte faciam, ut semper horti pulchritudine et usu fruar.*

Sulpicius: Farewell, Polla! I will do my best to always enjoy the beauty and use of the garden.

De Vita Familiae Romanae – Disputatio de vita domestica et muneribus familiaribus

Lucius: *Salve, Octavia! Hodie tecum loqui volo de rebus domesticis et familia nostra Romana. Vidi enim te saepe diligenter in curanda domo operam dare. Quid tibi videtur de vita familiari? Quomodo munera inter viros, feminas et liberos distribui debent?*

Lucius: Hello, Octavia! Today I want to talk with you about domestic matters and our Roman family. I have often seen you diligently working to take care of the household. What do you think of family life? How should the duties be distributed among men, women, and children?

Octavia: *Salve, Luci! Vita familiaris Romana multos labores et sollicitudines habet, sed etiam magno gaudio completur. Feminae domus curas gerunt, ut familia bene alatur et omnia pulchre administrentur. Viri autem plerumque res foris et officiis publicis agunt. Ita unusquisque suo loco pro familia prodest.*

Octavia: Hello, Lucius! Roman family life has many tasks and worries, but it is also filled with great joy. Women handle the care of the house to ensure that the family is well-nourished and everything is managed beautifully. Men usually deal with matters outside, such as public duties. Thus, each one contributes in their own way to the family.

Lucius: *Recte dicis, Octavia. Viri quidem suas partes in foro aut in agris plene explent, sed sine feminarum studio et diligentia domus ipsa stare non potest. Dic mihi, quid censes de muneribus liberorum? Quomodo pueri et puellae in familia Romana educari debent?*

Lucius: You're right, Octavia. Men fulfill their roles fully in the forum or in the fields, but without the care and diligence of women, the household itself cannot stand. Tell me, what do you think of the duties of children? How should boys and girls be educated in a Roman family?

Octavia: *Liberi summa cura et disciplina educandi sunt. Puellae matrum exemplum sequuntur, discuntque res domesticas, lanificium, et diligentiam in servanda familia. Pueri autem a patre ipso ad officia viri et civis praeparantur. Militia, leges, et honores in re publica administranda eorum studium esse debent. Nihil tamen maius quam virtus et pietas docenda sunt.*

Octavia: Children must be raised with great care and discipline. Girls follow their mother's example, learning domestic tasks, spinning, and diligence in maintaining the household. Boys, however, are prepared by their father for the duties of a man and citizen. Military service, laws, and honors in public administration should be their focus. However, nothing is more important than teaching virtue and piety.

Lucius: *Ita vero, Octavia. Pietas enim fundamentum est familiae Romanae, et cum pietate honores et officia bene geruntur. Cerno autem hoc tempore in urbe multas familias quasdam curas neglegere, puerosque nimia indulgentia educari. Quid de ea re putas?*

Lucius: Indeed, Octavia. Piety is the foundation of the Roman family, and with piety, honors and duties are managed well. However, I notice that at this time in the city, many families are neglecting certain responsibilities, and children are being raised with excessive indulgence. What do you think about this?

Octavia: *Quaestio gravis est, Luci. Multae matres et patres vitiosa indulgentia nimium liberos molliunt. Ita fit ut liberi nec diligentia nec virtute digni fiant. Sine severa disciplina sperare non possumus ut liberi ad honestam vitam progrediantur.*

Octavia: It is a serious issue, Lucius. Many mothers and fathers spoil their children too much with harmful indulgence. As a result, the children become neither diligent nor virtuous. Without strict discipline, we cannot hope that the children will progress toward an honorable life.

Lucius: *Admodum probo quod dicis. Familia Romana tamen fundamentum urbis et imperii est. Si familia non bene regitur, quomodo possumus sperare rem publicam bene geri? Ex parva domo magnae res oriuntur.*

Lucius: I fully agree with what you say. The Roman family is the foundation of the city and the empire. If the family is not well-governed, how can we expect the republic to be well-managed? From the small household, great things arise.

Octavia: *Nulla vera est divisio inter familiam et rem publicam. Civitas ipsa ex singulis familiis constat. Si pater, mater et liberi pietate, industria, et honesta vita vivunt, urbs et imperium etiam florent. Sed dic* *mihi, Luci, tu curas familiae tuae bene gessisti? Ut saepe te in foro vidi, qualia tibi videntur officia tua domi?*

Octavia: There is no real division between the family and the republic. The state itself is made up of individual families. If the father, mother, and children live with piety, industry, and an honorable life, the city and the empire will also flourish. But tell me, Lucius, have you managed the duties of your family well? As I have often seen you in the forum, how do you see your responsibilities at home?

Lucius: *Domi me esse plerumque curas feminae reor, sed semper paratus sum de re familiari consultare. Patrem enim censeo non solum praecepta dare, sed etiam exemplum virtutis liberis suis proponere. Si patrem recte agere vident, ipsi quoque sequuntur.*

Lucius: I usually think that the household is mostly the responsibility of women, but I am always ready to consult on family matters. I believe a father should not only give instructions but also present an example of virtue to his children. If they see their father acting rightly, they will follow.

Octavia: *Bene sapis, Luci. Virtus enim maxime per exempla traditur. Utinam familiae Romanae semper dignas progenies habeant, quae rem publicam sustineant! Gratias tibi ago quod de hac re mecum colloqui voluisti.*

Octavia: You are very wise, Lucius. Virtue is indeed passed down mostly through examples. May Roman families always have worthy descendants to uphold the republic! Thank you for wanting to discuss this matter with me.

Lucius: *Grates tibi, Octavia, quod sensus tuos tam clare expressisti. Vale nunc, et spero familiam tuam semper florentem videre!*

Lucius: Thank you, Octavia, for expressing your thoughts so clearly. Farewell for now, and I hope to always see your family flourishing!

Octavia: *Vale, Luci! Quam primum iterum colloquamur!*

Octavia: Farewell, Lucius! Let us speak again soon!

In Itinere ad Romam – Disputatio dum iter fit ad Romam

Servius: *Salve, Marcia! Longum quidem iter habemus, sed exspectatio Romae perveniendi me magna laetitia complet. Quam diu putas iter nostrum fore? Nonne iam prope urbem sumus?*

Servius: Hello, Marcia! We do indeed have a long journey, but the anticipation of arriving in Rome fills me with great joy. How long do you think our journey will take? Are we not already near the city?

Marcia: *Salve, Servi! Ita profecto, longum iter fuit, sed nihil iucundius est quam Romam pervenire, urbem omnium pulcherrimam! Cogito nos post meridiem in portas urbis intraturos esse. Via Appia admodum bona est, quamquam interdum lapides incommodi sunt.*

Marcia: Hello, Servius! Yes, indeed, it has been a long journey, but there is nothing more delightful than arriving in Rome, the most beautiful city of all! I think we will enter the city gates by the afternoon. The Appian Way is quite good, although sometimes the stones are a bit uneven.

Servius: *Via Appia quidem praeclara est! Eam saepe iter feci, sed numquam non admiror. Quanta vis est in opere huiusmodi—quomodo milia passuum per montes et valles exstructa est, ut tam longum iter sine labore ingrato faciamus!*

Servius: The Appian Way is indeed remarkable! I have traveled it many times, yet I never cease to admire it. What a marvel it is—how it stretches for miles over mountains and valleys, allowing us to make such a long journey without undue hardship!

Marcia: *Vere dicis. Viae nostrae Romanae sicut venae per corpus imperii discurrunt, et sine iis ne Roma ipsa quicquam proficiat. Ego tamen, cum iter ad finem appropinquat, magis de spectaculis et urbis splendore cogito. Estne prima tua visitatio Romae?*

Marcia: Truly said. Our Roman roads flow like veins through the body of the empire, and without them, even Rome itself would not progress. Yet, as our journey nears its end, I think more about the spectacles and splendor of the city. Is this your first visit to Rome?

Servius: *Non prima quidem, sed urbs semper tamquam nova mihi apparet. Quotiens ad urbem redeo, novas res video et antiqua semper* *miror. Sed te rogo, Marcia, quid primum spectare cupis cum Romam advenerimus? Fori magnitudo, templorum maiestas, an populi ipsius tumultus tibi maxime placet?*

Servius: Not my first visit, but the city always seems new to me. Every time I return, I see new things and always marvel at the ancient sights. But tell me, Marcia, what do you most wish to see when we arrive in Rome? The grandeur of the Forum, the majesty of the temples, or the bustle of the people?

Marcia: *Omnia mihi delectamentum offerunt, sed Fori magnitudinem et pulchritudinem semper primo loco pono. Videbis templum Iovis Capitolini, ubi summus honor deis datur. Nihil est tam maiestatis plenum quam illae columnae marmoreae sub caelo patenti stantes.*

Marcia: Everything delights me, but I always place the grandeur and beauty of the Forum first. You will see the Temple of Jupiter on the Capitoline, where the highest honors are given to the gods. There is nothing as full of majesty as those marble columns standing beneath the open sky.

Servius: *Sic est! Nihil urbis Romae pulchrius aut magnificentius quam templum Iovis aut Fori multitudo. Ego autem saepe ad Circum Maximum descendo, ubi currus et aurigae suas vires ostendunt. Roma ipsa ibi populi animos accendit, et nihil magis movet quam clamor spectantium.*

Servius: Indeed! Nothing is more beautiful or magnificent in the city of Rome than the Temple of Jupiter or the crowds of the Forum. I often go down to the Circus Maximus, where the chariots and drivers show their strength. There, Rome herself stirs the spirits of the people, and nothing moves me more than the roar of the spectators.

Marcia: *Circum Maximum etiam mihi magnam delectationem affert. Sed ego, cum ad urbis sermones deducor, non possum non cogitare de Theatro Pompei, ubi et arte et scaena delectamur. Nonne hoc quoque tibi cordi est?*

Marcia: The Circus Maximus also brings me great pleasure. But when I think about the city's discussions, I can't help but think of the Theatre of Pompey, where we are delighted by both art and the stage. Do you also hold this dear?

Servius: *Mihi quidem placet! Ars scaenica Romae sicut virtus belli laudanda est. Ibi spectare possumus fabulas praeclaras, quae non solum delectant, sed etiam animos movent ac sapientia implent. Et fortasse aliquando etiam philosophia imbuemur, ut Plato vel Seneca hortantur.*

Servius: I do indeed! The theatrical arts in Rome deserve as much praise as the valor of war. There, we can watch famous plays, which not only delight but also move our spirits and fill us with wisdom. And perhaps we will sometimes be imbued with philosophy, as Plato and Seneca encourage.

Marcia: *Ita vero, sapientiae et iucunditatis non decet oblivisci. Roma non solum imperium, sed etiam sedem doctrinae et artis praeclaram habet. Sed audisne, Servi? Equi procumbunt. Brevi perveniemus!*

Marcia: Indeed, we must not forget wisdom and pleasure. Rome holds not only the empire but also the seat of learning and esteemed art. But do you hear, Servius? The horses slow down. We will arrive soon!

Servius: *Ita est, Marcia! Finis itineris appropinquat, et Roma portas suas pandit. Mihi gaudium est tecum hanc urbem omnipotentem visere. Valeamus simul, cum in portas ingrediemur!*

Servius: Yes, Marcia! The end of our journey is near, and Rome opens her gates. I am filled with joy to visit this mighty city with you. Let us be well as we enter through the gates together!

Marcia: *Vale, Servi! In urbe nos diutius commorabimur et plura spectabimus. Fiat, ut Roma semper novis oculis cernatur!*

Marcia: Farewell, Servius! We will stay in the city for a long time and see many more things. May Rome always be seen with fresh eyes!

De Ludis Gladiatoriis – Disputatio de vita gladiatorum

Sextus: *Salve, Rufine! Nuper spectavi ludos gladiatorios in amphitheatro Flavio, et miratus sum quanta virtus et audacia in certaminibus gladiatorum ostendatur. Num tu saepe huiusmodi spectacula adis?*

Sextus: Hello, Rufinus! I recently watched gladiatorial games in the Flavian Amphitheater, and I was amazed at the great courage and bravery displayed in the gladiators' contests. Do you often attend such spectacles?

Rufinus: *Salve, Sexte! Saepissime ad ludos gladiatorios prodeo. Nihil est, ut mihi videtur, quod aeque spectatores excitet. Gladiatores vere sunt exempla fortitudinis, et cum mortem ipsam sub oculis habeant, nullum tamen timorem praeferunt.*

Rufinus: Hello, Sextus! I very often go to gladiatorial games. There is nothing, in my opinion, that excites spectators as much. Gladiators truly are examples of courage, and though they face death itself, they show no fear.

Sextus: *Vere quidem. Sed sic cogito, quam terribilis eorum vita sit. Tot pericula cotidie subeunt, nullam spem fugae. Dic mihi, Rufine, num tibi videtur huiusmodi vita digna esse viris talibus? Num semper tales ludos crudeles approbare debemus?*

Sextus: Truly. But I wonder how terrible their life must be. They face so many dangers every day, with no hope of escape. Tell me, Rufinus, do you think such a life is worthy for men like them? Should we always approve of such cruel games?

Rufinus: *Est quaestio difficilis, Sexte. Gladiatores saepe servi aut captivi sunt, qui hanc fatorum sortem patiuntur. Sed multa gloria in eo certamine est. Si quis satis fortiter pugnat, populi favorem ac praemia magna consequitur. Alii, post multa certamina, etiam libertatem adipisci possunt.*

Rufinus: It's a difficult question, Sextus. Gladiators are often slaves or captives who suffer this fate. But there is much glory in the contest. If someone fights bravely enough, he wins the favor of the people and great rewards. Some, after many contests, can even achieve freedom.

Sextus: *Ita, non nego multos favorem et libertatem adipisci posse, sed quam saevum est hanc libertatem per sanguinem quaerere. Gladiatores saepe a dominis impelluntur ut in arenam exeant, et vitam suam propter voluptatem aliorum periclitentur. Quid censes de hoc? Nonne saevitia plus quam virtus videtur?*

Sextus: Yes, I don't deny that many gain favor and freedom, but how cruel it is to seek that freedom through blood. Gladiators are often driven by their masters to enter the arena, risking their lives for the entertainment of others. What do you think of this? Doesn't it seem more like cruelty than virtue?

Rufinus: *Recte dicis, sunt qui hoc genus ludorum saevum et inhumanum putent. Sed hoc quoque meminisse oportet: populus Romanus semper bellatoribus et virtuti militari studuit. Gladiatores, quasi exempla militum in arena, populo demonstrant quid sit fortitudo et constantia sub periculis. Ludi non tantum crudelitas, sed etiam exercitatio est ad animorum robustorum constantiam.*

Rufinus: You're right; some do think these games are cruel and inhumane. But we must also remember this: the Roman people have always admired warriors and military valor. Gladiators, as examples of soldiers in the arena, show the people what courage and endurance under danger look like. The games are not just cruelty; they're also a test of the strength of spirit.

Sextus: *Sic fortasse est, sed ego tamen plus misericordiae in hoc videre velim. Milites in proeliis necesse est ut pugnent, sed gladiatores pro ludo certant. Multi viri magni perierunt sub gloria falsa. Sed ne omnino condemnemus—quid dicas de gladiatoribus ipsis? Nonne quidam ex eis sunt praeclari viri, qui et honore et virtute digni sunt?*

Sextus: Perhaps that's true, but I would still like to see more mercy in this. Soldiers must fight in battles, but gladiators fight for entertainment. Many great men have died under the illusion of false glory. But let's not condemn it entirely—what would you say about the gladiators themselves? Aren't some of them famous men, worthy of both honor and virtue?

Rufinus: *Sane, Sexte! Sunt ex gladiatoribus qui magnam gloriam adepti sint, ut Spartacus, qui etiam exercitum servorum duxit. Quidam etiam* *liberti facti sunt et post gladiatoriam vitam in societate honorem habuerunt. Quidquid dicas de ludis, nihil negare potes virtutem eorum qui tam saepe victoriam de morte ipsa reportant.*

Rufinus: Certainly, Sextus! Some gladiators have achieved great glory, like Spartacus, who even led an army of slaves. Some have even become freedmen and held honor in society after their gladiatorial life. Whatever you may say about the games, you can't deny the courage of those who so often win victory over death itself.

Sextus: *Hoc non nego. Virtus eorum certe laudanda est. Sed tamen miror, Rufine, utrum ipsi gladiatores hanc vitam suam libenter accipiant. Nonne plures malint alios modos libertatis quaerere, si facultas esset?*

Sextus: I don't deny that. Their courage is certainly praiseworthy. But I still wonder, Rufinus, whether the gladiators themselves willingly accept this life. Wouldn't most of them prefer to seek freedom in other ways, if they had the chance?

Rufinus: *Certe plerique malint liberi esse sine ludorum periculis. Sed ubi quis semel gladiator fit, necesse est ut fato suo contendat. Fatum eorum, ut dicunt, in arena perficitur. Gloria, favor populi, et fortasse libertas post longum certamen—haec sunt eis spes maxima.*

Rufinus: Certainly, most would prefer to be free without the dangers of the games. But once someone becomes a gladiator, he must contend with his fate. Their fate, as they say, is fulfilled in the arena. Glory, the favor of the people, and perhaps freedom after many contests—these are their greatest hopes.

Sextus: *Itaque, quidquid sentiamus, gladiatorum vita semper erit exemplum inter vires et pericula. Ego tamen, sicut tu, Rufine, cum ludos spectare soleam, non possum non admirari et simul dolere. Vale nunc, et fortasse iterum ludos simul spectemus.*

Sextus: So, whatever we may think, the life of a gladiator will always be an example of strength and danger. Still, like you, Rufinus, when I watch the games, I can't help but admire and feel sorrow at the same time. Farewell for now, and perhaps we'll watch the games together again.

Rufinus: *Vale, Sexte! Quotiens in arenam venerimus, semper de fortitudine et fato humano cogitabimus.*

Rufinus: Farewell, Sextus! Whenever we go to the arena, we will always reflect on the courage and fate of mankind.

De Imaginibus et Statuis – Disputatio de imaginibus et statuis Romanis

Flavia: *Salve, Faustine! Nuper in domo Quinti fui et praeclaras statuas atque imagines antiquas vidi. Quanta artis peritia in illis operibus adhibita est! Ego vere stupefacta sum. Dic mihi, quid tibi videtur de his imaginibus et statuis, quae tam multum in domibus Romanis ponuntur?*

Flavia: Hello, Faustinus! Recently, I was in the house of Quintus and saw magnificent statues and ancient images. What great artistic skill was applied to those works! I was truly amazed. Tell me, what do you think of these images and statues, which are so commonly placed in Roman homes?

Faustinus: *Salve, Flavia! Ita vero, statuae et imagines magnam partem consuetudinis Romanae efficiunt. In omnibus locis, tam publicis quam privatis, artificia haec videmus. Est aliquid divini in conspectu statuae, praesertim cum magni viri aut dei repraesentantur. Sed quid tibi de imaginibus domesticis videtur? Non pauci censeant eiusmodi imagines esse memoriae familiae sacrae.*

Faustinus: Hello, Flavia! Indeed, statues and images form a great part of Roman customs. We see these works everywhere, both in public and private places. There is something divine in the sight of a statue, especially when great men or gods are represented. But what do you think of domestic images? Many believe such images serve as sacred memories of the family.

Flavia: *Plene assentior. Imagines avorum et maiorum in atriis domuum non solum ornamentum sunt, sed etiam testimonia laudis et virtutis. Eae enim maiorum exempla posteris proponunt. Quotiens procedo ante statuam avi mei, sicut vivum eum videre videor. Quid mirabilius?*

Flavia: I completely agree. The images of ancestors and forefathers in the atria of houses are not only decorations but also testimonies of praise and virtue. They present the examples of our ancestors to future generations. Whenever I walk past the statue of my grandfather, it feels as if I see him alive. What could be more wonderful?

Faustinus: *Id est pulcherrimum consuetudinis nostrae argumentum, Flavia. Cum vultus maiorum nostrorum in marmore expressos videmus,*

274

non solum memoria eorum tenemur, sed etiam ad virtutem incitamur. Est tamen quaestio peculiaris de re qua hodie cogito: quidam statuas et imagines ad deos respiciendos efficiunt, alii autem hominum praesentiam perpetuare videntur. Quid censes? Estne quaedam divinitas in his operibus?

Faustinus: That is a beautiful element of our tradition, Flavia. When we see the faces of our ancestors carved in marble, we are not only reminded of them, but we are also inspired toward virtue. However, there is a specific question I've been thinking about today: some create statues and images to reflect the gods, while others seem to immortalize human presence. What do you think? Is there something divine in these works?

Flavia: *Hoc sane discrimen non parvum est. Statuas deorum, ut Apollinis aut Minervae, cum reverentia maxima colimus. Ibi non tantum artifex, sed ipsa divinitas videtur praesens esse. Sed cum statua viri magni, ut Scipionis aut Ciceronis, ante oculos nostros stat, magis fortasse de humana gloria et virtute cogitamus. Utrumque tamen, ut mihi videtur, reconditum quiddam sacrum continet.*

Flavia: This is certainly no small distinction. We honor the statues of the gods, like Apollo or Minerva, with the greatest reverence. There, it's not just the artist, but the divine itself that seems present. But when a statue of a great man, like Scipio or Cicero, stands before our eyes, perhaps we think more about human glory and virtue. However, both, in my opinion, contain a hidden sacredness.

Faustinus: *Bene dicis, Flavia. Est quaedam sacra maiestas in forma deorum repraesentanda, sed etiam virtus hominum nemini praeferenda est. Quotiens statuas virorum illustrium cernimus, quasi admonemur quanti sit honor et gloria pro patria vel rebus gestis merenda. Hoc etiam non minus deorum exemplis docemur.*

Faustinus: You speak well, Flavia. There is a certain sacred majesty in representing the gods, but the virtue of men should not be underestimated. Whenever we see statues of illustrious men, it's as though we are reminded of how much honor and glory are earned for the country or through great deeds. We learn no less from the examples of the gods.

Flavia: *Sic est. Est etiam peculiare quod, cum imagines aut statuae ex marmore aut aeneo efficiuntur, diutius vitam nostram memoria continebunt. Marmor quidem aeternum esse videtur. Nonne pulchrum est, Faustine, quod virtus et memoria hominum tamdiu durent, dum nos ipsi longe abeamus?*

Flavia: That's true. It's also remarkable that when images or statues are made from marble or bronze, they preserve our memory for much longer. Marble, indeed, seems eternal. Isn't it beautiful, Faustinus, that human virtue and memory endure for so long, even after we ourselves are long gone?

Faustinus: *Prorsus! Imagines et statuae sunt quasi pactum inter praesentem aetatem et posteritatem. Quotiens spectas statuam Augusti aut Traiani, non vides tantum hominem, sed testimonium aeternitatis Romanae. Statua non iam est lapis iners, sed signum perpetuae laudis.*

Faustinus: Absolutely! Images and statues are like a pact between the present and future generations. Whenever you see the statue of Augustus or Trajan, you don't just see a man, but a testimony to the eternity of Rome. A statue is no longer just an inert stone, but a symbol of everlasting praise.

Flavia: *Hoc verum est. Quotiens ego ante statuam procedo, non solum admiratione afficior propter artem, sed etiam recordationem magnarum rerum gerendarum consequor. Curabo ut semper hae imagines familiares meae honores suos teneant.*

Flavia: That's true. Whenever I walk past a statue, I am not only struck by admiration for the art, but I also recall the great deeds done. I will ensure that these family images always retain their honor.

Faustinus: *Quam iuste! Statuas et imagines maiorum venerari non tantum propriae familiae honorem continet, sed etiam civitati nostrae prodesse potest. Vale nunc, Flavia, et utinam iterum sermones de artibus et virtute habeamus.*

Faustinus: How right you are! Honoring the statues and images of our ancestors not only upholds our family's honor but can also benefit our entire society. Farewell for now, Flavia, and may we discuss art and virtue again soon.

Flavia: *Vale, Faustine! Libenter iterum de his rebus colloquar.*

Flavia: Farewell, Faustinus! I will gladly talk about these things again.

In Foro Romano Cum Philosophis – Disputatio philosophorum in Foro

Aulus: *Salve, Rufe! Vidi te ad locum philosophorum in Foro Romano iterum convenire. Quid hodie disputatum est? Audivi eos saepe de natura boni et mali disserere. Quid sentis de ea re?*

Aulus: Hello, Rufus! I saw you once again gathering at the philosophers' place in the Roman Forum. What was discussed today? I often hear them debate about the nature of good and evil. What is your opinion on the matter?

Rufus: *Salve, Aule! Hodie animosa disputatio fuit inter duos praeclaros viros, Lucilium Stoicum et Hermarchum Epicureum. Lucilius contendit virtutem ipsam esse summum bonum, neque ceteras res ad felicitatem conferre. Hermarchus autem dixit voluptatem esse principium et finem vitae beatae. Ne cessarent in hac disputatione!*

Rufus: Hello, Aulus! Today, there was a lively debate between two famous men, Lucilius the Stoic and Hermarchus the Epicurean. Lucilius argued that virtue itself is the highest good and that nothing else contributes to happiness. Hermarchus, on the other hand, claimed that pleasure is the beginning and end of a happy life. They wouldn't stop arguing!

Aulus: *Semper miror quanta sit discordia inter Stoicos et Epicureos. Lucilium quidem laudo, quia virtutem ante omnia collocat. Sed dic mihi, Rufe, quid praecipue Lucilius argumento adferebat?*

Aulus: I'm always amazed at how much disagreement there is between the Stoics and the Epicureans. I do admire Lucilius for placing virtue above all else. But tell me, Rufus, what was Lucilius' main argument?

Rufus: *Lucilius firmissime docuit virtutem non ex extrinsecis rebus pendere, sed in ipsa voluntate ac ratione firmari. "Sapientem," inquit, "nihil posse perturbari, si modo virtutem adhibeat." Exemplum Ciceronis adhibuit, qui in magnis rerum publicarum tempestatibus tamen egregiam prudentiam servavit. Secundas res et adversas aequo animo tolerandas esse affirmavit.*

Rufus: Lucilius strongly taught that virtue doesn't depend on external things but is rooted in will and reason. "A wise person," he said, "cannot be disturbed if they rely on virtue." He used Cicero as an example, who, despite facing great political turmoil, maintained outstanding wisdom. He argued that both good fortune and adversity should be endured with a calm spirit.

Aulus: *Bene se habet illud principium, sed quid de Hermarcho dicis? Quomodo ille voluptati summum bonum tribuere potuit? Non videtur mihi dignum esse homini honores aut laudem adhaerere, si solum voluptatem petat.*

Aulus: That principle makes sense, but what about Hermarchus? How could he attribute the highest good to pleasure? It doesn't seem right to me for a person to be praised or honored if they only seek pleasure.

Rufus: *Hermarchus sapienter respondit, ut sibi videtur, voluptatem non carnalem aut inhonestam, sed tranquillitatem animi intellegendam esse. "Voluptas," inquit, "est absens dolor ac sollicitudo, et hic status, quo nihil timendum sit, nihil dolendum, summum bonum vocari potest." De hac tranquillitate animi multum disseruit, et aeris serenitatem ad otium sapientis comparavit.*

Rufus: Hermarchus responded wisely, at least in his view, that pleasure shouldn't be understood as something carnal or dishonorable, but as the tranquility of the mind. "Pleasure," he said, "is the absence of pain and worry, and this state, where there is nothing to fear or suffer, can be called the highest good." He spoke at length about this peace of mind, comparing it to the clear sky enjoyed by a wise person at rest.

Aulus: *Id quidem sophisma Epicureorum semper admirari soleo. Voluptas animi dicitur, sed tamen multi primum carnis voluptatem intellegunt. Stoici honestius argumentantur, cum de officio et virtute disputant, et ideo praefero eorum doctrinam. Virtus autem ipsa per se vivere potest, etiam si corpus laboret aut patiatur.*

Aulus: That Epicurean argument has always seemed like sophistry to me. They speak of pleasure of the mind, but many first think of bodily pleasure. The Stoics make a more honorable argument when they discuss duty and virtue, and that's why I prefer their philosophy. Virtue itself can survive, even when the body suffers or endures hardship.

Rufus: *Non omnino dissentio, Aule. Virtus quidem summa laude digna est, et ego quoque Lucilio plus faveo. Tamen non negandum est Epicureos aliquam sapientiam habere, praesertim cum de fugiendis angoribus et perturbationibus loquuntur. Fortasse quaedam mediocritas inter utramque doctrinam est quaerenda.*

Rufus: I don't entirely disagree, Aulus. Virtue is certainly worthy of the highest praise, and I, too, lean more toward Lucilius. But we can't deny that the Epicureans have some wisdom, especially when they talk about avoiding anxieties and disturbances. Perhaps some middle ground between the two doctrines should be sought.

Aulus: *Forsitan mediocritas sit, sed ego magis inclino ad sententiam Lucilii. Est quiddam maius in virtute quam solum timorem aut dolorem effugere. Virtus non propter voluptatem colenda est, sed propter honorem et dignitatem. Ut Seneca ait, "Vita sine virtute mortis imago est."*

Aulus: Perhaps there is a middle ground, but I lean more toward Lucilius' view. There is something greater in virtue than just avoiding fear or pain. Virtue shouldn't be pursued for the sake of pleasure, but for honor and dignity. As Seneca said, "Life without virtue is the image of death."

Rufus: *Sapienter pronuntias, Aule. Philosophi non numquam curas vitae levare student, sed neminem errare putem, si virtuti et officio se totum dedicat. Valde me iuvat disputatio huiusmodi. Cur non plus saepe convenimus ad locum philosophorum, ut alios sermones exaudiamus?*

Rufus: You speak wisely, Aulus. Philosophers often seek to lighten the worries of life, but I don't think anyone goes wrong by fully dedicating themselves to virtue and duty. I greatly enjoy discussions like this. Why don't we meet more often at the philosophers' place to hear more debates?

Aulus: *Valde libenter, Rufe! Nihil tam me delectat quam inter homines doctos et sapientes versari. Hic locus vere est fons sapientiae, et multum discimus. Vale nunc, et cras iterum conveniamus!*

Aulus: I'd be delighted, Rufus! Nothing pleases me more than being among learned and wise people. This place is truly a fountain of wisdom, and we learn a great deal. Farewell for now, and let's meet again tomorrow!

Rufus: *Vale, Aule! Cras in Foro philosophorum verba audire ne praetermittamus!*

Rufus: Farewell, Aulus! Tomorrow, let's not miss the chance to hear the philosophers speak again!

In Senatu De Bello – Disputatio de bello in senatu

Lentulus: *Patres conscripti, tempus est ut de bello consilium capiamus. Hostes nostros non iam longius tolerare possumus. Prope limites imperii nostri iam castra posuerunt et multas civitates nostras populantur. Nullum dubium est, nisi bellum prompte gerimus, periculum immane urbi ipsi imminet.*

Lentulus: Senators, it is time for us to decide on war. We can no longer tolerate our enemies. They have already set up camps near the borders of our empire and are ravaging many of our cities. There is no doubt that if we do not wage war promptly, an immense danger will threaten the city itself.

Sulpicius: *Lentule, verba tua audivi, sed prudentiam ante celeritatem praeferre debemus. Bellum facile initur, sed difficile terminatur. Quaero: num satis parati sumus ad tantum certamen? Exercitus nostri in aliis partibus occupati sunt, et opes nostras hac tempestate laborare cerno. Num vere cogitasti quid hoc bellum populo Romano constet?*

Sulpicius: Lentulus, I have heard your words, but we must prioritize wisdom over haste. War is easily started, but difficult to end. I ask: are we truly prepared for such a conflict? Our armies are occupied elsewhere, and I see our resources strained at this time. Have you truly considered what this war will cost the Roman people?

Flaminia: *Patres conscripti, ego Lentulo pro sententia sto. Cunctatio semper periculorum maiorum fons est. Hostes progrediuntur, et si non statim resistimus, audacia eorum augebitur. Bellum iustissimum est, quoniam non ipsi hostes lacessivimus, sed ipsi nos oppugnant. Consilia longinqua et morae exercitum fessum efficiunt; nunc agendum est, non deliberandum.*

Flaminia: Senators, I stand with Lentulus' opinion. Hesitation is always the source of greater dangers. The enemy advances, and if we do not resist immediately, their boldness will increase. This war is most just, for we did not provoke the enemy, but they are attacking us. Long deliberations and delays will only exhaust our forces; we must act now, not delay further.

Fabius: *Flaminia, perinde ac tu censeo, audaces et promptos esse oportet. Sed num obliviscimur quanti bellum civitati constet? Ut Sulpicius ait, opes nostras iam non satis vires ad tantam expeditionem ducunt. Cur non prius legati mittantur, qui cum hostibus de pace tractent? Si bellum vitari potest, nonne melius est res tranquillitate quam ferro componere?*

Fabius: Flaminia, like you, I believe we must be bold and swift. But are we forgetting how much this war will cost the state? As Sulpicius said, our resources are not sufficient for such an expedition at the moment. Why don't we first send envoys to negotiate peace with the enemy? If war can be avoided, isn't it better to resolve matters through peace rather than through the sword?

Lentulus: *Fabii, nimis speras. Legati iam non utiles sunt cum hostes nostros nec pacem nec legationes accipiant. Propono ut, antequam urbes et agri a barbaris vastentur, nos ipsi bellum provocemus. Hoc modo et honorem nostri imperii conservabimus et cives tutos reddemus.*

Lentulus: Fabius, you are too hopeful. Envoys are no longer useful since our enemies neither accept peace nor negotiations. I propose that, before our cities and fields are devastated by the barbarians, we ourselves declare war. In this way, we will preserve the honor of our empire and ensure the safety of our citizens.

Flaminia: *Consentio cum Lentulo. Bellum hoc non est nobis optio, sed necessitas. Cunctatio et spes falsae de pace perniciem afferent. Melius est arma capere quam exspectare dum hostes portas nostras pulsant. Si non statim bellum gerimus, gloriam Romanam ipso ignaviae dedecore amittimus.*

Flaminia: I agree with Lentulus. This war is not a choice for us, but a necessity. Hesitation and false hopes for peace will bring ruin. It is better to take up arms than to wait for the enemy to knock on our gates. If we do not wage war immediately, we will lose the very glory of Rome to the shame of cowardice.

Sulpicius: *Nemo nostrum ignavus est, Flaminia. Nemini placet procedere in bellum sine causa iusta. Sed hoc quaero: estne hic noster ultimus recursus? Omnia remedia debent prius temptari, et si bellum inevitabile est, tum demum arma capiamus. Ut plurimum sensi, debemus* *etiam populi voluntatem respicere. Non omnia in senatu iudicari oportet, sed etiam ex ipsa civitate.*

Sulpicius: None of us is cowardly, Flaminia. No one wants to go to war without a just cause. But I ask this: is this truly our last resort? All remedies must first be tried, and if war is inevitable, only then should we take up arms. I believe we must also consider the will of the people. Not everything should be decided in the Senate; we must also listen to the voices of the people themselves.

Flaminia: *Patres, tempus fugere videtur. Non possumus semper populi suffragia exspectare. Respondistis hostes iam prope esse? Morae omnes belli exitium afferent, et nos dubitando civibus nocebimus.*

Flaminia: Senators, time seems to be slipping away. We cannot always wait for the people's votes. Did you not hear that the enemy is already near? All delays in war will bring destruction, and by hesitating, we harm our citizens.

Fabius: *Ego tamen, Flaminia, postulo ut ultimum consilium tenemus. Pacem prius temptandam censeo. Si hostes pacem repudiant, tum bellum iustissimum erit. Non est honos tantum arma capere, sed etiam sapienter procedere.*

Fabius: Even so, Flaminia, I insist that we hold to the final course of action. I believe peace must first be attempted. If the enemy rejects peace, then war will be most just. There is no honor only in taking up arms but also in proceeding wisely.

Lentulus: *Ergo statuamus: pro bello decernendum est! Bellum iustum, necessarium, et honorificum erit, si ad nostram dignitatem defendendam armis nos provexerimus. Civitatem nostram servare debemus.*

Lentulus: So let us decide: we must declare war! The war will be just, necessary, and honorable if we take up arms to defend our dignity. We must protect our state.

Sulpicius: *Si bellum necessarium est, nullam aliam viam video. Di superi prodent nostra consilia, et Romam invictam servabimus!*

Sulpicius: If war is necessary, I see no other way. The gods above will favor our plans, and we will keep Rome undefeated!

Flaminia: *Nunc agendum est, Patres! Ad arma!*

Flaminia: Now is the time to act, Senators! To arms!

In Palaestra – Disputatio de exercitatione in gymnasio

Marcellus: *Salve, Sulpicia! Video te saepe in palaestra exerceri. Quid agis hodie? Num corpus levibus exercitationibus firmans an gravioribus ludis contenta es?*

Marcellus: Hello, Sulpicia! I see you often exercising in the gym. What are you doing today? Are you strengthening your body with light exercises, or are you content with more strenuous activities?

Sulpicia: *Salve, Marcelle! Hodie quidem graviores exercitationes mihi proposui. Umeros ac bracchia validiora facere volo. Curare enim oportet ut corpus non solum ad speciem, sed etiam ad valetudinem firmetur. Tu autem, quid hic facis? Num consuetudo tua tibi placet?*

Sulpicia: Hello, Marcellus! Today, I have planned for heavier exercises. I want to make my shoulders and arms stronger. It's important to ensure that the body is strengthened not just for appearance, but also for health. But you, what are you doing here? Are you satisfied with your routine?

Marcellus: *Ego quoque valde studeo ut corpus robustum habeam. Hodie me luctando et pila iacienda exercui. Mihi videtur horum ludorum ratio non solum vim, sed etiam agilitatem augere. Sed dic mihi, Sulpicia, quid de salute tua censes? Num exercitatio corporis an cibus magis ad valetudinem pertinere tibi videtur?*

Marcellus: I also strive to have a strong body. Today, I exercised by wrestling and throwing a ball. It seems to me that these activities not only increase strength but also agility. But tell me, Sulpicia, what do you think about your health? Do you believe exercise or diet is more important for maintaining good health?

Sulpicia: *Utrumque profecto necessarium est. Sine exercitatione, corpus languet; sine iusto cibo, vires non conservantur. Ego conor medio modo inter utrumque vivere: neque nimium leniter, neque nimio rigore. Sed discipulos in palaestra saepe vidi, qui, fessi quidem, sed gloria contenti, nimis exercerentur. Quid tu de hac re sentis?*

Sulpicia: Both are certainly necessary. Without exercise, the body weakens; without proper food, strength cannot be maintained. I try to live in moderation between both: not too lightly, nor too strictly. But I have often seen students in the gym who, though exhausted, still push themselves too hard, driven by a desire for glory. What do you think about this?

Marcellus: *Hoc verum est. Nonnulli nimium fervore se contundunt, quidam etiam fruges corpori necessarias neglegunt. Exercitatio moderata, ut dicis, optime valet ad salutem. Ego ipse, quamquam certamine delecter, curo tamen ut ne nimis me fatigem. Prudenter agendum est!*

Marcellus: That's true. Some push themselves too hard with excessive fervor, and others even neglect the nourishment their body needs. As you said, moderate exercise is best for health. I, though I enjoy competition, make sure not to exhaust myself too much. One must act wisely!

Sulpicia: *Ita, sapientia provisum esse oportet, Marcelle. Exercitatio quidem corpus fortem facit, sed si mens quoque non reficitur, nihil ad integrum bene fiet. Neque enim fructus ullus ex labore melius est quam temperantia. Tu numquam nimium festinare vis, sed aequa ratione te defendis, ne vires celeriter deficiant.*

Sulpicia: Yes, wisdom must guide us, Marcellus. Exercise indeed makes the body strong, but if the mind is not also refreshed, nothing is truly done well. No benefit from effort is better than moderation. You never want to rush too much, but you wisely pace yourself, so your strength doesn't quickly fail.

Marcellus: *Plene assentior! Etsi enim athleta strenuus vires suas saepe ad ludos provehit, tamen frangitur, nisi temperantia corpus suum regit. Sed dic mihi, Sulpicia, quaenam exercitatio tibi maxime placet? Num pila lusus an currendo magis delectaris?*

Marcellus: I fully agree! Even though a vigorous athlete often pushes their strength for the games, they break down if moderation doesn't guide their body. But tell me, Sulpicia, what exercise do you enjoy most? Do you prefer playing ball or running more?

Sulpicia: *Mihi quidem currendo maxime delector. Libet animam per aerem et campos latos effundere. Tunc enim mentem ac corporis motus coniunctissime se habere sentio. Sed pila lusus quoque iucundus est, quoniam et levitatem et celeritatem simul requirit.*

Sulpicia: I really enjoy running the most. I like letting my spirit flow through the air and across open fields. In those moments, I feel my mind and body are in perfect harmony. But playing ball is also fun because it requires both lightness and speed at the same time.

Marcellus: *Currere et pila ludere sunt exercitationes quibus optime corpus movetur. Sed videsne quomodo in palaestra hic certent? Luctari videtur etiam maximam partem eorum delectare. Ego autem minus luctandi studio teneor, nam satis dure agitur et saepe vulnera affert.*

Marcellus: Running and playing ball are exercises that move the body most effectively. But do you see how many here compete in the gym? Wrestling seems to please most of them. I, however, am less attracted to wrestling, as it's rather rough and often leads to injuries.

Sulpicia: *Luctari, quamquam laboriosum et periculosum, nonnullis quidem placet. Sic fortasse vires melius probari constat. Sed, ut dicis, vulnera etiam exspectanda sunt, quae non semper feliciter curantur. Ego autem prudenter exercitationes moderatas praefero, ut diu corpus validum teneam.*

Sulpicia: Wrestling, though laborious and dangerous, pleases some. It may indeed be a better way to test strength. But as you said, injuries are to be expected, and they aren't always easily healed. I, however, wisely prefer moderate exercises, so I can keep my body strong for a long time.

Marcellus: *Sapienter loqueris, Sulpicia. Prudentia et moderatio semper in omnibus rebus servanda sunt. Vale nunc, et bona fortuna in palaestra tibi sit!*

Marcellus: You speak wisely, Sulpicia. Prudence and moderation must always be kept in everything. Farewell for now, and good fortune to you in the gym!

Sulpicia: *Vale, Marcelle! Tibi quoque bonam valetudinem et strenuitatem opto!*

Sulpicia: Farewell, Marcellus! I wish you good health and strength as well!

De Consilio Sapientis – Disputatio de sapienti consilio et monitis

Cornelius: *Salve, Valeria! Nuper me multae res sollicitant, et consilium tuum sapientis quaerere volo. Scio te saepe bene consuluisse amicis tuis. Dic mihi, quid tibi videtur: utrum melius sit prudentiam in rebus agendis usu perdiscere, an consilium alienum quaerere?*

Cornelius: Hello, Valeria! Recently, many things have been troubling me, and I want to seek your wise counsel. I know that you have often given good advice to your friends. Tell me, what do you think: is it better to learn wisdom in handling affairs through experience, or should one seek advice from others?

Valeria: *Salve, Corneli! Ego quidem censeo sapientiam partim ex proprio usu, partim ex consilio sapientium adhibendam esse. Nemo enim satis prudens est ut omnia sua sponte provideat; multum enim iuvabit aliorum iudicium et experientia. Sed dic mihi, quid te nunc angat? Quid consilii quaeris?*

Valeria: Hello, Cornelius! I believe that wisdom should be drawn partly from personal experience and partly from the counsel of the wise. For no one is wise enough to foresee everything on their own; the judgment and experience of others help greatly. But tell me, what is troubling you now? What advice are you seeking?

Cornelius: *Quaestio mihi difficilis est. Cogito utrum me ad magistratum petendum promoveam, an potius a re publica abstineam. Magni honores quidem magnam gloriam adferunt, sed simul multa pericula et sollicitudinum plena sunt. Nescio an melius sit otium quam negotium petere.*

Cornelius: The question is difficult for me. I am considering whether I should pursue public office or rather abstain from involvement in the state. Great honors indeed bring great glory, but they also come with many dangers and are full of anxieties. I am unsure whether it is better to seek a quiet life or to pursue public service.

Valeria: *Quaestio gravis est, Corneli. Magistratus quidem provident honorem, sed in eos etiam multae curae cadunt. Hoc tamen consilium tibi darem: si tu ipse sentis te patriae commodum ferre posse, petendum est.*

Non enim semper vitae tranquillae opes maximae laudis sunt. Diligentia et officium in re publica, si recte geritur, summum proficit.

Valeria: It is indeed a serious question, Cornelius. Public office does provide honor, but it also brings many burdens. However, I would give you this advice: if you feel that you can bring benefit to the state, you should pursue it. A tranquil life does not always bring the greatest praise. Diligence and duty in public service, if done rightly, achieve the highest success.

Cornelius: *Sapienter mones, Valeria. Sed nonnumquam video viros praeclaros, qui in magistratibus summis fuerunt, a calamitatibus gravissimis oppressos esse. Fortuna enim saepe non favet bonis. Quid censes? Estne fata Romana tam incerta ut nemo tutus sit, etiam si iuste ac prudenter agat?*

Cornelius: You advise wisely, Valeria. But sometimes I see great men, who have held the highest offices, oppressed by the gravest misfortunes. Fortune often does not favor the good. What do you think? Is the fate of Rome so uncertain that no one is safe, even if they act justly and wisely?

Valeria: *Vere loqueris. Fortuna semper variabilis est, neque certum est quid quis propositum habeat, etiam si virtute praestat. Sed hoc tibi monendum est: ei qui prudentiam et iustitiam sequuntur, et si fatis adversis occurrant, honorem tamen aeternum sibi comparant. Non tantum res exitiosas metue, sed gloriam virtutis persequere.*

Valeria: You speak truly. Fortune is always changeable, and it is never certain what one will face, even if they excel in virtue. But let me remind you of this: those who follow wisdom and justice, even if they encounter adverse fates, still earn eternal honor for themselves. Do not fear only ruin, but pursue the glory of virtue.

Cornelius: *Hoc quidem mihi ad cor loquitur. Melius est honorifice conari et, si necesse sit, casus ferre, quam ignava desidia vitam agere. Valde me movet quod dicis de gloria et honore aeterno.*

Cornelius: This speaks to my heart. It is better to strive honorably and, if necessary, face misfortune, than to live a life of lazy inactivity. I am deeply moved by what you say about eternal glory and honor.

Valeria: *Ita est, Corneli. Vita ipsa breve tempus habet, sed fama bonorum virorum diu manet. Magistratum petere non debet ex cupiditate honorum, sed ex cupiditate bene faciendi. Si animus tibi deditus est ut rem publicam bene geras, honorem non exspectes, sed bonos conatus propositum habeas.*

Valeria: That is correct, Cornelius. Life itself is brief, but the reputation of good men lasts for a long time. You should not pursue public office out of a desire for honors, but out of a desire to do good. If your spirit is dedicated to governing the state well, do not expect honor but have good intentions as your goal.

Cornelius: *Valeria, gratias tibi ago pro consilio sapienti. Me multum adiuvisti ut hac in re prudentiam caperem. Pareo igitur tuo monito: magistratum petam, et, si dis placet, virtute, non fortuna, geram.*

Cornelius: Valeria, thank you for your wise counsel. You have greatly helped me to gain wisdom in this matter. I will follow your advice: I will seek public office, and if the gods allow, I will govern by virtue, not by fortune.

Valeria: *Bene facis, Corneli! Sic semper rationem habe, ut honos et officium iustitiam sequantur. Spero ut tibi omnia prospere eveniant, et virtus tua praeclara sit in servanda patria. Vale!*

Valeria: You are doing the right thing, Cornelius! Always keep in mind that honor and duty must follow justice. I hope everything turns out well for you, and may your virtue shine in serving your country. Farewell!

Cornelius: *Vale, Valeria!*

Cornelius: Farewell, Valeria!

In Ludis Publicis – De ludis publicis spectandis

Numerius: *Salve, Septimia! Quam opportune advenisti! Ludi publici iam incipiunt, et populus Romanus avide spectat. Nonne haec celebritas tibi maxime placet?*

Numerius: Hello, Septimia! How timely you've arrived! The public games are about to begin, and the Roman people eagerly watch. Don't you find this celebration the most enjoyable?

Septimia: *Salve, Numeri! Ita vero, ludos publicos semper maxima cum laetitia specto. Nihil iucundius est quam videre tot cives gaudio plenos. Sed quid hodie praebeatur, nondum scio. Num currus certamen spectabimus?*

Septimia: Hello, Numerius! Yes indeed, I always watch the public games with great joy. There's nothing more enjoyable than seeing so many citizens filled with happiness. But I don't yet know what's being presented today. Will we watch a chariot race?

Numerius: *Certe! Hodie sunt ludi circenses, et aurigae quattuor factionum certabunt: albi, russati, virides, et caerulei. Ego viridibus faveo, nam eorum auriga, Celer, praeclarissimus in re currendi est. Tu autem cui faves?*

Numerius: Certainly! Today there are circus games, and the charioteers of four factions will compete: the whites, the reds, the greens, and the blues. I support the greens, as their charioteer, Celer, is most famous in the art of racing. But whom do you support?

Septimia: *Ego semper russatis faveo! Auriga eorum, Crispus, saepe palmas tulit, et populo valde amatus est. Miror tamen, quid de deorum cultu factum sit. Ante certamen solent deis sacrificia offerri. Nonne id iam vidisti?*

Septimia: I always support the reds! Their charioteer, Crispus, has often won the prize and is greatly loved by the people. But I wonder, what has been done regarding the worship of the gods? Before the race, sacrifices are usually offered to the gods. Have you seen that yet?

Numerius: *Ita est! Sacrificia iam facta sunt in aede Iovis Optimi Maximi. Augures aves bona ominia promiserunt, et sacerdos Iovi tauro* *sacrificavit. Totus populus spectavit, et signum felix datum est ad certamen incipiendum.*

Numerius: Yes, indeed! The sacrifices have already been performed in the temple of Jupiter Optimus Maximus. The augurs observed the birds and promised good omens, and the priest sacrificed a bull to Jupiter. The whole crowd watched, and a favorable sign was given to start the race.

Septimia: *Bene quidem! Nihil gravius in talibus ludis quam favere deorum voluntati. Sed dic mihi, quid de his certaminibus sentis? Nonne aliquantulum crudeles videntur?*

Septimia: That's good indeed! There is nothing more serious in such games than gaining the favor of the gods. But tell me, what do you think about these competitions? Don't they seem a little cruel?

Numerius: *Fortasse, Septimia, sed ludi circenses partem maximam rerum popularium habent. Est enim gaudium videre aurigas tanta peritia et audacia currus regere. Crudelitas non est in ipso certamine, sed periculum magis. Aurigae per virtutem vincunt, non per vim.*

Numerius: Perhaps, Septimia, but the circus games hold a major place in public affairs. It's a joy to see the charioteers guide their chariots with such skill and daring. The cruelty isn't in the competition itself, but more in the danger. The charioteers win through virtue, not through force.

Septimia: *Recte fortasse dicis. Ego tamen magis de ludis scenicis delector, ubi fabulae et saltationes non tantum corporis vires, sed etiam ingenium et ars celebrantur. Praeterea, mulieres in theatro commodius spectant quam in circo tumultuanti.*

Septimia: You might be right. But I enjoy scenic performances more, where plays and dances celebrate not just physical strength but also intellect and art. Besides, women find it more comfortable to watch in the theater than in the noisy circus.

Numerius: *Quidem, ludi scenici suae pulchritudinis habent, sed circenses alio quodam genere excitant. Aurigae pro gloria certant, et nullum spectaculum mirabilius est quam cum currus ad metam pervolant. Quid tamen de gladiatoriis ludis sentis? Multi eos vehementer laudant, sed ego crudeles nimis esse puto.*

Numerius: Indeed, scenic games have their own beauty, but the circus games excite in a different way. The charioteers compete for glory, and there is no spectacle more marvelous than when the chariots race toward the turning point. But what do you think of the gladiatorial games? Many praise them highly, but I think they're too cruel.

Septimia: *Gladiatoria certamina vere mihi minus placent. Saepe vires et audacia laudentur, sed nimis multa sanguinis effusio est. Crudelitas omni modo in huiusmodi ludis apparere videtur. Ego magis ad spectacula quae animum et corpus sine violentia movent convertor.*

Septimia: I truly like gladiatorial contests less. Strength and bravery are often praised, but there is too much bloodshed. Cruelty seems to appear in every way in such games. I am more drawn to spectacles that move the mind and body without violence.

Numerius: *Bene loqueris. Ludi tamen, sive gladiatorii sive circenses, suum locum in vita civitatis habent. Sed, audisne clamores? Signum certaminis datum est, aurigae iam prodeunt!*

Numerius: You speak well. However, whether gladiatorial or circus games, they have their place in the life of the city. But, do you hear the shouts? The signal for the race has been given, and the charioteers are now coming out!

Septimia: *Video! Specta! Populus clamare incipit. Videamus utris primum palmam ferent: russati an virides! Fortuna eis faveat quibus cordi sunt!*

Septimia: I see! Look! The crowd is starting to shout. Let's see who will win the prize first: the reds or the greens! May fortune favor those they hold dear!

Numerius: *Fortuna tamen viridibus favebit! Nunc spectabimus utrum virtus vel fatum praepolleat. Ad certamen animum intendamus!*

Numerius: Fortune will favor the greens, though! Now we will see whether skill or fate will prevail. Let's focus on the race!

Septimia: *Ita vero! Spectaculum incipit—videamus quid deorum voluntas sit!*

Septimia: Indeed! The spectacle begins—let's see what the will of the gods may be!

De Moribus Veterum – Disputatio de moribus priscorum Romanorum

Laelia: *Salve, Aemiliane! Nuper multum cogitavi de moribus veterum nostrorum, praesertim de eo quomodo vivebant prisci Romani. Cura et industria vitam agebant, sine ea luxuria quae hodierno tempore plerumque videtur. Nonne tibi videtur eos meliores mores fovisse quam nos?*

Laelia: Hello, Aemilianus! Recently, I've been thinking a lot about the customs of our ancestors, especially about how the ancient Romans lived. They led their lives with care and hard work, without the luxury that seems so common nowadays. Don't you think they upheld better values than we do?

Aemilianus: *Salve, Laelia! Assentior tibi. Veteres certe maiorem reverentiam adhibebant ad res domesticas et publicas. Non tam divitias aut voluptates quaerebant, sed virtutem, pietatem, et officium. Videsne quomodo in Roma antiqua magistratus honorem servabant, nec quicquam proprium lucri curabant?*

Aemilianus: Hello, Laelia! I agree with you. The ancients certainly showed greater reverence for both domestic and public affairs. They didn't seek wealth or pleasures as much as they sought virtue, piety, and duty. Do you see how in ancient Rome, magistrates preserved honor and didn't care about personal gain?

Laelia: *Ita vero, Aemiliane! Senatores ipsi prisci non tam ad gloriam suam quam ad rerum publicarum commodum spectabant. Curabant familiae honorem, res publicas administrabant magna cum gravitate, et deos omnes pie colebant. Multum enim valet religio in bonis moribus servandis, nonne?*

Laelia: Yes, indeed, Aemilianus! The ancient senators themselves didn't look for personal glory but for the benefit of the state. They cared for the honor of their families, managed public affairs with great seriousness, and piously worshipped all the gods. Religion plays a huge role in maintaining good morals, doesn't it?

Aemilianus: *Sane. Veteres, ut bene nosti, summa pietate ad deos et maiores suos spectabant. Non modo res domesticae, sed etiam res* *publicae sub auspiciis deorum gerebantur. Quid enim praeclarius quam Pompeius vel Cicero, qui non sine sacrificiis et ominibus auspiciisque omnem actionem in re publica agere coeperunt?*

Aemilianus: Certainly. The ancients, as you well know, looked up to the gods and their ancestors with utmost piety. Not only domestic affairs but also public matters were conducted under the guidance of the gods. What could be more illustrious than Pompey or Cicero, who never began any action in public life without sacrifices, omens, and auspices?

Laelia: *Cicero ipse saepe laudabat mores et disciplinam maiorum. In epistulis eius legimus quomodo vita moderata et simplicior praeferenda sit illi luxuriae et cupiditati quae posterioribus temporibus invaluerunt. Sed nunc multi Romani divitias et voluptates prae virtute et honestate collocant. Quid censes de hac re?*

Laelia: Cicero himself often praised the customs and discipline of our ancestors. In his letters, we read how a more moderate and simple life should be preferred to the luxury and greed that have gained power in later times. But now, many Romans place wealth and pleasures above virtue and honor. What do you think about this?

Aemilianus: *Haec quoque me valde angit, Laelia. Multi cives nostri iam vivere videntur ut res suas augeant, non ut rem publicam tueantur. Magnifica cenae, thesauri ingentes, et spectacula per totam urbem magis quam studium virtutis celebrantur. Cura antiqua temperantia iam cedit cupiditatibus novis. Sed quid putas facere oportere, ut mores veterum iterum colamus?*

Aemilianus: This troubles me greatly as well, Laelia. Many of our citizens now seem to live to increase their own wealth, not to protect the republic. Lavish dinners, immense treasures, and spectacles across the city are celebrated more than the pursuit of virtue. The ancient care for moderation now gives way to new desires. But what do you think we should do to revive the customs of the ancients?

Laelia: *Vix dicere possum, Aemiliane, sed fortasse revocanda est disciplina, primum in familiis. Pueri et puellae, ut olim, debent ab infantia virtutis exempla sumere. Parentes ipsi primum honorem, industriam, pietatemque colant, ut liberi iustas vitarum rationes discant.*

Laelia: I can hardly say, Aemilianus, but perhaps discipline must be restored, first in families. Boys and girls, as in the past, should learn examples of virtue from childhood. The parents themselves should first cultivate honor, hard work, and piety so that the children may learn the right way to live.

Aemilianus: *Sapiens consilium est! Nam si iuventus ad bonos mores bene instituatur, sperare possumus ut aliquando civitas totum orbem iterum virtute regat. Veteres praeceptores de virtute non modo loquebantur, sed etiam exemplis suis eam proponebant. Nos quoque eodem modo agere debemus.*

Aemilianus: Wise advice! For if the youth are well trained in good morals, we can hope that one day the state may once again rule the whole world with virtue. The old teachers not only spoke about virtue but also set it forth by example. We must act in the same way.

Laelia: *Ita est, Aemiliane. Veteres non tantum verba, sed facta colebant. Et si nos exemplum veterum sequemur, meliorem rem publicam atque societatem efficiemus. Vale nunc, et utinam semper maiorum nostrorum exempla ante oculos habeamus.*

Laelia: Indeed, Aemilianus. The ancients did not only honor words but also deeds. And if we follow their example, we will create a better republic and society. Farewell now, and may we always keep the examples of our ancestors before our eyes.

Aemilianus: *Vale, Laelia! Ad virtutem et pietatem semper properemus, ut digni filii Romae videamur!*

Aemilianus: Farewell, Laelia! Let us always strive for virtue and piety so that we may be seen as worthy sons and daughters of Rome!

In Iudicio – Disputatio in iudicio Romano

Iudex Marcellus: *Salvete, cives! Hodie in hac basilica rem gravem iudicabimus. Acusius, qui hic adsidet, Varium criminibus de peculatu et fraude accusat. Vari, dic mihi, quomodo te defendere velis? Negasne crimina, an culpam confiteris?*

Judge Marcellus: Greetings, citizens! Today, in this basilica, we will judge a serious matter. Acusius, who is seated here, accuses Varius of embezzlement and fraud. Varius, tell me how you wish to defend yourself. Do you deny the charges, or do you confess guilt?

Varius: *Salve, iudex. Omni fide et animo affirmo me innocentem esse. Nullam fraudem aut peculatum commisi. Praedonem me fingunt, sed res aliter se habent. Falsae accusationes mihi iniuria imponuntur.*

Varius: Greetings, judge. With all honesty and spirit, I declare myself innocent. I committed no fraud or embezzlement. They are making me out to be a thief, but the matter is different. False accusations have been unjustly placed upon me.

Acusius: *Non ita est, Vari. Me ipso teste, pecunia publica, cuius custodia tibi credita erat, subito deficere coepit. Ex numeris ipsis patent indiciorum documenta. Dicasne mirum casum accidisse, cum nemo alius nisi tu ad aerarium accessum haberet?*

Acusius: It is not so, Varius. I am a witness myself: the public money, of which you were entrusted with the care, suddenly began to disappear. The evidence is clear from the records. Would you claim that a strange coincidence occurred when no one else but you had access to the treasury?

Varius: *Acusi, erras. Tempus illud fuit plenum tumultus, cum res publicae perturbabantur. Non ego solus ad aerarium accessi. Multi alii, quibus fiducia publica erat, eadem officia gerebant. Quidquid defuit, fortunae casus fuit, non mea culpa.*

Varius: Acusius, you are mistaken. That time was full of chaos when the state was in turmoil. I was not the only one who accessed the treasury. Many others, who also had public trust, performed the same duties. Whatever was missing was due to misfortune, not my fault.

Iudex Marcellus: *Satis audivi utrumque. Vari, licetne tibi testes tuos vocare? Aliquem habes, qui te defendere possit aut testimonium ferat?*

Judge Marcellus: I have heard enough from both sides. Varius, may you call your witnesses? Do you have anyone who can defend you or give testimony?

Varius: *Ita, habeo. Lucius Valerius, vir summae probitatis, testabitur me semper recte administravisse et nullam fraudem admisisse.*

Varius: Yes, I do. Lucius Valerius, a man of the highest integrity, will testify that I always managed my duties properly and committed no fraud.

Lucius Valerius: *Salve, iudex. Varium ego longa annorum experientia cognovi. Non est is vir qui fraude vel inhoneste aliquid ageret. Cum aerarii custodiam haberet, semper integritatem praebuit. Crimina haec infirma sunt nec probari possunt.*

Lucius Valerius: Greetings, judge. I have known Varius for many years. He is not a man who would act dishonestly or fraudulently. When he had custody of the treasury, he always demonstrated integrity. These charges are weak and cannot be proven.

Acusius: *Sed testimonia numerosa contra clamant! Etiam servi publici testificati sunt pecuniam publicam a Vario minutam esse. Nihil potest huic falsitati obici. Probatio certa est.*

Acusius: But numerous testimonies shout against him! Even public slaves have testified that the public money was reduced by Varius. Nothing can be said against this falsehood. The proof is solid.

Iudex Marcellus: *Acusi, testimonia tua gravia videntur, sed non omnia sicco oculo cernere possumus. Vari, an alia tibi defensio est?*

Judge Marcellus: Acusius, your evidence seems serious, but we cannot judge everything without a discerning eye. Varius, do you have any other defense?

Varius: *Nisi hoc: omnia, quae contra me dicta sunt, falsa sunt. Nemo, nisi ex mala voluntate, me culpavit. Innocentiam meam iudicibus relinquo.*

Varius: Only this: everything that has been said against me is false. No one has accused me except out of ill will. I leave my innocence to the judges.

Iudex Marcellus: *Causae argumenta ex utraque parte gravia sunt. Cives, qui in hac re iudicatis, diligenter cogitate. Ego tandem iudicium pronuntiabo.*

Judge Marcellus: The arguments from both sides are weighty. Citizens, who are judging this case, consider carefully. I will finally pronounce the judgment.

Lucius Valerius: *Spero, iudex, ut innocentia Vari clare pateat. Ne honorem viri probi calumniae obscurent!*

Lucius Valerius: I hope, judge, that the innocence of Varius will be clearly seen. Let not the honor of a good man be darkened by slander!

Iudex Marcellus: *Quod iudicium hodie feramus, ad vestram fidem et iustitiam pertinet. Reum Varium, criminibus peculatus et fraudis, absolvimus. Curiae gratia edicta est, neque amplius quaestionem hac de re submittam.*

Judge Marcellus: The judgment we deliver today depends on your faith and justice. We acquit Varius of the charges of embezzlement and fraud. The court is adjourned, and I will submit no further question on this matter.

Acusius: *(murmurans) Sed iustitia non sic voluit!*

Acusius: (muttering) But justice didn't wish it this way!

Varius: *Gratias ago, iudex. Fidelissime me defensum esse sensi. Valete omnes.*

Varius: Thank you, judge. I felt that I was defended most faithfully. Farewell, everyone.

Iudex Marcellus: *Valete!*

Judge Marcellus: Farewell!

De Pacis Studio – Disputatio de pace et legationibus

Aulus: *Salve, Lucilla! Nuper in Senatu multa de bello audivi, sed ipse mirum in modum ad pacem magis inclino. Dic mihi, quid tibi videtur de studio pacis? Num semper bellum ultimum rerum effugium esse debemus?*

Aulus: Greetings, Lucilla! Recently, I heard much about war in the Senate, but I am surprisingly more inclined toward peace. Tell me, what do you think about the pursuit of peace? Should war always be our last resort?

Lucilla: *Salve, Aule! Certe, pax praeferenda est bello, si conservari potest. Nihil enim est in bello nisi miseria et periculum. Sed non semper reges aut populi pacem volunt. Quidam bello gloriam quaerunt, alii opes. Ergo dic mihi, cur nunc tibi pax potior videatur?*

Lucilla: Greetings, Aulus! Certainly, peace should be preferred over war, if it can be maintained. For there is nothing in war but misery and danger. But kings and peoples do not always desire peace. Some seek glory in war, others wealth. So tell me, why does peace seem preferable to you now?

Aulus: *Cogito, Lucilla, quanta damna bellum afferat. Non tantum corpus et res periclitamur, sed etiam animus ipse violatur. Cives, qui in pace artes et leges colunt, in bello saevire discunt. Ita fit ut Roma ipsa suam non virtutem, sed crudelitatem patefaciat. Sic in multis populis non prosperitas sed timor imperium nostrum servat.*

Aulus: I am thinking, Lucilla, of the great harm that war brings. Not only do we risk life and property, but the soul itself is harmed. Citizens who cultivate arts and laws in peace learn to be savage in war. Thus, Rome shows not its virtue, but its cruelty. In many peoples, it is not prosperity but fear that sustains our empire.

Lucilla: *Verba tua vera sunt, Aule. Tamen non semper pax perpetua potest esse in rebus humanis. Multos iam annos Romani per arma et bellum constantiam suam ostenderunt. Et fortasse non bellum per se laudandum est, sed disciplina et fortitudo, quae per bellum exercetur. Sed non contradico tibi; pax bona semper quaerenda est.*

Lucilla: Your words are true, Aulus. However, perpetual peace is not always possible in human affairs. For many years, Romans have shown their resilience through arms and war. Perhaps it is not war itself that should be praised, but the discipline and courage exercised through it. But I do not disagree with you; peace should always be sought.

Aulus: *Hoc quidem fateor, Lucilla. Bellum saepe necessitatem affert, et virtus militaris non est contemnenda. Sed multi nimis saepe in bellum provolant, non propter necessitatem, sed propter cupiditatem. Ne vidisti quam multi duces bellum pro gloria sua quaerant, nec utilitatem civium curent?*

Aulus: I admit this, Lucilla. War often brings necessity, and military virtue should not be scorned. But many rush too often into war, not out of necessity, but out of greed. Haven't you seen how many leaders seek war for their own glory, not caring for the well-being of the citizens?

Lucilla: *Ita, saepe hoc fit. Multi duces ambitione sua rerum statum perturbant. Nonnumquam videtur bellum magis esse iudicium virium quam verus sermo de iure aut aequitate. Cur non magis usque ad finem de pace tractamus? Nonne apud Romanos legationes et oratores magnam potestatem habuerunt?*

Lucilla: Yes, this often happens. Many leaders, driven by ambition, disturb the state of affairs. Sometimes war seems more like a trial of strength than a true discussion of justice or fairness. Why don't we negotiate for peace until the very end? Haven't Roman envoys and diplomats always had great authority?

Aulus: *Sane. Romani semper oratores et legatos magno in honore habuerunt, quippe qui sermones civiles pro pace publica mire efficerent. Cur non nunc eosdem mores sequimur? Si in oraculis et pactis fidem habemus, multae clades evitari possunt. Quid mirabilius est quam vitam sine bello vivere?*

Aulus: Certainly. Romans have always held orators and envoys in high esteem, as they skillfully conducted civil discourse for the sake of public peace. Why don't we follow the same customs now? If we trust in treaties and agreements, many disasters can be avoided. What is more wonderful than living without war?

Lucilla: *Ego quoque laetor, si pax provisa est. Multae gentes, multi populi bellum fugient, si saltem iusti pacti leges sequantur. Quid de te censes, Aule? Quid faciamus ut pacis studium praevaleat?*

Lucilla: I too am glad if peace is secured. Many nations, many peoples will flee from war if at least the laws of a just treaty are followed. What do you think, Aulus? What should we do to make the pursuit of peace prevail?

Aulus: *Censeo ut semper primum consilium pacis quaeramus, priusquam bellum faciamus. Emittamus legatos, discutiamus iusta, et si omnia deficiant, tum demum ad arma veniamus. Sed praeclare moneo: pax pro sapientia, bellum pro necessitate.*

Aulus: I believe that we should always seek peace as the first course of action, before we resort to war. Let us send envoys, discuss justice, and if all fails, then, and only then, take up arms. But I strongly advise: peace for wisdom, war for necessity.

Lucilla: *Sapienter dicis, Aule. Pax sine dubio est beatior quam gloria ex bello. Servemus eam, ut Roma, quae imperium terrarum propagat, sit etiam exemplum moderationis. Vale nunc, et utinam pax semper prosperet!*

Lucilla: You speak wisely, Aulus. Peace is undoubtedly more blessed than glory from war. Let us preserve it so that Rome, which spreads its empire over the world, may also be an example of moderation. Farewell now, and may peace always prosper!

Aulus: *Vale, Lucilla! Si pacem sequemur, finem laetum Romae auguror.*

Aulus: Farewell, Lucilla! If we follow peace, I foresee a joyful future for Rome.

In Castris – Disputatio inter milites Romanos in castris

Manius: *Salve, Decime! Longum quidem iter habuimus, sed nunc in castris aliquantulum requiescere possumus. Quomodo te habes post tantum laborem?*

Manius: Greetings, Decimus! We indeed had a long journey, but now we can rest a little in the camp. How are you after so much effort?

Decimus: *Salve, Mani! Certe fessus sum, sed non est mirum post tot dies per montes et flumina iter facientes. Nihilominus, milites Romani nullum laborem fugiunt. Dic mihi, quid nunc exspectamus? Num proelium appropinquat?*

Decimus: Greetings, Manius! Certainly, I am tired, but it's no surprise after so many days traveling over mountains and rivers. Nevertheless, Roman soldiers never shy away from hard work. Tell me, what are we expecting now? Is the battle approaching?

Manius: *Ita vero. Dux noster, Fabius, dixit hostes non longe abesse. Aliquot exploratores hodie redierunt et nuntiaverunt eos castra haud procul posuisse. Cras proelium fore puto. Tu paratus es?*

Manius: Indeed. Our leader, Fabius, said the enemy is not far away. Some scouts returned today and reported that they have set up camp not far from here. I think the battle will be tomorrow. Are you ready?

Decimus: *Sicut semper, Mani. Miles Romanus non est nisi proelio paratus. Sed fateri debeo me paulum sollicitum esse. Hostes Galli dicuntur feroces esse et audaces in proelio. Non facile erit eos vincere.*

Decimus: As always, Manius. A Roman soldier is always ready for battle. But I must admit that I am a little concerned. The Gauls are said to be fierce and bold in battle. It won't be easy to defeat them.

Manius: *Galli quidem feroces sunt, sed nos, Decime, milites disciplina et ratione multo superiores sumus. Ferocitas sine arte et consilio parum valet. Nonne saepe in provinciis barbaros vicimus? Dux noster non solum vir strenuus, sed etiam sapiens est.*

Manius: The Gauls are indeed fierce, but we, Decimus, are soldiers far superior in discipline and strategy. Ferocity without skill and planning is worth little. Haven't we often defeated the barbarians in the provinces? Our leader is not only a brave man but also a wise one.

Decimus: *Sane, spero ut fatum et fortuna Romanis faveant. Ratio et disciplina virtutes sunt quibus civitas nostra gloriam adepta est. Sed saepe fatum in proelio miro modo vertitur. Curabimus tamen ut virtute nostra victoriam efficiamus.*

Decimus: True, I hope that fate and fortune favor the Romans. Strategy and discipline are the virtues by which our state has achieved glory. But often fate turns in strange ways during battle. However, we will ensure victory with our courage.

Manius: *Sic loqui decet virum, Decime! Fortuna quidem variabilis est, sed animus noster firmus manere debet. Nemo, nisi fortitudine sua, victoriam certam facit. Cur, igitur, Gallos metueremus, cum nos ipsi honore et consilio praeclari simus?*

Manius: That is how a man should speak, Decimus! Fortune is indeed changeable, but our spirit must remain strong. No one secures victory except through their own courage. Why, then, should we fear the Gauls when we ourselves are renowned for our honor and strategy?

Decimus: *Prorsus, Mani! Durum est proelium, sed nihil tam difficile est quod virtus non superet. Tune cogitas de domo, cum in castris es? Mihi saepe subit memoria familiae meae.*

Decimus: Exactly, Manius! The battle will be tough, but nothing is so difficult that virtue cannot overcome it. Do you think about home when you're in the camp? I often think of my family.

Manius: *Certe, saepe de domo cogito, sed in bello me omnes curae rei militaris tenent. Cum pro patria pugnamus, omnia alia ad tempus in alio loco relinquenda sunt. Tu tamen, de familia tua cogitans, maiore studio pugnare poteris, ut illi tuti sint.*

Manius: Certainly, I often think of home, but in war, all my thoughts are consumed by military matters. When we fight for our country, all other concerns must be set aside for the moment. However, thinking of your family might give you even more motivation to fight, so they remain safe.

Decimus: *Ita est. Nihil tam gratum mihi est quam defendere rem publicam nostram, ut familiam et patriam incolumes relinquam. Spero ut hoc proelium non longum sit et victoria celeri perficiatur.*

Decimus: Exactly. Nothing is more pleasing to me than defending our republic, so that I may leave my family and homeland safe. I hope this battle won't be long and that victory is swiftly achieved.

Manius: *Sic erit, Decime! Cras vincemus, ut semper Romani vicerunt. Nunc autem quiescamus, ut vires ad proelium receperimus.*

Manius: It will be so, Decimus! Tomorrow we will win, just as the Romans have always won. But now, let's rest so we can recover our strength for battle.

Decimus: *Ita, quiescamus nunc, ut cras cum summa virtute pugnemus. Vale, Mani!*

Decimus: Yes, let's rest now so that tomorrow we fight with the greatest courage. Farewell, Manius!

Manius: *Vale, Decime!*

Manius: Farewell, Decimus!

De Rebus Maritimis – Disputatio de proeliis navalibus et commerciis maritimis

Marcus: *Salve, Servili! Nuper de navali proelio apud Actium audivi, quod inter Octavianum et Antonium commissum est. Quantae vires maritimae in illa pugna exstiterunt! Mihi videtur navalia proelia non minoris gloriae esse quam terrestria. Quid tibi videtur de rebus maritimis?*

Marcus: Greetings, Servilius! Recently, I heard about the naval battle at Actium, which was fought between Octavian and Antony. What great naval forces took part in that fight! It seems to me that naval battles are no less glorious than those on land. What do you think about maritime matters?

Servilius: *Salve, Marce! Recte censes. Proelia maritima saepe non tanto honore conspiciuntur quam illa quae in terra geruntur, sed utilitas eorum maxime apparet. Nisi Octavianus apud Actium vicisset, Roma ipsa discrimen maximum subiisset. Quid enim est imperium sine dominatu maris?*

Servilius: Greetings, Marcus! You are right. Naval battles often aren't viewed with as much honor as those fought on land, but their importance is clear. If Octavian hadn't won at Actium, Rome itself would have faced great danger. What is an empire without control of the sea?

Marcus: *Ita vero! Nostrae classes non tantum proelia gesserunt, sed etiam mercaturas et commoda imperii firmaverunt. Nonne dicitur mare internum, quod Graeci Mare Nostrum appellant, esse viam mercatorum et opum ad totam oram terrarum?*

Marcus: Indeed! Our fleets have not only fought battles but also secured trade and the benefits of the empire. Isn't the Mediterranean Sea, which the Greeks call "Mare Nostrum," said to be the highway for merchants and wealth to every shore?

Servilius: *Sane! Mare internum est quasi via regia imperii Romani. Multa per maria vehuntur, ut frumentum ex Aegypto, vinum ex Gallia, oleum ex Hispania. Nostrae classes etiam praedones maritimos reprimunt, qui mercatores nostros vexare solebant. Numquam sine mari dominatu Roma tantam opulentiam adeptura erat.*

Servilius: Certainly! The Mediterranean is like the royal highway of the Roman Empire. Many goods are carried across the seas, such as grain from Egypt, wine from Gaul, and olive oil from Spain. Our fleets also suppress maritime pirates who used to harass our merchants. Without control of the sea, Rome would never have achieved such wealth.

Marcus: *Nihil verius dixisti, Servili. Quotiens memoro procurationem maritimam, semper mihi in mentem venit quanta sit peritia navigandi necessaria. Rectores navium soli cum ventis et fluctibus contendunt, vere praeclarum opus est. Tu numquam in classe militavisti?*

Marcus: You couldn't have said it better, Servilius. Whenever I think about maritime operations, I'm always reminded of the great skill required for navigation. Ship captains must face the winds and waves alone—it's truly a remarkable task. Have you ever served in the navy?

Servilius: *Militare in classe nullum honorem habui, sed saepe de virtute eorum, qui in navibus pugnaverunt, audivi. Maxima laude digni sunt, qui in medio maris periculo rem suam fortiter gerunt. Fortuna maris saepe furtim vertitur, sed virtus pro certissima stat.*

Servilius: I've never had the honor of serving in the navy, but I've often heard about the courage of those who fought at sea. They are truly worthy of the highest praise, for they bravely carry out their duty amid the dangers of the sea. The fortune of the sea often changes suddenly, but courage remains steadfast.

Marcus: *Fortasse multi putent navalia proelia minus certa esse quam terrestria, sed, ut dicere solet, ratio et ars in omnibus rebus valent. Pugna ad Actium, ratio Octaviani vicit, cum callidissime Antonium circumvenit et classes eius dissipavit. Dux bonus in mari tam necessarius est quam in campo.*

Marcus: Some may think naval battles are less certain than those on land, but as the saying goes, strategy and skill prevail in all things. In the battle at Actium, Octavian's strategy won when he cleverly surrounded Antony and scattered his fleet. A good leader is as necessary at sea as on land.

Servilius: *Prorsus assentior. Quid plus valent milites in terra in proeliis, nisi dux eorum sapienter imperat? Idem est in mari. Sed quis scire possit* *ubi venti vertantur aut undae emergant? Itaque navigatio audaciam requirit, nec est res timidis apta.*

Servilius: I completely agree. What are soldiers worth in land battles if their commander does not lead wisely? It's the same at sea. But who can predict where the winds will shift or where the waves will rise? Therefore, navigation requires bravery, and it's not a task suited for the timid.

Marcus: *Ita quidem. Fortuna maritimorum semper pendet in multis incertis, sed eadem audacia quae in terra spectatur, etiam in mari laudanda est. Multum virtutis requirit, ut procellas et tempestates superes. Sed etiam memorandus est mercatus maritimus—quaenam plurima merces per mare vehuntur?*

Marcus: Exactly. The fate of sailors always depends on many uncertainties, but the same bravery that is admired on land is also praised at sea. It takes great courage to overcome storms and tempests. But we must also remember maritime trade—what are the most important goods transported by sea?

Servilius: *Multae sunt! Ut ante dixi, frumentum ex Aegypto, vinum et oleum ex Hispania, sed etiam marmora ex Graecia, aurum ex Africa, piper et aromata ex India vehuntur. Mercatores non solum rem facere curant, sed etiam ipso imperio serviunt, quoniam sine maritimis commerciis, totam terram nostram inopia pressam videremus.*

Servilius: There are many! As I mentioned earlier, grain from Egypt, wine and olive oil from Spain, but also marble from Greece, gold from Africa, and pepper and spices from India. Merchants are not only concerned with their profits but also serve the empire itself, for without maritime trade, our entire land would suffer from scarcity.

Marcus: *Vere loqueris! Re vera, mercatura maritima firmamentum est nostri imperii. Sine mari non solum proelia, sed etiam commoda, amicitiae, et opes interciderent. Valde me iuvat haec disputatio. Spero ut semper Roma maris dominatum teneat.*

Marcus: You speak the truth! Truly, maritime trade is the foundation of our empire. Without the sea, not only battles but also goods, friendships, and wealth would vanish. I greatly enjoy this discussion. I hope that Rome will always maintain control of the sea.

Servilius: *Ita fiat! Dum classes nostras fortes et firmas retineamus, imperium non tantum in terris, sed etiam in maribus servabimus. Vale, Marce!*

Servilius: So may it be! As long as we keep our fleets strong and firm, we will preserve our empire not only on land but also at sea. Farewell, Marcus!

Marcus: *Vale, Servili!*

Marcus: Farewell, Servilius!

In Officina Fabri – Disputatio in officina fabri

Tullius: *Salve, Crispine! Nuper vidi te in officina fabrum strenue operantem. Quanta vi et peritia clavos ac ferramenta fabricas! Sed ego hodie veni ut gladium meum corrigas. Non satis acutus videtur nec in pugna satis firmus fuit.*

Tullius: Hello, Crispinus! Recently I saw you working hard in the blacksmith's workshop. With such strength and skill, you forge nails and tools! But today I've come to have my sword fixed. It doesn't seem sharp enough and wasn't strong enough in battle.

Crispinus: *Salve, Tulli! Bene venisti. Gladius est fortissimum arma militis, et nulla excusatio accipi potest, si non recte conficiatur. Ostende mihi gladium tuum, videamus quid faciendum sit.*

Crispinus: Greetings, Tullius! You've come at the right time. A sword is the strongest weapon of a soldier, and no excuse can be accepted if it's not made properly. Show me your sword, and let's see what needs to be done.

Tullius: *Ecce! Vidistine? Ferrum aliquantulum debilitatum est, et acies obtusa. Fortasse in proelio nimis duram armaturam percussit.*

Tullius: Look here! Did you see? The metal is somewhat weakened, and the edge is dull. Perhaps in battle, it struck armor that was too hard.

Crispinus: *Ita videtur, ferrum percussum est. Sed ne cures de tota ferramenti laesura: ego te iuvabo. Hoc genus damnum ex duro belli labore saepe fit. Opus erit ut rursus incendium excitemus, gladium calefaciamus, et formam eius reddamus. Paulo patientiae, et mox erit tibi gladius novus.*

Crispinus: It seems so, the metal has been struck. But don't worry about the damage to the weapon: I will help you. This kind of damage often happens in the hard work of battle. We'll need to rekindle the fire, heat the sword, and restore its shape. A little patience, and soon you'll have a new sword.

Tullius: *Credo tibi, Crispine. Miror semper quomodo fabri tali arte ferrum doment. In cunctis rerum condicionibus, ferox tamen fidus gladius* *nobis militibus maxime necessarius est. Multi fortasse curant de hastis aut arcubus, sed mihi semper gladius princeps est.*

Tullius: I trust you, Crispinus. I am always amazed by how blacksmiths can tame iron with such skill. In all situations, a fierce yet reliable sword is most necessary for us soldiers. Many may care about spears or bows, but for me, the sword is always paramount.

Crispinus: *Recte dicis, Tulli. Gladius est anima militum Romanorum. Tamen, non satis est ferrum bonum habere; oportet etiam aciem semper curare. Si uno ictu hostem non prosternis, omnia subito periculo exponuntur. Iucundum mihi est, cum video militem virtute sua et armis perfectis firmum esse.*

Crispinus: You're right, Tullius. The sword is the soul of Roman soldiers. However, it's not enough to have good steel; the blade must always be kept sharp. If you don't strike down the enemy with one blow, everything is suddenly exposed to danger. I take great pleasure when I see a soldier firm with both his skill and well-prepared weapons.

Tullius: *Et ego quidem non solum gladium, sed etiam scutum meum reparari volo. Longis certaminibus concussum est. Potestne hoc quoque reparari in officina tua?*

Tullius: And indeed, I also want my shield repaired. It has been battered by long battles. Can this also be fixed in your workshop?

Crispinus: *Certe. Scutum tuum, quamquam gravi ictu afflictum, restitui poterit. Hic in officina nullum opus neglegenter perficitur. Custodiemus soliditatem ferri et ligni, ut rursus pugnis et periculis resistat.*

Crispinus: Certainly. Your shield, although struck heavily, can be restored. In this workshop, no task is done carelessly. We'll ensure the strength of both the iron and the wood, so it will again withstand battles and dangers.

Tullius: *Bene, Crispine! Fiducia magna mihi est in te. Si gladius acutus et scutum solidum sic parata sunt, nihil metuo in proelio. Hoc scio: sine bono fabro nec bonum militem esse posse.*

Tullius: Good, Crispinus! I have great confidence in you. If my sword is sharp and my shield solid, I fear nothing in battle. I know this: without a good blacksmith, there cannot be a good soldier.

Crispinus: *Recte cernis, amice! Sine artifice bonum ferrum non prodest. Sed iam tempus est operi manum admovere. Paulo temporis opus erit, et tuus gladius iterum micabit acumine. Vale interea, Tulli!*

Crispinus: You see rightly, my friend! Without an artisan, good iron is useless. But now it's time to get to work. It will only take a little time, and soon your sword will gleam with sharpness again. Farewell for now, Tullius!

Tullius: *Vale, Crispine! Mox revertar ut gladium et scutum recipiam, parata ad omnia certamina!*

Tullius: Farewell, Crispinus! I'll return soon to retrieve my sword and shield, ready for any battle!

De Luce et Tenebris – Disputatio philosophica de luce et tenebris

Spurius: *Salve, Cornelia! Dum hodie solem occidentem specto, cogitationes meae ad lucem et tenebras convertuntur. Multum mihi videtur in hoc mundo inter contraria pendere: inter lucem, quae omnia illustrat, et tenebras, quae omnia obtegunt. Quid tibi videtur de hac re? Nonne, ut multa aliter videmus in luce, ita alia ratione sub tenebris cogitamus?*

Spurius: Hello, Cornelia! As I watch the sun setting today, my thoughts turn to light and darkness. It seems to me that much in this world depends on opposites: between the light, which illuminates all, and the darkness, which covers all. What do you think of this? Isn't it true that just as we see many things differently in the light, we also think differently in darkness?

Cornelia: *Salve, Spuri! Quaestio tua magnam in se doctrinam continet. Lux et tenebrae, ut mihi videtur, non solum res corporeae sunt, sed etiam metaphorae. Lux saepe veritatem et sapientiam significat, cum tenebrae errores et ignorantiam referant. In luce omnia clara et manifesta sunt; in tenebris omnia dubia et obscura. Videre possumus quod in aperto est, sed ubi tenebrarum caligine involvimur, nemo certe scire potest.*

Cornelia: Hello, Spurius! Your question contains great wisdom. Light and darkness, as I see it, are not only physical things but also metaphors. Light often signifies truth and wisdom, while darkness refers to error and ignorance. In the light, everything is clear and evident; in darkness, everything is doubtful and obscure. We can see what is open, but when we are wrapped in the fog of darkness, no one can know for sure.

Spurius: *Ita est. Lux etiam ad nos ipsos intrinsecus pertinere videtur. Nam, cum ratio bene agit, omnia nobis quasi in luce posita videntur. Sed ubi animi perturbantur, sicut si tempestas in mentem incidat, totus mundus quasi in tenebras mersus videtur. Nonne philosophi saepe de hac distinctione disputabant?*

Spurius: Exactly. Light also seems to pertain to us internally. For when reason functions well, everything seems placed before us in the light. But when the mind is troubled, as if a storm hits the soul, the entire world seems plunged into darkness. Didn't the philosophers often debate this distinction?

Cornelia: *Sane. Plato, ut scis, multum de idearum luce locutus est. In illo praeclaro mytho de caverna, homines in tenebris versari dicit, nisi verarum rerum cognitio ad lucem emergat. Eodem modo, cum philosophiam sequimur, ab obscuris mentis statibus ad sapientiam et lucem accedimus. Estne tibi umquam ita visum, Spuri, ut in ipsa vita tenebris involutus te sentires?*

Cornelia: Certainly. Plato, as you know, spoke a great deal about the light of ideas. In his famous allegory of the cave, he says that people live in darkness unless the knowledge of true things emerges into the light. Similarly, when we follow philosophy, we move from the dark states of the mind to wisdom and light. Have you ever felt, Spurius, that you were enveloped in darkness in your own life?

Spurius: *Est profecto. Multis temporibus vitae meae, cum propositum mihi obscurum esset, sentire coepi me quasi per tenebras ambulare. Nulla ratio clara, nullum iter apertum erat. Sed postea, cum ratio in animo meo resplendere inciperet, omnia sicut ex illa caligine emergebant. Nihil tam laetum est quam illuminatio mentis post multas dubitationes.*

Spurius: Indeed, I have. Many times in my life, when my purpose was unclear, I began to feel as if I were walking through darkness. No clear reason, no open path. But later, when reason began to shine in my mind, everything seemed to emerge from that fog. Nothing is as joyful as the illumination of the mind after many doubts.

Cornelia: *Vere loqueris. Quotiens ipsa cogitatio nos ex tenebris ad lucem ducit, vere animi gaudium sentimus. Sed nonne etiam ipsa natura simile monstrat? Nam solis ortus post longas noctes, quomodo mundum illustrat, nonne ita est sicut ratio hominis post longas errorum tenebras?*

Cornelia: Truly spoken. Whenever thought itself leads us from darkness to light, we feel true joy of the soul. But doesn't nature itself show something similar? For just as the sunrise after long nights illuminates the world, is it not the same as a person's reason after long errors of darkness?

Spurius: *Sic est, Cornelia. Sol et lux omnes mundi tenebras expellunt, ut ratio et scientia caliginem mentis dispellunt. Sed quaero: num sine* *tenebris ipsis lucem bene cognoscere possumus? Non estne necessarium ut contraria invicem exsistant, ut unum per aliud comprehendamus?*

Spurius: Exactly, Cornelia. The sun and light drive away all the world's darkness, just as reason and knowledge dispel the fog of the mind. But I wonder: can we truly understand light without darkness? Isn't it necessary that opposites exist together so that we can comprehend one through the other?

Cornelia: *Quidam philosophi etiam id censuerunt, Spuri. Sine tenebris ne lucem ipsam quidem cognoscere possumus. Ut sapientiam sine erroribus, ut fortitudinem sine periculis non probamus, ita lux ipsa sine tenebrarum comparatione mirari non potest. Contraria inter se cohaerent.*

Cornelia: Some philosophers have also argued that, Spurius. Without darkness, we cannot even know light itself. Just as we don't prove wisdom without errors, or courage without dangers, so too light cannot be marveled at without the comparison of darkness. Opposites are interconnected.

Spurius: *Hoc verum est. Quaedam enim necessitas in omnibus rebus esse videtur. Lux et tenebrae, tamquam ratio et errores, tamquam scientia et dubia. Ubi tandem invicem complent, ibi verae cognitionis sedes est.*

Spurius: That's true. There seems to be a certain necessity in all things. Light and darkness, like reason and errors, like knowledge and doubts. Where they finally complete each other, there lies the seat of true understanding.

Cornelia: *Ita omni modo. Philosophia ipsa nos docet ut inter lucem et tenebras media via quaeratur. Et ne obliviscamur, Spuri, non semper perfectam lucem attingere necesse est: satis est, si paulatim ad eam appropinquamus.*

Cornelia: Yes, in every way. Philosophy itself teaches us to seek the middle way between light and darkness. And let's not forget, Spurius, it's not always necessary to reach perfect light: it's enough if we approach it gradually.

Spurius: *Sapienter dicis, Cornelia. Quod per lucem et tenebras ambulamus, utrumque intellegere discimus. Gratias tibi ago pro hac disputatione iucundissima.*

Spurius: You speak wisely, Cornelia. By walking through both light and darkness, we learn to understand both. Thank you for this most pleasant discussion.

Cornelia: *Et ego tibi, Spuri. Semper gaudeo de his rebus colloqui. Vale!*

Cornelia: And I thank you, Spurius. I always enjoy talking about these things. Farewell!

Spurius: *Vale, Cornelia!*

Spurius: Farewell, Cornelia!

De Iure Civili – Disputatio de iure Romano et iuribus civilibus

Gnaeus: *Salve, Aemilia! Nuper in foro audivi de causa quadam quae multum de iure civili continebat. Curare coepi quantum ius et leges nostras urbem regant. Te scire puto de iuribus Romanis multum; quid sentis de iure civili et quomodo hodie in civitate nostra valeat?*

Gnaeus: Hello, Aemilia! Recently, I heard about a case in the forum that involved a lot of civil law. I've started to think about how much our laws and legal system govern the city. I believe you know a lot about Roman law; what do you think about civil law and how it functions in our society today?

Aemilia: *Salve, Gnaee! Ius civile est fundamentum totius rei publicae nostrae. Sine legibus et ratione iuris, nemini tutum esse posset, nec urbs ipsa diu stare potuisset. Leges non solum crimina puniunt, sed etiam iura singulorum civium tuentur. Sed quid de illa causa audivisti? Quid ibi disputabatur?*

Aemilia: Hello, Gnaeus! Civil law is the foundation of our entire republic. Without laws and the structure of justice, no one could feel safe, nor could the city itself last long. The laws not only punish crimes but also protect the rights of individual citizens. But what did you hear about that case? What was being debated?

Gnaeus: *Causa erat de hereditate. Quidam civis diutius in exsilio fuerat, et, cum mortuus esset, quaestio facta est utrum filius eius, qui civitatem Romanam iam non habebat, heres legitimus esset. Iudex tamen pro filio iudicavit, quamquam lex satis clara non videbatur.*

Gnaeus: The case was about inheritance. A certain citizen had been in exile for a long time, and when he died, the question arose whether his son, who no longer held Roman citizenship, was a legitimate heir. However, the judge ruled in favor of the son, even though the law did not seem entirely clear.

Aemilia: *Quidem hoc exemplum iuris et aequitatis plenum est. Multae causae, quae iure civili tractantur, non tantum legem scriptam spectant, sed etiam iustitiam, quae super legem ipsam stare debet. Iudex saepe in animo suo quaerit qui sit aequissimus exitus, etiam si verba legum aliqua dubitatione implicentur.*

Aemilia: Indeed, this is a perfect example of law and equity. Many cases in civil law not only look at the written law but also at justice, which should stand above the law itself. The judge often seeks within himself what the fairest outcome is, even if the wording of the laws is somewhat unclear.

Gnaeus: *Ita vero, sed saepe, ut mihi videtur, leges et iura nimis obscura sunt. Miror cur tam multae leges scriptae sint. Nonne simpliciores rationes praeferendae essent? Populus ipse non semper intellegit quod iuris periti disputant.*

Gnaeus: Yes, indeed, but it often seems to me that laws and rights are too obscure. I wonder why there are so many written laws. Wouldn't simpler methods be better? The people themselves don't always understand what the legal experts are debating.

Aemilia: *Recte dicis, Gnaee. Leges Romanae variis temporibus et causis ortae sunt, et ideo aliquando intricatae videntur. Multae vetustissimae sunt, et cum nova res publica mutatur, leges etiam mutandae sunt. Tamen, necesse est ut ratio scripta sit, ne omnes lites arbitrio iudicum solvantur. In certa iuris fundamenta stabilitas invenitur.*

Aemilia: You're right, Gnaeus. Roman laws have arisen in various times and for various reasons, and that's why they sometimes seem complicated. Many are very old, and as the republic evolves, so must the laws. However, it's necessary to have written rules, so not every dispute is left to the judgment of the courts. Stability is found in the firm foundation of the law.

Gnaeus: *Intellego. Leges scriptae ordinem civitati praebent. Sed videre mihi videtur aliis temporibus aequitas ipsa legem vincat. Quid censes de ratione aequitatis? Estne semper supra legem, an iudices magis legibus quam aequitati servire debent?*

Gnaeus: I understand. Written laws provide order to society. But it seems to me that at times, equity itself surpasses the law. What do you think about the principle of equity? Should it always be above the law, or should judges serve the law more than equity?

Aemilia: *Aequitas et lex inter se cohaerent, sed aequitas, ut sapientes aiunt, animus legis est. Leges scriptae sunt ut aequitatem firment, sed ubi* *lex nimis stricta vel dura videtur, iudices interdum aequitatem prae lege colere debent. Nihil tamen sine prudentia et iudicio fieri oportet. Iudex enim aequitatem pro arbitrio suo interpretari non potest, nisi ad legis rationem respicit.*

Aemilia: Equity and law are intertwined, but as wise men say, equity is the spirit of the law. The written laws are there to uphold equity, but where the law seems too strict or harsh, judges sometimes must uphold equity above the law. However, nothing should be done without prudence and judgment. A judge cannot interpret equity by his own will unless he considers the reasoning behind the law.

Gnaeus: *Iam clarius mihi fit. Leges sine aequitate saepe iniustae videntur, sed aequitas sine legibus incerta est. Dic mihi, Aemilia, quis tibi Romanorum iuris peritissimorum maxime videtur esse laudandus?*

Gnaeus: It's becoming clearer to me now. Laws without equity often seem unjust, but equity without laws is uncertain. Tell me, Aemilia, who do you think is the most praiseworthy of the Roman legal experts?

Aemilia: *Multi praeclari viri de iure scripserunt, sed ego Ulpianum magno in honore habeo. Is non tantum rationem legis praeclarissime exposuit, sed etiam de iustitia et aequitate subtilissime disseruit. Saepe memoriae mandavi quod ille dixit: "Ius est ars boni et aequi."*

Aemilia: Many great men have written about law, but I hold Ulpian in the highest esteem. He not only explained the reasoning of the law most brilliantly but also discussed justice and equity with great subtlety. I've often remembered what he said: "Law is the art of the good and the fair."

Gnaeus: *Pulcherrime dictum est. Ego quoque existimo ius non solum praeceptum esse, sed artem boni faciendi. Gratias tibi ago, Aemilia, pro hac disputatione. Multa cognovi quae mihi prius obscura fuerunt.*

Gnaeus: Beautifully said. I also think that law is not just a rule but the art of doing good. Thank you, Aemilia, for this discussion. I've learned much that was previously unclear to me.

Aemilia: *Et ego tibi, Gnaee, gratias ago. De iure semper libenter colloquor. Vale et utinam ius nostrum semper aequitate floreat!*

Aemilia: And I thank you, Gnaeus. I'm always happy to talk about the law. Farewell, and may our laws always flourish with equity!

Gnaeus: *Vale, Aemilia!*

Gnaeus: Farewell, Aemilia!

In Taberna Libraria – Disputatio de libris emendis

Gaius: *Salve, Lucili! Nuper de praeclara taberna libraria audivi, ubi optimorum auctorum volumina venire dicuntur. Cras Romam iter facere volo, ut novos libros emam. Nonne tibi quoque placet librorum mercatura?*

Gaius: Hello, Lucilius! Recently, I heard about a famous bookstore where volumes of the best authors are said to be sold. Tomorrow, I plan to travel to Rome to buy some new books. Do you also enjoy buying books?

Lucilius: *Salve, Gai! Certe mihi placet! Nihil melius est quam diem inter libros et volumina referta scaenis agere. Sed dic mihi, quem auctorem nunc quaeris? De philosophia, rerum gestarum, an carmina cupis?*

Lucilius: Hello, Gaius! Certainly, I enjoy it! There's nothing better than spending a day among books and volumes filled with stories. But tell me, which author are you looking for now? Are you after philosophy, history, or poetry?

Gaius: *Me plurimum philosophia delectat, praesertim cum de Stoicis aut Epicureis lego. Nuper audivi Ciceronis De Finibus expositionem, et magno studio nunc eum librum habere volo. Fortasse etiam Platonis opera quaeram, ut Graecos sapientes legam.*

Gaius: I'm most delighted by philosophy, especially when I read about the Stoics or Epicureans. Recently, I listened to Cicero's "De Finibus" being explained, and I'm eager to have that book now. Perhaps I will also seek Plato's works, so I can read the wise Greeks.

Lucilius: *Bene censes, Gai! Cicero non solum in re publica magnus fuit, sed etiam in philosophia excelluit. De Finibus magna cum laude celebratur. Plato autem, si Graece legeris, animum valde movebit. Scisne illam tabernam esse ubi multi ex his libris venduntur? Prope Basilicam Iuliam sita est.*

Lucilius: You're right, Gaius! Cicero was not only great in public affairs but also excelled in philosophy. *De Finibus* is praised with great acclaim. As for Plato, if you read him in Greek, he will deeply move you. Do you know the bookstore where many of these books are sold? It's located near the Basilica Julia.

Gaius: *Profecto! Hac taberna mihi saepe utendum est. Librarius, Faustinus, non solum peritissimus in arte librorum est, sed etiam novas chartas optime conficit. Quod si quaeris librum rarissimum aut scitum ex Graecia aut Alexandria, Faustinus id celeriter inveniet.*

Gaius: Absolutely! I often use that bookstore. The bookseller, Faustinus, is not only very skilled in the art of books but also expertly produces new manuscripts. If you're looking for a rare or special book from Greece or Alexandria, Faustinus will quickly find it.

Lucilius: *Haec mihi maxime placet. Multum commodarum mercium in ea taberna reperitur. Nonnullos dies cogitabam an procurarem exemplaria Livii aut Sallustii. Historiae enim multum gaudeo et miror quanta sit ars Romanorum in annalibus et historiis scribendis.*

Lucilius: I love that! There are many useful items to be found in that store. For a few days, I've been thinking about getting copies of Livy or Sallust. I greatly enjoy history and marvel at the skill of the Romans in writing chronicles and historical accounts.

Gaius: *Intellego, Lucili. Livius, cum res Romanas a conditione urbis usque ad suum tempus scriberet, summam in historia adeptus est. Sed quid de Vergilio aut Horatio censes? Nonne carmina quoque in animo habes?*

Gaius: I understand, Lucilius. Livy, when he wrote about Roman affairs from the founding of the city to his own time, reached the height of historical writing. But what do you think about Vergil or Horace? Don't you also have an interest in poetry?

Lucilius: *O, certe! Aeneis Vergilii est opus quod semper in manibus teneo. De Horatio autem, eius carmina mihi videntur sapientiam et levitatem mirabiliter miscere. Sed audivistine de Carmen Saeculare? Librarius mihi nuper indicavit novum volumen praeclare illustratum venire.*

Lucilius: Oh, certainly! Vergil's *Aeneid* is a work that I always have in hand. As for Horace, his poetry seems to blend wisdom and lightness wonderfully. But have you heard about the *Carmen Saeculare*? The bookseller recently told me that a beautifully illustrated new edition is coming in.

Gaius: *Audivi quidem! Multi nunc carmina Horatii admirantur propter elegantiam et doctrinam. Ego autem in Vergilio magnitudinem et gravitatem epicam praefero. Si librarius hoc volumen habet, libenter eo procedam ut id emam.*

Gaius: Yes, I've heard! Many now admire Horace's poetry for its elegance and insight. But I personally prefer the grandeur and epic weight of Vergil. If the bookseller has that volume, I'll gladly go there to buy it.

Lucilius: *Bene consulis! Non saepe occurrunt exemplaria optimae qualitatis in horreis. Si tamen Faustinus id habet, non dubito quin tibi offerat. Cras igitur simul ad tabernam eamus. Ego quoque in animum induxi pluribus libris operam dare.*

Lucilius: Good thinking! High-quality copies don't often come around in stock. If Faustinus has it, I have no doubt he'll offer it to you. So, let's go to the bookstore together tomorrow. I've also decided to devote more time to some books.

Gaius: *Libenter, Lucili! In taberna libraria inter volumina amicorum philosophorum versari nihil iucundius est. Cras igitur conveniamus. Vale interim!*

Gaius: Gladly, Lucilius! There's nothing more enjoyable than spending time among the volumes of our philosopher friends in the bookstore. Let's meet tomorrow then. Farewell in the meantime!

Lucilius: *Vale, Gai! Cras tabernam cum gaudio visitabimus.*

Lucilius: Farewell, Gaius! Tomorrow we'll visit the bookstore with joy.

De Virtute et Honore – Disputatio de virtute et honore in vita

Servilia: *Salve, Fabi! Nuper multum cogitavi de rebus quae in vita maxime ponderandae sint. Virtus et honor prae aliis omnibus mihi videntur. Sed quid tu censes? Utrum divitiae et potentia praeferendae sint, an potius integritas animi et honesta vita?*

Servilia: Hello, Fabius! Lately, I have been thinking a lot about the things that should be most valued in life. To me, virtue and honor seem to be above all else. But what do you think? Should wealth and power be preferred, or rather integrity of soul and an honest life?

Fabius: *Salve, Servilia! Vera loqueris. Non enim divitiae aut potentia finem vitae hominis efficiunt, sed virtus, quae quidem animo nostro firmitatem et dignitatem praebet. Multi divitias quaerunt ut sibi felicitatem parent, sed numquam iis satis est. Ego autem censeo honorem et virtutem esse fundamentum vitae beatae.*

Fabius: Hello, Servilia! You speak the truth. It is not wealth or power that defines the purpose of a person's life, but virtue, which indeed gives our soul strength and dignity. Many seek wealth to gain happiness for themselves, but it is never enough for them. I, however, believe that honor and virtue are the foundation of a blessed life.

Servilia: *Placet mihi quod dicis. Saepe video homines gloriam et opes frustra petere, quasi his rebus omnia bona compleantur. At tu quid sentis de eorum dictis, qui fortunam aut fata omnia regere arbitrantur? Nonne sapientia et virtus constantiam etiam in adversis praebere possunt?*

Servilia: I like what you say. Often, I see people chasing after glory and wealth in vain, as if all good things are found in them. But what do you think of those who claim that fortune or fate rules everything? Can wisdom and virtue not provide steadiness even in adversity?

Fabius: *Neminem fata effugere posse scio, sed tamen propria virtus et sapientia hominem in adversis sustentare valent. Ut Cicero saepe dicebat, virtus est quae se ipsa contenta est. Fortuna est caeca, sed homo, si virtutem coluerit, per illam instabilitatem semper invictus manebit. Quid plus quaerere possumus quam animum honestum et sine metu?*

Fabius: I know that no one can escape fate, but still, one's own virtue and wisdom can support a person in adversity. As Cicero often said, virtue is that which is content with itself. Fortune is blind, but if a man has cultivated virtue, he will remain undefeated through its instability. What more can we seek than an honest and fearless soul?

Servilia: *Quam pulchre dicis, Fabi! Ego quoque credo virtutem omnes casus vitae vincere posse. Nam si vitam honorifice et modeste gesserimus, non metus aut dedecus nos tanget, etiam si fortuna adversa fuerit. Sed dic mihi, quem praeclarum virum tu exemplo sequi malis?*

Servilia: How beautifully you speak, Fabius! I, too, believe that virtue can overcome all the trials of life. For if we live honorably and modestly, neither fear nor disgrace will touch us, even if fortune turns against us. But tell me, which great man would you most like to follow as an example?

Fabius: *Multi praeclari sunt, sed mihi semper in mentem venit Cincinnatus. Etsi summum imperium obtinuit, tamen, cum res publica servata esset, statim ad agrum suum arandum reversus est. Nec divitiae nec potestas eum corrupuerunt. Hic vir mihi exemplum optimi civis et virtutis prodigi est. Quid autem tibi videtur? Quem virum tu maxime admiraris?*

Fabius: There are many great men, but Cincinnatus always comes to my mind. Even though he held the highest power, when the republic was saved, he immediately returned to plowing his field. Neither wealth nor power corrupted him. To me, he is the example of the best citizen and an extraordinary display of virtue. But what do you think? Which man do you admire the most?

Servilia: *Cincinnatus profecto summus vir fuit. Ego autem praeclarissime Ciceronem admiror, quia virtutem cum sapientia coniunxit et Romam tam diligenter servavit, etiam cum inimici ei summum periculum attulerunt. Res publica ei carior fuit quam ipsa salus sua. Nihil mirum est quod talem virum magnopere veneror.*

Servilia: Cincinnatus was indeed a great man. But I most admire Cicero, because he combined virtue with wisdom and protected Rome so diligently, even when his enemies brought him the greatest danger. The republic was dearer to him than his own safety. It is no wonder I deeply revere such a man.

Fabius: *Ita est, Cicero summa cum dignitate et fortitudine actus suos gessit. Virtute et honore patriae suae servivit, et eius exemplo discere possumus quod nec potentia nec metus virum sapientem movere debet. Si hoc modo vitam agimus, vera laude digni erimus.*

Fabius: That's right, Cicero conducted his actions with the highest dignity and courage. He served his country with virtue and honor, and from his example, we can learn that neither power nor fear should move a wise man. If we live in this way, we will truly be worthy of praise.

Servilia: *Bene quidem! Quam dulcis est vita honesta et virtute plena! Ne gloriam falsam aut opes sectemur, sed semper ad bonum publicum et integritatem animi propense tendamus. Hoc est iter verae gloriae.*

Servilia: Indeed! How sweet is a life that is honest and full of virtue! Let us not chase after false glory or wealth, but always aim toward the public good and the integrity of the soul. This is the path to true glory.

Fabius: *Profecto! Vale, Servilia, et virtutem semper sequamur.*

Fabius: Absolutely! Farewell, Servilia, and let us always follow virtue.

Servilia: *Vale, Fabi! Virtus noster princeps sit.*

Servilia: Farewell, Fabius! Let virtue be our guide.

De Fortuna et Fato

Rufus: *Salve, Tiberi! Nuper multa de fortuna et fato cogitavi. Non solum de rerum humanarum instabilitate, sed etiam de modo quo homines fortunam suam effugiant aut accipiant. Dic mihi, quid censes: estne fortuna casus incertus, an fatum immutabile quod nemo effugere possit?*

Rufus: Hello, Tiberius! Lately, I have been thinking a lot about fortune and fate. Not only about the instability of human affairs, but also about how people either escape or accept their fortune. Tell me, what do you think: is fortune an uncertain chance, or is fate unchangeable, which no one can escape?

Tiberius: *Salve, Rufe! Quaestio gravis est. Ego quidem inclino ut credam fatum omnia regere. Nihil enim fit sine causa, nec ulla res sine certo ordine evenit. Quod homines "fortunam" vocant, saepius fati pars est, etiam si id non intellegimus. Ut philosophi dixerunt, omnia quodam modo providentia reguntur. Quid tibi videtur?*

Tiberius: Hello, Rufus! This is a serious question. I tend to believe that fate governs everything. Nothing happens without cause, and no event occurs without a certain order. What people call "fortune" is often part of fate, even if we don't understand it. As philosophers have said, everything is governed in some way by providence. What do you think?

Rufus: *Providentiam quidem esse fateor, sed videtur mihi fortuna multis in rebus dominari. Cur alii summa gloria et divitiis perfruuntur, dum alii inopes et miseri sunt, etiam si virtute et sapientia praestant? Num fatum tam iniustum esse potest?*

Rufus: I do admit that providence exists, but it seems to me that fortune dominates in many matters. Why do some people enjoy great glory and wealth while others are poor and miserable, even if they excel in virtue and wisdom? Can fate really be so unjust?

Tiberius: *Vere loqueris, Rufe. Fortuna saepe iniqua videtur, sed non ideo iniusta est. Curas humanas fatum procul dubio altius spectat quam nos possumus. Sapientes docuerunt non in fatum rebellare, sed illud, quicquid sit, aequo animo accipere. Nam si omnia volentem fatum regit, prudens homo suum locum in rerum ordine servare debet.*

Tiberius: You speak truly, Rufus. Fortune often seems unfair, but that doesn't mean it's unjust. Fate undoubtedly sees human concerns from a higher perspective than we can. The wise have taught us not to rebel against fate, but to accept it calmly, whatever it may be. For if fate rules everything with a purpose, the wise man should keep his place in the order of things.

Rufus: *Fortasse, sed estne igitur nihil quod nostra voluntate flectere possimus? Estne homo omnino subiectus fato, an aliqua libertas ei concessa est? Quaero enim utrum virtus ipsa fatum vincere possit, an omnia iam prompta et provisa sint.*

Rufus: Perhaps, but is there nothing we can change with our own will? Is man entirely subject to fate, or is some freedom granted to him? I wonder if virtue itself can overcome fate, or if everything is already set and predetermined.

Tiberius: *Libertas hominis, Rufe, non propter fatum exstinguitur. Immo, ut quidam credunt, virtus hominis se ad fatum accommodare potest. Libertas non est fatum vincere, sed intellegere et accipere quod eveniat. Quaedam est coniunctio voluntatis nostrae cum fato, ut sapiens sciat quid patiendum sit et quomodo id ferat.*

Tiberius: Human freedom, Rufus, is not extinguished by fate. On the contrary, as some believe, human virtue can align itself with fate. Freedom is not about overcoming fate, but about understanding and accepting what happens. There is a kind of connection between our will and fate, so that the wise man knows what must be endured and how to bear it.

Rufus: *Sapiens igitur non solum patiens, sed etiam se fato coniunctum esse intellegit. Hoc mihi videtur summa sapientia. Sed quid de iis dicis qui fortunam provocant et, quamquam adversa videtur, tamen in causis agendis perseverant? Estne hoc frustra?*

Rufus: So the wise man is not only patient but also understands himself as connected to fate. This seems to me the height of wisdom. But what do you say about those who challenge fortune and, even when it seems against them, still persist in pursuing their goals? Is this in vain?

Tiberius: *Nequaquam frustra, Rufe. Quod adversa fortuna saepe occurrit, non significat homines nihil agere debere. Virtus et fortitudo in ipsis adversis consplendescunt. Nam si omnia facile dederit fatum, nihil esset quod homines exerceret. Fortuna adversa magna discipula sapientiae est. Sed dum agimus, meminerimus semper sub fato esse.*

Tiberius: By no means in vain, Rufus. The fact that adverse fortune often arises does not mean that people should do nothing. Virtue and courage shine brightest in the face of adversity. For if fate gave everything easily, there would be nothing to challenge men. Adverse fortune is a great teacher of wisdom. But as we act, we must always remember that we are still under fate.

Rufus: *Vera quidem loqueris, Tiberi. Hoc mihi nunc clarius apparet: homines non omnino fortunam suam vincunt, sed neque omnino fato cedunt. Intellegentia fati et voluntas recta sunt quibus vita beata effici potest. Gratias tibi ago pro hac disputatione.*

Rufus: You speak truly, Tiberius. This is now clearer to me: people neither completely overcome their fortune, nor entirely yield to fate. It is through understanding fate and having the right will that a happy life can be achieved. Thank you for this discussion.

Tiberius: *Et ego tibi, Rufe. Nihil dulcius est quam de rebus altissimis sermonem habere. Vale et semper ad sapientiam propemur.*

Tiberius: And thank you, Rufus. There is nothing sweeter than having a conversation about such deep matters. Farewell, and let us always strive toward wisdom.

Rufus: *Vale, Tiberi!*

Rufus: Farewell, Tiberius!

In Flumine Tiberi

Quintus: *Salve, Albine! Hodie, dum per Tiberim navigamus, nihil mihi iucundius esse videtur quam haec tranquillitas fluminis et arborum umbrae, quae ripas decorant. Vere dicunt Tiberim animam urbis esse. Quid tibi videtur?*

Quintus: Hello, Albinus! Today, as we sail along the Tiber, nothing seems more pleasant to me than the calmness of the river and the shade of the trees adorning the banks. Truly, they say that the Tiber is the soul of the city. What do you think?

Albinus: *Salve, Quinte! Certe, Tiberis non solum urbis, sed etiam totius Romanae historiae testis est. Ex hoc flumine res Romana ortum cepit, et in ripis eius primi Romani habitaverunt. Dum per has aquas vehimur, mihi saepe venit in mentem quanta praeclara facta hic gesta sint.*

Albinus: Hello, Quintus! Certainly, the Tiber is not only a witness to the city but also to all of Roman history. From this river, the Roman state took its rise, and on its banks the first Romans lived. As we travel along these waters, I often think of how many great deeds were done here.

Quintus: *Ita est! Primi conatus Romanae civitatis, et etiam narrantur vetera de Romulo et Remo, hic in Tiberi aguntur. Hic est locus ubi legendae fontes reperiuntur. Quae memoria dignissima tibi veniunt in mentem dum hoc flumen cernis?*

Quintus: Indeed! The first efforts of the Roman state, and even the ancient tales of Romulus and Remus, take place here on the Tiber. This is the place where the sources of legends are found. What memories come to your mind as you gaze upon this river?

Albinus: *Multa quidem, sed saepe de Cloaca Maxima cogito. Tiberis, ut nosti, non solum rerum bellicarum testis fuit, sed etiam civilis ingenii. Romani, ut scis, Tiberim ad utilitatem urbis meliorem fecerunt; Cloaca Maxima omnem urbem purgavit et salutem populi servavit. Quot urbes alias flumen tam diligenter curaverunt?*

Albinus: Many things, indeed, but I often think of the Cloaca Maxima. The Tiber, as you know, was not only a witness to wars but also to civil engineering. The Romans, as you know, improved the Tiber for the benefit of the city; the Cloaca Maxima cleansed the entire city and preserved the health of the people. How many other cities have cared for their rivers so diligently?

Quintus: *Recte dicis, Albine. Virtus nostra non solum in bello, sed etiam in ingenio et arte administranda videtur. Sed nunc, dum ad alteram ripam propius appropinquamus, specta humiles naviculas mercatorum! Video quomodo frumentum, oleum, et alias merces vehant. Tiberis tam utilis est mercatui quam bello.*

Quintus: You speak rightly, Albinus. Our strength seems to lie not only in war but also in engineering and management. But now, as we draw closer to the opposite bank, look at the humble merchant boats! I see how they carry grain, oil, and other goods. The Tiber is as useful for trade as it is for war.

Albinus: *Ita, Quinte. Hae ripae fluminis vere sunt arteriae imperii. Mercatores per Tiberim ex variis partibus terrarum vehuntur. Aegyptus frumentum, Hispania oleum, Graecia vinum — omnia ad urbis necessitates portantur. Nonne admirabile est quomodo hoc flumen Romam opibus alat?*

Albinus: Yes, Quintus. These riverbanks truly are the arteries of the empire. Merchants travel along the Tiber from various parts of the world. Egypt sends grain, Spain oil, Greece wine—everything is brought to meet the needs of the city. Isn't it amazing how this river nourishes Rome with its resources?

Quintus: *Certe! Sine Tiberi, Roma ipsa non tam magnifica fieri potuisset. Cur non Tiberim quasi patrem urbis honoramus? Flumen hoc nutrimentum et opem nostris bellis atque pacem nostris commerciis praebet.*

Quintus: Certainly! Without the Tiber, Rome itself could not have become so magnificent. Why don't we honor the Tiber as the father of the city? This river provides sustenance and aid to our wars and peace to our trade.

Albinus: *Bene dicis, Quinte. Tiberis semper inter deos urbanos numerandus est, ut ipse deus qui urbem et cives alit. Sed videsne illas naviculas remigantes procul? Mercatores num ad portum Ostiae navigant?*

Albinus: Well said, Quintus. The Tiber should always be counted among the city's gods, as the very deity who nourishes the city and its citizens. But do you see those small boats rowing in the distance? Are the merchants perhaps sailing to the port of Ostia?

Quintus: *Fortasse. Ostia est summus portus urbis, unde omnia per Tiberim ad Romam vehuntur. Video illos navigantes celeriter; ventus plane secundus est. Num vis cras ipsam Ostiam visitare? Poterimus videre quomodo merces nostrae a mari ad flumen transferantur.*

Quintus: Perhaps. Ostia is the city's main port, from where everything is transported along the Tiber to Rome. I see them sailing quickly; the wind is clearly favorable. Would you like to visit Ostia itself tomorrow? We could see how our goods are transferred from the sea to the river.

Albinus: *Libenter cras Ostiam irem! Ille locus semper mihi placet, ubi mare et flumen confluunt. Ad portum spectare et remiges audire semper animo iucundum est. Hoc flumen tam plenum est vitae et commercii.*

Albinus: I would gladly go to Ostia tomorrow! That place always pleases me, where the sea and the river meet. Watching the port and hearing the rowers is always a delight to the soul. This river is so full of life and commerce.

Quintus: *Ita est! Vale nunc, Albine. Cras ad Ostiam conveniamus.*

Quintus: Indeed! Farewell for now, Albinus. Let's meet tomorrow at Ostia.

Albinus: *Vale, Quinte! Exspecto diem crastinum ut iter per Tiberim ad mare faciamus.*

Albinus: Farewell, Quintus! I look forward to tomorrow when we will journey along the Tiber to the sea.

De Divitibus et Pauperibus

Caecilia: *Salve, Opimi! Hodie, dum per forum ambulabam, multos divites vidi auro et purpura ornatos, sed etiam multos pauperes ad eorum ianuas mendicantes. Quaesivi apud me ipsam quidnam sit quod homines in tam diversas fortunas ferat. Quid tibi videtur? Estne fortuna omnino iniusta, an quadam ratione divitiae et paupertas dantur?*

Caecilia: Hello, Opimius! Today, as I walked through the forum, I saw many wealthy people adorned with gold and purple, but also many poor people begging at their doors. I wondered to myself what it is that leads people into such different fortunes. What do you think? Is fortune entirely unjust, or are wealth and poverty granted according to some kind of reason?

Opimius: *Salve, Caecilia! Quaestio tibi gravis est. Ego quidem puto homines divitias non semper meruisse. Saepe fatum videtur sic hominibus obici, ut alii in summis opibus vivant, alii in summa inopia. Divitiae saepe non ex virtute, sed ex casu veniunt. Non ideo tamen dicendum est pauperes minus meritos esse; saepe mala fortuna innocentes opprimit.*

Opimius: Hello, Caecilia! Your question is a serious one. I believe that people do not always deserve their wealth. Often, fate seems to bestow it upon some, so that some live in great wealth while others are in deep poverty. Wealth often comes not from virtue, but from chance. That doesn't mean the poor are any less deserving; often, bad fortune oppresses the innocent.

Caecilia: *Bene dicis, Opimi. Mihi quoque videtur fatum nescio quo modo mortalium aequalium curam neglegere. Sed quid de eorum dictis, qui dicunt pauperes ipsos esse suae inopiae causam, dum divites industria sua opes congesserint? Nonne interdum hominum studium et labores locum habent in his rebus definiendis?*

Caecilia: You speak well, Opimius. It seems to me, too, that fate somehow neglects the care of mortals as equals. But what about those who say that the poor are responsible for their own poverty, while the wealthy have gathered their riches through hard work? Don't human effort and labor sometimes play a role in defining these matters?

Opimius: *Est aliquantum veritatis in illis dictis, Caecilia. Certe industria et sapientia aliquando efficiunt ut aliqui opes sibi parent. Sed id minime sufficit ad universam condicionem explicandam. Sunt plurima exempla eorum qui, nihilo minus labore et industria, summa tamen in paupertate manent. Civitas ipsa aliquando curam ad divitias adhibet, alios neglegit.*

Opimius: There is some truth in those statements, Caecilia. Certainly, hard work and wisdom sometimes lead people to acquire wealth for themselves. But that doesn't fully explain the entire situation. There are many examples of those who, despite their hard work and diligence, remain in deep poverty. The state itself sometimes favors wealth and neglects others.

Caecilia: *Ita, et mihi videtur hac de re non solum hominum industriam, sed etiam iniustas societatis partes culpare oportere. Quomodo, exempli gratia, agri Romani tam magnorum possessorum manserunt, dum multitudo pauperum vix vitam ducere potest? Nonne aliquod remedium huic iniustitiae inveniri potest?*

Caecilia: Yes, and it seems to me that we should blame not only human effort but also the unjust aspects of society for this. How, for example, have the lands of Rome remained in the hands of such large landowners, while a multitude of the poor can barely survive? Can't some remedy be found for this injustice?

Opimius: *Quaestio ista praeclara est, Caecilia. Multi in senatu de agris distribuendis cogitaverunt, sed magnorum possessorum opes resistunt. Ita fit ut pauperes terra careant, quamquam ager plenus manet. Remedium tamen facile inveniri non potest. Immutabiles videntur esse divitiae et potentia.*

Opimius: That is an excellent question, Caecilia. Many in the Senate have thought about distributing the land, but the wealth and power of the large landowners stand in the way. So it happens that the poor are left without land, even though the fields remain full. However, a solution is not easily found. Wealth and power seem immovable.

Caecilia: *Hoc ego valde doleo, quod in civitate nostra, quae iustitiam colere debet, tam multi divitiae frumenta cumulant, dum pauperes iusti nulla spe melioris vitae tenentur. Puto magistratus firmiores esse oportere in legibus aequitatis tuendis.*

Caecilia: I am deeply saddened by this, that in our state, which ought to honor justice, so many accumulate wealth while the just poor are held without any hope for a better life. I think the magistrates need to be stronger in upholding the laws of fairness.

Opimius: *Assentior tibi. Nisi aliquando magistratus rationem mutabunt, periculum est ne pauperes in maiorem calamitatem incidant. Sed ne obliviscamur etiam fortunam non semper favere, et fortunas hominum facile verti posse.*

Opimius: I agree with you. Unless the magistrates change their ways at some point, there is a danger that the poor will fall into even greater misfortune. But let's not forget that fortune does not always favor, and the fortunes of people can easily turn.

Caecilia: *Ita vero! Fortuna est tam incerta ut etiam divites suum statum semper metuere debeant. Nihil in hac vita firmum est, et id quod nunc altum videtur, cras humile fieri potest. Divitiae et potentia, quamvis magnae, saepe fluunt et refluent, quasi undae maris.*

Caecilia: Exactly! Fortune is so uncertain that even the wealthy must always fear for their position. Nothing in this life is stable, and what seems high today can become low tomorrow. Wealth and power, however great, often ebb and flow like the waves of the sea.

Opimius: *Sapienter locuta es, Caecilia. Divitiae sunt simillimae ventis et undis, quae in nulla certa sede manent. Meliorum temporum spero ut tandem aequitas praevaleat in civitate nostra. Vale nunc, et utinam tua semper fortuna stabilis sit!*

Opimius: You speak wisely, Caecilia. Wealth is very much like the winds and the waves, which never remain in one fixed place. I hope that better times will come and that fairness will finally prevail in our state. Farewell for now, and may your fortune always be stable!

Caecilia: *Gratias tibi ago, Opimi. Vale, et fortuna tibi quoque faveat!*

Caecilia: Thank you, Opimius. Farewell, and may fortune favor you as well!

In Urbibus Provinciarum

Lucius: *Salve, Publice! Nuper ex provincia Asia redii, ubi plurimae urbes provinciales Romana disciplina feliciter administrantur. Miror quomodo Roma tam longinquas gentes ita regat ut non solum pax servetur, sed etiam civitates ipsae floreant. Quid tibi videtur de vita in urbibus provinciarum?*

Lucius: Hello, Publicus! I recently returned from the province of Asia, where many provincial cities are successfully governed by Roman discipline. I marvel at how Rome can rule such distant peoples in a way that not only preserves peace but also allows the cities themselves to prosper. What do you think about life in the cities of the provinces?

Publicus: *Salve, Luci! Et ego multis in locis provinciales vitas vidi, praesertim in Gallia et Hispania. Mirabile mihi semper videtur quomodo populi tam diversae originis mores Romanos acceperint. Urbes Romanae, etiam in provinciis, simillimae sunt ipsi Romae: thermas, basilicas, theatra vidi quae nullo modo minoris dignitatis sunt.*

Publicus: Hello, Lucius! I too have seen the lives of people in many places, especially in Gaul and Spain. It always amazes me how peoples of such different origins have adopted Roman customs. The Roman cities, even in the provinces, are very similar to Rome itself: I have seen baths, basilicas, and theaters that are in no way less dignified.

Lucius: *Ita est! Cum Pergamum adveni, primum me quasi Romae esse credidi. Fora, templa, arcus triumphales—omnia ita magnifice aedificata sunt ut non multum Roma ipsa superet. Sed non solum aedificia, verum etiam mores civium Romani facti sunt. Iudico res publicas tam in urbe nostra quam in urbibus provincialibus aeque bene administrari.*

Lucius: Indeed! When I arrived in Pergamum, at first I thought I was in Rome. Forums, temples, triumphal arches—everything is so magnificently built that it's hardly surpassed by Rome itself. But it's not just the buildings; even the customs of the citizens have become Roman. I believe that public affairs are as well managed in our city as they are in the provincial cities.

Publicus: *Hoc etiam ego animadverti, Luci. Cum Massiliam visitarem, Galli ibi non tantum legibus nostris utuntur, sed etiam ritus et spectacula Romana cum suis commiscuerunt. Nuptiae, magistratus, etiam gladiatorii ludi prope ut Romae fiunt. Tamen videsne, numquid aliquid proprium manet in moribus provinciarum?*

Publicus: I've noticed that as well, Lucius. When I visited Massilia, I saw that the Gauls not only use our laws, but they have also blended Roman rites and spectacles with their own. Weddings, magistracies, even gladiatorial games take place almost as they do in Rome. But do you see if there's anything unique that still remains in the customs of the provinces?

Lucius: *Bene monuisti, Publice. Etiam cum Romani mores provincialium afficiunt, nullo modo omnes proprii mores exstinguuntur. In Asia, exempli gratia, veteres cultus et dii loci adhuc coluntur. Sacrificia ad deos locales perficiuntur, sed tamen etiam Iovem et Augustum honorant. Non est violenta coniunctio, sed quaedam communio.*

Lucius: You've made a good point, Publicus. Even though Roman customs influence the provincials, not all of their traditions disappear. In Asia, for example, the old cults and local gods are still worshipped. Sacrifices are made to the local gods, but they also honor Jupiter and Augustus. It's not a violent merging, but rather a kind of shared practice.

Publicus: *Idem dicere possum de Gallia. Vidi quomodo Galli suos antiquos deos cum Romanis dis miscuerint, ut Mercurius, quem Romani colunt, apud Gallos cum deo Lugone coniungeretur. Haec miscentia cultuum mihi magno dolore non est, nam denique pax et concordia inter diversos populos multum valent.*

Publicus: I can say the same about Gaul. I saw how the Gauls blended their ancient gods with the Roman ones, like how Mercury, whom the Romans worship, was joined with the god Lugus among the Gauls. This mixing of cultures does not trouble me, because, in the end, peace and harmony among different peoples are worth a great deal.

Lucius: *Profecto! Concordia debet esse summus finis imperii. Quod autem plus me delectat, est quomodo res ordinesque urbanae in provinciis firme custodiantur. Non multo postquam provincias* *ingredimur, Romana lex ibi viget. Cives Romani eadem fiducia in suis foris atque in rebus iudicandis utuntur.*

Lucius: Exactly! Concord should be the ultimate goal of the empire. What pleases me more, though, is how the order and structure of city life are firmly maintained in the provinces. Not long after we enter the provinces, Roman law is already in effect there. Roman citizens operate with the same confidence in their courts and legal matters as they do at home.

Publicus: *Iuste loqueris, Luci. Leges Romanae fundamentum sunt ut non tantum divitias et commoda, sed etiam iustitiam inter provinciales colantur. Urbes bene administratae semper pacem et prosperitatem provincialibus praebent. Nonne hoc est quod Romanos totum orbem temperare debet?*

Publicus: You speak rightly, Lucius. Roman laws are the foundation not just for wealth and prosperity, but also for justice among the provincials. Well-governed cities always provide peace and prosperity for the provincials. Isn't this what makes the Romans able to rule the whole world?

Lucius: *Ita est. Leges nostrae non solum arma tenent, sed etiam animos consociant. Cum provincialis ad regulam Romanam convertitur, in animo suo discit qui sit modus vitae civilis. Necesse est ut Romani non tantum dominentur, sed etiam provincialibus bonas rationes vitae ostendant.*

Lucius: Exactly. Our laws don't just hold power, they unite minds. When a provincial adapts to the Roman way, they learn in their soul the way of civil life. It's necessary for the Romans not just to rule but also to show the provincials the proper way of living.

Publicus: *Quid me mirum quod Imperium Romanum tam vastum et stabile sit? Urbes in provinciis florent, et denique Roma ipsa ex eis opibus alitur. Vale igitur, Luci! Utinam urbes provinciarum semper sub legibus Romanis feliciter stent.*

Publicus: No wonder the Roman Empire is so vast and stable! The cities in the provinces flourish, and in the end, Rome itself is sustained by their wealth. Farewell, then, Lucius! May the cities of the provinces always stand happily under Roman law.

Lucius: *Vale, Publice! Si concordia inter Romam et provincias colatur, imperium semper vigebit.*

Lucius: Farewell, Publicus! If harmony is cultivated between Rome and the provinces, the empire will always thrive.

De Sapientia Senum

Fabius: *Salve, Helvia! Dum hodie pro foro sedebam et senes in conversatione animadvertebam, coepi cogitare de sapientia eorum. Quanta videtur esse prudentia senum, qui tot annos experientiam colligunt! Nonne videtur tibi sapientia aetatis esse praeclarissima?*

Fabius: Hello, Helvia! As I was sitting in the forum today, observing the elderly in conversation, I began to think about their wisdom. How great the wisdom of the elderly seems, who gather so many years of experience! Don't you think that the wisdom of age is truly remarkable?

Helvia: *Salve, Fabii! Ita vero, quod dicis maxime mihi placet. Senes sunt velut viva exempla omnium acceptorum et cognitorum; eorum vita plena est doctrina et consiliis quae iuvenes adhuc discere debent. Etsi corpora laborant, tamen animi eorum clari manent ac saepe in eo consistunt exempla virtutis et gravitatis.*

Helvia: Hello, Fabius! Indeed, what you say pleases me very much. The elderly are like living examples of all that has been learned and known; their lives are full of teachings and advice that the young still need to learn. Though their bodies may tire, their minds remain sharp and often stand as examples of virtue and dignity.

Fabius: *Sane, Helvia. Cum audio senatores veteres in Curia loqui, non tam verba eorum quam ipsa dignitas aetatis me movet. Vide quid de Cicerone dicant! Etsi multorum annorum onera ferebat, tamen vi mentis suae et ratione non minus quam iuventute florebat.*

Fabius: Certainly, Helvia. When I hear the older senators speak in the Senate, it's not just their words, but the very dignity of their age that moves me. Look at what they say about Cicero! Even though he bore the weight of many years, he flourished with the strength of his mind and reason, just as he did in his youth.

Helvia: *Cicero profecto praeclarus erat, et sicut ipse dixit, senectus non est tempestas quae omnia auferat, sed potius temporis spatium ubi sapientia magis firmetur. Qui bene vixit, in senectute fructus suorum laborum percipit. Mihi quoque videtur senectutem non esse pondus, sed praeclarum tempus vitae.*

Helvia: Cicero was indeed remarkable, and as he himself said, old age is not a storm that takes everything away, but rather a time when wisdom is further strengthened. He who has lived well reaps the fruits of his labor in old age. I too believe that old age is not a burden, but a most distinguished time of life.

Fabius: *Recte censes. Sed nonne putas non omnem senectutem felicem esse? Sunt qui, cum annos multos habeant, tamen miseri sunt, quoniam aut corpora non valent aut se acta sua male gessisse sentiunt. Quid igitur facit ut senes felices sint?*

Fabius: You are right. But don't you think that not all old age is happy? There are those who, despite their many years, are still miserable, either because their bodies are failing, or because they feel they have lived poorly. So what do you think makes the elderly happy?

Helvia: *Fortasse iuste loqueris, Fabii. Sed, ut mihi videtur, qui bene vivit et sapienter, in senectute etiam magis sapientiam et tranquillitatem invenit. Nihil est dulcius quam recordari honesta facta aut bonas amicitias, nec minus est utile multis annis nato consilium dare iuvenibus. Est enim senibus suavis conscientia recte factorum, et gratissima societas proximorum.*

Helvia: You may be right, Fabius. But, as I see it, those who live well and wisely find even more wisdom and peace in old age. There is nothing sweeter than remembering honorable deeds or good friendships, and it's just as valuable for an elder to give advice to the young. For the elderly, the sweet reward of having lived rightly, and the cherished company of loved ones, bring much joy.

Fabius: *Quam vera dicis! Vita bene acta certe senectutem felicem reddit. Mihi autem placet etiam hoc cogitare: senes non solum pro propria sapientia coluntur, sed etiam quia exemplum ipsi iuvenibus sunt. Cum senex recte loquitur, non tam de verbis quam de ipsa dignitate discimus. Ut plurimum est, ut te exemplis melius regas quam doctrina sola.*

Fabius: How true your words are! A life well-lived certainly makes for a happy old age. But I also like to think about this: the elderly are honored not just for their wisdom, but because they are examples for the young. When an elder speaks rightly, we learn not so much from their words, but from their very dignity. It's often better to be guided by examples than by mere instruction.

Helvia: *Ita est! Exempla virtutis et iustitiae semper plus valent quam verba soluta. Si iuventus sapientiam senum sequitur, profecto et ipsa honorem vitae magis percipiet. Cogito saepe de nostris maioribus, qui non solum seditionibus rei publicae restiterunt, sed etiam familias suas sapientia et constantia regerunt. Non estne honorabilis dignitas talis?*

Helvia: That's right! Examples of virtue and justice are always more valuable than loose words. If the youth follow the wisdom of the elders, they too will surely gain a greater sense of honor in life. I often think of our ancestors, who not only withstood the upheavals of the Republic, but also guided their families with wisdom and steadfastness. Isn't such dignity worthy of great honor?

Fabius: *Certe! Senes qui aetatem suam honore et virtute plenam fecerunt, sunt decus familiae, urbis, et rei publicae. Itaque, Helvia, mihi videtur sapientiam senum non solum honorandam, sed etiam discendam esse. Hanc sententiam servemus: non anni, sed acta vitam beatam faciunt.*

Fabius: Certainly! The elderly who have filled their years with honor and virtue are the glory of the family, the city, and the Republic. So, Helvia, I believe that the wisdom of the elders should not only be honored but also learned from. Let us hold to this idea: it's not the years, but the deeds that make for a blessed life.

Helvia: *Bene locutus es, Fabii! Senes quidem merito honore digni sunt, sed etiam hoc discere possumus: quomodo vivamus, ut, cum senectutem agamus, et sapientiam et tranquillitatem habeamus. Vale igitur, et utinam senectus tua plena sapientia sit!*

Helvia: Well said, Fabius! The elderly are indeed worthy of honor, but we can also learn this: how to live so that when we reach old age, we may have both wisdom and peace. Farewell, and may your old age be full of wisdom!

Fabius: *Vale, Helvia! Tua quoque senectus sit tam felix quam digna!*

Fabius: Farewell, Helvia! May your old age also be as happy as it is dignified!

In Insula Graeca

Lysimachus: *Salve, Octavia! Hic in Graeca insula haud longe ab Athenis, nulla mihi videtur regio pulchrior. Maris caeruleum, montes excelsi, et ora tranquilla... omnia me delectant. Quid tibi videtur de his locis?*

Lysimachus: Hello, Octavia! Here on this Greek island not far from Athens, no region seems more beautiful to me. The blue of the sea, the towering mountains, and the peaceful shores... everything delights me. What do you think of these places?

Octavia: *Salve, Lysimache! Certe, hunc locum deorum donum esse puto. Quae caelum serenum et virescentes silvas in iugis montium specto, animus mihi levatur. Graecae insulae non tantum ob pulchritudinem suam, sed etiam propter historias et mysteria, nulli alii similes sunt. Nonne tibi praeclara videtur haec terra sapientiae?*

Octavia: Hello, Lysimachus! Surely, I believe this place to be a gift from the gods. As I look at the serene sky and the lush forests on the mountain ridges, my spirit is lifted. Greek islands are unique not only for their beauty but also for their history and mysteries. Doesn't this land of wisdom seem extraordinary to you?

Lysimachus: *Ita vero, Octavia. Haec loca olim philosophorum, poetarum, et rerum gestarum sunt plena. Memor sum quam saepe Graeci philosophi in locis talibus doctrinam suam tradiderint. Mihi primum venit in mentem Aristoteles et eius schola. Haec insula tam tranquilla est ut studio sapientiae aptissima sit.*

Lysimachus: Yes, indeed, Octavia. These places are full of the presence of philosophers, poets, and historic events. I remember how often Greek philosophers would teach their knowledge in places like this. Aristotle and his school come to my mind first. This island is so peaceful that it is perfect for the pursuit of wisdom.

Octavia: *Recte mones, Lysimache. In locis huiusmodi, multi non modo in philosophia, sed etiam in artibus excellebant. Ut vides, hic est templum, quod Pythagorae et eius discipulis dicatum est. Saepe me iuvat cogitare quomodo illi viri sapientiam in caelo, terra, et ipsa harmonia musica quaesierint.*

Octavia: You're right, Lysimachus. In places like these, many not only excelled in philosophy but also in the arts. As you can see, here is a temple dedicated to Pythagoras and his disciples. I often like to think about how those men sought wisdom in the heavens, the earth, and in the very harmony of music.

Lysimachus: *Mirabile est quam profunde Graeci naturam rerum cognoscere voluerunt. Nihil aliud nisi pulchritudinem et ordinem in omni re videbant. Et, ut Pythagoras credebat, omnia in numeris et musica iacent. Quid censes, Octavia? Num haec principia in vita nostra quoque locum habent?*

Lysimachus: It's remarkable how deeply the Greeks sought to understand the nature of things. They saw nothing but beauty and order in everything. And as Pythagoras believed, everything lies in numbers and music. What do you think, Octavia? Do these principles also have a place in our lives?

Octavia: *Nulla dubitatio est! Etsi nunc temporis aliter vivimus, tamen haec principia aeternam vim habent. Non modo in philosophia, sed etiam in consiliis cotidianis, iustus ordo et musicae harmonia animorum requirenda est. Graeci non tantum docuerunt quomodo cogitare, sed etiam quomodo vivere.*

Octavia: Without a doubt! Even though we live differently now, these principles still have eternal power. Not only in philosophy but also in everyday decisions, a just order and harmony of the soul's music should be sought. The Greeks taught not just how to think, but how to live.

Lysimachus: *Sapienter loqueris, Octavia. Etsi mundus circum nos mutatur, haec antiqua principia semper manent. Fortasse id ipsum est quod hanc insulam tam mysticam facit: hic, inter hanc pulchritudinem, sententiae antiquae animorum non omnino perierunt. Haec loca semper sapientiam vetustam servant.*

Lysimachus: You speak wisely, Octavia. Even though the world around us changes, these ancient principles remain. Perhaps that's what makes this island so mystical: here, amidst this beauty, the ancient wisdom of the soul has not completely disappeared. These places always preserve old wisdom.

Octavia: *Ita est, Lysimache. Locus ipse nobis docet silentium et pacem mentis. Et non modo in hominum studiis, sed etiam in rerum natura hac in insula tranquillitatem invenimus. Vide maris fluctus, qui levi fremitu ad litus veniunt: sicut musica est, animo tranquillam quietem afferens.*

Octavia: That's right, Lysimachus. This place itself teaches us silence and peace of mind. And not only in the study of humans but also in nature itself, we find tranquility here on this island. Look at the waves of the sea, gently lapping against the shore: it's like music, bringing quiet peace to the soul.

Lysimachus: *Mirum est quomodo natura ipsa doctrinam afferat. Hic, ubi caelum et mare coniunguntur, quis non potuit de rerum natura aut fato cogitare? Gratias tibi ago, Octavia, quod me huc adduxisti. Mihi videtur me aliquid altioris intellegentiae hic accepisse.*

Lysimachus: It's amazing how nature itself offers wisdom. Here, where the sky and the sea meet, who wouldn't think about the nature of things or fate? Thank you, Octavia, for bringing me here. I feel as though I've gained some higher understanding in this place.

Octavia: *Gratias tibi, Lysimache. Etiam ego hunc diem memorabilem esse censeo. Sapientiam Graecorum hic melius intellegimus, et ipsi in nostra vita musicam et ordinem quaerere debemus. Vale nunc, et felices simus dum hic sumus!*

Octavia: Thank you, Lysimachus. I also think this day will be memorable. We understand Greek wisdom better here, and we too must seek music and order in our lives. Farewell for now, and let us be happy while we are here!

Lysimachus: *Vale, Octavia! Utinam semper hanc tranquillitatem animi retinere possimus.*

Lysimachus: Farewell, Octavia! May we always retain this peace of mind.

De Rebus Domesticis

Decimus: *Salve, Flavia! Hodie in villa mea quaedam domesticorum curae gestae sunt, quae mihi non satis bene videntur. Servi negligentius operantur, et res multas mendas habent. Cogitavi quid faciam ut ordinem meliorem in domo restituam. Nonne domesticis rebus maior cura adhibenda est?*

Decimus: Hello, Flavia! Today in my villa, some domestic tasks were carried out, which don't seem to have been done well. The slaves are working with less care, and many things are faulty. I've been thinking about what I should do to restore better order in the household. Don't you think greater attention must be paid to domestic matters?

Flavia: *Salve, Decime! Nulla quidem vitae pars est quae maiorem sollicitudinem requirat quam res domesticae. Etiam si in villa tua multi servi sunt, nisi diligentia et auctoritate agis, omnia in turbam cadent. Nonne tibi videtur praefectus domesticorum, vir fidelis et experimento probatus, praeponendus esse?*

Flavia: Hello, Decimus! There is certainly no part of life that requires more attention than domestic affairs. Even if there are many slaves in your villa, unless you act with diligence and authority, everything will fall into disorder. Don't you think it would be wise to appoint a house steward, a faithful man tested by experience?

Decimus: *Prorsus assentior. Cogito de Marco, qui diu fideliter mihi servivit. Videtur idoneus ad hoc opus, sed num satis auctoritatis habebit inter servos, qui saepe inter se dissentiunt? Auctoritatem meam interdum violare temptant.*

Decimus: I completely agree. I'm thinking of Marcus, who has served me faithfully for a long time. He seems suitable for the task, but will he have enough authority over the slaves, who often disagree among themselves? They sometimes try to undermine my authority.

Flavia: *Marcus, si tibi fidelis est et prudenter agere novit, certe officium suum bene faciet. Tamen, Decime, non satis est solum praecepta dare; auctoritas firma moderatione et, cum opus est, levi severitate servanda est. Nulla domus sine certa disciplina diu regi potest.*

Flavia: If Marcus is faithful to you and knows how to act wisely, he will certainly perform his duty well. However, Decimus, it's not enough just to give orders; authority must be maintained with moderation and, when needed, with gentle severity. No household can be managed for long without proper discipline.

Decimus: *Iuste mones. Scio me servis nimium saepe indulxisse. Mirarisne quod laborem subterfugiant, cum sciant me non satis severum esse? Tempus est, ut videtur, ut disciplina in villa mea firmetur. Tu quid agis de servis tuis? Nonne tibi quoque interdum difficultates oriuntur?*

Decimus: You're right. I know I've often been too lenient with the slaves. Are you surprised that they avoid work, knowing I'm not strict enough? It seems it's time for discipline to be strengthened in my villa. How do you handle your slaves? Don't you also face difficulties at times?

Flavia: *Est ita, sed mensura semper adhibenda est. Odi nimiam severitatem, sed interdum necesse est exigere, ut officium suum faciant. Multum interest ut servi sentiant non tantum metum, sed etiam iustitiam domini. Est etiam commendabile cum eorum necessitatibus benigniter agere.*

Flavia: Indeed, but balance must always be applied. I dislike excessive severity, but sometimes it's necessary to ensure they do their duties. It's important that the slaves feel not only fear but also the justice of their master. It's also commendable to act kindly toward their needs.

Decimus: *Quid igitur, Flavia, censes: quo modo optimum temperamentum inter iustitiam et severitatem conservem? Utinam sciam qua ratione mentes servorum conciliari possint sine continua monitione.*

Decimus: So, Flavia, what do you think is the best way to maintain a balance between justice and severity? I wish I knew how to win over the minds of the slaves without constant scolding.

Flavia: *Consilium meum est ut pace et constantia omnia agas. Servos lauda, cum meritum est, et castiga, cum opus sit. At etiam interdum praemia dare prodest, ut discant bonum laborem agere non sine spe aliqua. Ita fit ut et reverentia et studio laborare velint.*

Flavia: My advice is to do everything with calm and consistency. Praise the slaves when it's deserved, and punish when necessary. But it's also useful to give rewards at times so they learn that hard work isn't without some reward. This way, they'll work with both respect and motivation.

Decimus: *Recte loqueris. Laudes et praemia multo efficaciora esse videntur quam poenae solae. Marcum quidem praefectum domesticorum faciam, ut melius ordinem custodiat et labores disponat. Multum auctoritatis habet apud ceteros, et ego de eius fide nullam dubitationem habeo.*

Decimus: You're right. Praise and rewards seem to be much more effective than punishment alone. I'll appoint Marcus as house steward to better maintain order and assign tasks. He has a lot of authority among the others, and I have no doubt about his loyalty.

Flavia: *Ei fidens, Decime, certe meliorem ordinem in domo reddere poteris. Fides et moderatio in rebus domesticis sunt fundamenta omnium. Multum valet habere aliquem, cui res administrandae committi possint, qui et prudenter et honeste agat.*

Flavia: Trusting him, Decimus, you will certainly restore better order in the house. Trust and moderation are the foundation of all domestic affairs. It's very valuable to have someone to whom the management of things can be entrusted, who acts both wisely and honestly.

Decimus: *Gratias tibi ago, Flavia, pro prudentibus consiliis. Sentio me iam melius scire quid faciendum sit. Vale, et si umquam tibi operam meam in rebus domesticis necesse erit, libenter tibi auxilium feram.*

Decimus: Thank you, Flavia, for your wise advice. I feel I now have a better idea of what needs to be done. Farewell, and if you ever need my help in domestic matters, I will gladly assist you.

Flavia: *Gratias tibi, Decime. Vale, et utinam omnia bene prosperentur in domo tua!*

Flavia: Thank you, Decimus. Farewell, and may everything go well in your household!

In Ludis Puerorum

Paulus: *Salve, Rufe! Visne ludos hodie in foro agere? Ego tibi novorum iaculorum vel equitandi ludorum provocationem offero.*

Paulus: Hello, Rufus! Do you want to play games in the forum today? I offer you a challenge of new javelin throwing or horseback riding games.

Rufus: *Salve, Paule! Certe! Nullo modo iaculando vinceris; multis vicibus prius te superavi! Sed quid censes? Melius estne nunc ludere pilis aut certare cursu?*

Rufus: Hello, Paulus! Certainly! You are unbeatable in javelin throwing; I have defeated you many times before! But what do you think? Is it better to play ball now or race instead?

Paulus: *Mihi quidem magis placet certamen cursus! Ego certe celerior sum quam tu, Rufe, nisi forte nimis saturus hodie fuisti prandio. Quod si certare audes, in via longissima faciemus, et videbimus quis sit celerior.*

Paulus: I certainly prefer a running competition! I'm definitely faster than you, Rufus, unless perhaps you've eaten too much lunch today. But if you're willing to race, we'll do it on the longest track and see who is faster.

Rufus: *Hahaha! Ego saturus? Ne minime quidem! Sed curam habeo ne latrocinium tibi accidat, cum ego primus metam pertingam. Si autem me vincis, promitto me tibi duos globos pilorum donaturum esse.*

Rufus: Hahaha! Me full? Not at all! But I worry that you might experience a robbery when I reach the finish line first. However, if you defeat me, I promise to give you two balls as a reward.

Paulus: *Bene! Sed priusquam currimus, specta, Faustilla et Antonia sub arboribus pilas iactant. Felices videntur esse. Quid si post cursum pilis cum iis ludamus?*

Paulus: Good! But before we race, look, Faustilla and Antonia are tossing balls under the trees. They seem happy. What if we play ball with them after the race?

Rufus: *Libenter! Faustilla semper pilas melioribus modis excipit. Saepe eam vidi pilam tam praeclare in aere tenentem, ut putares eam volare* *posse! Sed, priusquam ad ludum pilorum eamus, videamus uter currendo primus fuerit. Paratus es?*

Rufus: Gladly! Faustilla always catches balls in the best way. I've often seen her holding a ball so well in the air that you'd think she could fly! But before we go to play ball, let's see who will finish the race first. Are you ready?

Paulus: *Semper paratus! Videam te in finem ad metam. Incipiamus!*

Paulus: Always ready! I'll see you at the finish line. Let's start!

(Paulus et Rufus cursu properant, dum Faustilla et Antonia subridens eos aspiciunt.)
(Paulus and Rufus rush to race while Faustilla and Antonia watch them with smiles.)

Faustilla: *Vide, Antonia! Rufi pedes tam celeres sunt ut vix eum videas! Sed Paulus quoque non est tardus—prope est!*

Faustilla: Look, Antonia! Rufus's feet are so fast that you can barely see him! But Paulus isn't slow either—he's close!

Antonia: *Certe! Spero tamen ne confligant in angustia! Vidi multos pueros in cursu labentes. Sed post cursum nos quoque pilas iaciemus, ut tu dixisti, Faustilla.*

Antonia: Certainly! But I hope they don't collide in the narrow part! I've seen many boys slip during races. But after the race, we will also throw balls, as you said, Faustilla.

Faustilla: *Ita est! Et ego pilam melius iactabo quam viri! Dum pueri currunt, nos etiam praeparamus nostras pilas.*

Faustilla: That's right! And I'll throw the ball better than the boys! While they run, let's prepare our balls too.

Paulus: *(Respirans) Rufe! Ego—fessus—sum! Sed video te paulum priorem esse! Hodie vicisti.*

Paulus: (Breathing heavily) Rufus! I'm—tired! But I see you were just a bit ahead! You've won today.

Rufus: *(Ridens) Dixitne tibi aliquis me celerem esse? Sed aeque bene cursu contendisti. Nunc ad Faustillam et Antoniam eamus, pilas parant! Te admiraturi sumus in alio certamine.*

Rufus: (Laughing) Did anyone tell you I'm fast? But you competed well in the race. Now let's go to Faustilla and Antonia—they're preparing the balls! We'll admire you in the next competition.

Paulus: *Bene! Sed memineris globorum meorum!*

Paulus: Good! But remember, you owe me those balls!

De Tempore et Aetate

Sulpicius: *Salve, Septimiane! Hodie, dum sub hac vetere quercu sedeo, cogitare coepi de temporibus et aetate nostra. Tempus tam celeriter fugit, ut videamur non diu ab infantia recessisse, sed tamen iam in iuventutem transiimus. Nonne videtur tibi tempus nos praeterfluere velut fluvius sine fine?*

Sulpicius: Hello, Septimianus! Today, while sitting under this old oak, I began to think about time and our age. Time flies so quickly that it seems we haven't long departed from childhood, yet we have already transitioned into youth. Doesn't it seem to you that time flows past us like a river without end?

Septimianus: *Salve, Sulpici! Ita est, consentio. Tempus, ut saepe philosophi dixerunt, sicut umbra effugit et numquam regredi potest. Quot anni nobis videbantur longi cum pueri essemus, sed nunc iam celerius quam animadvertamus declinant. Miror quomodo aetas in singulis diebus parum notetur, sed post paucos annos subito appareat.*

Septimianus: Greetings, Sulpicius! Yes, I agree. Time, as philosophers have often said, escapes like a shadow and can never return. How many years seemed long to us when we were children, but now they pass more quickly than we notice. I wonder how age is scarcely noted in individual days, but after a few years, it suddenly appears.

Sulpicius: *Bene monuisti. Saepe cernimus nos in rebus cotidianis occupatos esse, ut nihil sentiamus de hac mutatione. Tum, subito, quotiens speculum respicimus, videamus vultus nostros mutatos esse et capillos aliquantulum canescere. Est quasi latens viator, qui non ante notus fit quam longum iter fecerit.*

Sulpicius: Well said. Often we are so busy with daily matters that we feel nothing of this change. Then, suddenly, when we look in the mirror, we see our faces have changed and our hair has grayed a little. It's like a hidden traveler who is only noticed after a long journey has been made.

Septimianus: *Non omnino potest tempus victum esse, nec fugiendum. Sed quid censes, Sulpici? Estne aetas ipsa onus, an sapientiam et tranquillitatem secum fert? Videtur mihi senectus non semper esse dolenda, sed plena consilii et prudentiae, si bene viximus.*

Septimianus: Time cannot be entirely conquered, nor can it be escaped. But what do you think, Sulpicius? Is age itself a burden, or does it bring wisdom and tranquility with it? It seems to me that old age isn't always something to lament, but is full of counsel and wisdom if we have lived well.

Sulpicius: *Ego quidem censeo aetatem maturam plenam esse fructuum, quos iuventus per laborem et pericula colligit. Senectus non onus, sed donum est, si animum ad virtutem et sapientiam intendimus. Vide senes nostros in foro: eorum consilium et gravitas omnium animos movent. Sed hoc quoque verum est: nisi aetas bene a iuventute praeparatur, onus fieri potest.*

Sulpicius: I indeed believe that mature age is full of the fruits that youth gathers through labor and challenges. Old age is not a burden, but a gift if we focus our minds on virtue and wisdom. Look at our elders in the forum: their counsel and dignity move everyone's spirits. But it is also true that unless age is well prepared for in youth, it can become a burden.

Septimianus: *Sane, providere debet iuvenis, ut postea senex tranquillitatem inveniat. Etsi iuventus impetuosa est et fortis, tamen sapientiam colere oportet. Senectus autem, quam multi fugiunt, est velut portus tranquillus, ubi, post longas tempestates, animus requiem invenit. Sed nonne vides plurimos homines fato ac fortunae credere, potius quam ipsi virtutem colant?*

Septimianus: Indeed, a young man must prepare himself so that later, as an old man, he may find tranquility. Even though youth is impetuous and strong, wisdom must still be cultivated. Old age, however, which many fear, is like a tranquil harbor where, after long storms, the soul finds rest. But don't you see that many people trust in fate and fortune rather than cultivate virtue themselves?

Sulpicius: *Plurimi quidem ita faciunt, Septimiane, sed ego semper existimavi virtutem supra fortunam esse. Tempus, quamquam irrevocabile est, nullam vim habet adversus eos, qui integre vivunt. Virtus ipsa aeternam iuventutem animi praestat. Non est aetas, sed modus vivendi, quod vitam beatam facit.*

Sulpicius: Many do, indeed, Septimianus, but I have always thought that virtue is above fortune. Time, although irreversible, has no power over those who live with integrity. Virtue itself grants eternal youth of the soul. It is not age, but the way of living that makes life happy.

Septimianus: *Pulchre dixisti, Sulpici. Tempus corporibus imperat, sed non animis. Et, dum virtutis studium colimus, ne metuendum est quid tempus tollat, sed potius gaudendum est quod sapientiam addat. Vale, amice! Utinam semper tempus tibi faveat et animus tuus in aeterna iuventute maneat.*

Septimianus: Beautifully said, Sulpicius. Time rules over bodies, but not over souls. And while we pursue virtue, we should not fear what time takes away, but rather rejoice in what wisdom it adds. Farewell, friend! May time always favor you, and may your soul remain in eternal youth.

Sulpicius: *Vale, Septimiane! Quod si tempus subito fugerit, sciam te mihi ex sapientia per multos annos exemplum dedisse.*

Sulpicius: Farewell, Septimianus! And if time suddenly flees, I will know that you have given me an example of wisdom through many years.

In Flore Iuventutis

Livia: *Salve, Furi! Hodie, dum in horto ambulabam, multum cogitavi de vita iuventutis. Videntur mihi hi anni esse pleni gaudii et spei, sed simul etiam pleni dubitationum et curae. Quid tibi videtur? Nonne iuventus est tempus et gratiarum et laborum?*

Livia: Hello, Furius! Today, while walking in the garden, I thought a lot about the life of youth. These years seem to me to be full of joy and hope, but at the same time full of doubts and worries. What do you think? Isn't youth a time of both blessings and challenges?

Furius: *Salve, Livia! Certe, iuventus, quamquam plena est virium et spei, tamen habet suas difficultates. Est quasi flos, qui subito efflorescit, sed eodem tempore ventis et tempestatibus expositus est. Spei quidem plena est, sed etiam multum habet periculi, cum adhuc nesciamus quomodo optime vitam gubernemus.*

Furius: Hello, Livia! Certainly, youth, although full of energy and hope, also has its difficulties. It is like a flower that suddenly blooms, but at the same time is exposed to winds and storms. It is indeed full of hope, but also has much danger, as we still do not know how to best steer our lives.

Livia: *Bene dicis. Quoties cogito de variis consiliis quae iuvenes secum trahunt! In hoc annorum flore tam multae sunt viae ante oculos nostros, et tamen, quoties timemus ne falsa via eligatur. Itaque, dum iuventus dulcis videtur, est etiam tempus magnarum curarum.*

Livia: You speak well. How often I think of the many plans that young people carry with them! In this bloom of years, so many paths lie before our eyes, and yet we often fear choosing the wrong one. Thus, while youth seems sweet, it is also a time of great worries.

Furius: *Ita est. Multum quidem pendet ex sapientia nostra, sed plerumque iuventus ex impetu agitur, non semper ex ratione. Vide: iuvenes saepe plus virtutem quam cautelam spectant, propositis audacibus favent, sine metu periculorum. Quid censes: estne haec audacia iuventutis laudanda an reprimenda?*

Furius: Indeed. Much depends on our wisdom, but youth is mostly driven by impulse, not always by reason. Look: young people often value bravery over caution, favoring bold plans without fear of danger. What do you think: should this youthful boldness be praised or restrained?

Livia: *Mihi quidem videtur audacia interdum laudanda esse. Sine audacia, nihil grandium operum fieri potest. Sed necessario iungenda est prudentia, quarum utraque in iuventute raro iuncta invenitur. Non est facile in aetate tantae spei et virtutis rationem semper sequi. Fortasse tamen hoc ipsum certamen iuventutis est: discere quomodo audaciam et sapientiam componamus.*

Livia: I believe boldness should sometimes be praised. Without boldness, no great works can be accomplished. But it must necessarily be joined with wisdom, and both are rarely found together in youth. It is not easy, in an age of such hope and virtue, to always follow reason. Perhaps this is the very struggle of youth: learning how to combine boldness and wisdom.

Furius: *Praeclare locuta es, Livia. Certe non audaciam debeo contemnere, cum ipsa sit vis quae mundum mutet et res novas efficiat. Sed ratio, ut dicis, praecipua est, et id quod differt iuvenem bene praeparatum ab eo qui temere agit. Quaedam tamen iuventutis vitia sunt inevitabilia, nisi tempus ipsa docuerit.*

Furius: You have spoken excellently, Livia. I certainly must not scorn boldness, for it is the force that changes the world and brings about new things. But reason, as you say, is essential, and it is what distinguishes a well-prepared youth from one who acts rashly. Some of youth's flaws, however, are inevitable unless time itself teaches them.

Livia: *Vere dicis, Furi. Tempus est magister, qui iuventutem moderatam facit. Sed etiam gaudium et laetitiam, quae his annis inveniuntur, non omittenda sunt. Iuventus, cum sit incerta, tamen plena est gloriae rerum nondum tentatarum. Mihi saepe videtur melius esse periculum temptare quam omnino vita relicta nihil audeas.*

Livia: You speak truly, Furius. Time is the teacher that tempers youth. But the joy and happiness found in these years should not be overlooked either. Youth, though uncertain, is still full of the glory of things yet untried. It often seems to me that it is better to risk danger than to leave life behind without daring anything.

Furius: *Sane. Audacia saepe ipsa est causa progressus et laetitiae. Ego quoque, dum iuvenis sum, gaudeo vivacitate horum annorum, etsi scio me aliquando erraturum. Nihilominus, sine audacia et visione, etiam errare non possumus. Cur non amplectamur haec tempora et discamus ex cunctis vitae periculis?*

Furius: Indeed. Boldness itself is often the cause of progress and joy. I too, while I am young, rejoice in the vitality of these years, even though I know I will sometimes make mistakes. Nevertheless, without boldness and vision, we cannot even make mistakes. Why not embrace these times and learn from all the dangers of life?

Livia: *Nihil verius. Iuventus est tempus ut discamus et ex erroribus crescamus. Non semper sapiemus, sed, per errores, viam nostram reperiemus. Gaudium iuventutis et audaciam servemus, dum simul rationem colimus. Sic vere vivitur.*

Livia: Nothing truer. Youth is the time for us to learn and grow from our mistakes. We will not always be wise, but through errors, we will find our way. Let us keep the joy and boldness of youth while also cultivating reason. This is how we truly live.

Furius: *Ita est, Livia! Dum iuventus in manibus est, utamur ea, sed etiam meminerimus rationis. Vale, et fortunam in tuis audacibus semper habe!*

Furius: That's right, Livia! While youth is in our hands, let us use it, but also remember reason. Farewell, and may you always have fortune in your bold endeavors!

Livia: *Gratias, Furi! Et tibi quoque omnia ex audacibus bene cadant. Vale!*

Livia: Thank you, Furius! And may all your bold ventures succeed as well. Farewell!

In Foro Artis

Gaius: *Salve, Valeria! Hodie in foro circa statuam pulcherrimam incidi, quae vero opere mirabilis videtur. Sculptor, ut dicitur, ex Graecia ipsa advenit et suas statuas hic in foro vendit. Cur non venis et eam aspicis? Puto te quoque admiratione captam futuram.*

Gaius: Hello, Valeria! Today, in the forum, I came across the most beautiful statue, which truly seems marvelous in its craftsmanship. The sculptor, they say, has come from Greece itself and is selling his statues here in the forum. Why don't you come and see it? I think you will also be captivated by its beauty.

Valeria: *Salve, Gai! Mihi quidem dicere non opus est: iam multorum sermonibus audivi de praeclaris illis operibus, quae ex Graecia ad nostram urbem afferuntur. Multi dicunt Graecos summos artifices esse, praesertim in sculptura. Statuas eorum non modo pulchritudine, sed etiam vivacitate animorum completas esse dicunt. Quae autem statua te adeo admiratum est?*

Valeria: Hello, Gaius! You don't need to tell me: I've already heard many people talk about those famous works that are brought to our city from Greece. Many say that the Greeks are the greatest artists, especially in sculpture. They say that their statues are filled not only with beauty but also with the liveliness of the soul. But which statue impressed you so much?

Gaius: *Statuam vidi Apollinis. Tam perfecte effingitur ut videas ipsum deum vivere! Bracchia eius in levi motu sunt, vultus tranquillus et vivaciter expressus. Marmoris etiam lucebat candor. Non dubito quin hoc opus aliquando in aedibus principum locatum sit.*

Gaius: I saw a statue of Apollo. It's sculpted so perfectly that you can see the god himself alive! His arms are in gentle motion, his face calm and vividly expressive. The marble even shone with a bright luster. I have no doubt that this piece will one day be placed in the halls of nobility.

Valeria: *De Apolline dicis? Nihil pulchrius esse potest! Eius effigies semper maiorem gravitatem atque dignitatem reddit. Sed dic mihi: quanti statuas vendit? Solent Graeci pretium non leve exigere pro operibus talibus.*

Valeria: You're talking about Apollo? Nothing could be more beautiful! His image always adds greater gravity and dignity. But tell me: for how much is he selling the statues? Greeks usually ask a high price for such works.

Gaius: *Certe, pretium non est modicum. Sculptor quadringenta sestertia postulavit. Cum primum numerum audirem, haesitavi. Sed cum propius accederem et omnia sculpta perfectionis digna spectarem, coepi credere pretium iustum esse. Praeter hanc statuam, etiam figurae minores habet pro minori pretio, si forte cupias aliquid etiam minoris magnitudinis.*

Gaius: Certainly, the price is not modest. The sculptor asked for four hundred thousand sestertii. When I first heard the amount, I hesitated. But as I got closer and saw all the details, each one crafted with perfection, I began to believe the price was fair. Besides this statue, he also has smaller figures at a lower price, in case you prefer something smaller.

Valeria: *Quadringenta sestertia? Haud leve quidem pretium! Sed, si ars ita perfecta est ut dicis, fortasse dignum sit. Non saepe in foro tam praeclara opera invenimus. Cur non consideramus hanc statuam in hortum nostrum domi ponere? Multa iam ornamenta sunt, sed nihil tale.*

Valeria: Four hundred thousand sestertii? That's no small price! But if the art is as perfect as you say, it may be worth it. We don't often find such exquisite works in the forum. Why don't we consider placing this statue in our home garden? We already have many decorations, but nothing like this.

Gaius: *Haec cogitatio mihi placet. Hic Apollo certe in horto florenti bene staret, inter lilia et rosas, sub umbrosa arbore. Magnopere quidem hortus noster augeretur et gratiam sumeret. Sed quid censes tu? Nonne praeterea aliquas alias effigies spectandas putas?*

Gaius: I like that idea. This Apollo would certainly stand well in our flourishing garden, among the lilies and roses, under a shady tree. Our garden would indeed gain much beauty and charm. But what do you think? Don't you think we should also look at other statues?

Valeria: *Est quod dicis, Gai. Verum est Apollinem praeclarum esse, sed vellem quoque alia opera inspicere antequam certum consilium capiam.*

Audivi etiam prope thermas esse tabernas ubi alia marmora et figurae aliorum deorum expositae sunt. Fortasse Venus aut Minerva magis nos alliciat.

Valeria: You're right, Gaius. It's true that Apollo is magnificent, but I'd also like to see other works before making a final decision. I've heard there are shops near the baths where other marbles and figures of other gods are displayed. Perhaps Venus or Minerva would attract us more.

Gaius: *Bona idea! Venus quidem in horto nostro esset dignissima, pulchritudine sua omnia loca decorans. Itaque eamus ad illas tabernas prope thermas. Fortasse inveniemus aliquid quod et re visu dignum et pretio commodiore sit.*

Gaius: Good idea! Venus would indeed be most worthy in our garden, decorating every space with her beauty. So let's go to those shops near the baths. Perhaps we'll find something both worth seeing and at a more reasonable price.

Valeria: *Agamus! Ubi tam multa opera ex Graecia veniunt, certe inveniemus id quod admiratione et arte summa dignum sit. Valeamus modo ut haec auctorum praeclara opera in nostram domum accipere possimus.*

Valeria: Let's do it! With so many works coming from Greece, we will surely find something worthy of admiration and the highest artistry. Let us hope that we can bring such magnificent works into our home.

Gaius: *Vale! Eamus et videamus quid ars Graeca nobis offerat.*

Gaius: Farewell! Let's go and see what Greek art has to offer us.

De Tempore Futuro

Aemilianus: *Salve, Plautia! Nuper multum cogitavi de rebus futuris. Videtur mihi mundus sic in constanti mutatione esse, ut saepe quaeram quid posthac exspectandum sit. Dic mihi, quid tu sentis de tempore futuro? Estne res cuius cursum omnino providere possumus?*

Aemilianus: Hello, Plautia! Lately, I've been thinking a lot about future matters. It seems to me that the world is in constant change, so I often wonder what we can expect next. Tell me, what do you think about the future? Is it something whose course we can completely foresee?

Plautia: *Salve, Aemiliane! Mihi quidem videtur providentia futurorum rerum esse difficillima, nisi forte di immortales nobis aliquam visionem fecerint. Multa tamen ex iis quae nunc aguntur nonnumquam indicia dant quo modo futura eventura sint. Sed quid te hac de re sollicitum facit?*

Plautia: Hello, Aemilianus! It seems to me that predicting future events is very difficult, unless the immortal gods have given us some vision. However, many things happening now sometimes provide signs of how the future may unfold. But what is it that worries you about this?

Aemilianus: *Est vero quod dicis. Multa ex praeteritis signis provisum esse potest. Sed saepius cogito de imperii nostri fortunis. Cum videam quanta pericula foris et domi instent—belli minae, seditio populi—vereor ne res nostrae magno discrimine afficiantur. Futura autem obscura manent, et non satis certe dicere possum quo horum eventuum decurret.*

Aemilianus: What you say is true. Many things can be foreseen from past signs. But I often think about the fate of our empire. When I see how many dangers threaten us, both from abroad and within—threats of war, civil unrest—I fear that our affairs may be gravely affected. The future remains unclear, and I can't say for certain how these events will unfold.

Plautia: *Hoc tibi certe timendum est. Nihil tam fragile est quam fortuna imperii. Multae civitates quae aliquando floruerunt, velut Carthago aut Babylon, iam ruinae sunt. Sed spero tamen Romam, quae divinis consiliis et virtute patrum suorum fundata est, diu mansuram esse. Forsitan etiam res meliores effici possint, si prudenter et moderate agitur.*

Plautia: That is certainly something to be feared. Nothing is as fragile as the fortune of an empire. Many cities that once flourished, like Carthage or Babylon, are now ruins. But I still hope that Rome, founded on divine guidance and the virtue of its ancestors, will endure for a long time. Perhaps things can even improve, if we act wisely and with moderation.

Aemilianus: *Utinam ita sit! Sed homines ipsi saepe tam imprudenter agunt, ut multae occasiones frustra periclitentur. Vides quam civitas cupiditate divitiarum et gloriae trahatur, dum obliviscitur verae virtutis et disciplinae. Mihi videtur hoc vitium esse quod, nisi coerceatur, non parvum damnum feret.*

Aemilianus: I hope it may be so! But people often act so recklessly that many opportunities are wasted. You see how the city is driven by the desire for wealth and glory, while forgetting true virtue and discipline. It seems to me that this flaw, if not restrained, will cause significant harm.

Plautia: *Non ambigo. Saepe dixit Cicero virtutem esse fundamentum rei publicae, et ubi haec deficit, regnum cadere coepit. Sed tamen non omnes homines corrupti sunt; sunt etiam multi qui magna prudentia et recta mente res gesserunt. Forsitan ex his viris salus imperii aliquando oriatur.*

Plautia: I don't doubt it. Cicero often said that virtue is the foundation of the republic, and when this fails, the kingdom begins to fall. But not all people are corrupt; there are also many who have acted with great wisdom and a righteous mind. Perhaps the salvation of the empire will one day arise from such men.

Aemilianus: *Fortasse. Homines boni et prudentes semper spes aliqua sunt. Sed quid de technis et novis institutis censes? Videtur mihi haec tempora multa nova afferre—arcus maiores, aedificia altiora, mirabilia opera in aqueductis et portubus. Horumne progressuum signa fiduciae futurae sunt, an potius indicium exsuperantiae et superbiae?*

Aemilianus: Perhaps. Good and wise men are always a source of hope. But what do you think about technology and new institutions? It seems to me that these times are bringing many innovations—larger arches, taller buildings, marvelous works in aqueducts and harbors. Are these signs of confidence in the future, or rather indications of excess and pride?

Plautia: *Profecto haec nova opera ingenium Romanum mire ostendunt. Progressus technicus non per se malus est; immo, saepe prodest populo* *et urbi. Sed, si his rebus nimium confidimus, et si aestimamus nos diis gnatos esse propter nostram artem, tunc superbia nos corrumpet. Haec, ut semper, ratione et modestia regenda sunt.*

Plautia: These new works certainly display the remarkable ingenuity of the Romans. Technological progress is not bad in itself; in fact, it often benefits the people and the city. But if we rely too much on these things, and if we consider ourselves divine because of our craft, then pride will corrupt us. As always, these things must be guided by reason and modesty.

Aemilianus: *Ita, rationem et modestiam colere debemus. Nunc autem video spem meam tibi plus esse quam metum. Mihi quidem placet hac providentia quae modum et disciplinam praeferat. Non praevenimus omnes casus futuros, sed possumus certe ad meliora tendere, si virtuti et prudentiae incumbimus.*

Aemilianus: Yes, we must cultivate reason and modesty. Now, however, I see that your hope outweighs your fear. I'm indeed pleased by this foresight that favors moderation and discipline. We can't foresee all future events, but we can certainly strive for better things if we focus on virtue and wisdom.

Plautia: *Nihil verius! Futura obscura esse possunt, sed nostrum est ut earum cursum cum virtute et sapientia moderemur. Vale igitur, Aemiliane, et spes tibi semper sit melioris temporis.*

Plautia: Nothing truer! The future may be unclear, but it is up to us to guide its course with virtue and wisdom. Farewell then, Aemilianus, and may you always have hope for better times.

Aemilianus: *Vale, Plautia! Utinam futura nobis semper propitia sint.*

Aemilianus: Farewell, Plautia! May the future always be kind to us.

De Fabulis et Mythologia

Marius: *Salve, Albine! Hodie, dum in luco ambulabam, multa de nostris antiquis fabulis atque divinis legendis cogitavi. Romulus, Remus, et reges vetustissimi—non solum mihi admirationem movent, sed etiam quoddam mysterium. Quid tu de nostra mythologia sentis? Videnturne tibi haec esse plena sapientiae, an potius ficta ad populi animos movendos?*

Marius: Hello, Albinus! Today, while walking in the grove, I thought a lot about our ancient tales and divine legends. Romulus, Remus, and the earliest kings—they not only inspire admiration in me but also a certain mystery. What do you think of our mythology? Does it seem to you that these stories are full of wisdom, or rather fictional to move the minds of the people?

Albinus: *Salve, Mari! Fabulae nostrae mihi semper magnae visae sunt, et non sine causa. Etsi fortasse multae res fictae esse possunt, tamen saepe sub his legendis latent magna exempla virtutis et sapientiae. Romulus et Remus, ut scis, non tantum filii Martis dicuntur, sed etiam Romanam virtutem repraesentant: audaciam, fortitudinem, et condendi civitatis ardorem. Quid tibi videtur de talibus rebus?*

Albinus: Hello, Marius! Our stories have always seemed great to me, and not without reason. Although many things may be fictional, often under these legends lie great examples of virtue and wisdom. Romulus and Remus, as you know, are not only said to be the sons of Mars but also represent Roman virtue: bravery, strength, and the passion for founding a city. What do you think of such matters?

Marius: *Bene censeo, Albine. Certe, res fabulosae saepe ad monendos et docendos homines compositae sunt. Romulus quidem non solum urbis conditor fuit, sed etiam exemplum Romani impetus. Sed in memoriam mihi venit alia fabula: legenda Aeneae, quem Venus ipsa servavit. Nonne fabula Aeneae multa de fato et pietate docet?*

Marius: I agree, Albinus. Certainly, fabulous tales are often composed to warn and teach people. Romulus was not only the founder of the city but also an example of Roman drive. But another story comes to mind: the legend of Aeneas, whom Venus herself saved. Doesn't the tale of Aeneas teach us much about fate and duty?

Albinus: *Prorsus! Aeneas, ut Vergilius noster narrat, est exemplum summae pietatis. Ille, cum patriam suam Troiam videret flammis deletam, tamen fortiter divinum mandatum sequitur, novam urbem condere et populum ad novam spem ducere. Aeneas ostendit non solum fortitudinem in bello, sed etiam oboedientiam fato. Fortasse hae omnes praeclarae narrationes sunt, sed habent suam sapientiam.*

Albinus: Exactly! Aeneas, as our Vergil tells it, is an example of the highest duty. Even though he saw his homeland, Troy, destroyed by flames, he still bravely followed the divine command to found a new city and lead his people to new hope. Aeneas shows not only strength in battle but also obedience to fate. Perhaps all these are grand stories, but they contain their own wisdom.

Marius: *Quam pulchre dicis, Albine! Fatum, quod Aeneam pericula superare iussit, semper mihi videtur esse pars magna nostrarum fabularum. Vides ut in fabulis fatum sit potens, nec ullus homo fatum effugere possit, nec reges, nec heroes, nec di immortales. Sed quid de aliis fabulis censes, de legendis Minervae aut Mercurii?*

Marius: How beautifully you speak, Albinus! Fate, which ordered Aeneas to overcome his trials, always seems to me to be a major part of our stories. You see how, in the tales, fate is powerful, and no man can escape it—not kings, not heroes, not even the immortal gods. But what do you think of other stories, like the legends of Minerva or Mercury?

Albinus: *Minerva et Mercurius quoque magna exempla afferunt. Minerva, ut dea sapientiae, ipsa monstrat virtutem mentis et belli iusti, dum Mercurius, nuntius deorum, artem verborum et ingenii docet. Minerva Athenam, urbem praeclaram, tuetur, atque haec fabula suam dignitatem habet, nam ipsa urbs per sapientiam et iustitiam firmam potentiam obtinuit.*

Albinus: Minerva and Mercury also offer great examples. Minerva, as the goddess of wisdom, herself shows the virtue of the mind and just warfare, while Mercury, the messenger of the gods, teaches the art of words and cleverness. Minerva protects Athens, a famous city, and that story holds its own dignity, for the city gained its lasting power through wisdom and justice.

Marius: *Vereor ne homines has fabulas parum serio trahant. Sed, ut dicis, sub his fictionibus est semper aliqua insignis doctrina. Itaque consentio tecum. Numquam sine causa Romani has divinas narrationes coluerunt. Nonne etiam nostri mores et rerum publicarum moderatio in his fabulis referuntur?*

Marius: I fear that people may take these stories too lightly. But, as you say, beneath these fictions, there is always some notable teaching. So I agree with you. The Romans never honored these divine stories without reason. Don't our customs and the governance of the republic also find their reflection in these tales?

Albinus: *Sane! Per exempla fabularum et mythorum, populus non solum docetur de dis, sed etiam de virtutibus civitatis. Hoc exemplum virtutis debemus semper animo tenere. Vale igitur, Mari! Fortasse cras aliam fabulam discutiemus.*

Albinus: Certainly! Through the examples in these stories and myths, the people are taught not only about the gods but also about the virtues of the state. We must always hold this example of virtue in mind. Farewell then, Marius! Perhaps tomorrow we'll discuss another story.

Marius: *Vale, Albine! Semper mihi iucundum est de his rebus colloqui. Fabulae nos semper sapienter moneant!*

Marius: Farewell, Albinus! It's always a pleasure to talk about these things. May the stories always wisely remind us!

In Foro Marmoreo

Lucius: *Salve, Secunde! Vidi te iam antea hic in foro marmoreo versari. Quaerisne marmorem ad novum opus domi tuae, an forte statuam aliam spectas?*

Lucius: Hello, Secundus! I saw you here earlier in the marble market. Are you looking for marble for a new project at your house, or are you perhaps admiring another statue?

Secundus: *Salve, Luci! Ita est, hodie marmorem quaero ad implendas columnas atrii, quod apud me renovo. Oportet enim ut solidum et candidum sit, nec libenter nimis alta pretia solvam. Sed, ut vides, marmora variis qualitatibus offeruntur. Quae tibi videntur optima?*

Secundus: Hello, Lucius! Yes, today I'm looking for marble to complete the columns of my atrium, which I'm renovating. It must be solid and white, and I'd prefer not to pay overly high prices. But as you can see, marbles come in various qualities. Which do you think are the best?

Lucius: *Si bonum marmorem quaeris, ego semper commendo marmorem Lunensem. Is quidem candidus est et diuturnitatem habet. Sed, si pretia nimium gravia esse putas, marmora Tenestina ex Africa quoque digna sunt opera. Etiam minoris pretii sunt quam Lunense.*

Lucius: If you're looking for good marble, I always recommend the Lunense marble. It is white and durable. But if you think the prices are too high, Tenestine marble from Africa is also worthy. It's cheaper than Lunense as well.

Secundus: *Lunense, ais? Novi illum marmorem laudatum esse Romae. Fortasse eo utar, sed volo quoque scire de marmore Phrygio. Nonne splendidior aspectu est et magis decorum ad columnas ornandas?*

Secundus: Lunense, you say? I know that marble is praised in Rome. I might use it, but I also want to know about Phrygian marble. Isn't it more splendid in appearance and better suited for decorating columns?

Lucius: *Phrygium marmor certe pulchrum est, variae coloris divitias ostendit. Est aptum in locis ubi voluptas et spectaculum quaeritur, sed non ad diuturnas structuras, ut columellae, tam bene valet quam*

Lunense. Si ornamenta quaeras, praeclare aptum est; si stabilitatem, melius esset Lunense.

Lucius: Phrygian marble is certainly beautiful, showing rich variations in color. It's suitable for places where beauty and spectacle are desired, but it doesn't hold up as well for long-lasting structures, like columns, as Lunense does. If you want decoration, it's excellent; if you want stability, Lunense is better.

Secundus: *Intellego quid dicas. Fortasse erunt columnae ex Lunensi, sed frigidarium meum meliorem aspectum habere cupiam cum Phrygio marmore. O, quales censes tu, Luci, fuisse marmora in templis veterum? Audivi multa fuisse ex variis orbis terrarum partibus allata.*

Secundus: I understand what you're saying. Maybe the columns will be of Lunense, but I want my frigidarium to have a better look with Phrygian marble. Oh, what do you think the marbles in the temples of the ancients were like, Lucius? I've heard many were brought from different parts of the world.

Lucius: *Vere dicis. Veteres magnum honorem marmori debebant, et ex locis longinquis id importabant. Scisne templum Apollinis ex marmore Pentelico factum esse? Eius color sub luce solis fere aureus apparebat. Sed nihil, opinor, comparandum est cum marmore Porphyretico, qui tantum ad sacra et imperiales structuras adhibetur.*

Lucius: You're right. The ancients gave great honor to marble, importing it from distant places. Did you know that the temple of Apollo was made of Pentelic marble? Its color under sunlight appeared almost golden. But nothing, in my opinion, compares to the Porphyry marble, which is used only for sacred and imperial structures.

Secundus: *Sane, memini Porphyreticum laudari propter eius raritatem et magnificentiam. Sed nunc quaestio est: possumne haec omnia efficere sine nimio aere amittendo? Quanti aestimas marmora, utroque genere?*

Secundus: Certainly, I remember Porphyry being praised for its rarity and magnificence. But now the question is: can I do all of this without spending too much? How much do you estimate the price of the marbles, both types?

Lucius: *Bene, Secunde, si quaeris Lunense, quod solidum et candidum est, pretium eius decem sestertiis pro modio pendere solet. Phrygium, quia divitias coloris praebet, paulo plus constabit, quindecim sestertiis. Sed, si bene loquaris cum tabernario, fortasse aliquantum imminuere potes pretium.*

Lucius: Well, Secundus, if you're looking for Lunense, which is solid and white, its price usually runs at ten sestertii per measure. Phrygian, because of its rich colors, will cost a bit more, at fifteen sestertii. But if you negotiate well with the merchant, you might be able to lower the price somewhat.

Secundus: *Multas tibi gratias ago, Luci! Bene sensi te esse hominem, qui non solum pretia bene cognosceret, sed etiam consilium prudentissimum proferret. Nunc opus est ut tabernarium quaeram.*

Secundus: Many thanks to you, Lucius! I had a feeling that you were someone who not only knows prices well but also offers the wisest advice. Now I need to find the merchant.

Lucius: *Quidquid de marmore decernas, Secunde, certo scio te sapienter electurum. Vale, amice, et felicem tibi diem opto in marmore condendo.*

Lucius: Whatever you decide about the marble, Secundus, I'm sure you will choose wisely. Farewell, my friend, and I wish you a successful day in selecting your marble.

Secundus: *Vale, Luci, et gratias iterum ago.*

Secundus: Farewell, Lucius, and thanks again!

De Bello Romano (Ein Kampf um Rom), opus notissimum Felicis Dahn, nunc Latine redditum, lectoribus antiquitatis amatoribus novam lucem de gestis Gothorum et Romani Imperii in saeculo sexto obicit.

www.briansmith.de

Libri Latini

Emilio Salgari

Carthago in Flammis

Filiae Pharaonum

Felix Dahn

Felicitas

Gelimer

Stilicho

Bissula

De Bello Romano

Arthur Conan Doyle

Legio Ultima et Aliae Fabulae Antiquae